Robert's Rules

4th edition

by C. Alan Jennings, PRP

for
dummies®
A Wiley Brand

Robert's Rules For Dummies®, 4th Edition

Published by: **John Wiley & Sons, Inc.,** 111 River Street, Hoboken, NJ 07030-5774, www.wiley.com

For general information on our other products and services, please contact our Customer Care Department within the U.S. at 877-762-2974, outside the U.S. at 317-572-3993, or fax 317-572-4002. For technical support, please visit https://hub.wiley.com/community/support/dummies.

Wiley publishes in a variety of print and electronic formats and by print-on-demand. Some material included with standard print versions of this book may not be included in e-books or in print-on-demand. If this book refers to media such as a CD or DVD that is not included in the version you purchased, you may download this material at http://booksupport.wiley.com. For more information about Wiley products, visit www.wiley.com.

Library of Congress Control Number: 2021952532

ISBN: 978-1-119-82458-9

ISBN 978-1-119-82459-6 (ebk); ISBN 978-1-119-82460-2 (ebk)

SKY10032198_122821

Robert's Rules

4th edition

by C. Alan Jennings, PRP

for
dummies®
A Wiley Brand

Robert's Rules For Dummies®, 4th Edition

Published by: **John Wiley & Sons, Inc.**, 111 River Street, Hoboken, NJ 07030-5774, www.wiley.com

For general information on our other products and services, please contact our Customer Care Department within the U.S. at 877-762-2974, outside the U.S. at 317-572-3993, or fax 317-572-4002. For technical support, please visit https://hub.wiley.com/community/support/dummies.

Wiley publishes in a variety of print and electronic formats and by print-on-demand. Some material included with standard print versions of this book may not be included in e-books or in print-on-demand. If this book refers to media such as a CD or DVD that is not included in the version you purchased, you may download this material at http://booksupport.wiley.com. For more information about Wiley products, visit www.wiley.com.

Library of Congress Control Number: 2021952532

ISBN: 978-1-119-82458-9

ISBN 978-1-119-82459-6 (ebk); ISBN 978-1-119-82460-2 (ebk)

SKY10032198_122821

Contents at a Glance

Table of Contents

CHAPTER 9: Subsidiary Motions: Helping to Process the Main Motion 175

Introduction

Welcome to the fourth edition of *Robert's Rules For Dummies* — a book with "Robert's Rules" in the title that doesn't pretend to be a substitute for Robert's Rules! It's written to serve as your personal guide to the principles of parliamentary procedure found in *Robert's Rules of Order Newly Revised,* (12th edition) and as found in *Robert's Rules of Order Newly Revised In Brief* (3rd edition).

Just so you know, in this book, whenever I use the term "Robert's Rules," I'm referring to the 12th edition of *Robert's Rules of Order Newly Revised,* not to one of the many other books with "Robert's Rules" in the title. The 12th edition of Robert's Rules is the current edition. It contains at least 90 changes of some sort from the 11th edition. And that is the big reason why I've updated *Robert's Rules For Dummies*; I want you to be able to put two-and-two together with the latest, greatest, Robert's Rules.

I doubt that you *really* want to know anything about parliamentary procedure. But I'm pretty sure you're looking to get some quick information to help you participate more effectively in meetings, to serve in an office to which you've recently been elected, or both. Whatever your situation, if using parliamentary procedure is a must, then this book will go a long way toward helping you master the rules of Robert's Rules.

I was in a similar situation in 1989 when I joined a local unit of the National Association of Parliamentarians in Baton Rouge, Louisiana. I didn't join because I wanted to be a parliamentarian or because I wanted to be a member of another organization; I joined because I wanted to learn enough to get a new organization off the ground. I needed some specific information, and I didn't even realize that everything I needed to know but didn't even know enough to ask about could be found in a book titled *Robert's Rules of Order Newly Revised* (at that time, it was in its eighth edition, but the ninth edition was about to be published).

At first glance, the real Robert's Rules appeared to be naught but a tome of arcane spells to intimidate the masses and empower the erudite. But thanks to several very knowledgeable and experienced parliamentarians, I found that quite the opposite was true. Robert's Rules is actually a great reference book that provides a proper procedure for practically any parliamentary predicament.

So, when I was offered the opportunity to write this book, I thought it would be nice to pay forward all the personal help I've received over the years from the parliamentarians in the Louisiana Association of Parliamentarians, the National Association of Parliamentarians, and the American Institute of Parliamentarians. If I've accomplished my goals for this book, then you can keep *Robert's Rules For Dummies* handy and use it as if it were your own personal consulting parliamentarian.

But it comes with a very important caveat: When you need to make a point in a meeting, be prepared to cite the real Robert's Rules. That is, *Robert's Rules of Order Newly Revised* (12th edition) Whatever you do, please don't go waving *my* book around to your presiding officer unless your bylaws say that your parliamentary authority is Jennings's *Robert's Rules For Dummies* (which they should not!). Of course, I'm delighted that you've bought this book, but it's not a parliamentary authority. It's a book *about* one.

About This Book

To get the most out of this new edition of *Robert's Rules For Dummies,* use it to introduce yourself to the fundamental concepts that are covered in comprehensive detail in *Robert's Rules of Order Newly Revised.*

Don't try to read this book cover to cover. Instead, dive right into the chapter containing the information you need. Read it and you'll have a good and thorough overview of that particular topic. If I've done my job, you'll be well oriented to the subject matter. When you turn to the corresponding pages in the 2020 edition of *Robert's Rules of Order Newly Revised,* the in-depth treatment of a particular subject will make much more sense to you, and you'll be able to apply it to your particular situation.

What's new with this fourth edition? In particular, I include information about electronic meetings and using electronic voting in your in-person meetings. In this edition, I cover

- Meeting electronically.

- Voting using electronic keypads.

- putting together special rules for holding your business meetings electronically.

Other updates of note include the following:

- Rules governing the sending of meeting notices

- Clarification of the rules applicable to meeting in executive session

- Expansion of rules about when points of order can be raised

(Not So) Foolish Assumptions

Because you picked up this book, I assume a few things about you:

- You've heard of Robert's Rules, but you have little (or no) formal training or study in parliamentary procedure.

- You're a member of an organization that uses Robert's Rules.

- You want to participate effectively in meetings.

- Much of what you know about parliamentary procedure is what you've picked up here and there in meetings.

- You may sometimes feel not confident about how to participate effectively at some point in a meeting, so you keep your mouth shut and later wonder what maybe you could have done if only you had known what to do and how to do it when it could count.

- You have to deal with others who attempt to minimize the importance of using proper procedures in meetings.

>> You want to have a better understanding of Robert's Rules so that others can't take advantage of you in meetings.

>> If you're an officer or director, you want to understand the proper way to handle your duties in the organization.

I also assume that you *will not try to use this book as a substitute for Robert's Rules*. It's *not* written to be a parliamentary authority. It's written to give you the perspective you need to make the best use of the real Robert's Rules when you need it.

That being the case, my final assumption is that you will obtain a copy of the real Robert's Rules. The right book is the 12th edition of *Robert's Rules of Order Newly Revised.* Get a copy if you don't already have one. You can pick up a copy at your favorite bookstore, or you can order it online from the National Association of Parliamentarians store at `www.parliamentarians.org/`.

Icons Used in This Book

Icons are these peculiar little pictures that surface in the margin from time to time in each chapter to let you know that the following topic is special in some way. *Robert's Rules For Dummies* utilizes the following five icons:

TIP

When you see the Tip icon, you know you're about to read a helpful hint or tip that can save you some time or trouble. The tip may make things easier for you when you're in the thick of some difficult parliamentary situation.

WARNING

When you see this icon, pay close attention. It lets you know that trouble, problems, or exceptions may be lurking, but you can avoid the trouble by taking the right precautions or paying heed to some advice born of experience in the school of hard knocks.

TECHNICAL STUFF

This one doesn't get a lot of use here, because just about everything in this book qualifies as technical stuff. So if you see this icon, it's sure to be the most technical of the technical stuff.

REMEMBER

I use this icon a good bit, but that's only because there's a lot to remember in this book. But the good news is that you don't have to memorize it because you can flip to the page and go straight for the icon. But generally, this icon highlights key points of whatever discussion you're reading.

EXCEPTION

An important aspect of knowing the rules is knowing the exceptions. Whenever there's an important exception to an otherwise pretty hard-and-fast rule, I call it to your attention with this icon.

Beyond the Book

If you need more help with Robert's Rules, I encourage you to check out additional resources available to you online:

>> You can download the book's Cheat Sheet at www.dummies. com. Just search for "Robert's Rules Cheat Sheet." It's a handy resource to keep on your computer, tablet, or smartphone.

>> I also include helpful forms and sample documents on Dummies.com. All you have to do is point your browser to www.dummies.com/go.robertsrulesfd4e, download the files you want, and they'll show up on your computer ready for you to customize, save, and print.

Where to Go from Here

Get with it! You bought this book for a reason, so look up whatever it is you need to understand about Robert's Rules. After you've read the discussion, turn to your copy of *Robert's Rules of Order Newly Revised* if you want or need to know more. Immerse yourself in an in-depth treatment of a topic as written by the somewhat droll but definitely learned authors. On the National Association of Parliamentarians website at www.parliamentarians.org, you'll find a bookstore with a great collection of parliamentary procedure titles that you can order direct.

Don't stop there! It's the very nature of parliamentary law that knowledge about one topic leads to interest in another. Learning a little more will make you that much more effective in your meetings and service as a leader. It feels good to gain a stronger grasp of the Robert's Rules principles.

If I can help at any time, let me know. I can be reached by email through the contact page on my website. Go to www. alanjennings.com, click on "Contact," and type in a message. I make every effort to respond to all my email, so please drop me a line if there's something you need clarified or expanded upon.

Parliamentary procedure education in your area

If you really want to find out as much as you can, check with one or both of the following organizations and ask for information about the nearest local unit or chapter of parliamentarians. These local units have regular program meetings and offer educational programs in the community. They also usually have registered or professional members that can tailor-make a workshop for your group to help you have better meetings or develop leadership skills.

The National Association of Parliamentarians

213 South Main St.

Independence, MO 64050-3850

Phone: 888-627-2929

Website: www.parliamentarians.org

American Institute of Parliamentarians

1100 E. Woodfield Rd., Suite 350

Schaumburg, IL 60173

Phone: 888-664-0428

Website: www.aipparl.org

Hiring a professional parliamentarian

More and more groups are looking to professional parliamentarians for training, consulting, or on-site meeting services.

If you have a large group and want to have more orderly and productive meetings, or if your staff is overwhelmed when putting together your meetings and could use some help, you will probably benefit greatly by retaining a professional parliamentarian for specific services.

And even if your group is small and local and is just interested in fixing some bylaws, you save a lot of time and angst if you enlist the help of a local certified, registered, or professional parliamentarian.

No matter the size of your organization, when you find yourself in a rough situation and you just can't get past a particular issue, you may be able to break the impasse by asking a professional parliamentarian to give you a consultation and advise you on how to proceed.

1

It's Parliamentary, My Dear: Participating Effectively in Meetings

Discover the rules of parliamentary procedure.

Get familiar with the bylaws of any organization you belong to.

Understand the basic requirements for a valid meeting.

Follow the standard order of business.

» Defining parliamentary law

» Understanding the rules of parliamentary procedure

» Recognizing the personal benefits of learning Robert's Rules

Chapter **1**

Following the Rules (Robert's, That Is)

A re you the kind of person who sees meetings as a wonderful and personally fulfilling activity that you look forward to with great anticipation?

I didn't think so. If you were, you probably wouldn't be reading this book. Truth is, I haven't met many folks who love meetings and can't wait for the next one. But I *have* met plenty of people who dread meetings and attend only because they're afraid of what may happen if they're absent. Attitudes like this develop most frequently when nobody in the group (especially the presiding officer) really knows how to run a good meeting.

Luckily for you, I've found a remedy for anti-meeting attitudes. Try out a well-run meeting conducted by a presiding officer who takes the time to learn and use the principles of parliamentary procedure in Robert's Rules. It really does work wonders!

Keeping Things Informal

For anyone reading this book who thinks that Robert's Rules is all about being stiff and formal in meetings, I hope you disregard that notion right away. Robert's Rules is about conducting good meetings without any more formality than is absolutely necessary to protect the rights of everyone and keep things orderly. The rules are there to help, not hinder, business. General Robert (though not a general at the time) said, in advising inexperienced chairmen in his original edition:

Know all about parliamentary law, but do not try to show off your knowledge. Never be technical, nor be any more strict than is absolutely necessary for the good of the meeting. Use your judgment; the assembly may be of such a nature, through its ignorance of parliamentary usages and peaceable disposition, that a strict enforcement of the rules, instead of assisting, would greatly hinder business; but in large assemblies where there is much work to be done, and especially where there is liability to trouble, the only safe course is to require a strict observance of the rules.

The general's point must be taken to heart. Sprinkled throughout Robert's Rules are details of procedures that are available when you need them. The key theme of *Robert's Rules For Dummies,* as with Robert's Rules in general, is that you don't need to be any more formal than necessary. But you never want to be so informal that you compromise any rights — whether those of the individual, the minority, or the group as a whole.

Making Meetings Meaningful

One of the most marvelous points about Robert's Rules is that it makes meetings meaningful. I first experienced a true understanding of how Robert's Rules can really work to a group's advantage in a meeting of my state association of parliamentarians many years ago.

At that meeting, the president of the National Association of Parliamentarians, Kathryn Scheld, presented a workshop titled "Making Meetings Meaningful." I was really taken with that presentation, and I have since made it my goal in service as a parliamentarian to help my clients see their meetings as events that can and should be meaningful experiences for the members who invest their time and money in attending and participating. Those three words — *making meetings meaningful* — so clearly describe the most immediate benefit to learning and applying the principles of parliamentary procedure contained in Robert's Rules.

Using *Robert's Rules For Dummies* as a handbook for making your meetings meaningful can give you a real edge on the knowledge that can help you put your organization on the fast track to greater success.

A Brief History of Robert's Rules

Robert's Rules is practically synonymous with *parliamentary procedure.* My colleagues conservatively estimate that more than 80 percent of all organizations use Robert's Rules as their parliamentary manual. But *Robert's Rules of Order Newly Revised* is just one of a number of parliamentary manuals. And because copyrights expire and the name *Robert's Rules* has assumed a generic usage, many books are published with *Robert's Rules* in their titles. But they're not the real thing.

Robert's Rules of Order was the cover title of a book first written in 1876 by Henry Martyn Robert. The actual title was *Pocket Manual of Rules of Order for Deliberative Assemblies.* The author was a civil engineer in the U.S. Army. In 1863, when he was 26 years old, he had been called on to preside at a church meeting. He was reluctant to decline, but he didn't know how to properly preside. Despite his reservations, he accepted the duty, hoping that his lack of knowledge wouldn't be an embarrassment to himself or a disservice to those at the meeting.

No one knows exactly what happened at that meeting that historians describe as "turbulent," but Robert came away determined to learn something about parliamentary procedure before he even *attended* another meeting.

Some years later, Robert, who at the time held the rank of major, was stationed in San Francisco and found himself working with different organizations having memberships composed of persons from all over the country. Thanks to different local customs, wide disagreement arose over "correct" meeting procedures. Major Robert saw the need for uniformity and immersed himself in study of the parliamentary law of the day. He developed a pocket manual of parliamentary procedure that was published in 1876, known as *Robert's Rules of Order.* Since then, the manual has seen two revisions in a total of 11 editions.

THE EDITIONS OF ROBERT'S RULES

"Robert's Rules of Order" refers to the most current edition of the parliamentary authority described by any of the following titles:

- *Robert's Rules of Order* (RO) (1st, 2nd, and 3rd editions)
- *Robert's* Rules *of Order Revised* (ROR) (4th, 5th, and 6th editions)
- *Robert's Rules of Order Newly Revised* (RONR) (7th, 8th, 9th, 10th, 11th, and 12th editions)

All the revised editions are revisions by the original copyright holder or his successor trustees of the copyrights. The original *Robert's Rules of Order* is out of copyright and, consequently, has been republished or rewritten by numerous authors and sold with the name *Robert's Rules* or *Robert's Rules of Order* in the title.

This updated fourth edition of *Robert's Rules For Dummies* is intended as your guide to the current (12th) edition of the work, which is now titled *Robert's Rules of Order Newly Revised.* That book is based on the most current rules, not on the old and outdated rules of earlier editions.

General Robert's heirs continue to be actively involved in the current edition. The Robert's Rules Association, the National Association of Parliamentarians, and the American Institute of Parliamentarians recognize *Robert's Rules of Order Newly Revised* (RONR) as the authoritative work on parliamentary procedure whenever "Robert's Rules" is designated as the parliamentary authority.

Being Empowered at Meetings

In groups where a presiding officer becomes truly knowledgeable about correct parliamentary procedure, things change for the better. When I hear someone complain about how "parliamentary procedure" causes problems, I'm hearing from a member of a group that uses parliamentary procedure incorrectly. The parts that members dislike about the so-called process aren't even accurate parliamentary procedures. The procedures they're using are usually just somebody's self-serving double-talk that snookers members who don't know better into accepting them at face value.

After hearing things like that the authors and editors of the real Robert's Rules wrote *Robert's Rules of Order in Brief*. Limited in scope to the specific rules applicable to meetings, it's an in-a-meeting handbook useful for presiding officers and members alike. Although not a parliamentary authority because of the limited scope, it's consistent with *Robert's Rules of Order Newly Revised* and affords one quick and easy access to the meeting rules found in RONR. Every serious participating member of a deliberative assembly (see Chapter 3) whose parliamentary authority is Robert would do well to keep *In Brief* right beside *Robert's Rules For Dummies* when in a meeting.

When conducting meaningful meetings, you're successful only if you empower yourself by gathering the right information. But just as important as *having* this information is *knowing when to use it.*

REMEMBER

The rules in Robert's Rules aren't set up to give one side an edge over the other. They exist to help you arrive at the true will of the assembly, with due consideration for all points of view. Adding a few basic rules of procedure to your arsenal puts you more in control. Preparation helps you know when to insist on technicalities and when not to worry about them.

Understanding What Parliamentary Procedure Is

You'll enhance your understanding of the principles in this book if you take a few minutes now to go over some of the basics. *Parliamentary procedure* refers to the practices used in meetings to keep things orderly and give everybody a fair chance to be heard for at least as long as it takes for everybody to realize that nothing new is being said and that a large majority is ready to make a decision and move on to other business.

Parliamentary procedure actually goes a lot farther than that, but you've probably guessed as much. It takes a book or two to really cover the subject. You're on your way, though, and you'll have a much better understanding of the process after you've worked through some concrete examples like the ones in this book. The following sections give you a quick overview.

General parliamentary law

Parliamentary procedure is based on *parliamentary law.* Specifically, parliamentary procedure is the parliamentary law you follow in your organization, along with any special rules of order that you institute just for your group.

The broad concept of *parliamentary law* (although not actually law in the sense of statutes and jurisprudence) is the body of accepted rules and practices of *deliberative assemblies* of all types and sizes. (Flip to Chapter 3 for more details on deliberative assemblies.)

If the term *parliamentary* conjures images of men in scratchy wigs crying "Hear, hear!" you may think this has little to do with you. But if you've come together as a loosely knit group of friends (or enemies), chances are good that you follow some rules even if you haven't written them down and given them a name. You know what I mean — rules like "Only one person speaks at a time," "Don't interrupt the person talking," or "Let's decide what to do about this before we go on to something else."

The most basic rules about interacting with others form the basis of what you may hear referred to as the *common parliamentary law.*

It's a collection of rules and customs, many of which you know, understand, and use every day, even though you never really think about them much.

REMEMBER

Robert's Rules isn't a law book. When you see the terms *legal* and *illegal* in this book, they usually refer to the propriety of a procedure or action under parliamentary procedure. Parliamentary law isn't statutory law. It's just the body of rules that, written or unwritten, you use when you're assembled and discussing your business.

Principles of parliamentary law

Robert's Rules is generally regarded as the codification (or systematic arrangement) of general parliamentary law. Robert's Rules is written to be a concise but thorough treatment of the vast amount of interrelated information on parliamentary law.

The rules in Robert's Rules are soundly based in principles of parliamentary law that take into account the rights of the majority, the minority, the individual, any absent members, and the collective rights of all these groups.

Robert's Rules is grounded in the principle that a deliberative assembly (see Chapter 3) is a body, usually autonomous, that enjoys the freedom to conduct its business in accordance with its own provisions for the rights of its members and itself as an assembly. It's free to enact its own rules, choose its leadership, delegate to its leadership all or part of its authority, and retain whatever control over its business it wants.

Another guiding principle is the "one person, one vote" principle. Although members of an assembly commonly hold more than one position in the group, one person still gets only one vote. You may be both the club treasurer and the chairman of the program committee, but you don't get to vote twice at board meetings.

Members only

When you hold *membership* in a deliberative assembly, which is a fancy way of saying "a group of people debating an issue," you're entitled to all the rights and privileges associated with that membership. Generally, members have the following rights:

- » To attend the meetings of the assembly
- » To make motions, which are formal proposals that the assembly take some kind of action in the name of the group
- » To participate in debate
- » To vote

These are fundamental membership rights that can't be taken from you without disciplinary action through due process (see Chapter 18), unless provisions set out in your bylaws define limitations on these rights within specific classes of membership.

TIP

Although these rights apply to the majority of members, different levels of membership, which can carry with them varying privileges, may be provided for in your bylaws. In this book, however, just like in Robert's Rules, when I talk about "members" or "membership," I mean the class that has all rights, including the right to attend meetings, make motions, speak in debate, and vote.

Membership carries with it basic duties, such as the duty to vote on questions on which the member has an opinion. The *duty* to vote, however, exists alongside a right to *not* vote, that is, to *abstain.* (For more on abstention, see Chapter 8.) Membership often carries with it other duties and obligations as well. You can resign your membership if you want to end your obligations and duties to the assembly, but you can be compelled to fulfill any duties and obligations that you incurred as a member. However, a member who is in good standing can't be compelled to continue membership to the extent that additional obligations accrue.

One of the more common duties that go along with membership is to be of service to your organization. The organization's bylaws specify membership duties specific to the organization or assembly. If you haven't found out already, you'll surely find out someday that the honor of getting on a prestigious board includes the duty to give service on a committee — and maybe even to give a little extra money to your organization from time to time.

REMEMBER

The term *membership* also refers to the assembly, or to the group of people who have basic membership rights. In this book, as in Robert's Rules, the term *membership* is often used when referring to the assembly, as in, "That's a question that has to be decided by the membership."

You may have heard the phrase "member in good standing." Well, that has special meaning according to Robert's Rules. A member who is in good standing is one whose membership rights haven't been suspended through due process or based on the application of specific bylaws to the member's standing. If you haven't paid your dues, but you're in a bylaw-specific grace period, then the fact that you haven't paid the dues doesn't besmirch your status of being "in good standing."

Fundamental principles of parliamentary law

Some rules are so fundamental that Robert's Rules has labeled them *fundamental principles of parliamentary law*. These principles are at the foundation of all the rest of the rules. The rules that embody these principles can never be suspended, even by a unanimous vote. If you want to avoid having these rules apply to your group, you need to provide as much in your bylaws (more on those in Chapter 2). Those fundamental principles are as follows:

>> Basic rights of a member can't be suspended. Unless a particular member is subject to rules of discipline, all members' rights to attend meetings and exercise other rights of membership can be inhibited only by procedural rules that affect the entire assembly — rules such as ones that limit or close debate.

>> Rules protecting absentees can't be suspended. Therefore, business conducted in a special meeting must conform to what is specified in the call of the meeting (see Chapter 4).

>> A member is entitled to one, and only one, vote on any question before the assembly. This rule can't be suspended to allow for cumulative voting (see Chapter 8).

>> The right to vote is limited to the members who are present in a meeting during the time a vote is actually taken. Therefore, on any question before the assembly,

rules can't be suspended, even if the vote is unanimous, to allow a nonmember or an absentee to vote.

>> Only one motion can be considered at a time. (You can, however, have several motions *pending* at one time.)

>> The majority rules, but not until the opportunity for full and free debate has occurred. No member, or any minority, can be denied the right to participate in debate unless by two-thirds vote the assembly has decided to limit or end discussion or debate. (Take a look at Chapter 7 for the details on limiting or closing debate, and check out Chapter 9 for details on the motions that you use to do it.)

Other principles of parliamentary law

Parliamentary law also includes the following general principles:

>> Even though it's not always wise to do so, every person and minority faction has the right to use all available rules and procedures in their efforts to have their positions adopted by the group. However, these measures can't be undertaken in a manner that disrupts the peace of the entire group.

>> A higher voting threshold is required to change something than to adopt it in the first place. (See Chapter 12 for more details on readdressing issues.) This requirement protects against the instability of rules that may be changed easily when there are minor shifts in attendance from meeting to meeting.

Achieving Personal Goals

The benefits of understanding the principles of parliamentary law in Robert's Rules go beyond just running (or participating in) a meeting. Taking the time to better understand the ins and outs of Robert's Rules can save you a lot of time during meetings and help you use motions to get your ideas on the fast track.

Understanding motion-making techniques develops your ability to concisely state exactly what needs to be done. The better you are at making motions in meetings, the better you will be at processing your own particular action plans, both in and out of meetings.

Experiencing Personal Success

As you absorb tips on effective meeting participation, you're no doubt developing leadership skills you didn't even know you had. By focusing your knowledge of rules and your educated judgment of when and how to apply them, you'll find yourself successful in all your meetings. The education you get from a hands-on application of Robert's Rules in your meetings helps you more naturally listen to others before making a decision. Ask successful people whether they'd be where they are now if they hadn't learned how to listen and respect other points of view!

Chapter **2**

Defining the Organization: Bylaws and Other Rules

"*We the People...*" These famous words begin the definition of one of the greatest organizations in the world, the United States of America.

We, the people, adopted a rule early on that secures the right "peaceably to assemble." Your right to belong to an organization is based on the agreement of everybody that assembling is a natural and sacred right, and it's one of the first membership rules the founding fathers established. It was so important that they put it in the Constitution, making it sure to stay in force unless a large majority of Americans agree to change it. And that's not likely to happen anytime soon.

A country *is* its citizens, and your organization *is* its membership. The success of both depends on the members agreeing to the fundamental rules. If you think of your organization's rules as the framework for your mutual cooperation and benefit, you can understand bylaws and other organizational rules much more clearly.

In this chapter, I focus primarily on bylaws because this governing document establishes the real framework of your organization. My focus isn't intended to minimize the importance of other types of rules; instead, it's to emphasize that your bylaws are to your organization pretty much what the Constitution is to the United States of America.

Covering the Rules about Rules

C'mon now, admit it: You saw it in the Table of Contents, but you really didn't believe that a whole chapter could cover rules about the rules. Well, this is a book about a book full of rules, so this chapter shouldn't be a big surprise. But don't worry — it's not all that complicated.

When it comes to the rules about rules, one rule stands out: A deliberative assembly is free to adopt whatever rules it wants or needs, as long as the procedure for adopting them conforms to any rules already in place or to the general parliamentary law (which Chapter 1 defines).

The reason for having rules in the first place is to enable you and your fellow group members to agree on *governance* (that is, who your leaders are, how you choose them, when you have your meetings, and so forth), *procedures* for arriving at group decisions, and *policy* that covers the details of administration for your organization.

Without rules, you won't last long as a group; you'll be unable to avoid conflicts, and you'll experience disagreements on points as basic as whether a particular assembly of individuals can really decide something in the name of the group. You won't know for sure whether some procedure used is inappropriate for arriving at an important decision. And without a way of classifying the different rules, you'll find yourself not knowing which rule takes precedence and when. Robert's Rules sets up some basic classifications to help you avoid these complications.

Classifying your rules

Different situations call for different types of rules. Robert's Rules classifies the different governance rules based generally on their application and use and on how difficult they are to change or suspend.

Robert's Rules classifies rules for deliberative bodies as follows:

>> **Charter:** The charter may be either your *articles of incorporation* or a *charter issued by a superior organization,* if your group is a unit of a larger organization. A corporate charter is amendable as provided by law or according to provisions in the document for amendment. A charter issued by a superior organization is amendable only by the issuing organization.

>> **Bylaws:** The *bylaws* are fundamental rules that define your organization. Bylaws are established in a single document of interrelated rules. (I discuss bylaws in detail in the section, "Uncovering Bylaw Basics," later in this chapter.)

>> **Rules of order:** *Rules of order* are written rules of procedure for conducting meeting business in an orderly manner and the meeting-related duties of the officers. Because these rules are of a general nature about procedure rather than about the organization itself, it's customary for organizations to adopt a standard set of rules by adopting a parliamentary authority such as Robert's Rules. Most of the rules in Robert's Rules and the other chapters of this book are *rules of order.* Rules of order can be customized by adopting *special rules of order* to modify or supersede specific rules in an adopted parliamentary manual. For example, the rule of order in Robert's Rules limiting speeches in debate to ten minutes can be superseded permanently by adopting a *special rule of order* providing that speeches are limited to three minutes.

EXCEPTION

Robert's Rules makes an important exception to the rule that a special rule of order can supersede a rule in the parliamentary manual (whew!): If the parliamentary manual states that some particular rule in the manual can be changed only by amending bylaws, the rule in the parliamentary manual can't be superseded merely by adopting a special rule of order. You have to amend your bylaws to change it.

» **Standing rules:** These rules are related to the details of administration rather than parliamentary procedure. For example, suppose your group adopts a motion that directs the treasurer to reimburse the secretary for postage up to $150 per month, provided that the secretary submits a written request accompanied by receipts for postage purchased and a log of items mailed in the name of the organization. That policy becomes a standing rule. Motions that you adopt over the course of time that are related to policy and administration are collectively your *standing rules.*

» **Custom:** Your organization probably has some special ways of doing things that, although not written in the rules, may as well be etched in stone on your clubhouse door. Unless your bylaws or some written rule (including the rules in Robert's Rules) provides to the contrary, a practice that has become custom should be followed just like a written rule, unless your group decides by majority vote to do something different.

Ranking the rules

When you're dealing with different types of rules, you need to know when to follow which rule. Among the more fundamental rules are rules about which rule takes precedence over other rules, which the following sections discuss.

Finishing first: Charter

The charter, if you have one, reigns supreme. Nothing except a judge or the law of the land supersedes it. Fortunately, a charter is usually pretty succinct and operates like a franchise. It's a grant of authority by the state (if your group is incorporated) or a superior organization (if your group is a constituent unit of a larger body). A charter usually lists the few conditions under which you must operate, but it usually provides for your organization to be subject to bylaws specifically tailored to your organization but which may not conflict with provisions of the charter.

WARNING

When your organization is incorporated, your state's corporation statutes will most certainly contain rules of procedure. Often, the statutes will authorize the corporation's charter, bylaws, or other rules to supersede a statute. But probably just as often, the statute will supersede anything to the contrary you have in your bylaws. Things get complicated for organizations (incorporated or otherwise) that are governed by various other state statutes and codes. If your organization is a homeowner association or a condominium association, it's likely subject to some pretty specific state laws defining how the organization must operate. Things can get even more complicated when deeded covenants and restrictions come into play. If your organization is one that is governed by such laws and court filings, it can be difficult to know just what rules might apply in your situation. In those cases, only a lawyer licensed to practice in your state can give you the birds-eye lowdown on the applicability of the various and sundry laws that may pertain to your situation.

Coming in second: Bylaws

Even though the bylaws contain the most important single set of rules for defining your organization and its governance, the content of the bylaws remains binding and enforceable only to the extent that it doesn't conflict with your charter. If your group isn't incorporated or isn't subject to a charter, the bylaws are the highest-ranking rules of your organization. No matter what, no rules of order or standing rules can ever be enforced if they conflict in any way with your bylaws.

Because bylaws define specific characteristics of the organization itself — including (in most cases) which parliamentary authority the organization uses — bylaws are of such importance that they can't be changed without previous notice and the consent of a large majority of your members.

Tying for third: Special rules of order and standing rules

Special rules of order and *standing rules* have completely different applications and uses, but they rank together as immediately subordinate to bylaws because they have one particular point in common: They comprise individual rules (each of which is usually adopted separately from the other rules in the class) based on the specific need of the organization to accomplish a specific purpose for which the rule is adopted.

Coming in fourth: Robert's Rules (parliamentary authority)

Robert's Rules is a parliamentary manual, and if your organization has adopted it as your parliamentary authority, Robert's Rules is binding on your group. But it's binding only to the extent that it doesn't conflict with the charter, bylaws, special rules of order, or standing rules.

Last place: Custom

By *custom*, I mean procedures that aren't written anywhere but are followed in actual practice just as if they're written rules. Custom has its place, and any practice that's taken on the standing of an unwritten rule is just as binding as if it were written, with one exception: If a written rule exists to the contrary, even in the parliamentary authority, the custom must yield as soon as the conflict is pointed out to the membership through a point of order; the only way around this exception is if a *special rule of order* is adopted to place the custom formally in the body of written rules.

So when Mr. Meticulous shows you the bylaw that requires all elections to be conducted by ballot vote, from then on, you have to have ballot votes, even if your organization's custom has been to elect unopposed candidates by acclamation. In that case, you can no longer claim that custom has any standing.

TIP

Custom is known by another name: The "we've always done it that way" rule. When a written rule contradicts the "we've always done it that way" rule, the custom absolutely yields to the written rule — unless, that is, you change the written rule to make it agree with the way you've "always done" whatever it is you're doing.

Laying down rule requirements

Fundamental differences exist in the procedures you use to adopt or amend each class of rules. Table 2-1 lists the rules by class and the requirements for their adoption, amendment, and suspension. (See Chapter 11 for rules on suspending rules.)

TABLE 2-1   ## Rule Classifications and Requirements

Class of Rule	Requirements to Adopt	Requirements to Amend	Requirements to Suspend
Charter	Instrument initially adopted by majority vote or as provided by law or chartering authority	As provided in charter	Can't be suspended unless the charter or applicable law allows it to be suspended
Bylaws	Instrument initially adopted by majority vote	As provided in bylaws or by two-thirds vote with previous notice if bylaws are silent	Can't be suspended unless provisions for suspension are included for a particular rule or are clearly in the nature of a *rule of order*
Special rules of order	Previous notice and two-thirds vote or a majority of the entire membership	Previous notice and two-thirds vote or a majority of the entire membership	Two-thirds vote, subject to limitations (see Chapter 11)
Standing rules	Majority vote	Majority vote with notice, two-thirds vote without notice, or a majority of the entire membership	Can't be suspended if application is outside a meeting; can be suspended for the particular session by majority vote if application is in a meeting
Rules of Order (parliamentary manual)	Initially adopted by specifying in bylaws, but may be adopted by special rule of order	Not amendable, but special rule of order or standing rule takes precedence	Two-thirds vote, subject to limitations

When you know the basics about the different classes of rules, it's time to drill down to bylaws. Your bylaws are the heart of your organization's structure.

Uncovering Bylaw Basics

Your *bylaws* comprise the fundamental rules that define your organization. They include all the rules that your group determines are of such importance that

>> They can't be changed unless the members get previous notice of any proposed change, and a large majority (commonly two-thirds) is required to enact any proposed change.

>> They can't be suspended (see Chapter 11), even by a unanimous vote.

REMEMBER

A particular bylaw may be suspended if the bylaw provides for its own suspension or if it's a rule that otherwise would be considered a *rule of order* as I define in the section "Covering the Rules about Rules," earlier in this chapter. An example of such a bylaw that can be suspended is a provision that "the president shall preside at all meetings of the assembly." Because this bylaw is specifically a rule related to the duty of an officer in a meeting, it would otherwise be classed as a rule of order; it could, therefore, be suspended. I discuss procedures for motions to suspend the rules in Chapter 11.

WARNING

The exception permitting bylaws to be suspended in these cases must be narrowly construed. If any doubt exists about whether a rule in the bylaws can be suspended, it probably can't be suspended.

Because bylaws are such a closely interrelated and customized set of rules, they're gathered in a single document. With the exception of any laws governing your organization or your charter (if your organization is incorporated or is a unit of a larger organization), the bylaws take precedence over any and all other rules you adopt.

The nature of bylaws is sufficient to establish a contract between members and define their rights, duties, and mutual obligations. Bylaws contain substantive rules relating to the rights of members whether or not they're present in meetings. The bylaws detail the extent to which the management of the organization's business is handled by the membership, a subordinate board, or an executive committee.

REMEMBER

Whenever the U.S. Congress enacts a law that treads on the fundamental rights of a citizen, that citizen can take 'em to task and show Congress just how the law is unconstitutional. Well, bylaws are like that, in a way. Adopting a motion or taking any action that conflicts with your bylaws is wrong — and, under Robert's Rules, any such action is null and void.

You don't have to go to all the trouble of taking your violation to the Supreme Court, however. You just have to take it to the membership by raising a point of order (see Chapter 11). Although the membership is considered supreme, it can't even use a unanimous vote to make legal something that conflicts with the bylaws without amending the bylaws; to do so violates the rights of the absentees.

TIP

Because of the nature and importance of bylaws, and because members' rights are spelled out there, a copy of the bylaws should be given to every member upon joining your organization. Anyone who is considering joining your organization must also be given a copy of the bylaws upon request. By joining, your prospective members agree to be bound by these rules, and it's reasonable for them to want to look over the bylaws in advance. For just that reason, I usually request a copy of an organization's bylaws before making a commitment to become a member. I figure that there's nothing wrong with looking at what I may be getting myself into!

ORIGINS OF THE CONSTITUTION AND BYLAWS

As stable as Robert's Rules are, styles change over time. In times past, an organization more commonly had two separate governance documents — the *constitution* and the *bylaws*. Now it's usually preferable to combine all the articles from both into one document called the *bylaws*. (A very old organization sometimes wants to keep its constitution, for historical reasons.)

Then . . .

Once upon a time, organizations customarily established two sets of rules to define themselves. The higher-ranking rules were called the *constitution,* and the rules that ranked just below the constitution in importance were called the *bylaws.*

The constitution usually contained the articles establishing the name and object of the organization, articles defining the qualifications of members and officers, and articles spelling out the essential details of meetings. (If the society was to be incorporated, the corporate charter contained these articles and the society didn't adopt a constitution.)

The bylaws, then, contained any other rules that the organization required that couldn't be changed without previous notice. These rules included details related to meetings that weren't included in the constitution; the quorum requirement; and any provisions for executive boards, committees, and parliamentary authority.

Both the constitution and the bylaws contained specific provisions for amendment. The constitution was a little more difficult to amend.

And now . . .

The only substantive difference between then and now is the recognition that, unless some compelling reason exists to have separate governance documents, or a real purpose is served by having two documents, with one more difficult to amend than the other, it's unnecessary to have a separate constitution and bylaws.

In fact, the only time a separate constitution is absolutely necessary is when some law requires it.

Robert's Rules now includes in the bylaws all the articles once placed in the two separate documents. Furthermore, whenever the term *bylaws* is used in Robert's Rules (or in *Robert's Rules For Dummies,* for that matter), it refers not only to bylaws, but also to the constitution (when one exists).

Breaking Down the Content of Bylaws

Your bylaws may have more articles than the basic list Robert's Rules provides. (And that's okay, unless you're adding a lot of stuff that you shouldn't.) In any case, the following list outlines the articles you need to have in your bylaws (and the order in which they need to appear) to cover the basic subjects common to most organizations:

1. **Name:** Specify the official name of your organization in this article.

2. **Object:** This article includes a succinct statement of the object or purpose for which your society is organized. This statement should be broad enough to cover anything your group may want to do as a group, but it should avoid enumerating details. When you list items, anything you leave out is deemed excluded.

3. **Membership:** Begin this article with details of the classes and types of membership, as well as the voting rights of each class. If a class of members doesn't have full membership rights, be sure to specify which rights that class *does* have (to prevent headaches later). If you have eligibility requirements or special procedures for admission, include them under this article. Also include any requirements for dues, including due dates, rights or restrictions of delinquent members, explanations of when members are dropped from the rolls for nonpayment, and reinstatement rights. Any rules related to resignations and any intricate requirements related to memberships in subordinate or superior societies are included here, too.

4. **Officers:** This article is the place to explain specifications about the officers that your organization requires and any duties beyond those duties established by rule in your parliamentary authority (see Chapter 15). Sections including qualifications of officers; details of nomination, election, and terms of office (including restrictions on the number of consecutive terms (or total terms in a lifetime, if any); and rules for succession and vacancies are appropriately placed in this article. You may include a separate article to describe the duties of each officer.

5. **Meetings:** This article contains the dates for all regular meetings. Authority for special meetings, if they're to be allowed, must appear in the bylaws. Details related to how and by whom special meetings can be called, and the notice required, are included here. Also, the quorum for meetings needs to be included in a section of this article.

6. **Executive board:** If your organization plans to have a board of directors to take care of business between your regular meetings (or all the time, if that's the way you set it up), your bylaws *must* include an article establishing the board and providing all the details regarding the board's authority and responsibility. Be clear and specific about who is on the board, how board members are elected or appointed, when the board is to meet, any special rules it must abide by, and, of course, specific details of the board's powers.

WARNING

The powers and duties of boards vary widely from one group to the next, and problems arise for many organizations whenever the members and the board have different ideas about the role and duties of the board. This article, therefore, must be developed or amended only with the greatest care.

It's common not only to have an *executive board* to handle the business of the organization between membership meetings, but also to have an *executive committee* (that reports to the board) composed of selected officers who are authorized to act for the board in the time between board meetings. The same amount of care must be taken when establishing the composition and power of an executive committee as when establishing a board. Furthermore, as with the executive board, no executive committee can exist except as the bylaws expressly provide for it.

7. **Committees:** All regular standing committees that your group anticipates needing to carry out its business are defined under this article, each in its own section. The description of each standing committee needs to include the name of the committee, how its members are selected, and its role and function in the organization. If other standing committees may be needed, this article must contain an authorization for the formation of additional standing committees. Otherwise, the bylaws must be amended to create a standing committee.

8. **Parliamentary authority:** Adopting a parliamentary authority in your bylaws is the simplest and most efficient way to provide your group with binding *rules of order* under which to operate. The statement adopting the parliamentary authority needs to define clearly any rules to which the rules in your parliamentary authority must yield. Robert's Rules contains tried-and-true bylaw language for making Robert your parliamentary authority. You'll find it in the sample bylaws available online at www.dummies.com/go/robertsrules4e.

9. **Amendment:** The bylaws specify the precise requirements for previous notice and size of the vote required to change the bylaws. If your bylaws say nothing about amendment, and if Robert's Rules is your parliamentary authority, then amending your bylaws requires previous notice and a two-thirds vote or the vote of a majority of the entire membership.

Making Sure Your Bylaws Are Complete

If your bylaws include at least the basic articles I outline in the previous section, you're at least able to say that you have a set of bylaws. But a basic set of bylaws often isn't enough. Some things you just can't do unless you make provisions for them in your bylaws, and other bylaws you need because your membership includes constituent organizations. These sections identify a number of bylaw provisions to consider depending on the nature and needs of your organization.

Express-permission needed bylaws

The actions in the following list are collected from throughout Robert's Rules, but this list is by no means a complete one. It's accurate, though, and it may help you if you're wondering whether you can (or can't) do something in your own organization.

If your bylaws don't specifically authorize it, you can't do the following:

» Elect officers by plurality, cumulative, or preferential voting

» Submit absentee votes (including votes by mail, fax, email, or proxy)

» Hold a runoff between the top two candidates

» Suspend a requirement for a ballot vote

» Suspend a bylaw (unless the bylaw is in the nature of a rule of order or provides for its own suspension)

» Limit in any way the right of the assembly to elect officers of its choice, including officers who aren't members of your organization

» Restrict the right of a member to cast a write-in vote

» Keep a vice president from assuming the office of the president if a vacancy occurs in the office of president

» Designate persons as honorary officers or honorary members

» Allow honorary officers or honorary members to vote

» Create an executive board

» Appoint an executive committee

» Impose financial assessments on members

- ≫ Suspend a member's voting rights or drop a member from the rolls for nonpayment of dues or assessments without due process (see Chapter 18)

- ≫ Hold meetings by telephone conference, videoconference, or (heaven forbid) email

- ≫ Hold special meetings

Special bylaw provisions for convention-holding organizations

If your organization is one that comprises subordinate bodies and which meets as a convention of delegates (see Chapter 20), your bylaws will probably serve you better if they include the following:

- ≫ Authorization for periodic convention and the frequency it shall convene

- ≫ Definition of the powers and duties of the parent organization

- ≫ The convention quorum

- ≫ Details of the composition of the voting members, including qualifications for delegates and alternates and details of how delegates and alternates are chosen

- ≫ Details about the notice (call) of the convention, including when, how, and to whom the notice is sent

- ≫ Details as to what constitutes good standing of a subordinate unit for participation in the convention

- ≫ Provision for officers elected at the convention to assume office at the end of the convention

- ≫ Any other information essential to the organization and operation of the convention

Amending Your Bylaws

No matter how good a job you've done in creating your bylaws, sooner or later, you'll need to change something. If you followed all the guidelines and instructions for creating proper bylaws, amending them won't be so difficult that you can't consider and make changes within a reasonable time when necessary — but they won't be too easily amended. These sections explain in plain English what you need to do to amend your bylaws.

Setting the conditions for amending your bylaws

Normally, amending something previously adopted (see Chapter 12) takes a majority vote if previous notice is given, a two-thirds vote without any previous notice, or a majority of the entire membership (see Chapter 8).

But amending a previously adopted bylaw is a different story. You want to ensure that the rights of all members continue to be protected. The surest way to provide this protection is to prevent bylaws from being changed without first giving every member an opportunity to weigh in on a change. And bylaws ought never be changed as long as a minority greater than one-third disagrees with the proposal.

Just think: If you can amend your bylaws by a majority vote at any meeting without notice, then Pete Sneak, Mabel Malevolent, and Connie Slink can assemble a small group on a slow night and, by excluding everyone not present from the right to vote, push through changes that allow the evil threesome to effectively take over all the group's bank accounts.

This worst-case scenario illustrates why you make it a little more difficult to amend bylaws than to amend anything else. And you should always specify in your bylaws the exact requirements for their amendment.

WARNING

According to Robert's Rules, you should, at the very least, require a two-thirds vote *and* previous notice to make any change in your bylaws. The previous notice ensures that anybody who cares about a bylaw amendment knows it's going to be voted on at a particular meeting and can attend the meeting to help the vote reach (or fail to reach) the threshold. The rule also makes sure that if more than one-third of the members voting are opposed to the change, then they win and nothing changes. When deciding what amendment requirements to put in your bylaws, consider two points: the *details of the previous notice* and the *vote threshold required to adopt the change.* For detailed information concerning previous notice of motions, turn to Chapter 6; you can find a discussion of voting thresholds in Chapter 8.

Giving notice of bylaw amendments

Bylaws are important to orderly, productive organizations, so even if you don't know many specifics about them, you can probably guess that bylaw amendments are pretty serious undertakings. Amending bylaws essentially changes the contract you've made with your fellow members about how your organization operates, so you need to be really technical and precise. The proper notice for a bylaw amendment contains three fundamental components:

>> The proposed amendment, precisely worded

>> The current bylaw

>> The bylaw as it will read if the amendment is adopted

Additionally, the notice commonly includes the proposers' names and their rationale for offering the amendment. It may also include other information, such as whether a committee or board endorses or opposes the amendment.

I furnish an example form for a bylaw notice at www.dummies. com/go/robertsrules4e.

TIP

Robert's Rules recommends organizations that meet only once a year include in their bylaws a provision for some minimum number of days' previous notice for a proposed bylaw amendment. For example, "Previous notice of proposed bylaw amendments must be sent to the members in writing no less than 30 days in advance of the meeting."

Handling a motion to amend bylaws

When the time comes to deal with the amendment on the floor, you're handling a special application of the motion to *Amend Something Previously Adopted* (see Chapter 12). The bylaw amendment is subject to all the rules for that motion except for the following:

>> The provisions for amendment contained in your bylaws determine the requirements for previous notice and the vote required to adopt a bylaws amendment. Robert recommends that bylaws include provisions for their amendment that require previous notice and a two-thirds vote. But if your bylaws have no provisions for their amendment, the requirement is a two-thirds vote with previous notice or, without notice, a majority of the entire membership.

>> Primary and secondary amendments to your proposed bylaws amendment can't exceed the *scope* of the notice. For example, if the proposed amendment was noticed as one to raise the dues by $10, then you can't amend the proposal to increase the dues by more than $10. (Nor can you amend the proposal to lower the dues by any amount!) But you can amend the proposal to increase the dues only $8, because an $8 increase is within the scope of notice.

>> After you've adopted an amendment, that's it — you can't reconsider the vote. (But if the amendment fails, you can reconsider *that* vote.) See Chapter 12 for more information on the motion to *Reconsider*.

>> The rule against considering essentially the same question twice in a meeting doesn't apply when you're amending bylaws. Members may offer different approaches to accomplishing similar goals, and all bylaw amendments included in the notice are eligible for consideration.

WARNING

Even though other amendments addressing the same issue have to be considered if proper notice has been given, you can't get around the possibility that, after you adopt a particular bylaw amendment, other proposals may become moot because any change in the bylaws may make a yet-to-be-considered amendment impossible to enact.

Amending specific articles, sections, or subsections of your bylaws

Proposed amendments to bylaws are main motions, which means that the amendments are themselves open to primary and secondary amendments.

When you're amending parts of your bylaws, you propose the amendment as a main motion and specify one of the same processes used for any amendment. The processes of the motion to *Amend*, which Chapter 9 describes in detail, are as follows:

>> Strike out words, sentences, or paragraphs.

>> Insert (or add) words, sentences, or paragraphs.

>> Strike out and insert (or *substitute*) words, sentences, or paragraphs.

Any primary or secondary amendments to the proposed bylaws amendment must be within the scope of notice, as I describe it in the previous section. However, when your amendment is noticed as a substitution of an article or section, and some part of the substitution is no different from the original bylaw, then you're prohibited from amending that particular part when considering the substitution. When no change is proposed, any change is considered outside the scope of the notice.

Making a series of isolated changes to accomplish one purpose

Sometimes, handling a series of amendments separately is impractical. Consider those cases where, for example, you want to change the name of the office of secretary to the office of clerk, it would make no sense to go through your bylaws and handle separate amendments for each occurrence of the word "secretary." It's appropriate in those cases to offer the motion in such a way that it takes care of it all in one motion. That motion would be that "we amend the bylaws by striking out the word 'secretary' and insert the word 'clerk' throughout the bylaws."

WARNING

It's not always going to be a simple one-sentence amendment. You may have to include a little more than that in the proposed amendment. But because bylaw amendments require thoughtful preparation even before notice is given, you may be able to take care of these kinds of changes with one carefully written motion to amend. Take your time and prepare your proposed amendment in writing so that you avoid unintended consequences of adopting a poorly thought-out amendment.

TIP

This procedure isn't limited to bylaw amendments. It's okay to accomplish a similar series of changes in anything previously adopted, or even when amending a pending motion for that matter. Flip to Chapter 9 for a more specialized discussion of the motion to amend.

Tackling a full revision of your bylaws

A *revision* to bylaws is an extensive rewrite that often makes fundamental changes to the structure of the organization.

By considering a revision of your bylaws, you're proposing to substitute a new set of bylaws for the existing ones. Therefore, the rules regarding scope of notice that limit primary and secondary amendments don't apply. Your group is free to amend anything in the proposed revision before it's adopted, as if it were considering and adopting the bylaws for the first time.

WARNING

The membership may properly consider a proposed bylaw revision only when it has been prepared by a committee that the organization's membership itself has appointed for the purpose of preparing a draft bylaw revision. Such a committee, however, can be appointed by an executive board that has been specifically authorized to create and appoint a bylaw revision committee.

Recording the results of the vote

Bylaws amendments (requiring a two-thirds vote) are handled as a rising vote (see Chapter 8) unless the amendments are adopted by unanimous consent. However, because of the importance of bylaws and the impact of their amendment, unless the vote is practically unanimous, the best and fairest procedure is to count the vote and record the result in the minutes.

Interpreting Bylaws

Your bylaws belong to your group, and only your group can decide what they mean. A parliamentarian can help you understand the technical meaning of a phrase or a section, but when you come across something ambiguous (meaning that there's more than one way to *reasonably* interpret something), the question needs to be answered by the members of your organization by a majority vote at a meeting.

TIP

If your group has to adopt a specific interpretation to resolve an ambiguity, make the interpretation. But as soon as you can, follow up by amending the bylaws to remove the ambiguity. Making the adjustment to the bylaws keeps you from having to go round and round with the same issue, depending on who attends the meeting.

Robert's Rules lists some *principles of interpretation* to help you determine what's truly ambiguous and what's just a matter of following a rule for interpretation. I list and discuss these principles here in the context of bylaws, but the principles apply to other rules, too.

>> Bylaws are subject to interpretation only when ambiguity arises. If the meaning is clear, not even a unanimous vote can impute to them a different meaning. In other words, if you want a bylaw to have a different meaning, you have to amend it.

>> When bylaws are subject to interpretation, no interpretation can be made that creates a conflict with another bylaw. You're also obligated to take into account the original intent of the bylaw, if it can be ascertained.

>> If a provision of the bylaws has two reasonable interpretations, but one interpretation makes another bylaw absurd or impossible to reconcile and the other interpretation doesn't, you have to go with the one that doesn't have a negative effect on existing bylaws.

>> A more specific rule takes control when you have a conflict between the specific rule and a more general rule. For example, if your bylaws say that no relatives are permitted at meetings and another individual bylaw says that you can

bring your spouse to the annual meeting and barn dance, be prepared to buy your spouse a new dress or a new tie before the festivities begin.

>> When bylaws authorize specific items in the same class, other items of the same class aren't permitted. For example, if your bylaws allow members to enter cats, dogs, hamsters, and ferrets in the annual pet parade, then elephants are off-limits.

>> When a bylaw authorizes a specific privilege, no privilege greater than the one that's authorized is permitted. For example, if your bylaws say that your board can provide refreshments for the members at meetings, that doesn't mean the board can host a banquet at the Ritz.

>> If a bylaw prohibits something, then everything beyond what's prohibited (or limited) is also prohibited. However, other things not expressly prohibited or not as far-reaching as the prohibition are still permitted unless they're improper for some other reason. For example, if your bylaws say that you can't throw rotten fruit at the presiding officer during a meeting, but fails to rule out catapulting a spoonful of fresh stewed okra in their direction, you still should avoid hurling the okra. But you won't be in violation of the bylaw if you sneer fiercely.

>> If a bylaw prescribes a specific penalty, the penalty can't be increased or decreased except by amending the bylaws. For example, if you say that members shall be expelled for speaking ill of the Grand Mazonka, then members who call the GM a louse must be expelled. But you can't kick those members on the backside as they head for the exit.

>> If a bylaw uses a general term and then establishes specific terms that are completely included in the general term, then a rule that's applicable to the general term applies to all the specific terms. For example, if your bylaws define a class of membership as Royal Pains and that class includes Hot Shots and Know-It-Alls, then a rule applying to Royal Pains applies to both the Hot Shots and the Know-It-Alls as well.

DEALING WITH BYLAWS OF SUPERIOR AND SUBORDINATE ASSOCIATIONS

No shortage of organizations exist that comprise multiple subordinate organizations. National organizations are made up of state or regional organizations; state or regional organizations are made up of regional and local organizations. You get the picture.

Frequently, the superior organization will require that the bylaws of its subordinates "conform" to those of the superior organization. But under Robert's Rules, such "conformity" doesn't mean that the subordinate's bylaws must contain all the same provisions. What's essential in this consideration is the need for the subordinate's bylaws to be free from conflict with the bylaw provisions bylaws of its parent organization. Avoiding conflicts, however, doesn't mean that the bylaws have to all match up.

For example, if the National Nailbiters' bylaws require its officers to be members of the national association, it doesn't automatically mean that the Southeastern Nailbiters must restrict their own officers to members of their association. But if National's bylaws or policies specify that all subordinate associations' officers must be members of National *and* the subordinate body, then Southeastern's bylaws may not provide otherwise. If they do, then there's a conflict and the subordinate body's conflicting bylaws are unenforceable.

Publishing Your Bylaws and Other Rules

As I explain in Chapter 15, one of the duties of the secretary is to maintain a record book containing the current bylaws and rules of your group. This book needs to be available at meetings for easy reference.

Furnishing all members with a copy of the bylaws when they join the organization is good practice. Because special rules of order are indispensable to a member's effective participation in meetings, it's customary for special rules of order to be printed with, but under a separate heading from, the bylaws.

Standing rules, which are, for the most part, policies related to the details of administration and operations, are maintained as a current list. They're updated as rules are added, amended, or rescinded. It's customary to furnish a copy of the standing rules to new members along with the bylaws and special rules of order. Members who are actively involved in the organization will benefit from having easy access to up-to-date versions of the standing rules.

Some organizations periodically publish an updated booklet containing all their rules except rules that appear in the parliamentary authority. By publishing this type of booklet, you communicate that you intend for your rules to mean something. You encourage your members to know and understand the rules, and that helps them become more effective participants in your meetings. Everybody wins when you foster a high level of respect for and awareness of the rules of your organization.

Chapter **3**

Meetings: Making Group Decisions

Meetings are the official gatherings of your group. In them, you make the decisions that bind your organization. Not everybody agrees on every issue every time, but that's just part of the process.

With Robert's Rules, everybody wins in some way because you have an agreed-upon deal: You may not win, but you do get your say. This premise is the key to what makes your group a *deliberative assembly,* and meetings are the time and place for your assembly (group) to conduct its deliberations (discussions and decisions).

This chapter contains everything you ever wanted to know (and more) about the meetings of a deliberative assembly. Meetings. Ya gotta love 'em.

Defining the Deliberative Assembly

You're probably familiar with all the types of groups for which Robert's Rules generally comes into play. These time-tested rules of parliamentary procedure apply to meetings of several types of assemblies. Examples include the organizational meeting for a new society, a local meeting of a service club, a monthly meeting of the board of directors of your neighborhood association, or maybe even the national convention of your professional association.

Most of these groups are what are known as *deliberative assemblies.* Robert's Rules was designed to assist the meetings of these groups and the bodies subordinate to them.

Your group is a deliberative assembly in these cases:

>> You meet to act together in the name of the group, and you make your decisions after thorough *deliberation* (that is, an airing of the pros and cons). The majority gives the minority full opportunity to present its case and increase its number to a majority.

>> Your meetings are attended in one physical location where all the participants can hear each other. This stipulation includes teleconferences or videoconferences and other types of technology-aided gatherings, as long as your group's bylaws have authorized the use of these technologies in holding meetings. (For more on bylaws, turn to Chapter 2.) The point is that members *must be able to participate simultaneously* in the discussion.

>> Your members are free to use their own judgments in connection with making the group decisions, and each member's vote counts the same.

>> You don't have to quit or resign from the group if you don't concur in the final decision.

>> You have rules protecting the rights of absentees, and you require some absolute minimum number of participants to be present before taking action in the name of the group.

Robert's Rules uses the word *session* as another word for a meeting, particularly when so much needs to be accomplished that the group needs more than one meeting to get it all done. A session, therefore, is a meeting *or series of meetings* that gets your assembly through all the business it needs to take care of at one time.

In general, the groups I discuss in this book are divided into two types of deliberative assemblies (and the committees subordinate to them):

>> **The local assembly of an organized society:** You're probably most familiar with this kind of deliberative assembly. For the most part, the material in this book is geared to this type of assembly; examples include your civic or service club, your neighborhood association, and a professional or trade association meeting at the local (or maybe state) level.

>> **The board:** The board is an administrative or management group whose members are appointed or elected. It may be an executive board that is subordinate to a larger assembly, or it may be an autonomous body elected in public elections, appointed by public officials or government agencies, or appointed by the membership of a private organization.

Three other general types of deliberative assemblies exist: *mass meetings, conventions of delegates,* and *legislative bodies.* The legislative body includes lawmaking bodies like state and national legislatures. Except for small legislative bodies such as city or town councils that are run like the boards described earlier, legislative bodies operate under specialized parliamentary rules and authority. Robert's Rules wasn't written for them, so I don't discuss them beyond this mention.

(Un)Tying the Hands of the Assembly in Future Sessions

Although an assembly is free to make just about any decision it can agree to in a session, it isn't free to limit the ability of a majority to make any particular decision during the next session — at least, not without adopting a bylaw amendment or creating a special rule of order. (Flip to Chapter 2 for more on that.)

Robert's Rules provides that, when you get into a new session, you can revisit anything you've talked about before, whether you've made a decision or just talked about it and decided to decide later (if at all).

BONING UP ON TERMS OF ART

Terms with precise parliamentary definitions, such as *meeting* and *session,* often are used in everyday speech without giving much thought to their precise parliamentary meaning. The same is true for terms like *recess* and *adjournment.*

For example, many groups call their two- or three-day annual session an *annual meeting* and refer to the meetings in the session as *sessions* (as in "the Friday morning session"). Or they may call the time between those separate meetings a *recess,* even though they really *adjourned* the morning meeting.

For a more complete glossary of parliamentary terms, skip to the Appendix of this book. The following list defines meeting-related terms as they're used in this book:

- A *meeting* is any official convening of the members for any length of time to transact official business, with no break in the proceedings for more than a few minutes. Such a break is called a *recess,* not to be confused with an *adjournment.*

- A *recess* is a short break in a meeting, but declaring a recess does not adjourn the meeting.

- An *adjournment* ends a meeting, but it doesn't necessarily end the *session.* For a session that carries over to more than one meeting, when any but the last meeting of the session adjourns, that meeting is said to "adjourn to meet again at [specify a time]." The act of adjourning is termed an *adjournment,* and the next meeting is called an *adjourned meeting,* or an *adjournment of* the previous meeting.

- A *session* refers to a meeting or series of meetings working completely through an entire agenda or order of business (see Chapter 5). If the session is more than one meeting, each meeting picks up where the previous one left off.

For example, imagine that you've just figured out in July that you don't have enough money to buy an air conditioner for the clubhouse, so you propose to "postpone until next summer" any talk about buying an air conditioner. Your chair should rule the motion to *Postpone* "out of order" because a motion can't be postponed beyond the next session. No motion to *Postpone* is in order if it would limit your assembly's ability to make a decision to buy an air conditioner when things get hot at your August meeting.

The rule that keeps your group from tying its own hands in a future session also makes it possible to revisit a motion that failed at an earlier session and start over with no restrictions. Nothing prohibits any member from making a motion again, even if it failed in your last session.

TECHNICAL STUFF

When you're in a new session, it's too late to make a motion to *Reconsider*, but a motion to *Reconsider* that was made at the earlier meeting can be called up (see Chapter 12). If a motion failed at your last meeting, you can just try again. If a motion passed that you want to get rid of it, you can move to *Rescind* or *Amend Something Previously Adopted*. Either way, it doesn't matter what side you were on in the earlier meeting.

Understanding Types of Business Meetings

In most deliberative assemblies, meetings are classified as one of the following types.

Regular meetings

Regular meetings are just that: regular! You can count on having one every week, month, quarter, or whatever your schedule calls for. Your bylaws probably spell out the days when you hold regular meetings, and if you've done the smart thing, you've even established place and time of your meetings by adopting a standing rule or two. Regular meeting times can be established in other ways, but if the times and places aren't fixed in the rules in some way, you'll need to provide for adequate notice of the day, time, and place of the meeting. I cover some important details about for meeting notices in Chapter 4.

Regular meetings are generally conducted to complete a standard order of business (see Chapter 5), so your meeting and the session are the same thing. Any business that the assembly needs to handle can be dealt with at a regular meeting. However, any motions that require previous notice (such as bylaw amendments) must be noticed in strict accordance with your bylaws or rules of order.

Special meetings

Special meetings, sometimes referred to as *called meetings,* are held for the purpose of taking up business that requires the urgent attention of your group and that can't wait until the next regular meeting. Special meetings are also used if your group needs to dedicate an entire meeting to dealing with one or more specific issues.

REMEMBER

Your group can't hold special meetings unless your bylaws specifically authorize them or unless your group needs to schedule a special meeting for a trial. (Flip to Chapter 18 for the straight-and-skinny on trials.) Bylaws need to clearly specify just how a special meeting may be called.

Commonly, bylaws provide that "special meetings may be called by the president, and shall be called on the request of any five members." The exact number isn't that important, but it's a good idea to have some number of members who can demand a special meeting, especially if there's a need, say, to chastise the president for extreme misfeasance (or just plain obtuse recalcitrance!). After all, presidents aren't likely to call such meetings on their own initiative.

Special meetings always require notice to the members a reasonable time in advance. The notice must include not only the time and place of the meeting, but also the specifics of the business to be transacted. I go into detail about meeting notices in Chapter 4, so be sure to read that chapter before you call any special meetings!

WARNING

In a special meeting, only properly noticed business can be taken up. Other than the application of secondary or incidental motions that might be needed to deal with the business for which a special meeting is called, *nothing* can be done in a special meeting if it wasn't specifically included in the notice, or *call*, of the meeting. This rule protects the rights of absentees and can't be suspended unless every single member of the organization is present.

TECHNICAL STUFF

Sometimes a special meeting notice lists a couple of items of business to be dealt with and then says, "and any other business that may come before the assembly." But this language in a notice for a special meeting is meaningless. Anything done in a special meeting that wasn't *specifically* declared in the notice as business to be considered is null and void.

Adjourned meetings

An *adjourned meeting* is a continuation of a meeting (regular or special) that has adjourned without completing its agenda or order of business. Adjourned meetings come about in two ways:

>> **Unplanned:** Adjourned meetings come about as a result of a decision you make in one meeting to close the meeting for now, but to reconvene later and pick up where you left off. Such an adjourned meeting turns what you probably thought would be a one-meeting session into a two-meeting session.

>> **Planned:** Adjourned meetings are commonly scheduled within a session of several meetings.

No matter how it is created, an adjourned meeting's purpose is to continue the order of business you were involved in during an earlier meeting. In the adjourned meeting, the order of business continues at the point where it left off in the previous meeting (except that minutes of the previous meeting are read before the meeting continues).

Adjourned meetings are appropriate when it's important to con-tinue the business of a particular meeting before the beginning of the next regular meeting (session).

Suppose that you're in your annual meeting in the middle of elections, and balloting is taking an unusually long time. Your group wants to complete the election without having to wait until your next regular meeting, but everyone is tired. If you don't stop soon, you'll lose your quorum and have to quit anyway.

So you move to *Fix the Time to Which to Adjourn* (see Chapter 10) before actually adjourning your meeting. By adopting that motion, you've established an *adjourned meeting* to be held next week. Next week, you hold your adjourned meeting and continue your election process; you conclude the session when you finally adjourn that meeting.

TECHNICAL STUFF

The term *adjourned meeting* also applies to the prescheduled meetings that make up a *session* of several meetings; each successive meeting in a session is an *adjournment of* the previous meeting.

Annual meetings

Two kinds of annual meetings exist. I explain both here.

Some groups have only one meeting of the membership each year. At this meeting, they elect officers, an executive board, or both. They hear a lot of reports and approve the auditors' report, have some refreshments, and go home. After this *annual meeting*, the new officers and the board run the show for the next 12 months, until it's time for another annual meeting. Minutes of annual meetings of this sort should be approved as soon as possible, and it's customary for the members to appoint a special committee for that purpose.

REMEMBER

If your group operates with only one such annual membership meeting and you find yourself unable to accomplish something required to be done at your annual meeting, you should take steps to provide for an adjourned meeting to deal with the matter.

Other groups have membership meetings more often than annually, but still have a meeting known as the "annual" meeting at which the officers and standing committees present annual reports, and the members elect new officers. With the exception of *special orders of business* (see Chapter 5) designated in the bylaws to be handled at the annual meeting, the organization handles its usual order of business, including approving the minutes of the previous regular meeting.

REMEMBER

If your members meet under this kind of schedule and conditions prevent handling some required annual-meeting business, it's acceptable to postpone whatever the required business is to your next meeting. If you don't get to it at all, and don't postpone it, it's just unfinished business (or unfinished special order, as the case may be) at your next regular membership meeting.

Executive session

An *executive session* is any meeting or part of a meeting in which the proceedings are considered secret and nonmembers are excluded (unless they're invited for specific purposes of providing information to the assembly). Commonly, fraternal lodges conduct all their meetings in executive session. Nothing that occurs in executive session may be revealed to nonmembers except for the nonmember wo attended the meeting with the permission of the assembly.

REMEMBER

With the exception of public bodies required by law to hold meetings open to the public, no assembly (whether that of the organization's full membership, its executive board, or just a committee) is obligated to admit any nonmember to its proceedings unless ordered to do so by a superior body. The key element of "executive session" isn't so much about who can attend. It's about the confidentiality of what is said and done once executive session is invoked.

WARNING

Secrecy is everything when it comes to what happens in an executive session. The only time information can be revealed to a nonmember is when the action has to be revealed to carry it out. For example, if you expel Jack the Jerk for conduct that casts your organization in a bad light, keeping that a secret isn't going to be easy. Even this fact may be revealed only to the extent necessary to protect the organization or other organizations. But you still better not tell anybody about all the things you had to talk about to arrive at the decision to show him the door. A member who violates the secrecy of executive session can be held to account under the procedures for disciplining members for misconduct. Chapter 18 covers that not-so-pretty consequence.

The restrictions on the secrecy of discipline are stricter than the normal executive session rules.

The body that went into executive session can lift the secrecy requirement by adopting a motion to lift the secrecy restriction under the rules applicable to the motion to *Amend Something Previously Adopted* (see Chapter 12).

Conducting Your Business

Everything you do in meetings revolves around using Robert's Rules to get your business taken care of so that, ultimately, you can go home. And the whole purpose of parliamentary procedure is to facilitate the conduct of business in your meeting so that the deliberate will of the majority is achieved, while still protecting members' rights.

In the following sections, I go over the planning and execution of a business meeting and give you some guidance on how to decide the level of formality you need to get your group's business done. I also offer a few tips on effective meeting participation and presiding.

Giving notice and getting people to the meeting

The first requirement for any meeting is members — enough members that the decided-upon action is, in all likelihood, representative of the wishes of the entire group. Robert's Rules calls that minimum number a *quorum*. Part and parcel to achieving a quorum is making sure that all the members know about the meeting. After all, it's hard to show up if you don't know about the meeting, right? You need to send a meeting notice to your members. I discuss notice and quorum in detail in Chapter 4.

The only persons who have a right to attend a meeting are members of the body that is meeting. If you're a board, only board members have a right to attend. If you're a committee, only committee members have a right to attend. The body that is meeting, however, may open its meetings to any nonmembers it chooses by a majority vote. Sometimes bylaws have provisions that allow members who aren't on the board to attend board meetings as observers. But unless your organization is subject to open meeting laws, the right to be in the room where a meeting is held is controlled completely by the members of the body that is meeting.

Getting some help up front

In addition to having a room full of members, your meeting needs a minimum of two people to officiate. A presiding officer and a recording secretary are essential to holding a meeting and creating a record of what was done. If you don't already have officers, or if your regular officers can't attend the meeting, you need to know how to select temporary replacements. I cover officers and their duties in Chapter 15.

Planning the work

To conduct a productive and efficient meeting, you need a plan, or *agenda* — a schedule of what's going to be discussed and when. Find out all you need to know about using an agenda to get through your order of business in Chapter 5.

Getting down to business

If a meeting were a banquet, this would be the point at which the server shows up with your first course. After an appetizer of opening ceremonies and the soup and salad of reports, you get to the main course of making your decisions by making motions and voting, followed by adjournment (always a great dessert!).

Making motions

Nothing can get done until somebody has an idea and shares it with the group. You do this by making motions. I discuss the process of making main motions in Chapter 6.

HOW FORMAL DOES IT HAVE TO BE?

One of the concerns I hear from members and presiding officers alike is, "We don't like to get too formal with all this parliamentary procedure stuff." I understand. But usually one of these groups has a Puggy Knuckleknocker in attendance at its meeting.

Puggy is somewhat of a bully who likes to show off his knowledge of parliamentary procedure (that he remembers from the fifth grade). As elementary and convenient as his knowledge may be, he has a way of intimidating the members and the presiding officer. He's able to control the meeting because the other members don't even know enough to show him just how little he really knows. The only way they can disarm him is to just avoid using parliamentary procedure or anything that sounds too formal; the goal is just to keep him from being able to insist on having his way because he knows how to holler, "Point of order!" or "I move to table that motion!"

But the best way to handle Puggy is not to avoid making good use of Robert's Rules — it's to learn them so that you can't be buffaloed.

I can almost guarantee that if you master a few of the basics, including the secondary motions and their rank (discussed in Part 2), and if you start handling business (especially recognizing members and assigning the floor) with a little formality, ol' Puggy won't know what hit him. And as a bonus, you'll have more meaningful meetings.

Discussing and debating

Nobody's idea is perfect. Some members may want to improve it, and some may want to just forget about it. Chapters 7 through 10 cover debating motions, making amendments, and voting.

Adjourning

Probably the best part of any meeting is when the chair declares the meeting adjourned. If you've had a good meeting, you're glad you were a part of it, and you feel a great sense of accomplishment. If you've had a bad meeting, you're probably even happier that it's over!

Participating in Meetings as a Member

Fundamental to effective meeting participation is knowing how to get the attention of your presiding officer, which the following sections discuss, so that you can be recognized and permitted to speak. Just as important is understanding the way to avoid getting personal in debate by asking questions of the other members through the chair. (Jump to Chapter 7 for more information on debate decorum.)

Addressing the presiding officer

In meetings, your presiding officer needs to be addressed by title, such as "Madam Chairman" or "Mr. President." Robert's Rules provides that an officer's title is properly used as defined in the *bylaws*, or the rules of order. In Robert's Rules, "Chairman" is considered as gender neutral as "Director" or "Governor." (Not many female members of a board of directors or a board of governors want to be called "Directrix" or "Governess," the traditional feminine forms of "Director" and "Governor.") But courtesy demands honoring a person's preference in the usage of title. Accordingly, "Madam Chair" or "Madam Chairperson" isn't incorrect if it's the pleasure of a woman holding the position of presiding officer.

A vice-president is addressed as Mr. President or Madam President when actually presiding. If the president is only temporarily out of the chair and is still present at the meeting, Mr. Vice-President or Madam Vice-President are the appropriate addresses. Any other person temporarily occupying the chair is properly addressed as Mr. Chairman or Madam Chairman.

TIP

When addressing the presiding officer, avoid the second person, as in "Madam Chairman, are you sure that . . .?" Instead, use "Madam Chairman, is the *chair* certain of . . .?"

Speaking through the chair

When addressing another member, you never go wrong by speaking through the chair. Refrain from using the member's name, if you can avoid it. Respect is conveyed by depersonalizing comments made in debate. For example, "Mr. Chairman, does the member who just spoke have information on the cost of his proposal?" works much better than, "Dang it, Fred, have you thought about how much your stupid idea is gonna cost us?" Formality has its benefits.

Waiting for recognition before speaking

Before you launch into your speech, get recognition. When you and your fellow members properly seek recognition and refrain from speaking until the chair has recognized you, you allow the presiding officer to do his job. A presiding officer who understands the rules for preference in obtaining recognition (see Chapter 7) and applies them impartially has the control necessary to conduct balanced debate. This control gives them the respect due to the station.

Presiding over Meetings with Style

When you're *in the chair* at a meeting, your job is to always maintain the appearance of impartiality. The quickest way to lose control is to allow your personal agenda to control the decisions you make while presiding. You can run the organization from day to day, and you can even have an agenda, but your floor leaders have to stand on their own when you're in the chair. Otherwise, you're sunk. To ensure that you're seen as the leader of your group, keep these tips in mind:

>> **Speak of yourself in the person of your position.** Say, "The chair rules the point not well taken," not, "Oh, come on, George, get real!" Or say, "Your president is proud to announce that . . .," not "I just found out that . . .."

>> **Avoid directing instructions to members by name.** Say, "The member will please take his seat," not "Puggy, sit down and shut up!" However, using a member's name is appropriate when assigning the floor, as in, "The chair recognizes Mr. Phister." When delegates represent specific constituencies, it's appropriate to recognize them by delegation, as in, "The chair recognizes the member from Tribble County."

>> **Know your bylaws and rules of order.** Probably the single most dutiful thing you can do as a presiding officer is to become intimately familiar with your organization's charter, bylaws, special rules of order, and sections in your parliamentary authority related to serving in the leadership position you have accepted.

Relaxing the Rules at Meetings

Maintaining a degree of formality of proceedings is essential to order and expediency. Nobody wants to get bogged down in minutiae or listen to a lot of mindless chatter in a business meeting. But sometimes things are just better suited to a little less formality, which I cover here.

This need for less formality occurs in meetings of ordinary assemblies when some issues need to be discussed with a little flexibility on the rules of debate. And in committees and small boards, when the group consists of as few as a dozen or so members, some aspects of formality can actually slow things down.

Considering things informally

A regular assembly, no matter how large or small, has some options to relax its rules and deliberate on any particular subject under the rules for committees and boards. It may do the following:

>> **Resolve itself into a committee of the whole,** in which the entire assembly makes itself one big committee and uses committee rules as the rules of debate on a particular subject.

Committee of the whole is the procedure commonly chosen by large bodies of more than about 100 members. This procedure officially turns the assembly into a committee; the presiding officer steps down, and a committee chair steps up to run the show. A committee of the whole is formed by motion and vote, as a variation of the subsidiary motion to *Commit* (see Chapter 9). When a committee concludes its work, it reports back to the group that appointed it. When a committee of the whole finishes, it "rises and reports," reconvening back into the regular meeting and voting as that group on the recommendation of the committee.

REMEMBER

To "rise and report" requires a motion, a second, and a majority vote. The motion is undebatable and can't be amended.

>> **Resolve itself into a quasi-committee of the whole,** which is much like a committee of the whole, except that it doesn't change presiding officers, and it doesn't actually *become* a committee, it just *acts* like one.

In both the quasi- and full committee of the whole, members aren't voting as the original assembly. Instead, they're voting on issues as recommendations to the full assembly, which they become when they rise and report to the assembly. Quasi-committee of the whole is used by groups of 50 to 100 members.

>> **Simply relax the rules and consider a particular subject informally.** This move essentially relaxes the limits on debate on main motions and amendments to main motions. Votes during informal consideration are votes of the assembly.

>> **Establish breakout groups.** This method requires some advance planning to appoint facilitators that bring back the results of these short committee meetings.

>> **Make it permanent.** Adopt a special rule of order to allow your assembly to use the relaxed rules of procedure Robert's Rules makes available to small boards. But do this only if your assembly is actually a small group. I explain what Robert means by "small" in the next section.

Taking it easy in small boards

For larger groups, the need for formality is more important, so you start off formally and use special procedures to relax formality in some circumstances. But smaller assemblies and committees work just the opposite: You start off with more relaxed rules and get formal only if such a change becomes necessary.

Boards are usually smaller than most deliberative assemblies. Depending on size, the board may operate as any deliberative assembly, but if not many more than a dozen members generally attend its meetings, the board may be able to hold meetings using more informal rules.

Your board meetings are generally subject to the same rules as the organization they serve. But you have some flexibility. Your board can adopt its own set of special rules of order and standing rules as long as those rules don't conflict with the organization's bylaws or other governing rules. Even so, many of the procedural rules important in large groups are relaxed in small boards.

Under the relaxed rules of procedure for small boards, the following apply:

>> You don't have to stand when seeking the chair's recognition. Just raise your hand while addressing the chair.

>> You can keep your seat while making motions and speaking.

>> Your motions don't have to be seconded.

>> You can speak in debate as often as you can politely obtain recognition, except during debate on an appeal (see Chapter 11). The regular rules for debate during an appeal still apply.

>> You can discuss things without a motion being on the floor.

>> Your chair (assuming they're a member) can make motions, participate in discussion, and vote. What's more, they don't have to stand when stating a question or taking a vote.

One more point about procedure in small boards is exemplary of the relaxed rules: A vote can be taken by assuming a motion, even where none has been formally made. If it's abundantly clear that a particular decision is pending, voting can be by show of hands, or the decision can be made by unanimous consent (see Chapter 8).

For example, suppose you've been talking about whether the fire truck you're recommending to the company commander should be red or white. Your board is sitting around the table, and you say, "The red one is cheaper. Besides, the white one will show more dirt." Bill says, "Yeah, I like red fire trucks better anyway." The chair then says, "Then I guess we go with the red fire truck. Any objections?" You've just decided to buy a red fire truck, or at least to recommend the purchase to your membership. Wasn't that easy? Similar rules apply to committee meetings. Flip to Chapter 16 for more information.

Meeting Virtually

Not many who are reading this book will have missed out on one of the greatest meeting adventures of the early 21st century: the virtual meeting. My guess is that you've already attended way to many such events in connection with your work. Knowing some of the folks with whom I've worked, I'd probably have to quit my job rather than to labor through an hour-long, "Where do I click to say something" questions from countless co-workers. But this section is here to give you some perspective on the application of technology to the ability to meet as a deliberative assembly.

Robert's Rules addresses this subject matter under the name "Electronic meetings," which, technically speaking, includes unsophisticated chat-rooms, email, and fax as well as teleconferencing and videoconferencing.

WARNING

Everything there is to say that's good about virtual meetings comes with a *huge* caveat: No virtual meeting truly meets Robert's Rules definition of a meeting of a *deliberative assembly* (see the section, "Defining the Deliberative Assembly," earlier in this chapter). At least not yet. But with careful planning, they can be given enough similarity to be an acceptable substitute. You just have to understand that some things just don't fit the mold. After you're outside the realm of the true deliberative assembly, you're outside the scope of a plethora of rules applicable to the deliberative assembly because they just don't fit in a virtual setting. Refer to the nearby sidebar for an example.

The benefits of meeting virtually are numerous, but in most cases, they come with some compromises that can affect the rights of members. If you're going to approach some degree of similarity to a deliberative assembly in the virtual world, you're going to have to look closely at the tools and rules available to help you avoid, as much as possible, compromising the protections that members enjoy in the true deliberative assembly.

Amending your bylaws to make virtual meetings possible

In order to have legal virtual meetings, you have to amend your bylaws to authorize electronic meetings. You have to decide what meetings are to be affected by the bylaw change: Meeting for the membership? For the board? For your committees? You also have to decide just what kind of electronic meetings you want to authorize. Teleconferences? Video conferences? With secure Internet-based balloting? Decisions, decisions, decisions!

WARNING

Amending your bylaws to allow for virtual meetings can't be done in a virtual meeting. You have to follow your current rules for amending bylaws to make the change. That means giving previous notice and having an in-person meeting to adopt (or reject) authority to conduct virtual meeting.

Until you amend your bylaws to allow virtual meetings, During the COVID pandemic, a group I know called a special meeting giving proper notice to all 200 of the members. The leadership beat the bushes to get a quorum in a room together, adopted the amendment, and was back in business. They're working on their special rules now.

Evaluating meeting platforms

You have to evaluate the various virtual meeting platforms being offered for your type of group. Maybe your group is small enough that you can do your work in an email thread. Maybe one of the popular free or low-cost online meeting services will be adequate, although not without its limitations and trade-offs. But your group might also be a sizeable convention of delegates, and to conduct a virtual business meeting will require highly specialized and expensive meeting software.

REMEMBER

"Expensive" is a relative term. A few thousand dollars spent on a well-managed virtual meeting might be negligible compared to the expense of securing a physical location for a large number of members to come together to take care of their business. Companies exist to produce such meetings with plenty of sophisticated tools to come pretty close to simulating an actual, genuine, real-life, in-person meeting.

Electronic meetings comprise chat-rooms, email, fax, teleconferencing, and videoconferencing, which I discuss in greater detail here. Each may find its place in your decision-making process, but always keep in mind that Robert's Rules is applicable to deliberative assemblies. Only teleconferencing and videoconferencing can approach sufficiently the kind of meeting that can be defined as that of a deliberative assembly.

Email, chatrooms, and fax

Although making group decisions through email, chatrooms, and fax is possible, using them isn't a process that can remotely resemble a deliberative assembly. Robert characterizes the results of such a collaboration as "consultative," In other words, using them is *not* a meeting, and no action binding on the organization can be properly adopted without further action by the body itself in a properly convened meeting.

EXCEPTION

Some states have laws applicable to corporations, LLCs, and the like that authorize the organization or its board of directors to officially act by "unanimous written consent" in lieu of a meeting. I've dealt with boards who had this kind of power, and it's useful and practical in many circumstances. But it's only useful when the group so authorized is small enough that achieving written consent by every member is possible. One holdout and you'll need a meeting and a majority vote.

Teleconferencing and videoconferencing

Teleconferencing is probably the most flexible term to use when you're providing bylaws that allow virtual meetings. That's because if you're teleconferencing, you don't need to be able to see each other.

Using a videoconferencing platform for teleconferencing is okay as long as it allows people to join the meeting by telephone. For a teleconference, all you have to do is ensure that everybody can hear each other. With or without active video of the participants, you fulfill a fundamental necessity of a deliberative assembly, being, as Robert so eloquently articulates, "simultaneous aural communication."

WARNING

Bylaw provisions that authorize only videoconferencing technology for virtual meetings will be problematic, because to meet the definition of videoconferencing under Robert's Rules, all the participants must be able to hear and see each other.

TIP

Bylaw provisions that authorize meetings to be conducted by teleconference should specify whether it's authorized for the general membership meetings, or is limited to the executive board, committees, or both. And just so you know, an organization can authorize committees that aren't established in your bylaws to meet electronically by standing rule or by the motion that creates the committee.

Adopting special rules of order

Meeting by teleconference isn't as simple as authorizing it in your bylaws. Just think about it for a minute and you'll be formulating some questions about how a meeting will work when the presiding officer might not be able to see Martha Meticulous who is in the meeting by telephone stand up hoping to be recognized. Plenty of questions need to be asked and answered about how things are going to work.

After you decide on the technology you want to try (and whatever you choose, you're in trial-and-error territory) you're ready to make your best attempt at putting together and adopting some special rules designed to bridge the challenges of virtual meetings with the benefits of the rules in your parliamentary authority. The rules you put in place to assist you in having virtual meetings should reflect your group's specific needs. Those needs vary depending on the type of group, its size, its nature as a legal entity, and, yes, the temperament of the members.

Head to Chapter 25 where I cover some basic considerations necessary to come up with a workable plan to help bridge the gap between the virtual meeting and the real, in-person meeting that you know and love.

Chapter **4**

Notice and a Quorum

It doesn't matter whether your organization is a three-member refreshment committee for the Myrtle B. Glutz chapter of the Georgia Crumpet Tasters Society, a 250,000-member General Assembly of the Congress of Delegates of *For Dummies* Readers International, or some group of some size somewhere in between. No matter how large or how small your voting membership is, you can't have a meeting in which you do anything in the name of the group unless you've given some sort of previous notice for the meeting. Even then, if too few voting members show up, you can't do much at the meeting.

In this chapter, I explain how to set requirements for notifying your members about meetings, and I help you figure out the minimum number of members who have to show up to do anything in the name of your group.

Giving Notice of Meetings

Robert's Rules says that if you expect to do business in the name of a group, every voting member has a right to *previous notice* of the meeting. It's easy to understand why: If you have a right to vote, then you have a fundamental right to attend. And you can't attend a meeting if you don't know about it, right?

This section discusses basic requirements for the content of meeting notices depending on whether the meeting is a regular meeting or a special meeting, the different forms available for giving the notice, and how it all works to protect the rights of the members.

Regular meetings

Regular meetings are just that — regularly scheduled and open for any regular business that needs to be discussed. The bylaws of your organization must include information on how often your organization's membership (and its executive board, if you have one) is supposed to hold regular business meetings.

The content and the delivery requirements of the notice for regular meetings depend mostly on the details of scheduling that your bylaws already address. For example, if your bylaws provide for your board to meet on the second Tuesday of every month, then your board may just fix the location and the hour by adopting a standing rule (see Chapter 2); no additional notice is required unless a change is necessary or some business is scheduled that requires special notice. But most bylaws are more general, narrowing meeting times to only a particular day if regular meetings are held monthly, or to a particular month (or season) if meetings are held quarterly or annually.

Spelling out notice requirements

Unless the bylaws include details on the hour and location of regular meetings (a fairly uncommon scenario), they need to provide specifics about when and how meeting notices are given. The lead time always must take into account the frequency and importance of a particular meeting and the distance members have to travel to attend. Voting members need enough notice to arrange their schedules so they can attend. You can, however, avoid having to give formal notice of regular meetings if your bylaws define the date of those meetings and you have established the meeting time and place by a standing rule.

Including special items of business

In addition to the hour and location, the content of the meeting's notice, or *call*, must specify all items of business that require previous notice under your rules. Common examples of such special items of business include proposals to amend bylaws, to adopt or amend special rules of order (see Chapter 2), to elect someone to fill a vacancy in an office (see Chapter 14), or to amend or rescind — by majority instead of two-thirds vote — something previously adopted (see Chapter 12).

REMEMBER

At the very least, notice for regular meetings must specify the hour and location of the regular meeting. It also can include additional information about what business is on tap for the meeting. This notice is referred to as the *call of the meeting*, and it must be furnished to all the voting members.

Special meetings

Special meetings (see Chapter 3) are, well, *special.* They're called only if

» Something important comes up that *must* be dealt with before the next regular meeting

» Some particular business matter(s) is important enough that it needs to be the exclusive reason for the entire meeting

After all, you're busy, so special meetings had better be important, right? Now, because these meetings are special, the notice announcing them is special as well. You have to take a little more care with notices for special meetings than you do for regular meetings.

E-NOTICE? THINK TWICE!

I get asked at least once a week whether it's okay to give notice of meetings using email or messenger programs such as Facebook's Messenger or Skype. Even though Robert's Rules says you can use electronic means to give notice, my answer is always, "It depends."

Despite the widespread use and convenience of email and other electronic communication, technologically challenged voting members still populate membership rolls in great numbers. Even the technologically gifted can find themselves at the mercy of a system that's nowhere near dependable enough for important time-sensitive, mission-critical communication.

Because notice is a fundamental right of members, my advice is always to make sure that the group's bylaws establish a policy for meeting notice lead time and method(s) of distribution, and add policy details either in bylaws or in standing rules.

Without clear policy, and even some written waivers of liability covering the possibility of email notice failure, you may find your whole meeting (and some important decisions made there) legally challenged on a claim of improper notice. For that reason, Robert's Rules requires a member's consent to receive notice electronically.

E-notice can be very convenient, especially if your group is small and all the members consent (and are able) to receive notices this way. But if your secretary has a long membership list to contend with and has to keep three lists to manage notices in different media, you'll be turning to my chapter about filling vacancies in office (Chapters 14 and 15) a lot more than you want to.

TIP

To be on the safe side and to eliminate doubt, I always recommend that my clients provide for written notice of special meetings to be *sent* within a specified time frame before the meeting. For example, your bylaws may state, "Notice of special meetings shall be mailed to the members at least 14 days but no more than 30 days before the meeting." The actual range for notice varies depending on the size of your group and the distance members must travel. The important point is that the range of dates for sending the notice must be reasonable, and everyone must be able to receive the notice in time to arrange their schedules to attend the meeting.

All the notice principles for regular meetings still ring true for special meetings, so I touch on just the additional material in this section. See the section, "Regular meetings," earlier in this chapter for more details.

You can't hold special meetings if your bylaws don't provide for them, so the information in this section may not even apply to your group. Check your bylaws before you worry about special meetings. If your bylaws don't provide for holding special meetings to handle issues that come up between regular meetings, skip to the next section. Otherwise, read on.

Calling a special meeting

If you need to have a meeting before the next regular meeting, go ahead and do so. But be sure that it's important and can't wait. And don't try to cover anything more than what is absolutely necessary. Write your notice, include the pertinent details, and get out the notice as far in advance as you can. (Hopefully, your bylaws dictate the lead time requirements for special meeting notice. If not, you need to amend the bylaws to include this info.)

Drawing up the special meeting notice

Make your notice simple and to the point. The subject of the meeting must be so urgent that it can't wait. Don't try to accomplish anything else at this meeting. Just write down exactly what you need to address and get the notice in the mail.

Suppose Peter Piper just applied for membership on your Parched Peanut Purveyors panel. Piper promised to pick a peck of pickled peppers for each of your panelists if he's permitted to petition for a position on the panel prior to the time his pickled pepper patch pays out.

Pickled peppers dry on the vine long before your next regular meeting. You really want Piper to belong to the club: Not only is he a person of patience and prestige, but you and the other panelists have postulated that the prospects for pickled peppers packed with parched peanuts is a profitable possibility. The opportunity to present Piper to the panel and permit his promise to perhaps profit the panel requires a special meeting. In accordance with provisions of your bylaws, you call a special meeting and send a notice to all the voting members of the panel that reads as follows:

Parched Peanut Purveyors Panel
Notice of Special Meeting

A special meeting of the Parched Peanut Purveyors Panel will be held at the Peanut Patch on March 22 at 3 p.m. to peruse the petition of Peter Piper and prognosticate on the possibility of permitting Piper to hold a permanent post on our panel.

Please plan to participate.

Sincerely,
Lilbo Peep
Secretary

© John Wiley & Sons, Inc.

As long as a *quorum* is present (the minimum number of voting members required to be present to validly conduct business in the name of the assembly), and provided that a majority of the panelists adopt the proposal, Peter Piper's petition will pass. That fact will then be placed in the proceedings of the panel. (For more info on quorum, check out the section, "Quorum Defined," later in this chapter.)

REMEMBER

Special meetings *always* require previous notice. Special meeting notices not only must include the date, time, place, and location, but also must *specify all the business to be included in the meeting*. *Nothing* other than this business, and the various motions that allow the meeting to take care of this business, can be considered in a special meeting if it's not included in the notice.

TIP

Be sure to call special meetings only when something must be addressed before the next regular meeting. Your time is important, so use this tool judiciously. Save everything that can wait for the next regular meeting.

Selecting forms of giving notice

Depending on the rules of the organization, previous notice can take any of several forms. Meeting notices can be given in these ways:

>> **By a simple announcement at a regular meeting:** Small, informal committees that meet frequently to work on a project often adopt this method. A simple "We'll meet same time, same place, next week" is a proper notice.

>> **By a fixed rule in the bylaws establishing a regular meeting time and place:** For example, "Regular meetings of the Second Thursday Club will be held on the third Wednesday of every month, at noon in Tuesday's restaurant."

>> **By mailing (or otherwise distributing) written notice of the time and place of the meeting a reasonable time in advance:** This method is the most common.

A requirement for previous written notice of a meeting is satisfied by a timely mailing via U.S. mail addressed to members at their last known addresses. It can also be satisfied by sending notice electronically, but only if the member has given consent to receive notices electronically.

TIP

Defining the time and method for giving notice in your bylaws makes this distribution much easier down the road. A good bylaw provision reads something like, "Notice of the time and place of the annual meeting shall be sent to each member at their address of record at least three weeks prior to the meeting. The notice may be sent by email or by other electronic means if the member has consented (in writing) to receive meeting notices via these means." In this example, the bylaw defines the method of distribution and the time in advance of the meeting that it is to be sent.

REMEMBER

The important point about giving notice is that everybody who has a right to be at the meeting must have a reasonable opportunity to be informed that a meeting will be held. If your group is a public body, like a school board or a town council, you probably face some legal requirement for *public* notice, too.

TIP

The officer responsible for sending notices of meetings must keep a careful record of the notice, to whom it was sent, and when it was sent, along with the method transmitted and the address to which it was sent. If a member later claims not to have received notice, a record of it having been sent can go a long way toward satisfying questions about whether proper notice was given.

Protecting the rights of absentees

According to Robert's Rules, members have the absolute right to expect that nothing except business specified in the call will take place in a special meeting. As a member, I still have rights, even if I decide not to attend the meeting.

For a good example of absentee rights, I use the Peter Piper petition scenario from the section "Drawing up the special meeting notice," earlier in this chapter. Suppose that I'm on the Parched Peanut Purveyors panel. Even though I want to be a good member who attends all meetings, getting to this special meeting is difficult for me for some reason. I have no particular objection to Peter Piper's petition, so I decide that my absence from this meeting isn't a problem for me or the other members. I'm okay with the action proposed, and I know that enough people will attend, so my presence isn't vital. I can miss the meeting, then, and continue to pull up peanuts in my peanut patch.

So what happens if the rest of the panel members attending the special meeting decide at that time to invest the panel's money in a pickled pepper packing machine? Why shouldn't they? Everybody's there but me, and they all want to do it! Why, indeed! If I'd had any reason to think that an investment discussion might take place, I would have definitely attended that meeting to stop such a stupid idea. I would have tried my darnedest to convince the others not to do it. Even if I wasn't successful, I have a right to decide whether I want to go to the meeting and make my point.

REMEMBER

Robert's Rules says that I don't have to worry about being absent from a special meeting. The rule requiring previous notice of the specifics of the business to be conducted at a special meeting protects me as an absentee. This rule is so important that even if the panel did decide to make the investment, the decision would be a null-and-void action (because it violates the absentee protection rule). If I'm too late to keep the money from being spent, I can probably force the other members to pay back the money to the treasury from their own personal funds. Oh, I may have to wave my Robert's Rules around and hire a professional parliamentarian (or even threaten to sue) to get things straightened out, but I'm right, and that's the point.

Quorum Defined

When you know how to notify everybody of the when, where, and what of your meetings, the last hitch to having your meeting hooked up and ready to roll is answering the question of how many, as in "How many members have to be there?"

Some number of members — more than one, but less than the total number of voting members of any deliberative assembly — is a magic number. That magic number, called a *quorum*, is the minimum number of voting members who must be present at a properly called meeting to validly conduct business in the name of the group.

If your bylaws don't define the quorum (and it definitely should), Robert's Rules fixes the quorum for you based on the nature of the assembly as follows:

>> In a mass meeting or if there's no reliable roll of members (think "church"), the quorum is the number of members present.

>> If the assembly is a convention of delegates, the quorum is a majority of the persons who actually registered as delegates at the convention, even if some have since left the convention.

>> Otherwise, if there is a reliable roll of members, Robert fixes the number at a *majority,* or more than half, of all the members.

Here I list several considerations addressing quorum requirements.

Determining how many is enough for a meeting

Robert's Rules is full of practical guidance when it comes to how many members you need to have present to hold a meeting. General Robert continues to guide readers with the same rule that he devised more than 100 years ago.

REMEMBER

According to General Robert, the bylaws should provide for a quorum "as large a number of members as can be depended upon for being present at all meetings when the weather is not exceptionally bad." In other words, at best, a quorum is just an educated guess.

Establishing a quorum

Some groups set a quorum as a percentage of membership; others use a fixed number. What's best for your organization is anybody's guess. In fact, you really need a track record for your group before you can come up with a number that doesn't allow too few people to spend all the money in the treasury and doesn't call for some number that's way too high. Unfortunately, most of the time, you don't have a track record to guide you when you're just getting started. So proceed with caution and think about your quorum carefully. Use common sense, and be willing to change the quorum frequently as your organization grows.

REMEMBER

Until you make a different decision for your group and include it in your bylaws, Robert's Rules sets your quorum at a *majority of the members.*

Counting ex-officio members in board and committee quorums

Your bylaws may specify a quorum for your committees or executive board, or they may be silent, making the quorum a majority of the board or committee membership. In either case, Robert's Rules provides you with rules for counting ex-officio members toward a quorum.

An ex-officio member of a board, when a member of the assembly superior to the board, has a duty to serve on the board and is counted toward, and when determining, the quorum. An ex-officio member who isn't otherwise a member of the assembly isn't counted toward, or when determining, a quorum.

An ex-officio board member who is also an officer of the board in all cases has a duty to serve and is counted towards, and when determining a quorum

When it comes to committees, the quorum rules for boards apply except in the case where the organization's president is designated in the bylaws as an ex-officio member of all the organization's committee. In that case, the president has the *right* to participate, but doesn't have an *obligation* to participate, and therefore is counted neither when determining the quorum nor when determining whether a quorum is present.

Knowing what you can do without a quorum

Regardless of the reason, sometimes too few members show up for a meeting. When this situation happens, you have options, but they're pretty limited. That's good, though. You don't want three of your members voting to divide the treasury among themselves and dissolve the association!

Consider an example of a quorum at work. The quorum for the Mountainview County Potbellied Pig Society is defined as 20 members. It wasn't always like that, though. When the society began, nobody thought much about fixing a quorum in the bylaws. A majority was fine, especially when the membership was low. As the membership grew, however, so did the quorum. By the time the members numbered more than 50, they were having problems (boring meetings and too many silly pig stories). Achieving attendance of more than 25 members became impossible.

The Mountainview County Potbellied Pig Society had a problem. After all, at a meeting without a quorum, you can't do much more than say you held the meeting. You can have the program, but you can't approve last month's meeting minutes, you can't adopt any committee recommendations, you can't deal with unfinished business, and you can't entertain new business. All isn't lost if you're quorumless, however. Robert's Rules lays out a few things you can do during a meeting without a quorum:

>> **Fix the time to which to adjourn.** Doing so makes it possible for the meeting to continue on a later day, after you've chased down enough people to achieve a quorum.

>> **Adjourn.** You can call it quits for now and wait for the next regular meeting.

>> **Recess.** Sometimes achieving a quorum is as simple as taking a short break to go into the hall and round up more members. You then can proceed with the business of the assembly. Recess is often used when attendees wander out of the meeting room in the middle of a meeting, and suddenly somebody notices that there aren't enough members in the room anymore.

>> **Take other measures to assemble a quorum.** For example, you can appoint a committee to make calls and round up enough members for your business meeting; while you're waiting for additional members to arrive, you can then continue with the program or scheduled speaker. A motion to take action to obtain a quorum is in order when no business is pending and can be treated as a privileged motion taking precedence over a motion to recess.

TECHNICAL STUFF

When you're without a quorum and are dealing with the previous motions, you can handle subsidiary and incidental motions (see Chapters 9 and 11) and motions to *Raise a Question of Privilege* or *Call for the Orders of the Day* (see Chapter 10), on the condition that it's all part of the handling of the motions or conducting parts of the meeting (like the program) that don't require a quorum.

TIP

In cases like the example of the Mountainview County Potbellied Pig Society, when you don't expect to achieve quorum, given your membership situation, the only real solution is to entice enough members to a meeting (or drag them, kicking and screaming, if need be) that you have a quorum and then amend the bylaws! You need to do so as soon as you realize you have a problem so that the default quorum doesn't continue to grow. True, you can go on just having program meetings, but until you change your bylaws to specify a quorum you know you can achieve, your group is helpless to conduct any business. You can't even decide to disband until you get a quorum!

Consider how the Mountainview County Potbellied Pig Society handled its problem: After having to adjourn three regular meetings because the group didn't have a quorum, the president and the founder asked the members to amend the bylaws to fix the quorum at 20, before the club grew any larger. With plenty of notice (and the promise of refreshments, including the president's famous lemon rum pound cake), a majority of the club's members showed up to a meeting and passed an amendment to the bylaws. Now the quorum is 20, which seems to be the magic number!

TIP

See Chapter 2 for the rules for amending bylaws; you need to know how to make these changes in case you ever have a problem getting a quorum for your meetings.

Handling emergencies quorumless

You can't get around the requirement that a quorum be present to take official action in the name of your group. The quorum rule holds fast even if everybody in attendance votes unanimously to do something. In fact, Robert's Rules says that *any* action (other than the few things discussed in the previous section) done by those in attendance at an inquorate meeting is *null and void*, at least as an action of the organization.

But what if you *have* to do something? I mean, you *really* have to do something? What if the circumstances are such that you call a special meeting to discuss making repairs to the heating system in your neighborhood clubhouse, and a snowstorm blows in and keeps everybody away except you and the other members who live no more than one or two doors away from the clubhouse. And while you're shivering in your boots in the clubhouse with your neighbors wondering what to do, a huge limb on the old tree next to the building breaks under the weight of its icy branches and crashes through the roof, leaving a gaping hole — and the snow, tree debris, roofing materials, and broken rafters are all over the place, and the storm is getting worse, and. . . .

The answer is really simple: You still can do nothing *in the name of the organization.* Even if you all agree that the clubhouse's heating system will have to wait on the quorum, but you decide that the roof must be fixed immediately at the expense of the group, you can't bind the group to pay the bill unless a quorum is present at a properly called meeting. You and the others can certainly make a decision to call in a roofer to make emergency repairs, but you do it *at your own risk.* If the membership doesn't agree that you did the right thing, or even if they agree but vote against a motion to ratify your action, you're "out in the cold," so to speak! In that case, the club doesn't have to pay the bill: You and your buddies do.

The motion to *Ratify* allows the group to approve, by majority vote at a regular meeting (or properly called special meeting) with a quorum, your action and adopt it as the action of the group. After that happens, you and the others are off the hook, and your action is no longer null and void. I discuss other applications of the motion to *Ratify* in Chapter 6.

REMEMBER

Things happen, and sometimes decisions must be made in the absence of proper authority. But the rule is that, without a quorum, or without proper notice, nothing done is binding on the organization unless and until the organization ratifies the action in a properly called meeting with a quorum present. And this rule can't be changed, even by a unanimous vote.

» **Understanding why matters are taken up in a particular order**

» **Using an agenda to plan your meeting and keep tasks on track**

Chapter **5**

Ordering Business: The Agenda

The meetings you attend are probably a lot like business trips. You want to finish the business and get back home or back to work or play. You probably don't even *consider* going on a business trip without some sort of itinerary — not unless you have all the time in the world and you don't care about the people you have to meet or the deals you have to make. My guess is that you *don't* have that kind of time and that you *do* care about others and about successfully handling your business.

In this chapter, I walk you through *order of business* — that is, the sequence you establish by rule to handle all the different issues that need to come before your members in the meetings. Then I show you how to develop an *agenda*, or itinerary, for your meeting and how to use it to work through your order of business. If you want to know how to get in and out of your meeting quickly and still get done everything you need to do, you're reading the right chapter.

Order of Business Sequence

At the foundation of every good meeting is a good meeting plan. And Robert is the man with the plan. His rule book provides your group with this standard *order of business*, which is simply a sequence for taking up each different class of business in the following order:

1. **Reading and approval of minutes:** Important actions happened in your previous meeting. Before you do anything else, make sure that everyone agrees with the record of that meeting.

2. **Reports of officers, boards, and standing committees:** Your leadership team likely is working in between membership meetings, and you need to hear what it's been up to before you venture into too many decisions.

3. **Reports of special committees:** If your group has appointed any special committees for specific purposes, you need their info, too. But these committees wait their turns and report after the standing committees make their reports.

4. **Special orders:** Sometimes you need to schedule particular items of business before you take up matters you've postponed from a previous meeting. And sometimes the bylaws require that you do something at a particular meeting; for example, maybe your bylaws include a "nominations in November" rule. Such items of business and bylaw requirements qualify as special orders.

5. **Unfinished business and general orders:** Before you do anything else, you need to finish what you've already started. Now is the time to get back to the postponed motions and any business that was pending when your previous meeting adjourned.

6. **New business:** If time permits, you can broach the subject of new business. You've taken a wise step by waiting until you've taken a shot at all the other stuff. It's sort of like cleaning your plate before you get dessert.

If you've adopted Robert's Rules, much of your meeting planning is done for you. This order of business framework is really all you need to develop your meeting agenda.

Approving the minutes

In the years before word processors and copy machines, the secretary wrote the minutes of meetings in a book kept for that purpose. When the next meeting rolled around, the secretary read the minutes, the chairman asked for any corrections, and the secretary made notations in the margins of the minutes being corrected.

Today technology has made its mark on meeting minutes. The secretary can now draft the minutes and easily send copies to the members for them to read before the meeting; then members can come to the meeting prepared with any corrections. You can still read the minutes aloud to the members in the meeting, if you want to, but if time is precious, distribute the draft of the minutes in advance.

WARNING

You need to be mindful that minutes drafted ahead of time aren't the official minutes *until the members approve them.* Because changes may be made in the minutes before they're approved, it's good practice for the secretary to note somewhere on the distribution copy that it's a "draft for approval" at the next regular meeting. Flip to Chapter 17 for the complete breakdown of how to write good minutes.

Members who make notes of any corrections to meeting minutes are able to keep accurate records if they keep their copies of the draft minutes on file (if a final version isn't automatically distributed to them at a later date).

Handling the approval of your minutes

Contrary to popular belief, a motion to approve minutes is unnecessary and a waste of time.

The process for approving minutes (as opposed to their correction after having been approved) involves only taking and disposing of proposed corrections followed by the presiding officer's declaration that the minutes are approved.

The presiding officer says, "The minutes have been [read/distributed] to you. Are there any corrections?" If corrections are offered, the chair handles each by offering the correction to the membership, just to be sure everyone agrees that the correction is accurate. When no (further) corrections are offered, the presiding officer says, "If there are no (further) corrections . . . (pause) . . . the minutes are approved as [read/distributed/corrected]."

That's all there is to it.

WARNING

It's never in order for a member to simply object to the approval of minutes. If a member has some objection to the content of the minutes, they must offer a correction. If disagreement arises about the correction, the correction can be amended using the rules for amendments. Check out Chapter 9 for details on procedures for handling amendments.

Approving minutes by committee

If the assembly isn't meeting again for a long time (if at all), such as in annual membership meetings, conventions of delegates, or the last meeting before a periodic change of some or all of the assembly's members, such as in a board or other elected body, the process of approving the minutes is delegated to a special committee or an executive board. This practice produces an approved and legal record of the meeting shortly after the meeting closes but before memories of what occurred in the meeting fade.

WARNING

If yours is a group that customarily deals with minutes by a motion to "dispense with the reading of the minutes," you need to make a change. Your intent is probably to approve them with that motion, but you don't actually approve anything. You just agree not to read them at that time. If you've adopted a motion to dispense with the reading of the minutes, you've not foregone their reading. You've delayed it.

TECHNICAL STUFF

When the minutes have been distributed in advance, no motion to omit their reading is necessary because the minutes aren't read if they have been distributed in advance. Well, not unless somebody requests it. A single member can demand that the minutes be read, even if the minutes have been distributed in advance.

Hearing the reports of officers, boards, and standing committees

After you've approved your minutes, your leadership team gets to bend your ears telling you what they think you need to know and what they think you need to do about it. Except for the big-deal annual meetings, when everybody likes to get into the act of telling you about all the hard work they've done during the year, this order of business is usually short, sweet, and to the point. For details on how to compose good reports, take a look in Chapter 17.

For the most part, the officers (except for the treasurer) don't usually have a report at regular membership meetings. Nor does the board, unless it's handling something that needs the membership's attention. Standing committee reports are the reports heard most frequently in this portion of the order of business. But despite their infrequency, reports from the leadership team tend to include items of high importance, so Robert's Rules places them second from the top in the standard order of business.

TIP

The prepared presiding officer knows in advance which officers and committees have reports, and they don't waste any time calling for reports unless they know someone has a report to give.

Under this order of business, reports (if there are any in this portion of the agenda) are taken up in this order:

1. **Officers:** Reports are taken up in the order the bylaws list the officers. If an officer's report includes recommendations, another member moves for the adoption of the recommendation or otherwise makes any appropriate motions that arise from the report. (It's not good form for the officer to move their own recommendations.)

2. **Boards:** After the officers' reports, the boards make their reports. If a board has recommendations, the reporting member makes the necessary motion. The motion doesn't require a second because the board is a body of more than one person. If the report gives rise to a motion by any member, it's in order to entertain that motion at this time.

3. **Standing committees:** Reports and recommendations of standing committees are made one by one, in the order the bylaws list the standing committees. Just as with boards, the reporting member makes any motions, which require no second unless a committee is a committee of one; if the report gives rise to a motion by any member, it's proper to entertain the motion at this time.

REMEMBER

Two types of standing committees have *completely* different procedures for properly handling their reports. They are *resolutions* committees and *nominating* committees. Not only are reports from these committees never adopted, but the committees' recommendations are never directly voted on.

WARNING

If an officer or committee report doesn't contain any recommendations, it really doesn't require any action. In these situations, I advise my clients generally to avoid *adopting* reports. Even a motion to *receive* a report isn't proper, because the report has already been received. Only motions dealing with report recommendations are in order.

If a report contains no recommendations, the proper handling of the report is for the chair to thank the reporting member and move on to the next item of business. However, because so many people (not you, thank goodness) still don't have a clue about good form and procedure in meetings, I usually recommend that presiding officers spell it out and say, at the conclusion of information-only reports, "Thank you. The report requires no action and will be placed on file. The next item of business is . . . ."

Receiving reports from special committees

If your organization has learned how to save meeting time and operate efficiently by making good use of committees, your meetings will often include special committee reports. Check out

Chapter 16 for details on working on committees. Also take a look at Chapter 17 for the info you need to produce great committee reports.

You consider reports from special committees in the order the committees were appointed. These reports are called for only if the committee has asked to report or is due to report based on its instructions. The rules for handling special committee reports are the same as for handling the standing committee reports.

Taking up special orders

After you've worked through the routine items, what's left to handle is an assortment of items of business that can cover a wide range of topics. But each item has a priority for consideration, based on what was done in earlier meetings. The class of business for items of this type with the highest priority is called *special orders.* This class refers to special items of business that have been given top priority by being made an *order of the day* through the express wishes of your members.

TECHNICAL STUFF

An *order of the day* is any item of business that your group is scheduled to consider at a particular session, meeting, day, or hour. A special order is one made with the condition that any rule (with a few rare exceptions) hindering its consideration at the specified time is automatically suspended.

Special orders (of the day) are considered in the following order:

1. **Unfinished special orders:** These are special orders that haven't yet been completed; they've been held over from an earlier meeting. Consideration starts with any special order that was pending when an earlier meeting adjourned; other orders are then taken up in the order they were made a special order.

2. **Items made special orders for the current meeting:** After you've disposed of your previously unfinished special orders, you can move on to those items that were made special orders for tonight's meeting. Those items include items provided for in the bylaws to be done at a particular meeting, such as the election of a nominating committee, selection of delegates to a convention, or the election of officers.

If a special order has been assigned a particular time (as opposed to those assigned only to a particular session, meeting, or day), it interrupts almost any business pending when the time arrives. The presiding officer will announce that the time has come for the particular business, and that business becomes immediately pending. The only way around this interruption is for the assembly to delay its consideration by a two-thirds vote (or unanimous consent). If the chair misses the mark, any member can cause the special order to rise to the top using the privileged motion *Call for Orders of the Day*. Flip ahead to Chapter 10 for discussion of this privileged motion.

Turning to unfinished business and general orders

Under this class of business, the next in order are motions that were before the assembly but not disposed of (for whatever reason) in earlier meetings, but that weren't made special orders. At this point in the order of business, items fall into two categories: unfinished business and general orders.

Unfinished business

Suppose you're considering a motion to lease a pink limousine for the Elvis impersonator scheduled to headline your annual talent show. Before you can finish your debate, the group adopts a motion to adjourn. You have unfinished business, and it's the first item you take up (after special orders) under this order of business in your next meeting. After you decide what to do about the limousine, you'll take up any business that was left under unfinished business in your previous meeting's order of business. *Unfinished business* includes the following items, which are considered in the order listed:

1. Any item (not a special order) that was pending when the previous meeting adjourned.

2. Business items that were on the "unfinished business" list in your previous meeting but still weren't taken up before adjournment.

3. **Items that were *general orders* (see the next section) in your previous meeting but were not reached during that meeting.** (They're considered now in the order in which they were made general orders.)

General orders

General orders are items that were made orders of the day by being postponed to a certain time (see Chapter 9) in the previous meeting so that they come up in this meeting. For example, you're considering a motion to install a second phone line at the neighborhood clubhouse and somebody moves to postpone the motion until next month's meeting. The postponed motion becomes a *general order* for next month.

And when you give notice of a bylaw amendment that you want to have considered at the next meeting, the proposed amendment becomes a general order for that next meeting. You can also make something a general order by adopting an agenda containing the item of business, or by adopting a motion by majority vote to consider a question that's not currently pending, such as, "I move that next month we consider a motion to host a picnic for all the soccer teams in our league."

Calling for new business

It's no accident that new business is the last order of business. After all, by the time you finish dealing with all the other business you have going on, you may not want to open any more cans of worms. But unless you just want to wind down your organization and disband, you need to provide the opportunity for members to introduce new items of business to the assembly. The chair is obligated to make the opportunity available; they do this by announcing that new business is in order and asking if any member has such business to present. At this time, it's in order for any member to make any main motion or to take from the table any item previously laid on the table.

REMEMBER

If it's been a long meeting, you may be getting the idea that tonight's new business may be showing up under unfinished business and general orders at your next meeting. But if you team the order of business with an agenda and good planning strategies, and if you spend quality time working in committees (as I discuss in Chapter 16), then you're on your way to making meetings meaningful (see Chapter 3).

Using an Agenda

It's 7 p.m. on a Tuesday. You're attending the regular monthly meeting of your neighborhood association. Your president, Prissy Gardner (who was elected because nobody else wanted the job), is ready to start the meeting. Prissy's really a stickler when keeping the petunias watered at the front entrance to your neighborhood, but she thinks the board is just one big beautification committee. So she starts off the meeting by going over last month's minutes — well, just the part about the new flowerbed she wants. When she finishes with that, she starts talking about the possibility of spending some money on a sprinkler system.

Despite the great organizational tools and techniques available in Robert's Rules, for some reason, meetings happen all the time in which presiding officers like Prissy fly by the seat of their pants — going over last month's minutes, rehashing old decisions, interspersing real discussions with commentary, and suppressing anybody who tries to move things along. If you're unlucky enough to be a member of one such organization, you already know the importance of knowing how to make a meeting run with a reasonable amount of dispatch. If not, believe me when I say that the future is now for anyone who can efficiently and effectively run meetings.

If Robert is your parliamentary authority, then you have a standard order of business on which you build your meeting program, or agenda. This section discusses the common components of an agenda based on that standard order of business.

Understanding the agenda

If you're like me, you know the only way to get the most out of your time is to spend it wisely, and you want to make every second you have count. When it comes to meetings, the way to be efficient and effective simultaneously is to prepare and make good use of an agenda. An *agenda* is essentially a program or listing of the events and items of business that will come before the meeting. It may be a detailed program covering several meetings in a session (see Chapter 3 for info on sessions), or it may be a short list of the items of business to be handled in a routine board meeting. The agenda may (but doesn't have to) indicate the hour for each event, or it may just show the total time allotted to each item.

TIP

The agenda may be *adopted* (that is, be made binding on the meeting), or it may simply be a guide to keep the meeting on track. Adopting your agenda is sometimes a good idea because it gets everybody in agreement with the meeting plan at the beginning of the meeting.

TECHNICAL STUFF

For an agenda to be binding, the assembly must formally adopt it at the beginning of the session. Its adoption can be by unanimous consent (which I cover in Chapter 8) or by a majority vote. Once adopted, the agenda can be changed only by a two-thirds vote or by a vote of a majority of the entire membership.

Using Robert's Rules' basic agenda

Robert gives an order of business but doesn't mandate any particular agenda. However, he does provide an agenda protocol that has been so widely used that it's almost universally accepted as a fundamental meeting plan. Not everything in the agenda shown here is necessary in every situation, and your agenda may even need to be more extensive and detailed. But in its own right, this basic agenda is a great arrangement of events, consistent with the standard order of business discussed throughout this chapter; you can find it at the heart of just about every good business meeting you attend. In the following section, I list the basics and add some commentary to help you put it to use in your organization as the need arises.

Call to order

Although technically not part of the agenda as far as Robert's Rules is concerned, this item heading shows up at the top of plenty of "Agendas." When the time comes, start the meeting on time.

A single rap of the gavel at the appointed hour and the declaration, "The meeting will come to order," is sufficient. You can't finish on time if you don't start on time, and everybody knows when the meeting starts. A good chairman is known for starting meetings on time and will always be respected for doing so.

Opening ceremonies

Your group may customarily open meetings with an invocation and a recitation of the Pledge of Allegiance. Maybe you sing a hymn or the national anthem. The protocol is "God before country" (meaning you invoke the deity before you salute the flag), so plan to make your invocation before you say the Pledge. This part of the agenda is also the place to include any special opening fraternal rituals, a greeting given by one of your officers, or anything else that may reasonably fall under the category of ceremony. You don't have to use it, of course, and in many types of meetings, you skip this item.

Roll call

If your group is a public body or if you have a rule that certain officers must be in attendance before the meeting can proceed, this is the time to call the roll. But if you don't have a rule requiring it, don't waste your time on this item.

Consent calendar

Robert's *consent calendar*, more often referred to as a *consent agenda*, is mostly used in specialized organizations such as public legislative bodies or a large professional society's house of delegates. A consent calendar quickly processes a lot of noncontroversial items that you can dispose of quickly by placing them on a list (the consent calendar) of items to be adopted all at once. The list can also contain special preference items to be considered in order at the appropriate time. This consent calendar is usually placed in an order of business by a special rule of order (see Chapter 2), and its placement is generally of relatively high rank.

TIP

Unless an organization's rules provide otherwise, a single member may demand that a particular item on a consent calendar be considered separately. Flip to Chapter 11 for everything you need to know about the incidental motion *Division of the Question*.

Standard order of business

Everything on the agenda outside the standard order of business is just ancillary to the meeting. All the business really begins with the approval of the minutes and ends when you're finished with any new business. Refer to the section, "Order of Business Sequence," earlier in this chapter for a detailed treatment of this agenda section, including a complete discussion of the six classes of business and the items included under each.

Good of the order

This time is set aside for members to offer comments or observations (without formal motions) about the society and its work. The good of the order is also the time to offer a resolution to bring a disciplinary charge against a member for offenses committed outside a meeting. (See Chapter 18 for more on discipline.)

Announcements

This portion of the basic agenda sets aside time for officers (and members, when appropriate) to make announcements. However, the fact that this is an agenda item doesn't prevent the chair from making an emergency announcement at any time.

Program

If you're offering some other general presentation of interest to your members, whether it's a film, a guest speaker, a lecturer, or any other program, it should be presented before the meeting is adjourned. If you would rather conduct the program at some other place in the agenda, it may be scheduled to take place before the minutes are read or, by suspending the rules, may be inserted within the standard order of business.

REMEMBER

Guest speakers are often on tight schedules, so it's quite proper for the chair to ask for unanimous consent to place the program at any convenient place on the agenda, even if the only convenient place is within the order of business.

Adjourn

This part of the agenda marks the end of the meeting. Yes, finally it's time to go home. But don't leave until the chair declares the meeting adjourned, or you just may miss something important. Chapter 10 contains everything you need to know about properly adjourning a meeting.

2

Motions: Putting Ideas into Action

Chapter **6**

Main Motions: Proposing Ideas for Group Action

You're sitting in a meeting, and that little idea light bulb that floats above your head starts flashing. You have a brilliant idea, and you're convinced that it will further the goals of your group. It may be a brand-new idea that your group has never considered, or it may be an idea to do something in a new or different way. No matter what the idea is, for your group to consider it, you have to offer your idea to the group as a proposal for action.

In parliamentary lingo, your proposal is called a *main motion.* In this chapter, I explain how to use a main motion to take action in the name of your group. I explain the different types of main motions, identify their characteristics, and give you some examples of how to use them in a meeting. I offer some basic information about other classes of motions as they relate to the main motion, and I walk you through the eight steps of handling a motion so that you feel comfortable and empowered to bring any idea to the floor in any meeting.

Understanding Motion Basics

A favorite saying among parliamentarians is, "When all is said and done, there's a lot more said than done!" This little quip packs a lot of meaning, though. The real reason your organization holds business meetings is to bring interested members together to talk about ideas for action and to make decisions and take action in the name of the group.

Even though it's the nature of meetings to have more said than done, Robert's Rules helps keep things on track by requiring that no discussion be undertaken until somebody proposes an idea for action.

Everything your group ever accomplishes gets its start through *motions.* So although it's more than just a truism that a lot more gets said than done in meetings, nothing can get done without the motion. Both the length of time you discuss something and the ultimate decision your group makes are based on your members' use and understanding of the nature of the different types of motions, their relationship to each other, and how the different motions are best used as tools for effective decision making.

Classifying motions

Motions come in all types and sizes, but they fall into five basic classes (and the first class breaks down into two types):

>> Main motions

- Original main motions

- Incidental main motions

>> Subsidiary motions

>> Privileged motions

>> Incidental motions

>> Motions that bring a question again before the assembly (Parliamentarians often use the term *bring-back motions* for this classification.)

Defining relationships between the classes

A member once asked me at a meeting, "Why don't you parliamentarians stop confusing us with all this stuff about motions and just teach people to say, 'Let's do this . . .' and then we can just talk about it?"

I replied that she made a really great point and that understanding "all this stuff about motions" can be viewed in precisely the terms she preferred. Using her suggestion, I explain the relationships between the classes and types of motions briefly here, and I refer you to other chapters for more detail.

Starting things off with main motions

The first class of motions, the *main* motions, is the most basic of all classes: The main motion introduces before your group a new subject for discussion and action.

A *main motion* says, "Let's do this about that."

Digging in deeper with secondary motions

The next three classes, subsidiary, privileged, and incidental motions, all help you process a pending main motion. Collectively, these three are termed *secondary motions:*

>> A *subsidiary motion* says, "Let's do this . . . to take care of the main motion."

>> A *privileged motion* says, "Let's do this . . . for the assembly or a member, even though there's a pending main motion (and maybe even pending subsidiary motions)."

>> An *incidental motion* says, "Let's do this . . . to better handle the pending motion."

Rebounding with bring-back motions

The fifth class, bring-back motions, is a special class of motion by which your group can undo or make changes to decisions it already made. This type of motion is a special tool used when changes to a decision become necessary "after the fact." You can find everything you need to know about these motions in Chapter 12.

A *bring-back motion* says, "Let's undo this and maybe do that instead."

Knowing when to use secondary motions

The main motion proposes action, but rarely is a motion decided without some discussion. After an idea is put before your group, the fun starts. Some folks completely support the idea; some are dead set against it. Others think it's a fine idea but want to consider a different approach.

You'd never get anything done if you didn't have a system for dealing with all the different points members offer in response to your idea. So Robert's Rules provides you with *secondary motions* — the tools you need to handle the different approaches members may want to take to arrive at a final decision.

TECHNICAL STUFF

Secondary motions fall into one of the following three classes:

>> **Subsidiary motions** are motions that apply directly to a pending main motion (or pending secondary motion) and help the group arrive at a final decision on the main motion. (For example, the motion to *Amend* is a subsidiary motion. You use it to propose a change to the main

motion. Another example is the motion to *Refer* the main motion to a committee. You use it when you don't want to spend all night talking about something that can be done at another time by people who are interested in working out the details.) I cover subsidiary motions in detail in Chapter 9.

>> **Privileged motions** are motions that deal with anything related to the comfort of the assembly or other situations that are so important that they may interrupt pending business and must be decided immediately by the chair or the members without debate. (For example, the motion to *Adjourn* is privileged when made if another motion is under consideration. You make this motion when you're ready to go home.) I cover privileged motions in detail in Chapter 10.

>> **Incidental motions** are motions that generally deal with procedures and help process other motions. (For example, raising a *Point of Order* during debate on a main motion is an incidental motion.) You use incidental motions to help the group conduct its business in meetings. I cover incidental motions in detail in Chapter 11.

TECHNICAL STUFF

Many individual motions make up these three classes of secondary motions. Collectively, secondary motions — and the bring-back motions in Chapter 12 — are often referred to as the *parliamentary motions.* I mention parliamentary motions here to illustrate their relationship to main motions, but I cover them more completely and provide examples of their applications in the individual chapters in Part 2.

Taking the Plunge with a Main Motion

The main motion is a proposal for specific action and marks the beginning of your group's consideration of a subject.

That's simple enough! You're a member, you're at a meeting, and you have an idea for action. All you have to do now is make a motion, and once it's seconded and stated by the chair, the group decides whether to accept your idea and authorize the action you propose. The following sections explain just what you need to know about making a main motion.

Examining examples of main motions

Suppose you're attending a monthly meeting of your community service club. Your speaker from the county library tells everyone about the new bookmobile program to make books available to community members who can't easily get to the library. Your club's president thanks the speaker and addresses the club members, asking if anyone has any new business. You think the club should make a donation to the county library to support the bookmobile, so you address the chair, are recognized, and suggest your idea by making a motion. You say, "Mr. President, I move that we donate $1,000 to the county library to purchase books for the bookmobile." You've just made a main motion.

Your motion is just one example. Main motions are also used to

>> **Express an opinion:** "I move that we commend the president for a job well done!"

>> **Authorize a purchase:** "I move that we buy a new computer for the club secretary."

>> **Create a policy or rule:** "I move that we limit the use of the swimming pool only to residents of the neighborhood and their preregistered guests."

>> **Adopt a recommendation made in a report:** "I move that we adopt the recommendation of the membership committee to advertise in the Sunday newspaper."

Understanding the main motion's purpose

The main motion is the starting point on the way to making a group decision. Essential for orderly decision making, the main motion's purpose is to introduce business for discussion. Ultimately, its result is a decision made in the name of your group.

REMEMBER

Until a motion is made, seconded, and stated by the chair, no discussion is in order. (I cover this and other rules about discussion in Chapter 7.) This rule of "motion before discussion" saves valuable meeting time. When you start off with a definite proposal ("I move that . . .") — and it's seconded and stated by the chair — your group discusses the motion's merits and all the details necessary to make a decision. During the discussion, you and the other members are free to alter your motion as much as necessary before you reach the final decision. This process is much more productive than just jabbering about some vague idea, hoping to work it out as you go, and then getting around to making a motion summarizing what you think you may have just proposed. That haphazard approach wastes meeting time and leaves your group confused.

WARNING

Brainstorming is great, but you need to do it outside your business meeting. Time is limited, and often many decisions need to be made at the meeting in a short time. The rule requiring you to have a motion on the floor before discussing it means that you need to have your idea fairly well thought out before you turn it over to the group for consideration.

Putting your motion in writing

Experience has taught me to write out my main motion before I stand up and make it in a meeting. Writing out the motion helps me organize my thoughts and compose a motion that's clear and covers the necessary details as concisely as possible. A well-prepared motion helps other members understand my idea and how I think the group should proceed.

TIP

If a member has something to bring before the group, writing it ahead of time is the thing to do. As often as not, however, ideas come during the meeting. An effective member works out a motion's wording before rising to make the motion. It's not always easy to follow along in a meeting *and* compose a motion, but that's what happens in meetings. As soon as a member gets to thinking about making a motion on the fly, writing it is the most effective way to compose one's thoughts.

REMEMBER

Putting your ideas in writing forces you to express your proposals as concisely as possible before any discussion occurs. You not only save time, but you also help the group reach the right decision (whether that's the decision you hoped for or the decision that's best for the group). A side benefit of being prepared and putting your motion in writing is that you don't find yourself grasping for words and delaying the meeting, especially if you have a long motion.

In fact, Robert's Rules gives the presiding officer the right to ask that you submit your motion in writing, and the secretary also may ask him to request your motion in writing. The secretary has the duty of recording all main motions in the meeting's minutes, but that duty doesn't involve transcribing your motion on the fly. For all but the simplest motions, handing the secretary your motion in writing (after you make it) is the thing to do. An important benefit is that offering your written motion eliminates the chance of error when the chair states your motion or when the secretary writes it in the minutes.

In any event, you achieve your goal more effectively if you state your proposal clearly without fumbling for words. You *sound* prepared because you *are* prepared — you've thought about exactly what you want the group to do and how best to propose that you do it.

Making your motion in proper form

TIP

In addition to writing your motions before you make them, you want to use proper form when stating your motion. Keep the following in mind:

>> **Do** use phrases like "I move that . . ." or "I propose that . . . ."

>> **Don't** use phrases like "I motion that . . ." or "I want to make a motion that . . . ."

- One of my mentors always responded to members who said, "I want to make a motion that . . ." by answering, "Okay then, make it!"

RESOLUTIONS: A MATTER OF FORM

Some main motions need to be expressed formally in writing, to attach a special level of importance to them. Because of the form — beginning with the word *Resolved* and following with either a statement of opinion or a statement authorizing or directing some action — such a motion is called a *resolution*.

Here's an example of a common resolution: "*Resolved,* That it is the sense of this assembly that the organization commend our city council for repairing our streets without raising our taxes."

You make this kind of motion by saying, "I move the adoption of the following resolution," and then you read the resolution.

Of course, your group can consider the same opinion if you make a motion stating, "I move we commend the city council . . . ." But casting the motion in the form of a resolution affords the group a way of adding emphasis to the expression.

Another point about resolutions is that, because they're formal, you get to add a preamble, if you want. A *preamble* is parliamentary lingo for all those *Whereas* paragraphs that precede the *Resolved* clauses. Using a preamble gives you a chance to list the reasons for the resolution and keeps you from having to use all your debate time justifying your motion.

When I was a student, I wondered a lot about the difference between a main motion and a resolution. After all, if they do the same thing, how do you know when to make your motion in the form of a resolution? My mentor told me, "Well, it's like this: You use a resolution when you want to make it like a law."

The difference has a lot to do with how you want the record to look when all is said and done. (I explain what the record is when I discuss minutes and reports in Chapter 17 and the duties of the secretary in Chapter 15.) Regardless of the differences, a resolution is still a main motion. It's just a matter of form.

Using proper form makes you sound natural, relaxed, and confident. Otherwise, you may sound like you don't know what you're doing, thus lessening your effectiveness in the meeting.

Breaking Down the Types of Main Motions

Main motions fall into these two classifications: original main motions and incidental main motions.

Original main motions

An *original main motion* is one that deals not so much with the internal business of the assembly as with the goals and objectives of the organization itself. Its most distinguishing characteristic is that, when made, the original main motion marks the beginning of a group's involvement in a substantially new question. Check out a few examples of original main motions:

>> "I move that we buy a copy of *Robert's Rules For Dummies* for our president."

>> "I move that we appoint a committee of three to plan a Christmas social for the residents of the senior center and to report its recommendations at the November meeting."

>> "I move that we adopt the following resolution: *Resolved,* That the Lakeside Acres Homeowners Association opposes the construction of a new causeway entrance across from the main entrance to Lakeside Acres subdivision."

Incidental main motions

An *incidental main motion* is a main motion that deals with things directly related (or *incidental*) to the business of the group, including previously made decisions and decisions yet to be made.

Distinguishing incidental main from original main motions

An incidental main motion is distinguished from an original main motion, in that

>> The incidental main motion deals with business that started as an original main motion and on which the group reached a decision. Now the subject matter is being revisited in some way and is the subject of further discussion or decision making.

Suppose that the committee responsible for planning a Christmas social for a senior center has found a caterer, but the caterer wants a $400 deposit before he will book the event. At the next meeting, the committee reports back to the group with a recommendation that the members authorize and direct the treasurer to issue a check for $400 to Party Hearty Catering Service. The chairman of the committee then makes an incidental main motion to adopt the recommendation of the committee.

>> The incidental motion to *Object to the Consideration of the Question* may only be applied to an original main motion, and it's never proper to use it to keep an incidental main motion from being discussed.

By definition, this kind of objection can be applied only to an *original* main motion. To understand this, just think of the previous incidental main motion example. Having the group vote on *whether to consider* the recommendations of a committee your group has appointed would make no sense. If a member is opposed to adopting the recommendation because he thinks $400 is too much to spend, his duty is to speak against the motion to adopt — not to stifle discussion about the recommendation. Chapter 11 fully discusses the motion to object to consideration of the question.

>> Motions that are related to parliamentary processes are incidental main motions.

Take a look at some examples of incidental main motions:

>> **Motion to *Adopt:*** "I move that we adopt the recommendations of the Christmas social planning committee to authorize and direct the treasurer to issue a check for $400 to Party Hearty Catering Service for our annual event for the senior center."

REMEMBER

If a committee comes up with a recommendation on its own initiative rather than as a matter of course in following up on previous instructions of the assembly, then a motion to *Adopt* that recommendation would be an original main motion, not an incidental main motion. As an example, when that Christmas social planning committee made its report last January after last year's Christmas party, its only recommendation was that the assembly authorize $100 for emergency repairs to the mailbox in front of the clubhouse where they had their meeting. Because that recommendation had nothing to do with any previous instructions from the assembly, the motion to adopt that recommendation was an *original* main motion, not an *incidental* main motion. (Let me tell you, the discussion on that motion was really interesting.)

>> **Motion to *Ratify:*** "I move that we ratify the decision made by the president to contract for emergency repairs to the clubhouse after the storm."

REMEMBER

The motion to *Ratify* is applicable to more than emergency actions. It can include other actions taken without proper authority in advance. For example, buying that swing set for the school's playground after a PTA virtual meeting when online meetings weren't authorized in their bylaws: "I move to ratify the purchase of the swing set for the playground made based on a decision made in the online meeting last month." Or how about when a member of the leadership team takes a chance to keep from missing a good deal: "I move to ratify the Town Fair booth rental contract that the membership committee member signed to take advantage of a 50 percent discount."

>> **Motion to *Recess* (made when no other motion is pending):** "I move that we take a ten-minute recess before we move on to the election of officers."

REMEMBER

If made when another main motion is pending, the motion to *Recess* isn't an incidental main motion, but is a *privileged motion* — a special type of secondary motion.

>> **Motion to *Limit Debate* (made when no other motion is pending):** "I move that we spend no more than 20 minutes tonight discussing the budget."

REMEMBER

>> If made when the budget is already under discussion, the motion to *Limit Debate* isn't an incidental main motion, but a *subsidiary motion* — a type of secondary motion.

>> ***Point of Order* (made when no other motion is pending):** "Mr. President, the bylaw amendment reported in the minutes as adopted last month was not included in the notice of that meeting. Bylaw amendments require previous notice and publication in the call of the meeting at which they are to be considered. Therefore, the action taken to adopt the bylaw amendment is null and void, and the bylaws were not amended."

REMEMBER

If a *Point of Order is* raised during consideration of a motion, it is not an incidental main motion, but an *incidental motion* — a type of secondary motion.

Distinguishing incidental main motions from incidental motions

An incidental main motion isn't the same as an *incidental motion*, which is one of the secondary motion types you can read about in Chapter 11. This section briefly highlights the differences between these motions.

The incidental *main* motion is, first and foremost, a *main* motion, and it's never made when another main motion is being made or discussed. By contrast, the *incidental* motion (notice the absence of the word "main") is about procedure. It might be about another pending motion, or it might relate to a motion that someone wants to introduce, or one that is about to be stated by the chair, but hasn't yet left his lips, or even one that has just been disposed of.

WINDING UP FOR THE PITCH: PREVIOUS NOTICE

When Casey was at the bat, he knew when the pitch was about to come because Pete the pitcher raised a foot, drew back his arm, and gave Casey a glare before he threw the ball. In other words, Pete gave notice that he was about to make his pitch. Some ideas (er, motions) that get pitched in a meeting are just too important to be initiated without some warning. In those cases, advance announcement, referred to as *previous notice,* is either necessary or at least highly desirable.

Previous notice of a motion is given at the meeting preceding that at which the motion will be introduced. Written notice may be required by an organization's rules.

Previous notice can help even when it's not required. For example, when you're looking to amend or rescind some previously adopted motion (other than bylaws or special rules of order), having given previous notice allows you to make the change with a majority vote. Without the notice, you'll need either a two-thirds vote or the affirmative vote of a majority of the entire membership (a nice option if it's a small membership).

Previous notice, therefore, might make it easier to pass the motion. But in all fairness, it might also put more people in the room to debate it. There. You're on notice! Refer to the section, "Giving Previous Notice of Motions" in this chapter for more information.

To understand the difference, consider these examples:

>> **Incidental main motion:** No motion is pending, and the election of officers is coming up. You rise, address the chair, are recognized, and say, "Madam President, I move that, when we vote on our officers, we vote by ballot." This motion is a *main motion* because it brings a new question before the group, and it's *incidental* to the business of the assembly.

>> **Incidental motion:** The election of the treasurer is pending, and there are two nominees. The chair proceeds to take the vote on the first nominee by voice, and it can't be determined whether the first candidate received a majority. You rise, address the chair, are recognized, and say, "Madam President, I move that we vote on the treasurer by ballot." This motion is a *motion* that is *incidental* to the currently pending election of an officer.

Giving Previous Notice of Motions

Previous notice of a motion involves either announcing at a meeting your intent to make a motion at the next meeting or providing written notice of the motion in the call of the meeting. Rules involving previous notice of motions are rules of order found in Robert's Rules, but your bylaws or special rules of order may also include requirements for previous notice for some motions.

A particular example common to many organizations is a requirement for previous notice for amending bylaws. When your bylaws require previous notice for their own amendment, then nobody can spring any organization-changing surprises on anybody.

Under Robert, previous notice of a motion is used to allow for a lower vote threshold to adopt the motion. For example, a motion to *Amend or Rescind Something Previously Adopted* (see Chapter 12) requires either a two-thirds vote or a vote of a majority of the entire membership for adoption unless you've given previous notice. If you've given previous notice, these motions can pass with a majority vote. But if you're talking about a motion to amend a bylaw, Robert's Rules recommends that you make previous notice, and a two-thirds vote, an absolute must.

The idea behind previous notice of motions is to make sure anyone interested in the result has time to make plans to attend the meeting, participate in debate, and vote. Except where previous notice is specifically required under your rules or bylaws, it's somewhat of a strategic decision when you're looking to make a change in something you've already decided whether to give the previous notice of the motion. It's a trade-off because of the voting threshold required to pass. Do you want to give the notice, alerting any opposition, but be able to get your motion passed with a majority vote? Or do you want to make your motion without any previous notice knowing it will take a two-thirds vote to pass?

Working within Limits: Basic Rules for Main Motions

To participate effectively in a meeting, you need to know some basic points about the various motions: Is the motion applicable in this situation? Can it interrupt a speaker? Does it need to be seconded? Is it amendable? Is it debatable? What vote is required to adopt it? Can it be reconsidered?

The answers to these questions make up what Robert's Rules terms the *standard descriptive characteristics* of motions. For a particular motion, these characteristics are made up of a concise set of rules that fairly describe when a motion is in order and what it takes to adopt such a motion.

The standard descriptive characteristics for main motions are the following:

>> A main motion takes precedence over nothing. Making a main motion is in order only when no other business is pending. Furthermore, a main motion must yield to almost all secondary motions.

>> A main motion is never "applied to" another motion, but all subsidiary motions can be applied to it.

>> A main motion that is made when someone else has the floor is out of order.

>> A main motion requires a second.

>> A main motion is debatable.

>> A main motion is amendable.

>> A main motion requires a majority vote to adopt except in these cases:

- Bylaws or special rules of order provide for a higher vote requirement, as they usually do for some special situations.

- Its adoption requires overriding any procedural rules in place or limits members' parliamentary rights. In such a case, the main motion requires a two-thirds vote.

- It has the effect of changing a decision already made. In such a case, the vote is the same as for bring-back motions (covered in Chapter 12).

>> A main motion can be reconsidered at the meeting at which it was decided (or on the next day in a session of more than one day), subject to some special rules about the motion to *Reconsider* (see Chapter 12).

Avoiding Out-of-Order Main Motions

No matter how good your idea may be, if you want to propose something that goes against the bylaws (or your charter or constitution, if you have either or both), your presiding officer has no choice but to rule your motion "out of order," which is a nice, succinct way of saying, "We can't go there now because, for some reason, it's against the rules."

Of course, if you're actually proposing to amend the bylaws, constitution, or charter in the manner provided for their amendment, then you've found the exception to this rule.

It's just as out of order to offer a motion again in the same meeting after a direct vote has obliterated it or it was "procedured" to death (and that's usually a big waste of time and not much fun). The parliamentary gurus will tell you that it's a fundamental principle of parliamentary law that you don't put members through the same discussion twice in the same meeting unless somebody who voted on the prevailing side moves to reconsider and a majority agrees to undo the vote and talk about it some more and vote again. (Refer to Chapter 12.)

Similarly, if the assembly has disposed of some motion temporarily, as happens when a motion is postponed to your next meeting or handed off to a committee for a thorough work-over, it's uncool to get sneaky. If old Fred deFumer offers a new motion that conflicts with the motion you postponed or committed, or that is nothing more than a convenient spin on the same question to try to start up the discussion all over again, your chairman can (and should) rule Fred's motion "out of order."

Another no-no is to move to do something that isn't copacetic with something you've already decided. Say you have a policy that forbids smoking and drinking on the property. Brazenly, Myrtle Marlboro moves to allow her husband's cigars-and-cognac club to use the clubhouse for its monthly social gatherings. If the chair is on their toes, they'll be quick to rule Myrtle's motion out of order because they know the club policy doesn't permit it. If Myrtle wants to get the clubhouse for her hubby's club, she has some other motions to get passed before her original motion is in order.

Finally, a motion to take some action that is outside the purposes for which your organization exists is out of order, too, unless two-thirds of the members present and voting agree to admit the motion. (Take a look at Chapter 11 to find out how to stop a motion that has nothing to do with what your organization is all about.)

TIP

Don't think you have to sit around and wait for the chairman to rule a motion out of order. You can speed things up by taking a little initiative by making use of the incidental motion *Point of Order*. I tell you all about that in Chapter 11.

Handling a Main Motion in Eight Easy Steps

When it comes to handling a main motion, Robert's Rules streamlines the process and saves your group a lot of time.

REMEMBER

Using the following eight steps to consider ideas brought to the group in a systematic and orderly manner doesn't guarantee that everybody gets their way, but it does guarantee that everybody has a say.

Step 1: The member rises and addresses the chair

Members have the right to make main motions during a meeting almost anytime no other business is pending. The chair's responsibility is to know whether a particular main motion is in order.

When the member is ready to make a motion, they make sure no one else has the floor and then they stand up and say, "Mr./Madam Chairman (or Mr./Madam President)."

Step 2: The chair recognizes the member

If the member is entitled to recognition by the chair, the chair responds by saying something along the lines of, "The chair recognizes the member from Elm Acres." (The chair needs to maintain the appearance of impartiality here. If the member from Elm Acres is a constant pain, the chair may have to work hard to avoid say anything like, "What is it *now*, George?" But that's the job!)

In some situations, when the chair needs to determine the purpose for which the member seeks recognition before recognizing the member, the chair says something like, "For what purpose does the member from Elm Acres rise?" In this case, the member responds, "I rise to offer a motion to . . . ." If the motion is in order, the chair proceeds by recognizing the member.

Sometimes several people rise at once to address the chair. When this happens, the chair follows the rules for preference in recognition. Chapter 7 discusses these rules.

Step 3: The member makes the motion

After the chair recognizes the member, the member offers the motion concisely (and with only minimal advance comment, if any at all) by saying, "Mr./Madam Chairman (or Mr./Madam President), I move that . . . ."

REMEMBER

For all but the simplest original main motions, the judicious member has written out the motion ahead of time and is prepared to immediately submit the written motion to the chair or the secretary after making the motion.

Step 4: Another member seconds the motion

Main motions must be *seconded*, meaning that a second member expresses a desire to have the group consider the motion.

TIP

Contrary to popular belief, a second isn't necessarily an endorsement of the idea. The procedure requires a second mainly to ensure that at least one other person thinks the motion should be discussed. A member who opposes the motion may want it to come before the meeting so the group can vote it down.

To second a motion, a member simply calls from their place, "Second!"

If no second is forthcoming, the chair asks, "Is there a second to the motion?" If a second still doesn't come, the motion is said to *fall to the ground* and simply doesn't come before the group. If this happens, the chair states it as the case and moves on to the next item of business.

However, if someone rises and starts making comments in support or opposition (even without being recognized by the chair or without saying "Second!"), the motion is considered seconded because another member has expressed interest in discussing the motion. The chair's duty when that happens is to ask the member whose speech is out of order to please be seated.

If you're the presiding officer when something like that happens and you want to do a little bit of education, after retaking the floor you may say, "I'll take that as a second."

Up to this point, the member who offered the motion still has complete control of the motion. If for some reason they want to withdraw it, they may do so. If they need to make a minor change, they may do so — and doing so doesn't require the permission of the assembly. But any suggestions that the member withdraws or changes a motion properly goes through the chair, who has the discretion to allow a brief exchange before moving on to Step 5.

If Zelda Zookeeper wants to suggest that Kelley Kindheart withdraw her motion to buy a pallet of camel food for the city zoo, she should rise and address Chairman Chelsea, and state that she would like to ask if Miss Millie would be amenable to withdrawing her motion given the fact that the zoo's beloved camel Clydette died this morning.

Or if the town kayak team's coach, himself a member of the club, wants to suggest that Moe Blabber change his motion that the club sponsor a pancake breakfast to raise money to send the town's canoe team up the river, he would address the chair and state that he wants to ask if Monty might be willing to change his motion to correctly reference the team as a kayak team.

It's the chair's responsibility to assist the member with their motion in making any such adjustments, when necessary. The time spent at this point is well worth the investment because it expedites business and helps the group arrive at its decision without being bogged down amending intricate details. The presiding officer, however, must not allow this sort of thing to become a discussion that more appropriately would occur during debate. Debate is a Step 6 thing, and you're just finishing Step 4.

Step 5: The chair states the motion

This step is, more often than not, simple. The chair says, "It is moved and seconded that . . ." and then reads the motion to the members. By then asking, "Is there any debate?" the chair puts the motion in the control of the group.

REMEMBER

The member who made the motion then needs the approval of the assembly to withdraw the motion or change it after the chair has stated the motion.

WARNING

Some motions, such as resolutions or motions referencing some paper for the assembly to adopt, involve longwinded verbiage. With any luck, copies of the motion, resolution, and any papers involved, have been distributed to the members in time for them to have read them. If not, you have to read the entire motion in this step because your job as presiding officer is to be sure that the full text of the motion, including any preambles to a resolution or papers to be adopted, has been read. You can get around this requirement if copies have been distributed in advance by obtaining the consent of the assembly to dispense with the reading and refer to the copies distributed to the members.

Think about that well-run meeting you attended where the presiding officer handled something like this so very well. The finance committee had reviewed the proposed budget and moved its adoption. The report containing the budget consisted of 16 pages of ten-point type. It had been made available to the members online and copies had been distributed at the meeting. When the committee chair moved the adoption of the proposed budget, Madam President said, "Unless someone wants me to read the budget in its entirety before we take up debate, the question is now on the adoption of the proposed budget just presented, copies of which have been distributed to you. Is there any debate?" Not even the member who is the technicality queen of the organization, insisted on a reading.

Or how about the time when Larry Loquacious moved to adopt a resolution with a preamble that took six long-suffering minutes to read. The moment he finished making his motion, his compadre Nick Short hollered, "Second!" That's when Madam President did a great job by saying, "The question is now on the adoption of the resolution just read. Is there any debate?"

After the chair states the motion and prompts for debate, the motion belongs to the group. However, Robert's Rules provides that the member who made the motion is entitled to be recognized to speak to the merits of their motion before any other member. I discuss preference in recognition in Chapter 7.

Step 6: The members debate the motion

The chair recognizes the member who made the motion by saying, "The chair recognizes the member from Elm Acres." The member now has the floor to explain their motion and the reasons behind its creation.

Other members may then seek recognition of the chair to speak for or against the motion. The member wanting to speak rises and addresses the chair by simply saying, "Mr./Madam Chairman/President" and waiting to be recognized.

During the discussion, any of the secondary motions may be considered — subject, of course, to the specific rules for their uses and applications.

Discussion or debate of the motion can be a complicated process. In Chapter 7, I cover the rules and procedures for this part of the process.

Step 7: The chair puts the question and the members vote

When all members who had anything to say have said it, it's decision time.

Putting the question

The presiding officer now asks the members whether they want to adopt the motion. The members vote on the motion by answering a yes-or-no question; hence, the term *question* is often interchangeable with *motion* in parliamentary usage.

For this step, assume that the motion is "To purchase a new copying machine for the staff at a cost not to exceed $600." The chair puts the question by saying, "The question is on purchasing a new copying machine for the staff at a cost not to exceed $600. [pause] Those in favor, say 'Aye.'"

After the ayes have been heard, the chair takes the negative vote by saying, "Those opposed, say 'No.'"

Clearly presenting exactly what the members are being asked to decide is important in this step. The chair should deliberately incorporate the actual language of the motion in the question.

The members vote

Motions are commonly decided by voice vote (or *viva voce*, in Robert's Rules), so the example for this step assumes that method. But the presiding officer may, on their own initiative, call for a rising vote or a counted vote. Additionally, before the voting actually begins, any member may offer an incidental motion to conduct the vote using a different method. Chapter 8 discusses voting procedures at length.

Step 8: The chair announces the result

It's all over now, and one side has prevailed. The chair's duty is to make the declaration of fact and announce the result. They say either "The ayes have it, and the motion is carried (or 'is adopted' or 'is agreed to')" or "The noes have it, and the motion is lost (or 'fails')." After an uncounted rising vote or vote by show of hands, the chair says, "The affirmative has it, and the motion is adopted (or 'carried' or 'agreed to')" or "The negative has it, and the motion is lost."

But that's not all. If the motion passes, the chair also needs to tell the assembly what will happen as a result. In the example used in this section, if the motion passes, the chair adds, "And we will purchase a new copying machine for the staff at a cost not to exceed $600." If the motion fails, nothing further is required in the announcement.

NAILING DOWN THE VOTING RESULT

So you're presiding at the annual meeting of the Reluctant Roofing Suppliers Society, and you have about a hundred rancorous roofers sitting in front of you. You've just taken the vote on a motion to donate enough supplies to the county park commission to help the county reroof its indoor swimming pavilion. Although you're pretty sure of the result, it's very close and you're concerned that the losing side won't gracefully accept the call.

Fortunately, you're prepared because you read your *Robert's Rules For Dummies* and found out that the way to start your announcement in a situation like this is to test the water by saying, "The ayes (or noes) seem to have it," and allow a few seconds for one of the members to call out "Division" (see Chapter 11), which is all it takes to require a rising vote. You know that if nobody jumps at the chance to challenge the call, you just proceed with confidence and declare, "The ayes (noes) have it, and the motion is adopted (fails)."

But suppose you're in the same meeting, same motion, but this time you have absolutely no clue which side is in the majority, and you don't want to guess. What do you do? Easy! You simply retake the vote as a rising vote.

After the rising vote is taken, if it isn't abundantly clear which side won, you retake the vote — again by a rising vote — but this time, you (or somebody everybody trusts) counts the heads. (You can also count the ears and divide by two, but that's like going around the block to get next door.)

The reasons you might be in doubt about the result of a vote can vary. Whether the inconclusive vote is a voice vote, or a vote taken by show of hands in a big meeting, or even when you have the sense that a substantial number of members didn't vote for any reason or no reason, taking a rising vote, counted when necessary, usually hits the nail on the head. Even if it isn't a roofing nail.

After the chair has announced the voting result and stated what will happen as a result of a motion's adoption, and assuming the vote isn't immediately challenged (see Chapter 8 for more about challenging a vote), all they have to do is to announce the next item of business and move the meeting along.

TECHNICAL STUFF

If the vote is viva voce and any member doubts the result, that single member may demand that the vote be redone by a rising vote. To make such a demand, the member simply rises and calls out "Division." Chapter 11 covers this incidental motion and its use.

» **Assigning the floor to the right person**

» **Focusing discussion on the merits of the question**

» **Interrupting a member who has the floor**

» **Knowing which motions are debatable**

Chapter **7**

Debate: Discussing the Pros and Cons of Ideas

When it comes to meetings, the fun doesn't really start until you're standing in front of everybody and, except for Mr. Boor rudely whispering to Miss Priss, they're all tuned in to hear what you've got to say. Some members are eagerly waiting to cheer you on; others are probably thinking about how to get everyone to listen to them instead. Either way, it's your turn to talk, and you need to make the most of it.

Whether you're the presiding officer or simply a member at the meeting, you won't last long without a working knowledge of the rules of debate. If you're the presiding officer, you need to know how to decide who gets to speak so that the meeting runs fairly. If you're part of the assembly, you need to know how to claim an opportunity to speak when you want to make a point.

This chapter guides you through the nuances of debating. For the presiding officer, it's about managing the floor. For the member, it's about listening and being heard. And for both, it's about being nice and professional when you're in the thick of it.

Understanding the Debate Process

Debate is Robert's Rules lingo for the time you spend discussing, amending, or otherwise dealing with a motion to arrive at its final disposition. Members take turns having their say, and in many cases, debate involves nothing more than spending a little time on a couple of amendments. However, it can also be a time when a lot of people have a lot to say about whether the group should agree on a motion and take the action it proposes.

When it comes to debating a motion in a meeting, you really have no such thing as pure and unencumbered freedom of speech. Because you're a deliberative assembly, you're concerned not only with the rights of individual members to have their say, but also with the rights of the group. Debate is thus subject to rules and limitations on who's allowed to speak on an issue, and how often and how long speakers can hold the floor. Protecting the rights of both the members and the group is also why rules for debate can be limited or extended, but only by a two-thirds vote.

REMEMBER

Rules for debate are designed to balance members' rights to speak with the assembly's right to make its decision and move on to something else.

To Debate or Not to Debate, *That* is the Question!

A quick look at the tables of subsidiary and privileged motions in Chapters 9 and 10 shows you that all the motions that rank above *Postpone to a Certain Time (or Definitely)* are undebatable. If you think about it, it makes perfect sense because everything of any higher rank is pretty much a yes-or-no question. Motions to *Limit Debate, Lay (a motion) on the Table,* or *Adjourn* just don't leave much room for question. Except for tweaks to the amendable motions, you don't really have anything to discuss.

The same is true for most incidental motions. As you can see in Chapter 11, incidental motions deal with questions of procedure. Except for appeals and resignations, procedure is procedure — what is there to discuss?

REMEMBER

When it comes to procedural motions, in most cases, you're either for the motion or against it, depending on the immediate parliamentary situation. So by defining a motion as undebatable, Robert's Rules is really just saying, "Take the vote and move on!"

Table 7-1 lays out the debatable motions and provides you with some key information about each one. You may find it ironic that meetings are all about discussing ideas and taking action, yet the list of debatable motions is really quite short. Of course, the advantage of a short list is that you don't have to remember much to know what's debatable and what's not. (Browse Chapters 6, 9, 11, and 12 for more information on these motions.)

TABLE 7-1 **Debatable Motions**

Motion	Key Points
Main motions	Debate is limited only by rules for length and number of speeches and, of course, rules of decorum.
Postpone Indefinitely	Discussion can encompass the merits of the main motion.
Amend	Debate is limited to merits of the proposed amendment. (Motion to *Amend* is undebatable if the underlying motion is undebatable.)
Commit	Discussion is limited to merits and details of referring.
Postpone to a Certain Time (or Definitely)	Discussion is limited to merits and details of postponing.

(continued)

TABLE 7-1 *(continued)*

Motion	Key Points
Appeal	Discussion is limited to the subject matter of the appeal. (But if debate serves no purpose and gets in the way of business, as is sometimes the case when the underlying motion is undebatable, then the motion to *Appeal* isn't debatable.)
Request to Be Excused from a Duty	Discussion isn't limited because each situation in which this motion is used is unique, and it's vital to have the information necessary to make a proper decision.
Rescind or Amend Something Previously Adopted (and Discharge a Committee)	Discussion can go fully into the merits of the subject matter.
Reconsider	Discussion can go fully into the merits of the motion to be reconsidered, unless that motion is undebatable.

QUESTIONING LIMITS ON DEBATE

I have to confess, one of my pet peeves is the obvious misuse of the rules of debate. Like when Member Smartypants wants to wax eloquent about how adopting a motion to *Limit Debate* violates the First Amendment or wants to argue about taking a recess. Some questions (in fact, *most* questions) are undebatable. I usually don't raise points of order about every little thing, even when I'm right. But when people start to debate an undebatable motion, I can't help myself. I almost always rise to a point of order, and if I'm presiding, I'm quick to rule improper debate out of order.

It doesn't take long for most of my fellow members to catch on to the list of debatable motions and to appreciate the time we save by cutting to the chase and voting them up or down without a lot of fuss. It's like starting a meeting exactly on time — sooner or later, people start actually showing up on time. When you start learning and following the rules of debate, you save time and have better meetings.

Presiding over the Debate

If you're a presiding officer, your leadership skills are clearly on display when you're chairing a meeting during the consideration of a motion on which a lot of people have a lot to say.

When it comes to presiding, your number-one duty is to know the rules. The rules for discussion and debate get quite a workout in meetings, so if you know the following rules, you'll do just fine. And if you don't know them, sooner or later, you'll wish you did.

Starting the debate

In meetings, discussion (also known as *debate*) is in order only when a motion is on the floor. A motion is on the floor after the presiding officer (also known as the *chair*) states the motion (see Chapter 6). For example, the chair may say something like, "It is moved and seconded to buy a fire truck for County Volunteer Company No. 2."

The discussion of ideas is the key component of any meeting. After the motion is on the floor, it's up to the members and you, as the presiding officer, to work as a team to figure out what, if anything, the assembly wants to do with the motion.

REMEMBER

Not every motion is as simple as the motion to buy a fire truck for County Volunteer Company No. 2. Some motions, such as lengthy resolutions or papers for the assembly to adopt, involve longwinded verbiage. Your job as presiding officer is to be sure that the full text of the motion, including any preambles to a resolution or papers to be adopted, have been read. As an alternative, where copies of the motion and related papers have been distributed, you can obtain the consent of the assembly to dispense with the reading and refer to the copies distributed to the members. See Chapter 6 for a brief discussion on handling the reading of resolutions and papers being considered for action by the assembly.

Your job while presiding is to keep up with who has spoken and who wants to speak. You control the assignment of the floor and handle discussion and secondary motions either until no further discussion is forthcoming or until members close debate or otherwise dispose of the motion.

The way you move things along is a matter of style. You call for debate by asking, "Is there any debate?" or "Is there any discussion?" or "Are you ready for the question?" Or, right after you've stated the motion, you can say something like, "Ms. Gliggenschlapp, do you wish to speak to your motion?"

You also need to know rules relating to discussion and debate, along with how to apply them, especially with regard to these actions:

>> Assigning the floor

>> Maintaining the appearance of impartiality

>> Handling an appeal

>> Taking the vote

Assigning the floor

Knowing that *members control decisions but the chair controls the floor* is at the heart of successful presiding.

Early in a discussion, the situation is pretty clear. Members rise and address the chair, and you basically want to take them in the order they seek recognition — first come, first served.

But deciding who gets the floor isn't always that easy. When the masses clamor for your attention, how do you decide whom to recognize? The needs and rights of the assembly are a big consideration in this decision. Knowing who's up first isn't enough; you often need to know why a member seeks recognition.

For example, you've just announced the result of the vote on buying a new outdoor grill for the clubhouse when Jumping Jack Gnash favors you with his favorite line: "Mr. Chairman! Mr. Chairman!" All his life, Jack has been the long-snouted me-first, and he is usually the same guy who jumps up to move to "reconsider" some vote when he voted on the losing side (flip to the important stuff about the motion to *Reconsider* in

Chapter 12). Jack, however, had jumped before the member who already had the floor had yielded it back.

And while Jack was jumping, Nola Nicely rose to her feet and called out pleasantly, "Mr. Chairman?" You ask the member why she seeks recognition of the chair, and she lets you know that she wants to move that you retake the vote on buying that new grill, only this time by ballot. And what Nola wants, Nola gets. In this case, it's because Nola's motion, if it is to be adopted, can't be decided later, like whatever Jack's great idea was.

If General Robert were here today, he'd be telling you that, by electing you to chair their meeting, the members have given you the job of making sure you put before them all the questions they need to decide. That task is what the job of assigning the floor really is all about.

But entitlement to preference in recognition depends not only on who wants to speak and why, but also on the parliamentary situation. The rules you'll follow depend on which of these situations applies:

>> No question is pending.

>> A debatable question is immediately pending.

>> An undebatable question is immediately pending.

When no question is pending

You've finished with a particular item of business, but you haven't moved on to the next order of business (see Chapter 5) or stated a new motion. So just what must a good presiding officer (and astute members) keep in mind when "what just happened" hasn't moved on to "what's on schedule to happen next?"

>> In a special meeting, if it has been arranged for a particular member to offer a motion for which the meeting was called, that member has preference in recognition over others who may offer competing motions. (See Chapter 3 for more information on special meetings.) The same is true in any meeting when it comes to important main motions that are planned and to be offered by a particular member.

>> When getting a motion before the group requires a series of motions, such as needing to lay a motion on the table to take up a more urgent motion, the member who made the intervening motion (in this case, the motion to *Lay on the Table*) is entitled to recognition so that they can make the motion they're trying to get on the floor.

>> If a motion is voted down because a member offers to make a certain motion if the assembly defeats a pending motion, that member is entitled to preference in recognition for the purpose of making the new motion.

>> Even when a member is entitled to recognition to make a main motion, if another member seeks recognition to do one of the following, that member must be recognized first:

- To make a motion to *Reconsider and Enter on the Minutes* (see Chapter 12)

- To make a motion to *Reconsider a vote* (see Chapter 12)

- To call up a motion to *Reconsider* (see Chapter 12)

- To give previous notice of a motion, or to make a motion for which previous notice was given (see Chapter 6)

- To make the motion to *Take from the Table* (see Chapter 12)

When a debatable motion is immediately pending

This situation applies most of the time during discussion and debate. As the presiding officer, you may often find yourself asking, "For what purpose does the member rise?" If it's not one of the following, your job is to inform the member, "That's not in order at this time," and move on to the next member seeking recognition:

>> A member rising to give notice is entitled to recognition (see Chapter 4).

>> The member who made the immediately pending motion is entitled to preference in recognition if they haven't

already spoken. (But, contrary to a somewhat common misbelief, a member who seconds a motion has no similar claim to preference in recognition.)

>> A member is entitled to speak a second time only after everybody else who wants to speak has done so.

>> The chair alternates recognition between proponents and opponents of the pending motion.

>> If the pending motion is one that was adopted earlier and is now being reconsidered for the purpose of being amended, the member who made the motion to *Reconsider* (see Chapter 12) — for the specific purpose of amending the motion now being reconsidered — is entitled to preference in recognition to move their amendment.

>> If the pending debatable question is on whether to sustain a ruling of the chair on an appeal (see the section, "Handling an appeal," later in this chapter) or a *Point of Order* (refer to Chapter 11) that the chair has turned over to the assembly to decide, the chair is entitled to speak once ahead of any other member and then again before closing debate. The chair gets this nifty privilege when the assembly is to make a decision usually made by the chair.

When an undebatable question is immediately pending

If a motion is undebatable, well, it's not in order to say much of anything. Only the following two situations give anybody any reason to claim the floor:

>> A member rising to give notice (see Chapter 4) is entitled to recognition.

>> A member rising to make a motion that takes precedence over the pending motion is entitled to recognition. For example, *Previous Question* (see Chapter 9) isn't debatable. But if a member wants to move to *Adjourn* (see Chapter 10), they're entitled to the floor.

When Nola seeks recognition for a purpose that entitles her to preference in recognition, but Geneva (who also had preference) was recognized and has begun to speak, Nola might be entitled to interrupt (through addressing the chair). Not many things give a member a right to interrupt, but some things are just that important. Refer to the section, "Knowing when it's okay to interrupt," later in this chapter for the list of motions that can interrupt a speaker who has the floor.

Deciding who to recognize

As the presiding officer, you decide which members get recognized and assigned the floor. And as with any other decision of the chair, if you're in doubt about who's entitled to recognition, you can ask the members and let them vote on whom to recognize.

When the chair asks the members to vote on who is to be recognized, the person seeking recognition who polls the most votes is entitled to be recognized. This is an exception to the general rule prohibiting a decision by a plurality absent a bylaw or special rule of order permitting it.

When the assembly is on the larger side and people are lining up at microphones all over the place, Robert's Rules allows you to make adaptations to the rules based on the situation, at least until you adopt the special rules you need to manage all the people who want to speak. But when it's not so big, the decision is usually routine.

If you're not sure whether an interruption by a member is in order, before recognizing the member, simply say, "For what purpose does the member rise?" Based on the response, you make your decision on whether to recognize the member; if their purpose is in order, you recognize them. If not, you inform them that their purpose isn't in order at this time.

In any case, if you err in assigning the floor, your assignment is subject to a point of order. And for the most part, the chair's ruling is subject to appeal (see Chapter 11).

A chair's ruling on a point of order in connection with assigning the floor isn't subject to appeal in mass meetings (see Chapter 19) or in assemblies that wish to prohibit it and adopt a special rule to that effect, such as is sometimes the case in large meetings or conventions.

Refraining from debate

Allowing yourself to be drawn into a debate is one of the surest ways to lose the confidence your members have in your ability to preside impartially. Your job is to facilitate the members making all the points, pro and con, on an issue. If you feel strongly about an issue, you'd better hope your political allies can handle advancing your goals from the floor. You must not give them any edge or advantage.

The *appearance* of impartiality is the key to presiding over debate. Nobody expects you to *be* impartial; chances are good that you were elected because you have a program you hope to advance. But when you're presiding, stick to the job at hand.

If you absolutely must engage in the debate, you're obligated to yield the chair to a vice-president or chairman *pro tem* and step down until the motion is disposed of.

Handling an appeal

The rules for assigning the floor during a debatable appeal (see Chapter 11) are generally the same as in any discussion, except that members may speak only once and you, as the chair, may speak not only once, but twice! You get to speak first — after the appeal has been moved and seconded — to explain your ruling. Then, after everyone else has had a say, you get to speak again to respond to the points made by the members and explain your ruling further before you take the vote on the appeal.

Closing debate and taking the vote

Your duty as a presiding officer is to enable the group to conduct a full and free hearing of both sides of an issue. However, debate isn't permitted to continue after voting begins. But because of the right of members to enjoy all the time the group is willing to spend in debate, it's not in order to move so quickly to the voting as to silence a member who legitimately seeks the floor to speak or make a secondary motion.

DISCUSSION WITHOUT A MOTION

The rule that no discussion is in order unless a motion is before your group has two exceptions that can make it easier for your group to arrive at some decisions:

- One exception occurs when the subject of discussion isn't particularly complex and the group isn't large. In this case, the purpose of the discussion isn't to debate the pros and cons of a motion, but rather to frame a motion that the group wants to adopt. For example, a member in a board meeting may say, "You know, we've all been talking about setting up a scholarship for a member to attend our convention. Can we take a minute now to compose a formal motion and adopt it?" Situations in which this exception comes into play are limited, and usually it's better to just make a motion to establish a special committee to compose the motion outside the meeting.

- The other exception occurs when a member wants to briefly discuss a subject and conclude their remarks with a motion. Technically, when they start explaining the reasons for a motion they haven't yet made, their discussion is out of order. However, if you have a clear idea of what's coming and can tell that it doesn't abuse the rule against speaking while no motion is on the floor, unanimous consent is all you need to suspend the rule.

  Watch out, though, because a fine line lies between making an exception to a rule and abusing the members' rights to have a proposal before them before spending any time on discussion.

  But these two exceptions, in the right place and at the right time, can help your members arrive at good decisions with a minimum of fuss.

Robert's Rules calls this practice of silencing members *gaveling through,* and it's looked upon as particularly contemptible. If you ignore a member who seeks recognition before voting starts and proceed to take a vote, the vote must be disregarded and debate reopened, even if the result has been announced. However, when you've made sure the members have a full opportunity to claim the floor before you move on to the voting, it's too late to reopen debate after voting has begun.

WARNING

The debate remains closed even if the vote isn't conclusive and if additional votes are necessary to determine the result. Only by unanimous consent can debate be resumed in such a case.

Debating As a Member

Knowing the rules of debate as they apply to a presiding officer and his duties isn't enough. Whether you're presiding or participating as a member, it's to your advantage (if not your duty) to know the following rules for members' participation in debate.

Taking your turn

You've been patiently waiting for the chair to recognize you. You've listened to everybody else so you won't waste time repeating points already made. Now you're ready to have your say.

If members try, as sometimes they do, to shut you out by making demands for adjournment or calls to table, they're out of order. As long as you've been assigned the floor, your presiding officer has a duty to help you have your say. Motions from those other members who haven't been recognized and assigned the floor are just hot air.

Seeking recognition and obtaining the floor

Seeking recognition is at first as simple as rising and addressing the chair with the statement "Mr./Madam President!" And unless someone else has preference in recognition, the chair says, "The chair recognizes Ms. Goodsense."

You may be competing for recognition, and the chair may need to ask why you seek recognition. Be prepared to answer that question, and take care only to seek the floor for a purpose that's in order at the time. And if you think the chair has improperly recognized another person when you're entitled to preference in recognition, you can make a point of order, forcing the chair to stop whatever else is happening and listen to your concern.

You have to follow a timeliness requirement to make a *Point of Order* (see Chapter 11). If you're entitled to preference in recognition, you must make your point before the other person begins to speak.

Because the chair has the prerogative of assigning the floor, you need to be aware of what entitles you to preference in recognition. (Refer to the section, "Assigning the floor," earlier in this chapter for an explanation.)

Recognizing limitations on debate

Unless your group has adopted special rules of order (see Chapter 2), you come to every meeting entitled to speak twice on every motion, with a limit of ten minutes per speech. That's 20 minutes per person, per motion, per meeting. It's a wonder meetings don't last for weeks!

Well, not really. Limits exist within the limits, and your group always has access to one of the most useful subsidiary motions: the motion to *Limit Debate*. I cover that motion in Chapter 9, and it's a great tool for keeping things short and sweet. In fact, it's not uncommon for a group to adopt a motion to limit discussion to a set period of time, to a set number of speeches for or against, to a shorter time per speech, or to some combination of these options.

To be sure you have your say, though, you need to be familiar with how the limitations on debate work.

>> **Speaking a second time:** Under Robert's Rules, you can't speak a second time until everybody else who wants to speak has done so. If Mr. Smartypants has spoken once and the chair lets him speak again while you're attempting to be recognized, you have every right to claim the floor, even if you have to rise to a point of order (see Chapter 11) to do so.

>> **Requesting an extension of time:** The chair is responsible for letting you (or any other member) know when your time is up, and it's your duty to honor the chair's polite notice that your time has expired and immediately conclude your remarks. If you need more time, you can ask for it, or if the chair deems it appropriate, they can offer the members the opportunity to consent to an extension.

>> **Yielding time:** You can't transfer time. When you yield the floor, you waive your remaining time, but that remaining time doesn't get added to another member's time. Yielding for a question counts against your time.

REMEMBER

As with many elements of Robert's Rules, the limits on debate aren't completely without exceptions, which include the following:

>> **Giving committee reports:** Time limits don't apply when a committee report is being given. But if the reporting member speaks to a motion to enact one of the committee's recommendations, that discussion is on the clock.

>> **Making secondary motions:** Introducing a secondary motion isn't considered debate on the pending motion unless a member goes into the merits of the pending motion before making the secondary motion.

>> **Debating secondary motions:** When secondary motions are debatable, limits on debate apply anew to debate on the merits of the secondary motions, but debate on the secondary motion may not go into the merits of the main motion except for the motion to *Postpone Indefinitely* (see Chapter 9).

>> **Sessions of more than one day:** If a member exhausts their rights to speak on a motion and the motion is carried forward to a meeting on the next day, their rights to debate the motion are completely restored.

Getting around the rules by changing the limits of debate

By using the motion to *Limit or Extend the Limits of Debate* (see Chapter 9), you have some options to change the default rules of ten minutes per speech and two speeches per person.

You can make changes as follows:

>> **Adopt a special rule of order.** Taking this approach (see Chapter 2) can establish a different length for speeches or change the number of speeches permitted. A special rule of order makes the changes basically permanent because special rules supersede Robert's Rules. However, they can still be changed temporarily, just like Robert's Rules.

>> **Adopt a rule for a single session.** By a two-thirds vote without notice at any meeting, your group can adopt an incidental main motion to change the rules for time and length of speeches per person for one session only. You also can set a period for debate and a time for the vote.

>> **Adopt a rule for a particular motion.** With this approach, you can change the limits of number and duration of speeches or the total time for debate of the motion; you can also set a time for debate to close, or set a limit for the number of pro and con speakers, or determine a workable combination of these. Adopting a rule for a particular motion takes a two-thirds vote.

Knowing when it's okay to interrupt

Most people were taught (or, at least, were told) that it's never polite to interrupt someone who's speaking. That etiquette rule works when it comes to interviews, dinner parties, and the like, but not when you're dealing with Robert's Rules. During debate in a business meeting, interrupting a speaker is often necessary to protect your rights or the rights of the other members.

Your presiding officer's duty is to know when interruptions are permissible and to recognize you for such things as points of order or giving notice. Recognized members who have begun to speak are entitled to their time, but they can be interrupted (using the motions in the following list) for specific purposes, if urgency requires it:

>> **Motions that can interrupt a speaker who is speaking and that don't require a second:**

- Call for the Orders of the Day

- Point of Order/Call a member to order

- Call for a separate vote on a series of independent resolutions or main motions dealing with different subjects that have been offered under one main motion

- Requests (or motions to grant another member's request)

- Parliamentary Inquiry

- Request for Information (sometimes called Point of Information)

- Call for Division of the Assembly

- Raise a Question of Privilege

>> **Motions that can interrupt a speaker who is speaking but that must be seconded:**

- Appeal

- A motion to grant the maker's own request

>> **Motions that are in order when another speaker has been recognized but has not yet begun to speak:**

- Notice of intent to make a motion requiring such notice (no second required)

- Objection to Consideration of the Question (no second required)

- A motion to *Reconsider* (but not reconsideration itself; must be seconded)

- A motion to *Reconsider and Enter on the Minutes* (must be seconded)

Playing Nice: Decorum in Debate

Nothing stands to ruin an organization's spirit and sense of group pride quicker than an acrimonious debate. When debate gets heated and personal, good members quit, and the antagonists generally don't have what it takes to keep the organization going.

Nobody likes acrimony, and nothing need keep you from having a spirited debate while still keeping discussion focused on the issues. The following list contains some points to keep in mind when the soup gets thick at meetings where you talk about a dues increase or what to do with a budget surplus:

>> **Listen to the other side.** You expect the presiding officer to protect your right to speak even if it turns out that you're a minority of one. You also expect the other members to hear you out and to allow you the same time as everybody else to get in your two cents' worth. Give your fellow members their rightful turn. Listen to them — you may hear something that affects the way you think.

>> **Focus on issues, not personalities.** You don't want somebody across the aisle saying about you, "I don't see how that idiot who just spoke can even hold a job, with as much sense as he has about spending money!" It's much better to just stick to the issues. You may disagree with the point, but you won't feel personally attacked if your opponent simply says, "If we make this purchase at this time, we'll have less money in the treasury than I think we need to maintain."

>> **Avoid questioning motives.** It's not a good idea to say, "Mr. Chairman, the dweeb who just spoke is obviously trying to raise the executive director's salary because he wants to get the director fired and hire his own brother-in-law." The dweeb may, in fact, be glad to see the director go, and he may indeed be working to set up a raise for the

next employee, hoping it's his brother-in-law. But when you're in the meeting, express your opinion based on the proposal's merits. Try saying, "Raising the executive director's salary is unwise at this time because we haven't yet completed the assessment of a performance review."

>> **Address remarks through the chair.** One of the ways things can deteriorate quickly is by forgetting the rule that requires you to address the chair, not a member directly, during debate. Instead of turning to the member who made the motion to buy a fire truck and asking, "Just how much money do you think we need to spend on the fire truck?" try, "Madam Chairman, I'd like to ask how much money the member suggests we allocate to the purchase of the fire truck."

>> **Use titles, not names.** Things are more likely to stay impersonal if you avoid using names during debate. Refer to "the secretary" instead of "George." Refer to "The member who offered the motion" rather than "Myrtle." It feels a bit formal, but the idea is to keep the focus on issues, not individuals.

>> **Be polite.** Don't get the floor and start reading some paper, don't argue with the presiding officer except by legitimate appeal, and don't do anything that otherwise disturbs the assembly.

TIP

At some point, you've probably been in a meeting listening to something of interest, and Mr. Sluggo behind you isn't the least bit interested. He starts talking about how his pet parakeet is better looking than the member at the microphone. He's disturbing the assembly with his distracting chatter, but Robert's Rules comes to your rescue with a way to remind Sluggo that his chatter isn't appropriate. If you have to handle such a disturbance and you can't deal with it quickly and quietly in your place, rise to a *Question of Privilege* that the buzz and chatter are affecting your ability to hear the speaker, and let the chair help you out. See Chapter 10 for more details on this privileged motion and how to use it.

Dealing with Disruption: Dilatory and Improper Motions

The purpose of Robert's Rules (and parliamentary procedure in general) is to facilitate the transaction of business and to achieve the deliberate will of the majority after giving the minority a full hearing of its position, with full consideration of the rights of all the members, whether present or not.

However, some people learn about a few different types of motions and think they can use them to force their will on the group or to thwart the process that rules of order are designed to protect.

Everybody has run into the meeting bully, that antagonistic malcontent who stirs up trouble and tries to get their way by raising baseless points of order and appeals, or by making motions to adjourn every few minutes. These motions have their rightful place in the big picture, but if they're used to hinder business instead of help it, they're properly termed *dilatory* and should be ruled out of order by the chair. After all, it's the presiding officer's job to protect the assembly from these types of members.

Dilatory motions include motions that are

>> Misused with the purpose of obstructing business (such as the meeting bully's motions just described)

>> Absurd in substance

>> Frivolous, especially amendments

>> Unwarranted (such as calling "Division" when the result is clear)

Just as disruptive are the motions Robert describes as improper. *Improper motions* are those that

>> Are inconsistent with the organization's charter, bylaws, or procedural laws

>> Conflict with an adopted motion that hasn't been rescinded

>> Present essentially the same question that was defeated earlier in the same meeting

>> Present a question that the membership still has within its reach (as it has when something has been postponed or referred to a committee, or is the object of a motion to *Reconsider*)

>> Are outside the scope of the purpose of the organization (unless the motion is agreed to be considered by a two-thirds vote)

REMEMBER

A meeting's success depends upon the good faith of the members and leaders to give everybody their say, but not at the expense of letting a troublemaker take over.

In his book *Parliamentary Law* (1923), General Robert says, "The greatest lesson for democracies to learn is for the majority to give to the minority a full, free opportunity to present their side of the case, and then for the minority, having failed to win a majority to their views, gracefully to submit and to recognize the action as that of the entire organization, and cheerfully to assist in carrying it out until they can secure its repeal." That excerpt says it all!

Chapter **8**

Making Group Decisions: Voting on the Motion

Voting is the heart of the deliberative process. Your group has discussed, debated, changed, and tweaked a proposal for action. Now everybody's ready to make a decision and get on with it.

In this chapter, I cover some general principles about voting and tell you about all the different methods of voting you can use. Even more important, I share with you when you should (or shouldn't) use each one.

Of course, after you've voted, you have to figure out the result and determine what it means. Believe it or not, it's not always as simple as "the majority wins." I cover here the different options for deciding the result of your vote.

Robert's Rules gives a good bit of coverage to the voting process and your rights in that regard. I summarize the voting process rules in this chapter, but you can also find references throughout the book that refine these concepts as they apply to specific situations.

Knowing Your Voting Rights and Responsibilities

Before I get into too much detail about the different methods of voting and the specific procedures for each method, I want to cover some fundamental points about voting in general. This section deals with your rights and responsibilities when it comes to voting. Knowing these points helps you keep the voting process fair and efficient.

Voting as a duty

Voting isn't just a right of membership; it's your duty to vote when you have an opinion about a matter being decided. I'm sure you've heard countless anecdotes about how important one vote can be, so I don't belabor that point here. Just remember that, if you fail to vote, you allow others to make the decision, which is usually the same as having voted for the prevailing side. Whether you vote or not, you're still responsible in some way for the decision that's made.

Abstaining from voting

Although it's your duty to vote when you have an opinion, you can't be forced to vote. You have the right to remain neutral! In fact, some situations demand that you refrain from voting, even if you have a legal right to vote.

According to Robert's Rules, you should abstain from voting whenever you have an interest in the outcome that directly affects you personally (or monetarily) in a manner not shared by the other members of your group. The key here is that the other members don't share your interest. For example, it's certainly okay for you to vote in favor of, say, holding a banquet, even though you have a direct personal interest. You benefit from having the association buy your dinner. But so does everybody else. However, if the motion decides whether to give your company the catering contract, good form compels you to abstain from voting.

REMEMBER

Just to be clear, the abstention rule is a *should* rule. Just as you can't be forced to vote, you can't actually be compelled *not* to vote. As a voting member, you can vote to swing the contract your way, but it's bad form if you do.

WARNING

Abstentions do not count. Let me say that again: *Abstentions do not count.* If you abstain from voting, you have not voted. The fact that you were in the room doesn't make any difference unless the result is based on the number of members present.

REMEMBER

Figuring abstentions into vote totals or noting them in the record is never correct unless the vote is a roll-call vote. Then it's important only that the record shows you were present. Your abstention still doesn't count as a vote.

Voting for yourself

The rule that you should abstain from voting on matters of direct personal interest to you doesn't apply if you're nominated for office. If your status as a member makes you eligible for the office, you're entitled to benefit from a vote as any other member would. So go ahead and vote for yourself, if you want to.

Interrupting a vote

After voting has commenced, no interruptions are allowed. The period covered is from the moment the first vote is cast until all members who want to vote have voted. Chairman Smith should brook no interruptions. Even a *Point of Order* regarding the conduct of the vote must wait until after the vote is over. It might even be in good form if the chair ascertains if any member who intends to vote hasn't done so before declaring the result of the vote.

When a vote is being taken by ballot, it's permissible to move on to other business before the balloting is completed. Whether this is appropriate depends on the circumstances, custom, or the will of the assembly.

Explaining your vote

When the group has moved on from the debate stage and voting is underway, you're not permitted to get a little debate in edgewise under the guise of explaining your vote. The right of free speech stops when the voting starts.

Changing your vote

When voting by any method except by ballot or other method providing secrecy, if the result of a vote has been declared, you can change your vote, but only with the unanimous consent of the assembly without debate. Otherwise, it's too late. However, you have an absolute right to change your (nonballot, nonsecret) vote at any time until the result is announced.

Making your vote count — once!

No matter how many constituencies you may represent at the convention or how many offices you hold, you have only one vote in the assembly of which you are a member. Secretary and treasurer may be two offices on the board, but even if you're serving in both offices, you don't get to vote twice. The rule of one person having only one vote is a fundamental principle of parliamentary law. You can flip over to Chapter 1 to read more about fundamental principles of parliamentary law.

Deciding questions of procedure

All questions related to the manner and methods of voting are within the control of your group except as your bylaws may dictate. Through the use of incidental *Motions Related to Methods of Voting and the Polls* (see Chapter 11), your group remains in control of its own voting procedures.

Taking Your Pick of Voting Methods

Whether voting on motions or holding elections, you have quite a selection of voting methods to choose from. Although many voting methods exist, they fall into two categories:

» **Usual voting methods for motions:** In most situations other than elections, you indicate your affirmative or negative vote by voice or by rising. The chair discerns the result and announces it, and then you move on to the next item of business. However, when using voice vote or rising vote, the judgment of the chair is subject to verification. A voice vote is verified by a rising vote either on the chair's own initiative or on the demand of a single member. A rising vote is verified by a counted vote either at the call of the chair or by a motion adopted by the membership.

» **Voting methods provided by rule or ordered by membership:** Depending on the type of organization or the nature of the decision, your rules or bylaws probably establish some particular methods of voting. For example, elections often require ballot votes so that members can vote without disclosing their choice of candidate. Similarly, representative assemblies often require roll-call votes because the representatives are accountable to their constituents.

It all gets down to just what you're deciding by your vote. With the six voting methods described in the following sections, you'll have no problem arriving at the will of your assembly.

Unanimous consent

Quite possibly the most efficient way of conducting a vote, *unanimous consent* is the voting method of choice because it saves so much time. The process involves simply asking the members whether anyone objects to adopting the motion. If no one objects, the motion is adopted.

REMEMBER

If even one member objects, you take a vote using one of the other methods explained in this section.

Unanimous consent can't be used in all situations, but it's perfect when a motion isn't controversial and it appears that you have universal agreement, or at least that the minority is likely to agree to the decision without protest. For example, proper form is to use unanimous consent to reach approval of the minutes: "If there are no corrections, the minutes are approved as distributed." Another example occurs when it's apparent that the assembly agrees to an amendment to a motion: "If there is no objection, the main motion is amended." Unanimous consent can be used even on complex motions or when a two-thirds vote is required: Unless you encounter an objection, the minority has, in effect, said, "Okay with us! Do it!"

Voice vote (viva voce)

Viva voce (pronounced *vie*-vuh *voe*-see — parliamentary lingo for voting "by voice") is the customary method for voting on motions that require a majority vote for adoption.

To initiate a voice vote, the presiding officer simply says, "Those in favor, say 'Aye,'" and then, "Those opposed, say 'No.'" This method handles votes effectively because it's efficient and because determining whether a motion carries isn't difficult unless the vote is close. When the vote *is* close, your presiding officer can retake the vote as a rising or counted vote on his own initiative.

If the chair doesn't think the vote is close enough to ask for a rising vote and declares a result that you doubt, you can demand a rising vote on your own initiative just by calling for a *Division* (see Chapter 11).

Rising vote

When a motion is to be decided by a two-thirds vote or some other proportion greater than a majority, or when a voice vote is too close to call, you have a more definitive method in your voting arsenal. A *rising vote* is just what the name implies. The chair says, "Those in favor will rise. [pause] Be seated." Then he says, "Those opposed, rise. [pause] Be seated."

What the ears can't discern, the eyes generally can. Odds are, everybody will be able to agree on whether the required threshold has been met. Only when the rising vote is too close to call do you need to move to a counted vote. (Jump to the next section, "Counted vote," for details on this method.)

The rising vote has some variations that generally depend on the size of the group.

>> **Voting by show of hands:** A vote by show of hands suffices when you're in a small group, such as a committee or a board meeting.

>> **Voting by voting cards:** In some assemblies (usually very large ones), members are given colored voting cards to hold up appropriately to signify their vote. In very large assemblies, voting cards are probably the most efficient means of deciding most questions because large groups require large rooms: A presiding officer may have difficulty discerning the result of a voice vote or determining who's standing and who's not.

REMEMBER

If the chair decides that the rising vote isn't conclusive enough, they must retake the vote as a counted vote to ascertain the result. However, if the chair is comfortable with the call, they're not required to take a counted vote unless the membership adopts a motion to order a counted vote. Such a motion requires a second and is adopted by majority vote (see Chapter 11).

Counted vote

In addition to the presiding officer's prerogative to order a counted vote, the assembly itself can order a counted vote by adopting an incidental motion to take a counted vote. A majority vote decides whether to take a counted vote, and it may be decided by a voice vote, a rising vote, or a show of hands.

The procedure for taking a counted vote is the same as for a rising vote, except that you ask the members to remain standing (or keep their hands or voting cards raised) until they can be counted. You also need to appoint someone, the *teller,* to do the counting. In a small meeting, the secretary usually handles the count. In a larger meeting, the chair appoints trusted members as tellers.

TIP

In very large meetings, you're probably better off conducting a ballot vote than a counted vote unless you're employing an electronic voting system. But no hard-and-fast rule determines when counting ballot votes becomes easier than counting heads. It depends largely on your group and the time available.

REMEMBER

With viva voce, rising, or counted votes, the presiding officer should always call for the negative vote (except, of course, for courtesy resolutions expressing appreciation, thanks, and so on). Even if it sounds like the ayes have it or it looks like enough members rise in favor, you need the comparison to decide whether you've really made the right call.

EXCEPTION

If the threshold for adopting a motion is based on the number of members *present* or requires a vote of the majority of the *entire membership*, the negative vote is irrelevant. See the section, "Crossing voting thresholds," earlier in this chapter.

Roll-call vote

Roll-call voting is used in representative assemblies in which the members represent constituencies and it's important for constituents to know how their representatives vote on particular issues.

If your group is a representative assembly, your bylaws should provide details on how and when roll-call votes are ordered. Many such groups require a roll-call vote to decide all main motions. Others provide that a specified minority may order such a vote. Without such provisions, a majority vote is required to order a roll-call vote. When a majority prefers *not* to have to go on the record, the constituents (especially those of the minority) can't know how their representatives are voting.

You can conduct roll-call votes by signed ballot or by voice. If by signed ballot, each member indicates their name and vote on the ballot. If by voice, the chair puts the question (see Chapter 6) and the secretary calls the members' names alphabetically (or according to some other adopted order), with the chair's vote taken last. Each member responds "Yea" for an affirmative vote, "Nay" for a negative vote, or "Present" if abstaining. The secretary repeats the name of each member and states the vote to ensure accuracy in recording.

In the interest of ensuring an accurate result, either the chair or the assembly can have the secretary then read the names of the members based on their votes, first reading the names of those who voted in the affirmative, then reading the names of the members who voted in the negative, and finally reading the names of the members who were willing only to admit to being present. This process, known to the erudite as *recapitulation,* is just a fancy way of talking about "double-checking" with the members in case a mistake was made.

REMEMBER

The record of how each member votes is recorded in the minutes.

Voting by ballot

Voting by ballot is used whenever it's desirable that the members' individual views on the matter being decided not be disclosed. The association of "secret" with "ballot" is technically a redundancy, but there's no shame in keeping the association intact. In fact, secrecy is such an important aspect of ballot voting that nothing that would compromise (either directly or indirectly) the ability of any member to maintain the secrecy of their views or vote would ever be permissible. If your bylaws require a vote to be by ballot, the rule can't be suspended.

Ballots, the slips of paper on which voters indicate their preferences, are understood to be *secret ballots* unless otherwise specified, such as with *signed ballots,* which may be used in connection with a roll-call vote (see the "Roll-call vote" section earlier in this chapter) or in voting by mail (refer to in the section "Voting by mail," later in this chapter) when secrecy is *not* required.

Ballot voting is not, however, always on slips of paper. (See the nearby sidebar.) Even so, the write-in vote is an essential component of a free and fair ballot election. If you're going to use electronic systems for voting in elections, you'll need to make some arrangement to collect and count write-in votes. Take a quick trip to Chapter 14 for a quick read on the importance of the write-in in a ballot election.

If your bylaws provide for ballot votes on any matter, it's to protect you, as an individual member, from having to disclose your vote. Because the rule protects the rights of an individual, it's a rule that can't be suspended (even by a unanimous vote), and no vote that would force you to disclose your views in order to protect that right is ever in order.

Ballots assume one of two general purposes: They either decide a motion or decide an election.

>> **If the ballot vote decides a motion**, the question is clearly stated by the chair, and you're instructed to mark your ballot *Yes* or *No* (or *For* or *Against*).

>> **If the ballot vote decides an election**, you're instructed to write the name of the candidate of your choice on your ballot.

Ballots with the options *Yes* and *No* (or *For* and *Against*) shouldn't be used when electing persons to office. If your election is by ballot, the only way you can vote *against* a candidate is to vote *for* another person.

In cases when the motion to be decided is known ahead of time or when the nominees are known, ballots may be preprinted to save time and make life easier for members at voting time.

A member has the fundamental right to vote for anyone, even if their candidate was not nominated. On a ballot, the voter does this with a write-in vote. On a roll-call vote, the voter simply announces their vote when called on. A vote for an ineligible candidate, however, is an illegal vote. See the section, "Counting the ballots," later in this chapter.

The actual process of voting by ballot, or *balloting* as it's sometimes called, involves several important considerations. I list them here.

Conducting the ballot vote

Depending on your organization and the decisions being made, balloting may take place during a meeting, or polls may be open during certain polling periods, including times when no meeting is in progress. In either case, you need to appoint tellers to hand out and collect ballots and to count the votes.

TIP

Tellers must be people known for their integrity. They don't have to be impartial, but whatever direct personal interest they have in the outcome should be the same as that of any other members. Some organizations appoint tellers representing each opposing side to ensure that all sides of the decision have complete confidence in the result.

Limiting ballot access to members

Only members entitled to vote are given ballots or are allowed to deposit ballots with a teller or place them in the ballot receptacle. If polling is conducted outside a meeting, members must verify their credentials with election officials when casting their votes at the polls, and members' names must be checked on a list showing who has voted.

In meetings where persons who aren't entitled to vote are present, take whatever measures are necessary to limit balloting to voting members. In this situation, the tellers distribute the ballots to the members, and the members return their marked ballots to the tellers.

Closing the polls

If a member arrives late and wants to cast a vote, they may not be completely out of luck. If polls haven't closed when they arrive, they're entitled to vote. If the polls have formally closed, they can vote only with the members' consent by majority vote.

Voting by the presiding officer

During a ballot vote, your presiding officer votes along with all the other members. This rule holds even if they've been absorbed in doing their job overseeing the election; if they fail to vote before the polls close, they need the permission of the members to vote.

WARNING

Your presiding officer is never allowed to cast a tie-breaker in a ballot vote. When the vote is by ballot, the presiding officer votes with the other members. If the vote winds up being tied in an election, the assembly votes again. The presiding officer doesn't get to vote a second time alone. Everybody, including the presiding officer, votes again. You just keep your fingers crossed that you don't have another tie.

Counting the ballots

When counting ballots, tellers need to keep a few key points in mind:

>> Blank ballots are treated as scrap paper and don't count.

>> *Illegal* votes cast by legal voters count toward the total votes cast, but they don't count for any individual choice or candidate. These votes are *illegal* votes:

- Unintelligible ballots

- Ballots cast for an unidentifiable candidate

- Ballots cast for an ineligible candidate

- Two or more marked ballots folded together (together they count as only one illegal vote)

>> If a marked ballot is folded together with a blank ballot, the marked ballot counts as one legal vote, and the blank ballot is considered scrap paper.

>> Each question on a multipart ballot is counted as a separate ballot. If a member leaves one part blank, the votes entered on the other questions aren't negated.

>> If a member votes for more choices than positions to be elected, the vote is considered illegal.

>> If a member votes for fewer choices than positions to be elected, the vote isn't illegal.

>> Small technical errors, such as making spelling mistakes or marking an X when a check mark is called for, don't make a vote illegal as long as the voter's intent is discernible.

>> Votes cast by illegal voters must not be counted or even included in the number of total votes cast. If illegal voters cast enough illegal votes to affect the result, and these votes can't be identified and removed from the count, the vote is deemed null and must be retaken.

Reporting to the chairman

After the votes are counted, the chairman of the tellers reads aloud to the membership the complete report of the vote counts, but that person doesn't declare the result. That job belongs to the presiding officer.

Declaring the result

After the tellers' chairman concludes the reading, the presiding officer reads the report again to the members, concluding with a formal declaration of the result. For example, the chairman may say, "Mr. Turkey is declared elected as the Birdbrain of the Year."

The minutes of the meeting must include the entire tellers' report.

Destroying the ballots

To avoid running up a storage bill or having the secretary quit because their spouse doesn't want so much junk in the house, destruction of the ballots and tally sheets should be ordered. When determining how long to hold these documents before destroying them, your main consideration is the possibility of needing a recount. After the period during which a recount can be conducted has passed, you need keep the ballots and tally sheets no more. The actual length of time you retain these records is usually set at the meeting when the vote takes place. Alternatively, your group can adopt a short retention period for ballots and tally sheets as a standing rule.

If you don't adopt a motion or standing rule addressing the retention or destruction of ballots, you're bound by Robert's Rules. Robert provides that when the voting is all over, the ballots and tally sheets are handed over to the secretary who seals them from prying eyes and hangs onto them until a recount can no longer be ordered. Flip to the section, "Recounting the vote," later in this chapter.

Allowing Absentee Voting

A fundamental principle of parliamentary law is that decisions are made only by the members present in a properly called meeting at which a quorum is present. This principle makes a lot of sense when you think about it: If you don't attend the meeting, you don't benefit from information that's presented during the discussion that precedes voting. If you haven't been exposed to any discussion or debate on the topic, you simply can't make a truly informed decision.

Whether voting by proxy, voting by mail, or even voting online, important considerations come into play when members are casting votes without being present in the meeting where the vote is taken. Here's the birds-eye lowdown on maintaining the integrity of the vote when your group wants to make its decisions without having all the voting members in the same place at the same time.

Voting by proxy

If anything's likely to cause trouble for a group, it's proxy voting. *Voting by proxy,* which is giving somebody a power of attorney to cast a vote for you, is inconsistent with the fundamental concepts that voting rights aren't transferable and that members must be present at the time a vote is taken.

WARNING

Proxy voting is so contrary to the principles of parliamentary law for deliberative assemblies that Robert's Rules strictly prohibits this method unless your bylaws or charter specifically authorize it or your state's corporation law requires it. (See the upcoming section, "Proxies in incorporated societies," for more details.)

Types of proxies

Proxies are powers of attorney, and they come in two types:

>> **General:** A person is authorized to cast your vote as she chooses.

>> **Limited:** A person is authorized to cast your vote on one or more particular matters or in a particular way. The actual authority depends on the document being used.

Proxies in incorporated societies

In several states, members of corporations have absolute rights under statute to vote on some matters by proxy unless the bylaws prohibit it. Just the opposite for board members, which commonly are absolutely prohibited from voting by proxy unless the charter specifically authorizes it. If your group is incorporated, you should ask a lawyer about how your state's laws apply to your corporation. Do this before you get taken by surprise at a meeting and find a few new members taking over your treasury.

Proxies in shareholder meetings

Proxy voting finds its most common application in business corporation shareholder meetings where shareholders have different voting power based on the number of shares. Usually the voting in these kinds of meetings relates to electing directors and approving recommendations of the board.

Proxies in membership meetings

For most groups (whether incorporated or not), proxies are rarely necessary if each member has equal voting power. If your group is authorizing any sort of voting by proxy, it's a good idea to specify how and when a proxy can be used.

WARNING

If your group is incorporated, you need to find out exactly what the corporation laws of the chartering state say about the use of proxies. If you ever experience the surprise of having a large faction someday show up represented by a member holding a block of proxies, you'll know why it's important to know the laws.

Consider the case of the Southside Sillysteppers. The group's bylaws were silent on proxy votes, and they depended on Robert's Rules' statement that proxies weren't allowed. That practice was fine until they were incorporated in a state where the law gives members of incorporated societies the right to vote by proxy unless the bylaws expressly prohibit it.

Nobody thought about it much until the election when Sally Slink slunk into the room with proxies from more than 100 absent members authorizing her to cast their votes for the stoop of Supreme Sillystepper. She slipped the proxies to the secretary and said she was casting 100 proxy votes plus her own for herself. The 70 other members present all stood up in protest. They were intent on electing Skipper Stoopstep. Skipper raised a point of order (turn to Chapter 11) about the proxies, and the point was ruled well taken because, according to their bylaws, Robert's Rules was the adopted parliamentary authority. Skipper was declared elected, but Sally took the decision to court; the judge said that, no matter what Robert said, the *bylaws did not expressly prohibit proxy voting.* So Sally Slink secured the stoop of Supreme Sillystepper, Skipper Stoopstep stepped down from the stoop, and the Southside Sillysteppers had to pay Sally's lawyer and the court costs.

To avoid surprise proxies and to make sure that only members who have made it to the meeting make your group's decisions, you can adopt clear and direct language in your charter or bylaws to prohibit proxy voting to the extent allowed by law. Otherwise, your group may wind up like the Southside Sillysteppers and have to deal with interpretations of laws, bylaws, or the proxy documents themselves so as to sufficiently put an election or some other decision in limbo until a judge decides the outcome. Not only is this complication no fun, it's also expensive and can cripple or ruin an organization.

WARNING

According to Robert's Rules, adopting a bylaw establishing Robert's Rules as your parliamentary authority is as good as adopting a bylaw to prohibit the use of proxies. In fact, it's the same thing — *unless your group is incorporated!* Then the law reigns supreme. My advice is to have your lawyer and your parliamentarian work together to help you coordinate provisions in your bylaws with your laws and articles of incorporation so that you have everything set up like you want it.

Voting by mail

Voting by mail is a trade-off: You give up the benefits of discussion and debate in favor of giving all your members an opportunity to vote. Voting by mail probably isn't worth the extra expense if most of your members can make it to meetings. But in large state, national, or international organizations that don't have some sort of delegate assembly, mail voting in elections (or to decide bylaw amendments) may make sense.

Mail voting is subject to the following considerations:

>> **The bylaws must authorize mail voting.** If your group wants to permit voting by mail, fax, or email, your bylaws must authorize whatever method you choose. You must also have provisions in place to ensure that such votes are verifiable as being cast by members entitled to vote.

>> **The question mustn't be changed at a meeting.** Any time your organization wants to allow members to vote by mail, you must be sure that you don't enable a decision on a question to combine mail votes with votes cast after discussion, amendments, or floor nominations at a meeting. A mail vote can decide something fairly only when *all* the votes cast are on the question as it was posed to members on the mail ballot.

For example, imagine that you poll your membership by mail on whether to hold a bake sale or a bingo game as your fundraiser. But then at your meeting, somebody moves to throw a raffle into the mix. How do you count the votes and be fair to the members who voted without the third option? It's just not possible.

>> **Mailing lists must be complete and accurate.** Ballots must go out only to members who are entitled to vote, so maintaining mailing list integrity is important when it comes to mail voting. If you're going to authorize mail ballots, you need to keep your address records up-to-date. When the time comes to send ballots to your members, your treasurer and secretary need to work together to make sure the mailing list is up-to-date and includes all the current members. They also need to ensure that purged members don't get ballots in error.

>> **The secrecy and integrity of the vote must be preserved.**
It's possible to preserve secrecy with mail voting (as opposed
to voting by fax or email), so that's the form to use if you're
extending absentee voting to a large membership. If your
group makes provisions for voting by fax or email, you don't
have any real means of ensuring that the votes you receive
are from people legally entitled to vote, unless the member's
name is somehow disclosed on the vote itself. Therefore,
avoid voting by fax or email unless secrecy isn't important. If
yours is a small group with considerable trust in each other,
the less secretive options shouldn't present a real problem.
But even then, explicit rules should cover when and how to
use these kinds of votes.

With mail voting, you have to be able to confirm that each vote
is from a member who's entitled to vote. But you also have to be
able to ensure that each member's vote can remain secret. Both
goals are accomplished by using a dual-envelope return system
and following a special procedure for opening and counting
ballots.

Sending the ballots to the members

For secret, mail-in ballots, each voter receives

>> **A ballot and all the information necessary for the
member to mark it properly and return it in a timely
manner.** The ballot needs to be folded in such a manner
that the member can mark it and refold it so that only the
tellers can see the vote when they open the ballot at the
meeting where it's being counted.

>> **A small envelope on which the voter signs and prints
their name and in which they place their folded,
marked ballot.**

>> **A separate, self-addressed return envelope into which
the sealed envelope containing the ballot is placed for
mailing back to the tellers.** This envelope needs to be
distinctive and recognizable as containing a sealed ballot so
that it's not inadvertently opened before the election.

>> Any additional information, such as brief statements from the candidates for elective office, or summaries or rationales related to items that are the subject of a vote.

If the ballot doesn't require secrecy, then the small ballot envelope isn't necessary. The ballot itself must have a place for the signature and printed name of the voter. (You still have to verify that the voter is entitled to vote though.)

Processing returned ballots

When the outer envelopes are returned, the designated recipient should keep them (unopened) until the election. At the meeting when the votes are to be counted, these envelopes are opened in the presence of the tellers. The signed inner envelopes are removed, and the name on each inner envelope is compared to the list of eligible voters. When your tellers confirm that the voter is eligible, that name is checked on the list as having voted. Only then does the teller remove the ballot from the signed envelope and deposit it, without unfolding it, into the ballot box.

Voting online

Just about everywhere I go and talk about parliamentary procedure, someone asks me whether it's okay to vote by email or by using a web-based service for Internet voting. The answer, as is so often the case with questions about parliamentary procedure, is "It depends."

First, unless you make provisions in the bylaws for absentee balloting, which I cover in the section, "Allowing Absentee Voting," earlier in this chapter, the answer is "No." The rule requiring that decisions in the name of a deliberative assembly must be made only by the members present in a properly called meeting at which a quorum is present is a fundamental principle of parliamentary law. To scrap such a rule in favor of voting absentee by mail, email, fax, or Internet requires specific authorization in your bylaws.

PREFERENTIAL VOTING

Preferential voting is a method of ballot voting that has excellent application in mail balloting because it avoids the cost of reballoting in the event of a tie. It also has considerable advantages over electing by plurality (see the section "Plurality," in this chapter) because it enables a group to make the best choice by taking into account each voter's second (or third, or fourth) choice. For example, suppose that you're voting by mail for your next president. You have a choice between Mr. I. M. Great, Ms. Raz M'tazz, Mr. Slug, and Ms. Gliggenschlapp. Mr. Great receives 91 votes, Ms. M'tazz receives 96 votes, Mr. Slug receives 35 votes, and Ms. Gliggenschlapp receives 75 votes. Who wins?

If you're electing by plurality, then Ms. Raz M'tazz wins. But out of 297 votes, 201 members want somebody else. So Ms. M'tazz is hardly the right choice for the group. She wins because only first choices matter in a plurality vote.

Now, imagine that you can redistribute based on the second choice of voters whose first choice was Mr. Slug. If all of them had Ms. Gliggenschlapp as their second choice, and you were using preferential voting, then she holds 110 votes, including secondary preference. That puts Mr. Great in last place. Now, if the members who voted him as their first choice had other ideas as their second choice, his votes could be redistributed to Ms. M'tazz and Ms. Gliggenschlapp, and one of the two of them would come out with the biggest stack of ballots. Preferential voting decides the election by taking into account everyone's preferences and thus avoids the cost of taking another mail ballot.

Preferential voting must be authorized in the bylaws to be used to elect officers. (So does plurality voting, for that matter.) For decisions other than elections, a special rule of order is sufficient to authorize these methods.

Preferential voting is a simple process, really. Members indicate their choices by order of preference, and the ballots are sorted based on the first choice listed, with each option having its own stack. The smallest stack is redistributed among the others, based on the second choice indicated on the ballot. The next round redistributes the remaining smallest stack based on the second or third choice indicated. This process continues until one choice receives a majority of the ballots, and that choice becomes the winner.

Preferential voting procedures come in all shapes and sizes. If you're going to benefit from this method of voting, you need to spell out your procedures in advance and in detail. Preferential voting comes closer than plurality in choosing the most desirable candidate or option. It's especially desirable when conducting elections by mail because it's less costly and less time-consuming than continuing to reballot until the group achieves a majority.

Robert's Rules' provisions for voting by mail (refer to the section, "Voting by mail," earlier in this chapter) emphasize ballot security and voting integrity; following Robert's procedures for mail balloting do a good job of ensuring election security and integrity. Email voting isn't as desirable as a substitute, but Internet balloting is fast becoming an efficient and less costly alternative to snail-mail balloting.

Email voting

Voting by email, like voting by fax, is particularly problematic for a number of reasons (I touch on them earlier in this chapter in the section "Voting by mail."). Although email voting might be workable with respect to small committees making some committee decisions, it isn't recommended for use in the place of voting in meetings or absentee balloting. The lack of security, including the inability to know whether a vote is cast by a legal voter, combined with the difficulty in managing the collection and tallying of the votes, makes email voting something to avoid at all costs. In any case, conducting *any* voting by email requires specific authorization in the bylaws, and you'll also need to adopt some special rules and policies for your organization ensuring its use doesn't create more problems than it solves.

Internet balloting

Internet balloting, on the other hand, has become an efficient alternative to mail balloting. Several Internet-based voting services now exist, offering levels of security and voting integrity similar to those of the voting-by-mail procedures. These services promise efficiency, automated result reporting, and a much lower cost per voter than snail-mail voting. Some of these services offer the option of preferential voting, which can be a real time- and money-saving method for conducting your elections. I cover the topic of preferential voting in a sidebar earlier in this chapter.

If your group currently conducts balloting by mail, you might benefit from adding provisions in your bylaws to allow you to also use a secure Internet balloting system. In researching these services, make sure that the system allows votes only from the members you designate as eligible voters. Additionally, if you decide to go this route, you'll still need to make sure that you provide your technology-challenged members the option to vote by snail mail using the procedures for mail balloting.

Determining Voting Results

You've no doubt heard the phrase, "The majority rules!" It's an age-old axiom, and in most cases, it's true. But according to the true definition and practice of democracy, *might* doesn't always make *right*. The primary democratic concept that everyone has an equal voice means that the minority, even a minority of one, has rights that must be respected. Robert's Rules are designed to protect the minority against the "tyranny of the majority."

Parliamentary law establishes two fundamental voting thresholds:

>> **Majority vote:** Except when governed by a specific rule to the contrary, a *majority vote* is the fundamental requirement to pass a motion. A *majority,* simply stated, is *more than half.* Not 50 percent plus one. Not one more than half. Just more than half. And a majority vote refers to more than half of the votes actually cast, not to more than half of

the votes that could be cast if everybody voted. Unless a motion receives a majority vote, the motion is lost. If the vote is tied, it doesn't receive a majority vote, so it's lost.

» **Two-thirds vote:** As a means of balancing the rights of the entire group with the rights of individuals, some decisions require the affirmative consent of at least twice the number of members as aren't in favor. This vote is called a *two-thirds vote* and refers to two-thirds of the votes cast. It protects any minority greater than one-third. As with a majority vote, the measure against which the two-thirds threshold is determined refers only to the number of votes cast, not the number of votes that could be cast if everybody voted.

According to Robert's Rules, a two-thirds vote is required:

- To suspend or change a rule already adopted

- To close or limit debate on a motion

- To prevent the consideration of a motion

- To close nominations or polls

Crossing voting thresholds

Voting results can also be determined according to a number of different variations on the basic majority and two-thirds votes. These variations relate not only to the threshold numbers required, but also to the number of members to be counted in determining that threshold.

Majority (or two-thirds) of the members present and voting

The *majority vote* and the *two-thirds vote*, if expressed without further qualification, are votes based on the total votes cast. These terms are often expressed with the phrases "a majority of the members *present and voting*" and "at least two-thirds of the members *present and voting*."

Majority (or two-thirds) of the members present

Sometimes by design (and often by mistake), a voting threshold is stated as "a majority (or two-thirds) of the members present." Making decisions based on the number of votes in relation to the number of members present is usually undesirable because it removes a member's right to remain neutral and it requires you to stop and count the number of members present to determine the result. If a member is in the room and chooses not to vote, the member's neutrality has the effect of a negative vote because the member's presence is counted when determining the result.

Majority of the entire membership

In some cases, permitting a question to be decided by a *majority of the entire membership* is just as protective of the rights of individuals as deciding that question by a *two-thirds vote.* Sometimes this threshold is used as an alternative to a two-thirds vote in matters for which no previous notice has been given. For example, a motion to rescind something previously adopted requires a majority vote with previous notice, or a two-thirds vote without previous notice, or a vote of a majority of the entire membership.

TIP

You can take a pass on calling for the negative vote when the threshold for passing a motion is based on the number of members present or when it *requires* a majority of the entire membership. When that's the case, the negative vote is just plain irrelevant.

Plurality

A *plurality vote* is the most votes cast for any choice in a field of three or more. The candidate or option receiving the most votes in such a situation has a *plurality.* A plurality isn't necessarily a majority; try to avoid it, because it can designate a winner that the majority of the members oppose.

According to Robert's Rules, when a ballot has more than two choices, balloting must continue until one choice achieves a majority. If reballoting isn't practical, such as when conducting a vote by mail, you really need to use some form of preferential voting. (See the nearby sidebar about preferential voting for more explanation.)

A plurality never elects unless your bylaws authorize it.

Cumulative voting

Some types of organizations, especially ones prone to factionalism, want to ensure that minority factions can achieve at least minimal representation on boards and committees. This aim is accomplished through *cumulative* voting. Using this approach, when several seats are to be filled, as on a board, each member may cast as many votes as there are seats to be filled; votes may be cast in any combination and for any number of candidates. For example, if five members were to be elected to the board, normally you would cast one vote each for up to five candidates. Under cumulative voting, you can cast all five votes for one or more of the candidates, distributing your five votes as you please.

Cumulative voting enables a faction to coordinate its voting to afford itself the greatest chance of electing some level of representation on a board. Although it violates a fundamental principle of parliamentary law because it allows members to transfer their votes, the method has its place. Still, it must be used judiciously and with a full understanding of its implications.

Cumulative voting can't be used unless provisions for its use are made in your bylaws.

Handling tie votes

Some of the folks in your group may think that the presiding officer must break a tie vote. But the solution isn't as simple as that. Because a tie vote isn't a majority, if your motion requires a majority vote, the motion is *lost* if it receives a tie vote. Therefore, a tie vote is as much of a decision as a majority vote in opposition.

The myth that the presiding officer votes to break a tie is only a partial truth. If the vote is by ballot, the presiding officer votes with everybody else, and a tie vote is either a lost motion or a failed election. If you're electing an officer or are filling a certain number of other positions, you must reballot until someone receives a majority.

However, if the vote is by voice, by rising, or by counted vote, the presiding officer properly casts a vote only after the results are known and if they want their vote to affect the outcome.

The presiding officer may want to break a tie, causing the motion to pass; or make a tie, causing the motion to fail. Similarly, with a two-thirds vote, the presiding officer may want to cause the motion to pass by adding their vote to reach the two-thirds threshold, or they may want to cause the motion to fail by adding to the minority to keep the two-thirds threshold from being met.

However, if they don't want to change the outcome, the presiding officer shouldn't vote at all; by reserving their vote, they preserve the appearance of impartiality while presiding. Maintaining that appearance is infinitely more important than casting a vote that makes no difference.

Challenging a vote

If you want to challenge a vote (not the same as challenging the action you voted on), you generally have to be fast. Any motion to challenge the conduct of the vote has to be initiated before any debate or business has started. Several options, which I discuss here, are available when the time is right.

Calling for a division of the assembly

This is the ground-level challenge. You hear the ayes and the noes, and you don't think there was any way to discern the winner from your group's utterance. So you call for a division, which is the presiding officer's cue to conduct a rising vote (or a show of hands in a small group). You don't even need to get recognized. I talk about the motion *Division of the Assembly* in Chapter 11.

Retaking the vote by another method

Just a little more involved, asking the presiding officer or the assembly to order a counted vote may produce a different result. And if the assembly thinks it would help, it can order that the vote be retaken by ballot. Or maybe the vote needs to be taken by roll call. In any case, the goal is to determine without doubt the will of the assembly. Timely action is required. As my parliamentarian friends say, "You snooze, you lose!" In any case, retaking a vote must involve taking it by another method. It's not in order to resolve a question about the outcome by taking any vote again using the same method.

Recounting the vote

Even though most everyone can count, people sometimes make counting mistakes. When you've voted by ballot, you may think it'd be easy to count the votes and get the numbers right as long as you've at least made it through the fifth grade (assuming that you're dealing with big numbers). But because even the smartest tellers get sidetracked, the membership can order a recount as late as the next regular session of the assembly (as long as it hasn't been so long as to constitute a *quarterly time interval*). (See the Appendix for the definition of quarterly time interval.)

Unless you've provided otherwise under a customized ballot retention policy, the opportunity for a recount is available until the end of the session when the result of the vote was announced. If the next session of the assembly is held within a quarterly time interval a recount can still be ordered. The assembly can also call a special meeting for the purpose of a recount if it is held within a quarterly time interval after the meeting where the result was announced and before the next regular session.

TIP

Whether your organization is one that would just as soon eliminate the possibility of the instability that can persist when election challenges can be advanced, or is one that enjoys the drama associated with the fracas of fighting factions, it's probably a good idea to take a close look at Robert's Rules on ballot retention as would apply given your regular meeting schedules, and decide whether you might benefit by customizing your ballot retention policy.

ALL IN FAVOR CLICK "YES"

Your organization may be one of those that has, or is considering, using electronic voting devices to speed up vote-counting and determining the result with precision. Most of you are probably familiar with the systems used by legislative bodies that vote almost exclusively by roll-call vote. But increasingly, especially in larger organizations, assemblies are using systems where each voting member has a keypad that is connected wirelessly to a control panel managed by the tellers, the secretary, or some other appointed member. These systems are especially useful when the need is for a rising vote, a counted vote, or a ballot vote. A time period can be assigned for voting on a question after which the result is announced.

One of the features of the electronic voting systems that members seem to appreciate is the ability to display the results for all to see. Projecting the number of votes cast, the number in the affirmative, and the number in the negative as the votes are cast can add to the confidence in the process. But it's usually a decision for the assembly as to when and whether to display results before the voting is over.

Other systems provide for centrally located voting machines where the members may cast their ballot just like we do when we vote in our governmental elections. These systems aren't much help in the meeting setting where immediate results are necessary, but they can be useful in elections or for questions that are no longer open for debate.

Both types of systems can provide the same voting secrecy as the ballot without the tellers' committee having to suffer the headaches of counting and recounting the ballots.

Warning: Using any electronic system for a ballot election needs to include a means by which members can cast write-in votes. That's not too difficult to arrange, but it does take a bit of planning.

Rules for the use of electronic voting devices and voting machines should be provided for in your special rules of order and should in all cases involving ballots provide for members' votes to remain absolutely secret.

Chapter **9**

Subsidiary Motions: Helping to Process the Main Motion

n a perfect world, when the chairman states your main motion and calls for the vote, people don't just say, "Aye!" Instead, they erupt in a loud and unyielding cheer, your name and picture adorn the front page of the next day's newspaper, and you get elected President of the United States — or at least get a phone call from him.

In other words, in a perfect world, your main motion is the perfect idea at the perfect time, stated in such a perfect way that no one can disagree with it.

But it's not a perfect world, and you're not always the one making the motions. So when somebody else comes up with a real dud of an idea, the closest thing to perfect is your small-but-powerful assortment of tools from Robert's Rules that helps you take a sad song and make it better.

Disposing of a Main Motion

One sure thing in the world of meetings is that, sooner or later, all motions are *disposed of*. No, that doesn't mean they're thrown out. (Well, some of them are, but that's not how we use the term here.) *Disposing* of a motion simply refers to making some decision about the motion so that you can move on to the next item of business — in other words, it's the end result of all the talk.

The *subsidiary motions* are the tools you use to help dispose of the main motions in your meetings.

For example, imagine that somebody in your volunteer fire company moves "to buy a new fire truck." During discussion, it becomes clear that the color can affect the price, and you don't want to make a decision (and thus dispose of the main motion) until you decide on the color. So you move to insert "green" before "fire truck" because you know the Hot Shot Fire Truck Catalog offers one on sale because nobody buys green fire trucks much anymore.

But before the group can dispose of the subsidiary motion to *Amend,* Lax Luster moves to amend the amendment by striking out "green" and inserting "red" instead. Unfortunately, your presiding officer, Chief Slow Pitch (who hasn't read Robert's Rules anyway), is getting confused.

But all isn't lost. Ben Dare (the member who usually drives to the fires) wants a new fire truck, and he wants the right one at the right price. He knows that the group needs to dispose of Lax's amendment before it can work on your amendment, and the group has to dispose of your amendment before it can get back to the original question of whether to buy a fire truck in the first place.

Ben also knows that the group doesn't have enough time to discuss the issue any further in this meeting, so he moves to *Refer* (a really handy subsidiary motion for complicated or time-consuming motions) the main motion and the pending amendments to a committee composed of himself, you, and Lax, with instructions that the committee report its recommendations next month. The motion to refer passes, and *voilà* — not only have you disposed of the motion to refer, but you've also disposed (temporarily) of the main motion and two subsidiary motions (the pending amendments). Now you can move on to the next item of business.

Arriving at a final disposition for a motion can (and often does) require one or more subsidiary decisions. Hence, Robert's Rules establishes the term *subsidiary motions.*

REMEMBER

Any or all of the issues specifically related to a motion itself are dealt with in an orderly manner through the use of the *subsidiary motions.*

The subsidiary motions (listed in order of rank, from lowest to highest) are as follows:

>> Postpone Indefinitely

>> Amend

>> Commit or Refer

>> Postpone to a Certain Time (or Definitely)

>> Limit or Extend Limits of Debate

>> Previous Question

>> Lay on the Table

Table 9-1 shows the most common use for each subsidiary motion. I discuss each of the subsidiary motions in more detail later in this chapter.

TABLE 9-1 **Common Uses for Subsidiary Motions**

If You Want To . . .	Then Use . . .
Avoid taking a direct vote on a motion	Postpone Indefinitely
Change the wording of the motion	Amend
Have a committee discuss a motion in detail and come back with a recommendation	Commit or Refer
Discuss a motion later in the meeting, or maybe put it off until your next meeting	Postpone to a Certain Time (or Definitely)
Provide for a certain amount of time for discussion of the motion, either for the subject matter or for each speaker	Limit or Extend Limits of Debate
End debate on the motion and vote now	Previous Question
Stop dealing with the motion temporarily to allow something of an urgent nature to be done immediately	Lay on the Table

Ranking the Subsidiary Motions

Each subsidiary motion has a specific purpose, and each has a rank, or a specific place in the order of things. They're outranked only by the *privileged motions*, which I cover in Chapter 10.

The established ranking of subsidiary motions is logical. For example, it doesn't make any sense to move to *Postpone Indefinitely* (kill) a motion, when a motion to *Amend* (change the motion) may make it better. But if a motion to *Amend* is currently being discussed, it makes perfect sense to consider referring the entire subject matter to a committee (motion to *Commit* or *Refer*).

To illustrate, suppose that your local duck lovers' club is considering a motion to petition the post office to issue a stamp commemorating the pea-brained coot. But Minnie Mutter thinks having a stamp for a pea-brained coot is so stupid that she wants to drop the idea altogether. She moves to *Postpone Indefinitely* (kill) the main motion. But you think the idea may fly if you change the motion to promote the flap-billed quacker instead of the pea-brained coot. So you offer an amendment to strike out "pea-brained coot" and insert "flap-billed quacker." Thanks to the *order of precedence* of subsidiary motions, Minnie's motion to *Postpone Indefinitely* has to go on hold until your amendment is considered because the amendment may remove or resolve Minnie's problem with the motion.

However, Gordy Flackflinger thinks both are bird-brained ideas; he jumps in before the vote on your amendment and makes a motion to *refer* the whole stamp motion to a committee to work out just which duck's head should go on a stamp and then come back next month with a recommendation. Again, because of the ranking of the motion to commit, Flackflinger's motion to *Refer* takes precedence over your motion to *Amend*.

TIP

Robert's Rules provides you with an orderly approach to handling the subsidiary motions by assigning them a relative rank, or *order of precedence,* which is shown in Figure 9-1. Each of the subsidiary motions is listed in order from highest rank to lowest rank. As you can see, all of them outrank the main motion, which has the lowest rank of all. Voting on the main motion is in order only when no subsidiary motion remains to be decided.

As Figure 9-1 depicts, when a subsidiary motion is being considered, the motions below it are out of order until the one being considered is disposed of. However, the motions listed above the motion in question can be moved and considered no matter what's pending in the lower ranks.

In the following sections, I discuss the seven subsidiary motions and cover the function of each in more detail.

			Can Interupt	Requires Second	Debatable	Amendable	Vote Required (M = Majority)	Can Reconsider
S E C O N D A R Y	P R I V I L E G E D	Fix the Time to Which to Adjourn		S		A	M	R
		Adjourn		S			M	
		Recess		S		A	M	
		Raise a Question of Privilege	I				Chair Decides	
		Call for Orders of the Day	I				Chair Decides	
	S U B S I D I A R Y	Lay on the Table		S			M	Neg. Only
		Previous Question		S			2/3	Neg. Only
		Limit or Extend Limits of Debate		S		A	2/3	R
		Postpone Definitely		S	D	A	M	R
		Commit (or Refer)		S	D	A	M	R
		Amend		S	D	A	M	R
		Postpone Indefinitely		S	D		M	Affirm. Only
Main Motion				S	D	A	M	R

FIGURE 9-1:
Motions table listing subsidiary motions according to rank.

© John Wiley & Sons, Inc.

Let's Vote but Say We Didn't: Postpone Indefinitely

The subsidiary motion to *Postpone Indefinitely* can help you avoid uncomfortable decisions because its adoption means that your group has agreed not to decide. The adoption of *Postpone Indefinitely* says that it's better not to decide than to decide. It kills the motion for the time being, and the motion can't be brought up again in the same session.

REMEMBER

After its adoption, the motion to *Postpone Indefinitely* can be reconsidered. And if it's reconsidered and then *fails*, the main motion that it "killed" is again as alive as Jason was in *Friday the 13th, Part 2*, when he sprang forth again to stalk unsuspecting campers. See Chapter 11 for information on the motion to *Reconsider*.

Using the motion to Postpone Indefinitely

Have you ever been in a meeting where a motion was made proposing an idea that sounded just fine on the surface but was later found to be problematic (to put it nicely)? Or worse, you were embarrassed to even have to consider it, much less vote on it?

This kind of uncomfortable situation often occurs when you're faced with a motion to express an opinion in the name of the organization and the subject matter is controversial. A decision can send the wrong message or even cause a split in the organization. The purpose of the subsidiary motion to postpone indefinitely is to defuse potentially damaging motions.

Make the motion to *Postpone Indefinitely* by simply rising, being recognized by the chair, and saying, "Madam Chairman, I move to postpone the pending motion indefinitely." (And just hope that your presiding officer doesn't ask you how the heck she's supposed to know when you want to get back to the question, if you're so vague!)

TIP

The motion to *Postpone Indefinitely* is a great tool for strategists. If you're opposed to the main motion, you can test the strength of your allies in opposition without risking the adoption of the main motion. Because debate on the motion to *Postpone Indefinitely* can go into the merits of the main motion, you can speak again even if you've exhausted your right to speak on the main motion. And if the motion to *Postpone Indefinitely* passes, you've effectively killed the motion for the present session. And if it fails, you're just back to the debate on the main motion.

GETTING OUT OF STICKY SITUATIONS

At a meeting of an educational organization I attended some years back, one member was trying to get the others to pass a resolution calling on the legislature to enact a mandatory continuing education requirement into state law.

Every member of the organization was a believer in continuing education. They even paid dues to get good prices on the educational programs their association offered. But a great variance of opinion existed on just how much everybody wanted the legislature to impose a particular requirement on them. The resolution was controversial because association members were all over the parking lot on the issue. Only one thing was certain: If the resolution in support of mandatory continuing education passed, the association could lose half its membership. And if the resolution failed, it would imply that the association was against continuing education, even though it certainly wasn't.

In this situation, it wasn't the motion to *Postpone Indefinitely* that got everyone off the hook. Instead of using that motion, the members just argued for an interminable period of time, went through all sorts of appeals on rulings of the chair, and ultimately avoided making a decision one way or the other only because the meeting adjourned with no meeting scheduled soon enough for the issue to become unfinished business in a later meeting (see Chapter 5).

The idea that hindsight is always 20-20 has a lot of truth to it. I'm sure now that if I had made the motion to *Postpone Indefinitely*, it probably would have passed, and the meeting wouldn't have been so frustrating for either side. I've tucked away this story in my "If I knew then what I know now" file so that I can benefit from the experience.

Six key characteristics of the motion to Postpone Indefinitely

A motion to *Postpone Indefinitely*

>> Can't interrupt a speaker who has the floor.

>> Must be seconded.

>> Is debatable (debate isn't restricted to the pros and cons of the motion to *Postpone Indefinitely*, but may go into the merits of the main motion).

>> Can't be amended.

>> Requires a majority vote for adoption.

>> Can be reconsidered if adopted (if the motion to *Reconsider* is adopted, the main motion is again pending, and the motion to *Postpone Indefinitely* is immediately pending).

Making a Change: Amend

The subsidiary motion to *Amend* is perhaps the most-used subsidiary motion. Use this motion whenever you want to change the wording of the motion under consideration. You can use it to make a good idea better or a bad idea more palatable. Amendments are really at the heart of the process of perfecting motions before a final vote, and the importance of understanding the basics of amending can't be overstated.

If an amendment is adopted, the motion to which it is applied changes. However, the amended motion itself isn't adopted until the motion, as amended, is voted on, and passes. If a motion to *Amend* fails, the original motion isn't changed in any way.

REMEMBER

The subsidiary motion to *Amend* applies to *pending* motions only. It can't amend bylaws, agendas, policies, or other motions that have already been decided. In those cases, the proper motion is to *Amend Something Previously Adopted*, which I cover in Chapter 12.

Most of the time, amendments bog down meetings because there's just so much to know. The section on amendments in *Robert's Rules of Order Newly Revised* is the longest section in the book, thanks to all the nuances and variations on basic forms of amendment. But a basic understanding of the forms of amending motions discussed here gives you the foundation you need to build your understanding. I encourage you to read this section with an eye on understanding the basic rules and forms, and to make it your practice to offer appropriate amendments in good form every chance you get. Practice makes perfect, and by learning to amend motions, you help your group adopt clear, concise motions that accomplish precisely what your group intended.

Six key characteristics of the motion to Amend

A motion to *Amend*

>> Can't interrupt a speaker who has the floor.

>> Must be seconded.

>> Is debatable if the motion to be amended is debatable (permissible debate is restricted to the pros and cons of the amendment, not to whether the main motion has merit).

>> Can be amended, but only one amendment to an amendment can be considered at any one time (see the nearby sidebar).

>> Requires a majority vote for adoption, even if the motion to be amended requires a different vote for its adoption.

>> Can be reconsidered.

Amending by the book

Here's one big rule for using amendments: An amendment must be relevant (or, as Robert's Rules describes, *germane*) to the motion it seeks to amend.

For example, a fire department council member can move to amend a motion to buy a green fire truck by striking out "green" and inserting "red." But it's not germane to amend the motion by adding "and send out for pizza" to the end. (Some firemen I know would consider that perfectly germane, and although the chairman at the meeting probably wouldn't, it *is* possible to appeal the chair's ruling and, by majority vote, declare the amendment germane.)

WARNING

A secondary amendment (see the nearby sidebar) has to be germane not only to the underlying motion, but also to the primary amendment to which it is being applied.

Another important rule to remember is that an amendment that does nothing but make the motion a rejection of the original motion isn't proper and is not in order.

For example, suppose that the pending motion is to endorse the incumbent mayor's candidacy for re-election. A motion to insert "not" before "endorse" would be out of order. If your group wants to "not" endorse him, it must simply reject the motion. However, this rule doesn't prohibit the amendment from striking out "endorse" and inserting "oppose" in its place. Although this change rejects the notion of supporting the incumbent, it goes beyond merely "not" doing something and instead proposes doing something else!

Amendments are out of order when they place before the meeting a question that has already been decided in some way in the same session. For example, if you've defeated, postponed, or referred to a committee a motion to "buy a new fire truck," and you're now discussing a motion to "overhaul the engine in our fire truck," it's out of order to move to amend the motion to overhaul the engine by striking out "overhaul the engine in our" and inserting "buy a new."

It's also just as improper to entertain an amendment that would cause the motion itself to be out of order. As an example, a motion to "censure Jack and Jill for tumbling down the hill" can't be amended to insert "who have no ethics or morals," after "Jill," because that insertion reflects on the character of Jack and Jill, and is beyond the pale (pun intended) of anything that would be proper to debate.

Understanding basic forms of amendments

Amendments enable you to make changes to pending questions in the following four ways:

>> By *inserting* (or *adding,* if placing at the end) words or paragraphs

>> By *striking out* words or paragraphs

>> By *striking out and inserting* words (with the words inserted replacing the words struck out, or with words struck out in one place and inserted in another)

>> By *substituting* (a form of striking out and inserting, applied to paragraphs or entire motions)

Each amendment form is distinct and subject to its own unique considerations. In the following sections, I outline the considerations particular to each form. But one consideration is true for all of them: Amending one form of amendment into another form isn't in order.

TIP

For example, suppose that an amendment is offered to insert words to a motion. It only complicates your life to try to amend the amendment into a motion to strike out words. If you're in a situation in which that seems like the thing to do, encourage the group to defeat the first amendment (to insert words) and consider another amendment to accomplish the desired result.

Inserting or adding words or paragraphs

Imagine that your neighborhood association is discussing a motion made on the recommendation of the building and grounds committee "that the association repave the parking lot around the clubhouse." Everyone seems to be concerned about how much the project will cost. The committee reports that it has obtained three estimates. It thinks the highest-priced estimate is probably too much, and it believes that the lowest bid came from a company with a questionable reputation. You can tell from the discussion that everyone's in favor of repaving the lot and probably will want to go with the middle bid. You decide to help the group cut to the chase by offering an amendment to the main motion.

You rise, address the chair, are recognized, and say, "Mr. Chairman, I move to insert the words 'accept the bid of the ABC company to' after 'association' and before 'repave.'

The presiding officer, when stating your motion, will repeat your motion and add, "so that if the amendment is adopted, we would be voting on a motion 'that the association accept the bid of the ABC company to repave the parking lot around the clubhouse.'"

Your motion is a *subsidiary motion to amend* a main motion by *inserting* words; it is a *primary* amendment (an amendment of the first degree) being applied directly to a main motion.

WARNING

After you've inserted or added words, you're not allowed to amend them by striking them unless you employ the motion to *Reconsider*. (See Chapter 12 for details on the motion to *Reconsider*.)

Striking out words, or paragraphs

At a board meeting of your service club, a motion is before the group to "make donations of $100 each to the Perfect Petunia Society, the Little Miss Muffet Pageant, the Mad Hatter's Artsy Crafts Fund, and the Four Corner Hammer Dulcimer Race Car Rally Fund."

You heard on the news last night that the manager of the Mad Hatter's Artsy Crafts Fund is under investigation, stemming from allegations that they stuffed the hats with cash from the fund, loaded the hats into their old footlocker, and bought a ticket to ride. You think that the group should wait and see what happens before making that donation. But you're okay with the other proposed donations.

So you rise, address the chair, and, when recognized, offer the following amendment: "Mr. Chairman, I move to amend the motion by striking out the words 'the Mad Hatter's Artsy Crafts Fund.'"

Your motion is a *subsidiary motion to amend* a main motion by *striking out words*; it is a *primary* amendment (an amendment of the first degree) being applied directly to a main motion.

WARNING

The motion to *Amend* by *striking out* can itself be amended only by striking out words from the primary amendment. This rule is one that sounds arbitrary, but it's logical because when you offer a primary amendment to strike out words, you're applying it to existing words with the purpose of removing them from the motion to which it is applied. Inserting words to be struck is impossible because you can't strike out what's not already there. Additionally, keep in mind that striking out words from an amendment to strike out words simply puts the words back in the original motion.

WARNING

A motion to amend by striking out words always refers to consecutive words. In the example set up in this section to strike out "the Mad Hatter's Artsy Crafts Fund," it isn't in order to also try to strike out the word "each" after "$100" in the same amendment. If you want to do that, you have to offer a separate amendment.

If all these strikes make you feel like you're in a bowling alley or at a baseball game, don't feel like you're alone in your confusion. Just think about it piece by piece — and trust me when I tell you that this rule is one for which the less said, the better.

Oh, alright. Here's an example.

Suppose that the motion at hand is to send membership invitations to John Green, Fred Black, Red McTavish, and Henrietta Violetta. But you don't like anybody but Henrietta. So you move to strike out the words "John Green, Fred Black, Red McTavish, and," which, if adopted, leaves only Henrietta on the list.

But I like Fred and Red, and I want to see only John excluded, so I move to amend your primary amendment by striking out (from your proposed amendment) "Fred Black, Red McTavish, and."

If my secondary amendment — to strike out the names in your primary amendment — passes, your amendment is left as an amendment only to strike out "John Green."

TECHNICAL STUFF

To help clarify why you can't insert words in a motion to strike out, consider how little sense it would make for me to move to insert "Finkley McFlatbush" between "John Green" and "Fred Black" in your primary amendment. I can't add Finkley's name to the strike-out list if he isn't anywhere in the main motion in the first place!

Striking out and inserting words

Changing something often requires more action than just adding words or removing them. Sometimes you need to replace one word (or group of consecutive words) with another.

For example, suppose that, during a board meeting of your professional association, one of the members moves to "authorize the executive director to buy a new computer for the bookkeeper."

You've been around a while, and you know that the bookkeeper has been complaining, but not about his computer. Actually, his complaints have to do with the computer's outdated software.

So you rise, address the chair, and, when recognized, offer the following amendment: "Mr. Chairman, I move to amend the motion by striking out 'computer' and inserting 'accounting software package.'"

Your motion is a *subsidiary motion to amend* a main motion by *striking out and inserting words*; it is a *primary* amendment (an amendment of the first degree) being applied directly to a main motion.

WARNING

Take care when amending by striking out and inserting words. The words to be inserted must relate to the words to be struck out. Trying to accomplish too much with one amendment can be problematic. Better to take it a step at a time, or you could wind up with a motion that needs to be addressed by another motion, called *Division of the Question.* You read about that one in Chapter 11.

TECHNICAL STUFF

A special variety of the motion to strike out and insert is a motion to move words or a paragraph from one place to another. Technically, the motion is to strike out words or a paragraph and insert the same (or if different, not *materially* different) somewhere else. If you need to transfer a paragraph in the text of the motion you're working on, you want to follow the general rules for striking out and inserting words. If you need to make changes to the words or paragraph after you move it, that's okay, too. But don't get in a hurry, or you're likely to get confused, not to mention having your motion to amend ruled out of order. If you need to move stuff, and amend the language you're moving, wait until you adopt the amendment that transfers the words or paragraph to the desired location before you propose to amend further the language you've moved.

Amending by substitution

The *amendment by substitution* is a special form of "strike out and insert" that's applied to paragraphs, sections, articles, or entire motions.

TIP

People sometimes use the term *substitute motion* when it comes to amending an entire motion by substitution, but I've found that if you can avoid that term in favor of "amend by substitution" or "motion to substitute," you can use this important form of amendment correctly and effectively.

The purpose of amending by substitution is to make several changes in the way something is stated without having to rewrite the motion one amendment at a time. Simply say, "I move to substitute the following for the motion currently under discussion . . ." and offer your changes in completely revised language.

When an amendment by substitution is proposed, both the original motion and the substitute can be amended before a decision is made on the motion to substitute.

Suppose a motion is on the floor that "the chair appoint a committee of four members to study the feasibility of purchasing an office building for the association headquarters, and to report back to the members at the next meeting."

Now, let me color in the background. The motion comes from a friend of the president who really wants to "invest" the surplus fund money by purchasing a building his brother-in-law has for sale. The association has the money, but concern abounds about the wisdom of the president's "investment" proposal.

You think the membership (and not the probably biased chairman) is best suited to choose committee members to look into how to invest the association's funds. An office building may be a good investment, but you and others think other investments may be more lucrative, considering that the association's offices are currently housed in rent-free space provided by a friend of the organization.

Instead of chopping away at the motion on the floor, you write up a motion to substitute. You rise, address the chair for recognition, and, when recognized, say, "Mr. Chairman, I move to substitute the following for the motion currently under discussion: 'that we elect a committee of six members to recommend a plan for investing the association's surplus funds, and that the committee report its recommendations as soon as possible, but no later than at the regular meeting three months from now."

Your motion is a motion to *Substitute,* or to *Amend by Substitution,* and it's nothing more than a primary amendment to a main motion. And even though its adoption makes major changes to the original proposal, it's really no different than a motion to strike out the pending motion and insert another motion in its place.

REMEMBER

Adopting the motion to substitute doesn't adopt what it proposes. The adoption simply replaces the original motion with a new motion.

Making a series of changes in a pending main motion

Robert has made it official in the 12th edition. Referred to as a *conforming amendment,* this procedure allows you to strike out and insert a single word or phrase wherever it occurs in a pending motion. For example, say that the pending question is on adoption of the finance committee's lengthy capital outlay resolution that makes frequent reference to First Bullmoose Bank as the depository for the capital outlay funds of the association. But Shane Sharp recalls that the capital outlay funds are deposited in the Elm Acres Credit Union. It's appropriate in a case like this to offer the motion to amend the pending resolution by striking out First Bullmoose Bank whenever it appears as depository for the capital outlay fund and to insert Elm Acres Credit Union in its place.

TIP

This procedure isn't limited to amending pending main motions. It's okay to accomplish a similar series of changes in bylaws or anything previously adopted. Check out the section on amending bylaws in Chapter 2 for details.

CREATING THE PERFECT SUBSTITUTE

A motion to *substitute* is nothing more than a primary amendment to an underlying motion. Therefore, secondary amendments (amendments to an amendment) are not only possible, but common.

The amendment process generally is known as *perfecting* the motion. So when you have a substitute motion (a primary amendment), you further perfect both the underlying motion and the substitute through secondary amendments. Only when each has been opened to further amendments and everybody is ready to make a decision is the vote taken on whether to substitute the new motion for the original one.

The chairman calls first for amendments on the original motion and then on the substitute. Only when the members are finished making changes to the original motion, does the chair open the floor to amendments on the proposed substitute.

When all secondary amendments have been made to each of the two, the chair then puts the question on the motion to substitute. If the majority votes in favor of the motion to substitute, it becomes the new motion.

After secondary amendments for the original motion and the substitute are handled, the chair gives members one more chance to offer amendments for the original motion or the substitute.

Examples are just that. It's optional whether to use this process. If, for example, no secondary amendments are offered for the original motion (or for the substitute, the chair might not use this process.

Because this action is the same as having struck out and inserted entire paragraphs, the only amendment that can be made to the new motion is to add to it, just as would be true for any part of any motion in which a word (or words) is struck out and replaced with different language.

If the majority is opposed to the motion to substitute, it fails; the original motion, as amended during the process of perfecting both motions, remains as the pending motion on the floor.

In either case, the pending motion is then subject to further debate and amendment.

Sending It to Committee: Commit or Refer

For all but the most simple and direct of motions, everyone's interests may be best served by referring a motion to a committee instead of spending a lot of meeting time discussing the subject. When a number of details need to be worked out and the motion needs to be discussed much more informally or at greater length than is possible in a regular meeting, refer the motion to a committee, or perhaps to the executive board of your group, by adopting the subsidiary motion to *Commit*.

Using the motion to Commit

It's a simple process, but before you make the motion, you need to give it a little thought and ask yourself these questions:

>> **Which committee are you referring the motion to?** A standing committee? A special committee dealing solely with this motion? (You find a complete discussion of committees in Chapter 16.)

Include the committee details in your motion. For example, you may say, "I move to refer the motion to the recreation committee," or "I move to refer the motion to a committee of six to be appointed by the president," or "I move to refer the motion to a committee composed of the officers."

>> **What do you want the committee to do?**

Even though there's no rule requiring it, at least give the committee an instruction on when to report. When establishing a committee, you can be as specific as you want. A specific instruction may be "to consider and recommend the time and place of the picnic and report back to the membership next month." Or you may just refer the motion with the instruction "to report its recommendations at the next meeting."

REMEMBER

If the motion to *Commit* doesn't include enough details, the chairman can't go on to the next item of business. The questions just listed have to be decided before you can move on.

TECHNICAL STUFF

Adopting a motion to commit requires only a majority vote even when giving the committee instructions that would conflict with rules of order under which it would normally operate. The usual two-thirds vote required to suspend the rules doesn't apply in that case.

TIP

Groups should use the motion to *Commit* more frequently because it provides the opportunity to take as much time as possible and necessary to gather information or consider alternatives before making a final decision. If you want to have good meetings where members make most of the decisions quickly and easily, use committees to hash out the details and come to the assembly with well-thought-out proposals.

This section discusses the motion to *Commit* as a *subsidiary motion,* but you can create a committee even when no motion is pending. Such a committee is most likely to be a *special* committee, and it's necessary to specify exactly what the committee is to consider. That's done in the motion creating the committee.

Delegating authority to a committee

If your group needs to make a decision before the membership can meet again, you can appoint a committee *with power,* giving it the authority to act for the membership without further membership approval. However, a committee with power must not exercise any more power than what was authorized, and the committee's authority can't exceed the power of the body that appointed it.

For example, if the body appointing the committee is the board, then the board may not empower the committee to do anything the board can't do on its own, and the committee reports to the board.

WARNING

A board can't delegate authority at all unless the bylaws authorize it to do so.

Six key characteristics of the motion to Commit

A motion to *Commit*

>> Can't interrupt a speaker who has the floor.

>> Must be seconded.

» Is debatable (permissible debate is restricted to the pros and cons of making the referral and to the appropriate details of the motion to commit, not to whether the main motion has merit).

» Can be amended (specifically, the type of committee, the committee selection details and any instructions given to the committee).

» Requires a majority vote.

» Can be reconsidered if it fails (until enough business or debate has transpired to as to make it a new question, in which case it is renewed instead), or if it is adopted and the committee has not begun its work. (If the group wants to terminate the committee's involvement with the subject after it has begun its work, the proper motion is to *Discharge a Committee*.)

Dealing with It Later: Postpone to a Certain Time (Or Postpone Definitely)

Although it pains me to admit it, in some ways, real life and meetings aren't all that different. Sometimes you just need to put things off.

I've attended more meetings than I can count, and I've found that groups don't always have all the information they need to reach a decision. As a result, continuing to consider particular motions becomes difficult.

Maybe you've been in a meeting and realized that some motion is taking up time better spent on something else. You know that the group needs to make a decision, but it doesn't need to do so right now; it also needs to take care of other issues before the meeting adjourns. Or perhaps it's officer election night, but the bridge across the river (to the side where most of the members live) is out, and you have barely enough members to make a quorum. Holding your election under these circumstances is unthinkable.

The motion to *Postpone to a Certain Time (or Definitely)* gives you a chance at having better luck the next time around. It doesn't kill the motion; it simply reschedules its consideration.

Using the motion to Postpone to a Certain Time

Moving to postpone a pending main motion to a definite time is easy. You just need to decide when you want to readdress the postponed motion. After obtaining recognition from the chair, you present your motion to postpone in one of the following ways, depending on when you plan to resume the discussion:

>> **Later in a current meeting:** "Mr. Chairman, I move to postpone the pending motion until 8:30 tonight."

>> **Another day in a session of more than one day:** "Mr. Chairman, I move to postpone the pending motion until the meeting tomorrow afternoon."

>> **Next regular meeting:** "Mr. Chairman, I move to postpone the pending motion until our next regular meeting."

>> **Future event:** "Mr. Chairman, I move to postpone the pending motion until after our speaker gives his presentation."

Limiting the time of postponement

Without limits on the time allowed to move back consideration of a motion, you could postpone something until two weeks before Bill Gates runs out of cash, killing the discussion as dead as the motion to *Postpone Indefinitely*. The idea behind postponing to a certain time is to afford yourself the luxury of a little more time before you act on a motion — not to kill it.

Postponing to the next regular meeting

A motion to *Postpone Definitely* can't move consideration beyond the next regular meeting. The membership then takes up the postponed motion as a *general order* unless a special provision is made to make it a *special order of business* — or *the* special order for a particular meeting. (Refer to Chapter 5 for a discussion of general orders and special orders.)

TECHNICAL STUFF

The term, "*The* special order . . ." refers to the single subject to be discussed when the assembly wants to dedicate an entire meeting (or major part of a meeting) to the subject. For example, if you call a special meeting to consider a motion to authorize the purchase of a new office building, that motion is "*the* special order for the meeting.

Postponing to a later meeting in a session

If the organization meets less often than quarterly, you can't postpone the main motion beyond sometime in the current session, which may be the current meeting only or may cover a few days, in some cases. (See Chapter 3 for specifics on the differences between a meeting and a session.) In such a case, however, the motion may be referred to a committee to report back at the next meeting.

Postponing to a time later in a meeting

A motion postponed to a time later in the same meeting can't be considered before that time except by a two-thirds vote or reconsideration.

Postponing to a time before the next regular meeting

Sometimes a postponed motion needs to be decided before the next regular meeting. In this case, you provide for an adjourned meeting by using the privileged motion to *Fix the Time to Which to Adjourn* and postpone the pending motion until then. Chapter 10 has a rundown of this type of privileged motion and how to use it properly.

WHEN THE BYLAWS SET THE TIME FOR ACTION

It's just plain out of order to decide in advance to postpone some item of business that your bylaws require to be done at a particular meeting. For example, if your bylaws provide that you elect the nominating committee in November, you can't decide to postpone it to December because it will be easier to do it then.

But if you do your best to make it happen at the meeting, and some problem keeps you from finishing the job, it's okay to complete the business at an adjournment of your meeting. It's even okay to postpone the action item to the next regular meeting, provided that you've begun consideration but some circumstance makes it impossible to dispose of the motion. The important point is that such an important and time-sensitive (according to bylaws) motion not be moved around willy-nilly, and that such motions get postponed only because the group has no other option at the time the item is on the floor at the specified meeting.

Six key characteristics of the motion to Postpone to a Certain Time

A motion to *Postpone to a Certain Time (or Definitely)*

>> Can't interrupt a speaker who has the floor.

>> Must be seconded.

>> Is debatable. (Permissible debate is restricted to the pros and cons of postponement, and to what time the question should be postponed. Debate may not go into the merits of the main motion.)

>> Can be amended (specifically, the details of the time to which the postponement is made and whether it should be made a special order — you can find details about special orders in Chapter 5).

>> Requires a majority vote (or a two-thirds vote if making a special order).

>> Can be reconsidered if adopted. (If the motion to *postpone to a certain time* fails, it can be reconsidered as long as there has been no material progress in debate or business, otherwise, the motion just needs to be renewed.)

How Long Can This Go On? Limit or Extend Limits of Debate

Robert's Rules allows a member to speak in debate twice on each motion per day, with up to ten minutes per speech. Even for small groups, that kind of rule can make for some l-o-o-o-ng meetings, especially if you're unlucky enough to have more than one know-it-all and an antagonist or two in your group. If you've got a hot debate and even one or two members who like to argue (or who otherwise like to impress you with their verbiage), you may be pulling an all-nighter. But don't panic just yet. You can use the subsidiary motion to *Limit Debate* and do just what the name implies.

In my experience, the motion to limit debate usually applies when time is short and debate is likely to be lengthy.

But many groups have adopted special rules of order (see Chapter 2) to limit the time allowed for speeches. If your group has this kind of special rule, you use the motion to *Extend the Limits of Debate* when a proposal really needs a thorough hearing and the rule hinders your ability to discuss it at length.

Using the motion to Limit or Extend the Limits of Debate

A motion to *Limit or Extend the Limits of Debate* can be used to change in your adopted rules for debate in several different ways, and the various modifications may be combined in a single motion. Some of this motion's more common uses are listed here:

» **To shorten, or lengthen, the maximum time members may speak in debate, or to extend a particular member's speech.**

"Madam President, I move that the discussion on this motion be limited to two minutes per member, per speech."

"Mr. President, I move that the member be granted two additional minutes to conclude his speech."

» **To set the number of times members may speak.**

"Madam Chairman, I move that no member be allowed to speak more than once on this motion."

» **To set the total number of speeches each for and against the motion and to set the maximum length for each speech.**

"Mr. President, I move that discussion be limited to two speakers for and two speakers against this motion, not to exceed three minutes per speech."

» **To define the total time allotted for discussion, or to define the time after which debate will be closed and voting will take place.**

"Madam Chairman, I move that we limit discussion on this motion to a total time of 20 minutes."

"Mr. Chairman, I move that, at 9 p.m., we close all debate on this subject matter and proceed at that time to vote."

Additional information

The motion to *Limit or Extend the Limits of Debate*

» Isn't allowed in committees.

» Can't be used to bring an immediate close to debate (if you want to stop debate and vote, the proper motion is *Previous Question,* which is describer later in this chapter).

>> Can generally be applied to any debatable motion or series of debatable motions and, if adopted, is termed an *order* limiting (or extending) debate (when it expires, the *order* is said to be *exhausted*).

>> Is often adopted by unanimous consent, but if a vote is required, requires a two-thirds (rising) vote for adoption.

TIP

This section discusses this motion as a *subsidiary motion*, but you can change the default limits of debate for a session, a meeting (or part of either) when no motion is pending. When you do so, this motion takes the form of an *incidental main motion*; when used in that manner, it is governed by the rules for incidental main motions, not subsidiary motions. I discuss incidental main motions in more detail in Chapter 6.

Six key characteristics of Limit or Extend the Limits of Debate

A subsidiary motion to *Limit or Extend the Limits of Debate*

>> Can't interrupt a speaker who has the floor.

>> Must be seconded.

>> Isn't debatable.

>> Is amendable, but amendments aren't debatable.

>> Requires a two-thirds vote (but is often adopted by unanimous consent).

>> Can be reconsidered if adopted, but only until the order to limit or extend the limit is exhausted, and only the unexecuted part if it is partly carried out. (However, the motion to reconsider is not debatable.) Reconsideration of a failed subsidiary motion to *Limit or Extend the Limits of Debate* is in order as long as no material debate or business has progressed on the main motion so as to make the motion a new question. If that's the case, a reconsideration vote isn't necessary. In that case, the motion to *Limit* or *Extend the Limits of Debate* just needs to be renewed.

SAVING TIME: CHANGING THE DEFAULT RULE

I recommend that my clients who use Robert's Rules consider adopting a *special rule of order* (see Chapter 2) to shorten the time a speaker may hold the floor, moving from ten minutes per speaker and two speeches per motion to something a little less.

Some groups, such as ones that have monthly meetings of 20 to 30 members, just adopt a special rule that limits speeches to three minutes instead of ten. Other groups with larger numbers may have a special rule that permits only two or three speakers for and two or three against any main motion, with a short fuse (two-, three-, or five-minute limit) on each speech.

I can't begin to tell you how much time you save with a special rule of order on this issue. You can always extend these limits with a two-thirds vote when you need to. But establishing a special rule of order makes the debate more concise, less redundant, and (most important, to some) much less inclined to wear your nerves thin.

Enough Already! Previous Question

How many times have you come home from a meeting exhausted because your group spent so much time beating a dead horse, as the saying goes? How can people find so many different words to repeat the same argument *ad nauseam*? If you can't count high enough to answer the first question, and if you're just rolling your eyes in familiarity of the second, *Previous Question* is the subsidiary motion for you.

Putting the damper on debate

Although the name doesn't quite speak for itself, *Previous Question* is simply a motion to end debate, allow no further discussion or subsidiary motions (except *Lay on the Table*) on the pending question (or series of questions, if, for example, a motion to *Commit* or an amendment is pending), and take the vote on all pending motions to which the order of the *Previous Question* applies.

Previous Question is one of the easiest subsidiary motions to use because it's not debatable, making it a quick decision. Because adopting it terminates members' rights to speak or hear more information, *Previous Question* requires a two-thirds vote. But very little can interrupt it, and when used properly, this motion can really save you and your group a lot of time. Why? Because if two-thirds of voters are ready to stop debate and vote on the pending motion (or motions), it's probably pointless to keep on with the debate.

Using Previous Question to stop debate and vote immediately

Despite its ease of use, *Previous Question* is one of the motions that winds up being handled incorrectly. (See the sidebar about misusing this motion in this chapter.) Members can't just call out "Question!" and expect the presiding officer to close debate on their demand.

Previous Question is a motion to close debate and can be made only by someone whom the chair has recognized. It also requires a two-thirds vote to adopt.

You start the process by first obtaining recognition by the chair. Then, when the chair recognizes you, you say for example: "Mr. Chairman, I move the *Previous Question* on the motion 'to buy *Robert's Rules For Dummies* for our president.'" The chair states the question and calls for the vote. If two-thirds are in the affirmative, debate stops and you vote on whether to buy *Robert's Rules For Dummies* for your president. If the *Previous Question* isn't adopted, you continue with debate until the cows come home or until nobody has anything else to say, whichever comes first.

The *Previous Question* may be ordered on the pending question or on a consecutive series of pending questions that includes the immediately pending question. For example, the immediately pending motion may be a proposed amendment to a main motion. If, during debate on the amendment, the *Previous Question* is moved without qualification, the decision before the group is whether to stop debate and vote *on the pending amendment.* However, if the *Previous Question* is moved and adopted for the entire series of pending motions, a vote is taken immediately on the pending amendment and then on the main motion (as amended or as originally stated).

Although the motion *Previous Question* isn't amendable, when the motion *Previous Question* is immediately pending and a series of questions is pending to which it could be applied, it can be made to apply to more or fewer pending questions provided that *if* it is applied to a series, it applies to a *consecutive* series of pending motions (such as pending amendments to a pending main motion) including the immediately pending motion.

If competing versions of the *Previous Question* are offered, they're voted on in order of the one covering the most motions to the least, until one is adopted or they've all been defeated. For example, say you're in the chair and you've got a pending main motion, a pending motion to refer it to a committee, a primary amendment to the motion to commit, and an immediately pending secondary amendment. Marsha gets the floor and moves to apply the *Previous Question* to the pending amendments. As you're beginning to handle Marsha's motion, John chimes in (it's okay for him to interrupt you at this point) and moves to apply the *Previous Question* to the pending amendments *and* the motion to commit. You should take a vote on John's version first because it covers the most motions. If it fails, then vote on Marsha's motion.

The presiding officer who knows their stuff can take advantage of the misuse of this motion as a teaching opportunity. No matter what form a member uses to move (or tries to move) the previous question, the presiding officer has the duty to protect the rights of the members to debate a question until they agree to move on to the vote.

When I'm in the chair and Miss Impatience hollers out "Question!", my practice is to take advantage of the opportunity to rewind the moment and simply say, "The chair recognizes Miss Impatience," and help her out with the motion. A couple of real-time lessons during a meeting will teach most members how to politely handle their eagerness to stop the blather and get to the vote.

MISUSING THE PREVIOUS QUESTION

Surely you've attended many meetings in which some impatient soul shouts, "Question!" or "I call the question!" To your dismay, you then hear the presiding officer respond almost automatically with, "The question has been called. All those in favor of buying *Robert's Rules For Dummies* for your president will say 'Aye.'"

If only the members and the presiding officer would stop to think, they would realize that no respectable book on parliamentary procedure permits one person to unilaterally stop debate by making a demand!

Still, it happens all the time. But ordering the *Previous Question* properly requires a member to be recognized by the chair, and after the motion is made and seconded, a vote of two-thirds of the members present and voting to decide to end debate.

The right to be heard can't be taken away from a minority that wants to keep on talking until at least twice as many members are ready to shut up and vote.

Six key characteristics of the motion Previous Question

The subsidiary motion *Previous Question* (to end debate)

>> Can't interrupt a speaker who has the floor.

>> Must be seconded.

>> Isn't debatable.

>> Isn't amendable (but you can have competing motions to apply *Previous Question* to more, or fewer, pending questions in a series in some cases, as discussed under "Using Previous Question . . ." earlier in this chapter).

>> Requires a two-thirds vote.

>> Can be reconsidered if adopted, but only if no part of the adopted order for the *Previous Question* has been executed. (If *Previous Question* fails, reconsideration is in order as long as no material debate or business has progressed on the motion or motions to which it was applied so as to make it a new question. If that has occurred, a reconsideration vote is unnecessary. The *Previous Question* just needs to be renewed.)

Doing This Now: Lay on the Table

In yet another scenario from a meeting from you-know-where (red hot, lots of fire), you've probably been in a meeting when Gerbil Strawbrain, who thinks he knows everything there is to know about parliamentary procedure, tries to kill a motion he opposes by saying, "I move to table!" Well, that may work in a legislature, but under Robert's Rules, the subsidiary motion to *Lay on the Table* refers to temporarily setting aside a pending motion (or a series of pending motions) to take care of something else deemed urgent.

The motion to *Lay on the Table* is, in fact, less about the business being discussed than about the assembly needing to handle something else immediately. And although the motion is just a temporary disposition of the pending business, no time is taken to decide in advance when to get back to the motion being laid on the table.

Using the motion to Lay on the Table

When something urgent comes up that requires the immediate decision by the assembly to set aside a pending motion, the motion to *Lay on the Table* is the motion to use.

After you're recognized by the chair, you say, "Madam President, because our speaker has arrived, I move to lay the pending motion on the table."

Making the motion is really that simple. If the circumstances don't clearly indicate why the motion is being made, the chair must ask what makes the motion appropriate.

REMEMBER

It's never in order to use the motion to *Lay on the Table* to kill a motion or to delay its consideration.

If the motion is made with improper intentions, the presiding officer simply clarifies the motion based on the maker's intent and, if in order at the time, puts the question not on *Lay on the Table*, but on *Postpone Indefinitely* or *Postpone to a Certain Time*, as the case warrants.

TECHNICAL STUFF

Anything pending when the motion to *Lay on the Table* is adopted goes to the table, too. So if a motion being laid on the table has a pending amendment or a pending motion to *Commit*, or is even under an order for the *Previous Question*, everything associated with the pending main motion goes to the table. And when the motion is taken from the table, it appears before the group in the same state as when it was laid on the table. However, if the motion isn't taken from the table until the next session, any adopted motions to *Limit or Extend the Limits of Debate*, or for *Previous Question* are no longer in effect.

WARNING

If the motion laid on the table isn't taken from the table (see Chapter 12) before the adjournment of the next regular session, provided that regular meetings are held at least quarterly, it evaporates quicker than hot water in you-know-where! If the meetings are held less frequently than quarterly, it needs to be taken from the table before the end of the current session.

Six key characteristics of the motion to Lay on the Table

The subsidiary motion to *Lay on the Table*

>> Can't interrupt a speaker who has the floor.

>> Must be seconded.

>> Isn't debatable, but it's proper (and often required) for the member to briefly explain his reason for making the motion.

>> Isn't amendable.

>> Requires a majority vote.

>> Can't be reconsidered if adopted because the motion to *Take from the Table* is easier to use for that purpose. But *Reconsideration* is permitted if *Lay on the Table* fails, as long as no material debate or business has progressed. If additional debate or business has occurred, a reconsideration vote is unnecessary. The motion to *Lay on the Table* just needs to be renewed. (You can also renew it if something urgent has arisen that was not known when the original motion was rejected.)

IN THIS CHAPTER

» **Dealing with special needs immediately**

» **Understanding the ranking of privileged motions**

» **Knowing when (and how) to use the right privileged motion**

Chapter **10**

Privileged Motions: Getting through the Meeting

O
ften meetings are interrupted by issues that are unrelated to the motion being discussed but that require immediate decisions. For example, your group may agree on a schedule for the business of the evening and then find that something is taking more than its allotted time and you want to get back on schedule. Or perhaps a problem develops that affects the comfort of the group. Or you may want to take a short break — or even quit, go home, and finish your discussions later.

When one of these situations arises, *privileged motions* help you take care of the problem and get on with your business.

REMEMBER Any or all issues specifically related to the meeting itself or to the comfort of members in attendance are dealt with in an orderly manner through the use of *privileged motions*. They're called *privileged* because, even when other business is pending, the real needs (regarding time, comfort, or other special needs) of the people in the meeting are considered important enough to be dealt with immediately.

The privileged motions (listed in order of rank, from lowest to highest) are as follows:

>> Call for the Orders of the Day

>> Raise a Question of Privilege

>> Recess

>> Adjourn

>> Fix the Time to Which to Adjourn

Table 10-1 shows the most common use for each privileged motion. I discuss the *privileged* motions in more detail throughout this chapter.

TABLE 10-1 Common Uses for Privileged Motions

If You Want To . . .	Then Use . . .
Get the meeting back on schedule	Call for the Orders of the Day
Deal with something that affects the comfort of the group or even a single member	Raise a Question of Privilege
Take a short break	Recess
End the meeting	Adjourn
Continue the current meeting on another day	Fix the Time to Which to Adjourn

Ranking the Privileged Motions

Each privileged motion has a specific purpose, and each has a rank or specific order in which they can be used. Privileged motions outrank *subsidiary motions*, which I cover in Chapter 9.

The established ranking of privileged motions is logical. For example, it doesn't make any sense to move to *Recess* (take a short break) when a privileged motion to *Adjourn* (end the meeting) is under consideration. Yet if the motion to *Adjourn* is on the floor, it's possible that members may want to establish a continuation of the current meeting rather than just end everything until the next regular meeting.

TIP

Robert's Rules provides you with an orderly approach to handling the privileged motions by assigning them a relative rank, or *order of precedence,* shown in Figure 10-1. Each of the privileged motions appears in order from highest rank to lowest. As you can see, these motions outrank even the *subsidiary motions.*

			Can Interrupt	Requires Second	Debatable	Amendable	Vote Required (M = Majority)	Can Reconsider
S E C O N D A R Y	**P R I V I L E G E D**	Fix the Time to Which to Adjourn		S		A	M	R
		Adjourn		S			M	
		Recess		S		A	M	
		Raise a question of privilege	I				Chair Decides	
		Call for Orders of the Day	I				Chair Decides	
	S U B S I D I A R Y	Lay on the Table		S			M	Neg. Only
		Previous Question		S			2/3	Neg. Only
		Limit or Extend Limits of Debate		S		A	2/3	R
		Postpone Definitely		S	D	A	M	R
		Commit (or Refer)		S	D	A	M	R
		Amend		S	D	A	M	R
		Postpone Indefinitely		S	D		M	Affirm. Only
Main Motion				S	D	A	M	R

FIGURE 10-1: Motion table showing privileged motions according to rank.

© John Wiley & Sons, Inc.

As Figure 10-1 depicts, when a motion is being considered, the motions below it on the list are out of order until the assembly has disposed of the one being considered. However, motions above the motion in question can be moved and considered no matter what's pending in the lower ranks.

Note in Figure 10-1 that none of the privileged motions is debatable, and only two of these motions are amendable (because you have to decide times and dates). These motions are all about making an informed decision without wasting time.

WARNING

This chapter discusses these motions in their privileged form, but the motions to *Recess,* to *Adjourn,* and to *Fix the Time to Which to Adjourn* can also be made as incidental main motions. When used in that manner, the rules relating to their order of precedence and privileged status change. I discuss these changes in more detail in Chapter 6.

Getting Back on Schedule: Call for the Orders of the Day

Your time is important. So is that of other members. Your meeting has a purpose and a goal of taking care of the group's business within a specific time frame. Meeting time is the time to get down to business, make decisions, and go home.

Recognizing the value of your time, Robert's Rules gives you a special motion to use to keep the meeting running on schedule. If you're in a meeting and see that the group isn't following the adopted agenda (or program, or order of business established by rule), or if the time has arrived for an item of business and the chair continues other pending business, you can insist that the schedule be followed.

In such a situation, the privileged motion to *Call for the Orders of the Day,* which the following section discusses, is just what you need. With this motion, the demand of a single member requires the group to resume the scheduled business immediately, unless the members decide otherwise by a two-thirds vote.

REMEMBER

This motion isn't permitted in a committee of the whole (see Chapter 3).

Using the motion to Call for the Orders of the Day

Calling for the orders of the day is appropriate in two situations:

>> When the time arrives for a special order to be discussed, but other business continues

>> When, for some reason, the group isn't addressing business in the proper order

To make this privileged motion, simply rise and say, "Mr. Chairman, I call for the orders of the day." You may also say, "Madam President, I demand that the regular order be immediately resumed."

Two situations exemplify the use of this motion:

>> **If the chairman, for whatever reason misses a general order, you can call for the orders of the day to get him on back on track.** But you have to make call before another item of business is underway. If you miss your chance, you have to wait until that item of business is concluded.

>> **If the time has arrived for a special order and the special order was neglected, then you can interrupt a pending question to call for the orders of the day and get that special order before the assembly.** Be prepared to inform the chair just what the special order is that it's time to handle. But don't volunteer it. The chair is supposed to know these things.

For the straight-and-skinny on general orders and special orders, flip to Chapter 5.

REMEMBER

Even if someone else is speaking, you can interrupt to make this motion because the privilege of the group is to be able to follow its schedule.

Your presiding officer is responsible for keeping the meeting on track, and when this motion is made, their duty is to proceed immediately to the proper item of business.

The chair responds to the member calling for orders of the day by saying, "Orders of the day are called for," and proceeding to announce the proper current item of business.

REMEMBER

When your program or agenda includes activities or events that occur outside of a business meeting, that event isn't subject to the motion to *Call for Orders of the Day*. The motion is applicable only to items of business scheduled inside a business meeting.

Setting aside the orders of the day

If the presiding officer or one of the members thinks that the members would likely rather continue the business currently before them, they can proceed as follows:

» Instead of proceeding immediately to the scheduled item of business, the chair can inform the assembly of the item of business that's in order and ask whether the members want to move on to that item. The members can choose to continue with the currently pending business by a two-thirds vote *in the negative*.

» A member can simply move that the time for consideration of the currently pending business be extended or that the rules be suspended (see Chapter 11) and that the group take up a particular matter. Either way, the motion requires a two-thirds vote in the affirmative.

Six key characteristics of the motion to Call for the Orders of the Day

The motion to *Call for the Orders of the Day*

» Can interrupt a speaker who has the floor.

» Doesn't need to be seconded.

>> Isn't debatable.

>> Can't be amended.

>> Requires enforcement on the call of any member unless the members, by a two-thirds vote, decide to continue with the currently pending business.

>> Can't be reconsidered.

It's Cold in Here: Raise a Question of Privilege

Plenty of situations can arise during meetings that keep members from being comfortable or able to concentrate on the business at hand. A good illustration of such disturbances plays out in a scene from my high-school days.

My chemistry classroom was near the band practice field, and during football season, the band tuned up at the same time my class started. The cacophony was deafening, and no one could hear the teacher explain the importance of not letting the sodium get wet. It was too hot to close the window and muffle the noise. Thankfully, the leader of the majorettes was able to talk the bandmaster into ordering an about-face while the tune-up continued, and the noise was abated because all the horns were suddenly tooting in the opposite direction. The class was able to proceed in a relatively quiet and well-ventilated classroom.

Such is the nature of meetings. Air conditioners are set too low or too high, there's noise out in the hall, or a group of members is abuzz about something and you can't hear the discussion. Anything that affects the comfort of the assembly can be dealt with on the request of one member who raises a *Question of Privilege*.

TECHNICAL STUFF

Robert's Rules labels *Raise a Question of Privilege* as a "device," but its application and use is still that of a privileged motion.

More often than not, the device *Raise a Question of Privilege* is made to solve some immediate problem of particular and immediate annoyance to the group. But this device covers other situations, too.

Here are the two types of questions of privilege:

>> **Questions dealing with matters that affect the entire group.** Examples include the physical comfort of members, questions about the organization, questions about the conduct of its officers or employees, and questions about the accuracy of published reports.

>> **Questions dealing with matters that affect an individual.** An example of this type is an inaccurate report of something a member has said or done.

Using the device Raise a Question of Privilege

There you sit, seventh row from the back in a small and crowded meeting hall. The meeting of the Association of Seersucker Beanbag Manufacturers is underway, and the group is debating an important motion. Some bonehead is out in the hall talking about his recent foot surgery, and you're not only disgusted, you're also unable to concentrate on the debate.

What to do? Easy! Raise a question of privilege! Stand up and (interrupting the current speaker because you just don't want to miss anything more of what's being said) say, "Mr. Chairman, I rise to a question of privilege affecting the assembly. There is a loud disturbance coming from the hall, and a large number of us can't hear or concentrate on the discussion."

The chair may respond, "Will the bonehead in the hall please shut up and take his foot with him?" No, sorry — I'm just kidding. That's probably what the chair would like to say, but as I discuss in Chapter 7, the chair must avoid getting personal and stick to the issue at hand.

The chair really should say, "Will someone please ask the members in the hall to remove the conversation from the doorway, and please close the doors to the hall?"

TECHNICAL STUFF

The device *Raise a Question of Privilege* rarely involves more than just a decision by the chair. But it may be used to introduce a motion that the group needs to decide immediately. Suppose you're in a board meeting, and the executive director and two committee chairs, none of whom is a board member, are present.

Some of your board members believe the executive director hung the moon, so when it's time for new business, one of them moves to increase the executive director's annual salary by $12,000, and another seconds the motion. The chair states the motion, and it's on the floor for debate. You're totally in shock. The executive director's performance has been on a downward spiral for months, and you've been thinking it's time to find a replacement. You want to speak freely in opposition to the motion, and you believe only the board members should be in the room for the discussion. So you raise a question of privilege relating to the assembly so that the group can decide immediately whether to go into executive session to consider the motion.

The question of whether to go into executive session is the question of privilege; the motion concerning the executive director's salary is a main motion whose private consideration is made possible by the question of privilege.

REMEMBER

Rarely is anything other than a motion affecting the physical comfort of the members in a meeting properly introduced by raising a question of privilege and interrupting the pending business. The other examples I provide in this section are most often handled as incidental main motions; they're the same motions, except that they're made while no other business is pending. (I discuss incidental main motions in Chapter 6.)

Six key characteristics of the device Raise a Question of Privilege

The privileged device *Raise a Question of Privilege*

>> Can interrupt a speaker who has the floor, but only if the motion's object would be lost by waiting.

>> Doesn't need to be seconded, but if the solution to the problem being addressed requires another motion, that motion needs to be seconded.

>> Isn't debatable regarding whether to allow the question of privilege to be addressed at that time, but if the question of privilege is handled as a main motion rather than a request, that motion is debatable.

>> Can't be amended regarding whether to allow the question of privilege to be addressed at that time, but if the question of privilege is handled as a main motion rather than a request, that motion is amendable.

>> Whether the question shall be allowed at that time is decided (ruled on) by the chair, but if the question is handled as a main motion rather than a request, that motion requires a majority vote.

>> The chair's decision on whether to allow the question of privilege to be addressed at that time can't be reconsidered, but if the question is handled as a main motion rather than a request, that motion can be reconsidered.

Taking a Break: Recess

No, it's not time to go out to the playground and climb the jungle gym. Well, maybe it feels like time for that kind of recess, but it's not likely to happen unless you're in class and this book is your parliamentary procedure textbook. *Recess*, in this sense, usually refers only to taking a break in the middle of a meeting. But I promise you that the feeling is the same. Recess is *recess!*

Well, almost. A motion to *Recess*, like other privileged and subsidiary motions, also has a form for use as an incidental main motion (see Chapter 6) and has a few different rules if it's made when nothing else is pending and the group wants to take a short break.

But the *privileged* motion to *Recess* is made to consider whether to take a short break *immediately while another motion is pending.* It can interrupt just about anything under consideration other than one of the privileged motions concerning adjournment.

REMEMBER

A recess doesn't close a meeting. When you reconvene from the recess, you take up business right where you left off.

Using the motion to Recess

I can't remember any time in my career, either as a member or as a parliamentarian, when a motion to take a recess failed. About the only time it may not go through is when somebody trumps the motion with a motion to *Adjourn.*

The motion to *Recess* provides for a short break in the proceedings, and the privileged motion is one that's used to get a recess immediately, even while you're in the middle of something. It can be used strategically to allow an opportunity for a caucus, or simply so you can step outside for a breath of fresh air.

Because a motion to *Recess* can't interrupt a speaker, you're required to wait for recognition by the chair. But the form is simple: "Madam Chairman, I move that we take a 15-minute recess," or "Mr. President, I move we take a recess until 3 p.m.," or "I move we recess until reconvened by the chair."

Unless your meeting is holding everyone rapt in enjoyment of the discussion, calls of "second" are likely to erupt from all corners of the room (and from the middle and sides, too!). Unless it appears that the motion to *Recess* may meet objection or perhaps an amendment to deal with the length of the recess, the chair can usually obtain general (or unanimous) consent (see Chapter 8). If objection arises or an amendment is offered, a voice vote is the way to go.

To resume business as usual, the chair calls the meeting back to order by saying something like, "The recess is ended, and the meeting will come to order."

That's it. You're back — refreshed, reenergized, regrouped, and ready to proceed.

Six key characteristics of the motion to Recess

The motion to *Recess*, as a privileged motion,

>> Can't interrupt a speaker who has the floor.

>> Must be seconded.

>> Isn't debatable.

>> Is amendable with respect to the length of the recess, with no debate permitted on such an amendment.

>> Must have a majority vote.

>> Can't be reconsidered.

Time to Get Outta Here: Adjourn

Those magic words, "I declare the meeting adjourned!" Who doesn't love 'em? Most of the time, nobody. In fact, as great as meetings can be when conducted by effective leaders who know what they're doing, adjourning is probably bad news only when your great idea is on the floor and is close to being adopted, and the opposition uses the motion to *Adjourn* to successfully close the meeting.

Interestingly enough, an actual motion to *Adjourn* is rarely necessary. Yes, you read that right. I elaborate here.

WARNING

In anticipation of adjournment, you and a few of the others in your meeting may already be beating a path to the to the door. But some business remains in order that you may not want to miss, so you may be doing yourself a big favor by hanging around long enough to actually hear the presiding officer declare the meeting adjourned.

Although it's rarely necessary to use the motion to *Adjourn* once your meeting is winding up, it's nevertheless important to know how the motion operates so that you can make good use of it when you want to shut a meeting down before it completes its order of business for whatever reason.

After the motion to *Adjourn* is made, and (except during voting) before the chair declares the meeting adjourned, any one or more of the following actions are permitted and in order:

>> Providing information about business that requires attention before adjournment

>> Making important announcements

>> Making (but not voting on) a motion to *Reconsider* (see Chapter 12)

>> Moving to *Reconsider and Enter on the Minutes* (see Chapter 12)

>> Giving notice for a motion to be made at the next meeting that requires previous notice to be given at a meeting

>> Moving to set the time for an adjourned meeting, if there is no meeting already scheduled for later in the session

In some situations, adjournment can take place without a motion. One is when the hour adopted for adjournment has arrived. At that time, the chair announces the fact, and unless you or someone else is pretty quick to move to *Set Aside the Orders of the Day* (refer to the section, "Setting aside the orders of the day," earlier in this chapter), the meeting may be adjourned by declaration.

Another instance in which adjournment doesn't need a motion is when some emergency or immediate danger makes hanging around for a vote a really knuckle-brained thing to do. For example, if there's a fire, your presiding officer should just break the glass to set off the alarm, and then declare the meeting adjourned to meet again at the call of the chair.

The other (more common) scenario in which adjournment can happen without a motion is when you've reached the end of the agenda. In that case, the chair may just ask whether there's any more business; if you don't speak up to make that motion you've been thinking about, and if no one else speaks up, the presiding officer can declare the meeting adjourned. Everybody can go out for coffee and beignets (I'm in Louisiana, and we love those little fried, square donuts!) before going home after the meeting.

A meeting isn't adjourned until the chair *declares* it adjourned, no matter how loud the "ayes" ring out when the vote is taken. So if you've nursed a controversial motion through debate and gotten it adopted, don't leave the room before the chair declares the meeting adjourned. Guess what happens if your majority leaves too early and your opposition can get a motion to *Rescind* on the floor at a time when it has two-thirds of the vote in the room. If you and your cohorts have ditched the meeting before it officially adjourns, you might be handing your opposition the control they need to lay to waste your hard-earned victory.

Using the motion to Adjourn

The motion to *Adjourn* is straightforward and simple. It comes in three basic forms:

>> **Adjourn now:** "Madam President, I move to adjourn."

Adopting the motion closes the meeting. At the heart of everyone making this motion is the bleeding desire to fold it up and go home! Unless a later time for adjourning the meeting has already been decided, this form of the motion is *always* privileged, meaning that even when nothing else is pending, the motion to *Adjourn* must be immediately disposed of by direct vote, unless the higher-ranking motion to *Fix the Time to Which to Adjourn* is made. (I discuss that motion in the final section of this chapter.)

This form of *Adjourn* is the only way in which the motion may be used as a privileged motion (meaning that it can be made while other business is pending).

If you're adjourning a meeting in a session with meetings still to be held, you pick up in the next meeting right where you left off when you adjourned (when you get past the usual meeting-opening rituals and any reading and approval of minutes). But if you adjourn and no meeting is going to occur until your next regular meeting, any motions not disposed of go forward as unfinished business.

REMEMBER

If your next regular meeting won't be held *within a quarterly time interval* (see the Appendix for that definition), or if a change in membership will occur because of expirations of terms of members (such as may be the case in an executive board), all motions pending and not disposed of (or sent to a committee) *fall to the ground.* If they need to be acted on, you just have to pick them up, dust them off, and introduce them again at the next meeting.

>> **Adjourn to continue the meeting later:** "Madam President, I move to *Adjourn* to meet again tomorrow at 8 a.m."

This form sets up a continuation of the current meeting. Tomorrow's meeting is called an *adjourned meeting* or an *adjournment of* the current meeting. At the heart of everyone making this motion is the same bleeding desire to get away from it all until they're dragged kicking and screaming back, being required by duty to continue an unfinished agenda.

>> **Adjourn sine die (without day):** "Mr. Chairman, I move to *Adjourn* sine die."

This form adjourns the assembly completely and is used to end the final meeting of a convention of delegates.

TECHNICAL STUFF

The second two forms aren't *privileged*, meaning that they're in order only as *main motions* and can be made only when no other business is pending. They're governed by the same rules as main motions, and not those for the privileged motion to adjourn.

Six key characteristics of the privileged motion to Adjourn

The privileged motion to *Adjourn*

>> Can't interrupt a speaker who has the floor.

>> Must be seconded.

>> Can't be debated.

>> Can't be amended.

>> Must have a majority vote.

>> Can't be reconsidered, but can be renewed if any business or material progress in debate has gone forward after a motion to *Adjourn* has failed.

REMEMBER

If the motion specifies when adjournment will occur, that aspect of the motion can be amended and debated because this form would be a main motion to *Adjourn*, not the privileged form of the motion to *Adjourn*.

Finishing on Another Day: Fix the Time to Which to Adjourn

The last of the privileged motions on the list, the motion to *Fix the Time to Which to Adjourn*, is the one that can be made at just about any time, no matter what else is before your meeting.

It may become clear at some point in the meeting that you need more time if you're to get everything accomplished that you intended. And you don't want to wait until the next regular meeting to finish things. You may be dealing with elections or just an overloaded agenda. You may not even have another regular meeting scheduled for a long time. When you find yourself in this situation, you want to provide for an adjourned meeting.

REMEMBER

An *adjourned meeting* refers to a meeting that continues the same order of business, or agenda, that wasn't concluded in an earlier meeting. Technically, it's a separate meeting, but it's a continuation of the same session. The adjourned meeting mostly takes care of important business that shouldn't (or mustn't) wait until the next regular meeting, but that can't go forward in the current meeting because of a lack of time (or perhaps a lack of a quorum). (Flip to Chapter 4 for a thorough discussion of quorum.)

Using the motion to Fix the Time to which to Adjourn

As soon as you realize that the work ahead of you is likely to consume more time than you have, the time is right to offer the motion to *Fix the Time to Which to Adjourn.* It's privileged when it's made while other business is pending, and because it's the highest-ranking motion, it takes precedence over just about everything, including a pending motion to *Adjourn.* That last little inclusion is great because it gives you or other judicious members of your organization one last chance to keep your good ideas alive and within reach of the membership before the next regular meeting. This consideration means a lot in the case of a group that meets only quarterly (or even less often).

This motion is introduced by saying, "Mr. Chairman, I move that, when we adjourn, we adjourn to meet again next Tuesday night at 6 p.m. at the clubhouse." Or, if you need to keep some options open, say something like "to meet next week at the call of the president."

This motion is commonly used when a motion is made that would benefit from having an evening to itself. In this situation, the motion to *Fix the Time to Which to Adjourn* is made as a way of postponing the motion until the assembly has enough time to handle it properly. You may even want to move to postpone the pending question to the adjourned meeting after adoption of the motion that sets the adjourned meeting. After adoption of the motion to postpone, the group can take up some other item of business in the current meeting before there's a motion to *Adjourn.* Or if you're running out of time, this privileged motion may be made to set up the time for an adjourned meeting just before making a motion to *Adjourn.*

TIP

When you're faced with a lack of *quorum* (enough people to legally conduct business), fixing the time to which to adjourn gives you another chance to complete the business that should have been completed on the original date but couldn't due to poor attendance.

Six key characteristics of the motion to Fix the Time to Which to Adjourn

The privileged motion to *Fix the Time to Which to Adjourn*

» Can't interrupt a speaker who has the floor.

» Must be seconded.

» Can't be debated.

» Can be amended only as to the date, hour, and place; such amendments cannot be debated.

» Needs a majority vote.

» Can be reconsidered.

REMEMBER

If this motion is made when no business is pending, it's a main motion and can be debated. It's subject to all the rules of an incidental main motion.

Chapter **11**

Incidental Motions: Dealing with Questions of Procedure

As you go through your day, you probably have some well-established routines that get you from one task to another. You get up, you have some coffee, and you get ready for the day ahead. You go to work or school, or otherwise go about your life. You come home, relax, and maybe do a little work in the yard. If you have time, you may read, study, watch a little TV, or do some surfing on the web. Soon enough, you tire, you retire, and you do it all over again tomorrow.

You may have your daily routine figured out, but you still have to make a lot of decisions about how to do the different things you do. Are you going to cook your breakfast or stop at the Greasy Spoon? Will you have your eggs sunny side up or scrambled? How are you getting to work? Will you drive, walk, or take the bus?

You make some decisions every time you deal with a particular situation, like deciding what to have for breakfast. Other times, you make a decision and stick with it until you make a change, like figuring out how you get to work. No matter what the big picture is, you have to make decisions just to be able to move from one thing to the next. It's not just about the main goals — the decisions you make to reach those goals are just as important. The same philosophy applies to meetings and the ways in which decisions are made.

Defining Incidental Motions

In your meetings, your group often needs to decide how to proceed in handling your business. Should you vote by ballot? Is the chairman correct? Does the treasury have enough money? Can your group say "Yes" to part of a motion and "No" to another part? Should your group even be talking about this? Also, when it comes to arriving at group decisions, it matters very much if things aren't handled correctly or in the manner agreed to by all, when improper handling results in the compromise of the rights of one, some, or all of the members.

Robert's Rules takes into account the need for members to make these kinds of decisions — to insist on strictly following the rules, to relax the rules for a special reason, or to decide to handle something in a particular way. These decisions are made by the introduction and consideration of what are called *incidental motions.* These motions help your group (or your presiding officer) decide a question about whether something is being done correctly, whether to get more information, or how to handle some aspect of business.

TECHNICAL STUFF

The term *incidental motion* refers to any of the motions described in this chapter when they're made in direct connection with a motion to be introduced, a motion that has been introduced but has not been stated by the chair (and is therefore not yet pending), a pending motion, or a motion that has just been pending. But when any of the motions described in this chapter are made as *main motions,* they're called *incidental main motions,* and even though the purpose is pretty much the same as described shortly, the rules for using them are a little different. Check out Chapter 6 for the rules regarding main motions.

Using Incidental Motions

The incidental motions in Robert's Rules cover most anything that can come up when you're in your meeting. They're listed here:

>> Point of Order

>> Appeal the Ruling (decision) of the Chair

>> Suspend the Rules

>> Objection to the Consideration of a Question

>> Division of a Question

>> Consider Seriatim (by paragraph)

>> Division of the Assembly

>> Motions Related to Methods of Voting and the Polls

>> Motions Related to Nominations

>> Request to Be Excused from a Duty

>> Parliamentary Inquiry

>> Request for Information

>> Request for Permission to Withdraw or Modify a Motion

>> Request to Read Papers

>> Request for Any Other Privilege

Table 11-1 lays out exactly which motions you use, depending on what you're trying to accomplish in your meeting. Each of these motions is discussed in detail in the following sections.

TABLE 11-1 **Common Uses for Incidental Motions**

If You Want To . . .	Then Use . . .
Enforce the rules	Point of Order
Overrule a decision of the chair	Appeal
Do something that violates a rule	Suspend the Rules
Avoid any consideration of an original main motion	Objection to the Consideration of a Question
Divide a motion into separate parts for debate and vote	Division of a Question
Discuss a long motion part by part before voting on the whole	Consideration by Paragraph (Seriatim)
Question the result of a voice vote	Division of the Assembly
Take a vote other than by voice, or open or close the polls	Motions Related to Methods of Voting and the Polls
Designate a method for taking nominations, or open or close nominations	Motions Related to Nominations
Avoid a compulsory obligation of membership or office or resign from membership or office	Request to Be Excused from a Duty
Ask a question about procedure	Parliamentary Inquiry
Ask for information pertaining to the business at hand	Request for Information
Withdraw or change a motion already stated by the chair	Request for Permission to Withdraw or Modify a Motion
Read something to the assembly	Request to Read Papers
Speak or make remarks when no business is pending	Request for Any Other Privilege

Following the Rules: Point of Order

The situation is inevitable: An important rule is ignored, over-looked, or just plain broken, and one or more members wind up with the short end of the stick. Any self-respecting book on rules provides a rule stating that any member who notices a breach of the rules has a right to call immediate attention to the fact and insist that the rules be enforced. Robert's Rules provides for this type of situation by giving you the procedure for raising a *Point of Order.*

Rising to a point of order

You're sitting there in your meeting waiting for the right moment to rise and get recognition of the chair (in this case, the president) to speak against the stupid idea that your service club support a proposition to increase the local sales tax. Suddenly somebody in the back of the room shouts, "Question! Question! I call for the question!" The president responds by saying, "The question has been called for. We'll stop discussion now and vote!"

You're dumbfounded. You thought your president knew by now that one member can't end debate by hollering out, "Question!" You know that *Robert's Rules For Dummies* explains the rules for ending debate (right there in Chapter 9, where I discuss the subsidiary motion *Previous Question*), your club just bought a copy for your president. Unfortunately, your president hasn't read it yet.

If you want to have your say on the issue, you need to stop the president from ending debate on the demand of this one member, and at least get the president to put a vote to the members on whether to end the debate. You rise — quickly, mind you, even if you interrupt a speaker, or you'll be too late — and say, "Point of order, Mr. President!" or "Mr. President, I rise to a point of order!"

Stating your point

The presiding officer says to you, "The member will state his point of order." In this case, you say, "Mr. President, the member did not obtain recognition of the chair, nor did his motion to end debate have a second, and we did not vote on whether we're ready to end debate."

Hearing the ruling of the chair

Now, if you're lucky and the president isn't trying to short-circuit the debate, the president says, "The point is well taken, and the previous question (or motion to end debate) is not before the membership. Is there any further discussion on the motion to endorse the sales tax increase?" You can then obtain recognition of the chair and proceed to speak against the idea.

You may be unlucky, though, and the president may simply rule your point well taken, ask for a second to the previous question, and then take a rising vote on whether to end debate. If two-thirds of the members vote to end debate, your point may be well taken, but the group is still tired of all the talk. However, because your president clearly doesn't know how to deal with previous question, they may say, "The point is not well taken, and I'm tired of all this talk." (If they do this, you'll be glad to know about your right to appeal, which I discuss in the next section of this chapter.)

A point of order can be raised at any time when any member notices a violation of the rules. The chair's duty is to make a decision, called a *ruling,* on the point of order. The president may need to check the rules or the bylaws, or ask the parliamentarian for advice, but in any case, a point of order is usually ruled on in one of two ways: The point is declared either "well taken" or "not well taken," and a short explanation of the ruling is given.

Proceeding when the chair is in doubt

Sometimes, however, the point being raised isn't as clear as whether the motion to end debate is being handled correctly. The point of order may, for example, be that a proposed amendment isn't germane to the main motion. In that case, the chair may reasonably be in doubt (or may just prefer to let the assembly decide the point, in the interest of harmony). In such a case, the chair responds, "The chair is in doubt on the member's point. Those who consider the amendment germane will say 'Aye' . . . opposed, 'No' . . . the ayes have it, and the amendment is germane."

TECHNICAL STUFF

If the chair refers the point of order to the assembly, it may or may not be debatable. If it is debatable, the rules for debatable appeals apply. Look for the section "Sorry, but I Disagree: Appeal" in this chapter.

Beating the clock on points of order

If you believe the rules aren't being followed, you need to speak up fast because points of order are subject to timeliness requirements. With few exceptions, if you let a breach of the rules pass without saying something when it occurs, you lose the opportunity to object. Parliamentarians like to call this the "You snooze, you lose" rule!

Reserving a point of order

If you think a motion may be out of order but you can't be sure until you hear something of what the maker has to say on the motion, you can *reserve a point of order.* After hearing the maker's speech, you have to either press the point or withdraw it. You can't wait until further debate has occurred. If you do, the chair doesn't have much choice but to rule your point of order as "not well taken," or "not in order."

Raising your point of order before it's too late

To raise a point of order correctly, you must raise it at the time the breach of order occurs. That rule is pretty straightforward. If some motion is out of order, if the vote isn't taken correctly, or if proper procedure is breached, you must raise the point of order at that time, or else you're out of luck. No second-guessing is allowed after the meeting, even for votes. If you want to raise a point of order about the conduct of a vote, you must do it before any debate or business has intervened, or the results declared by the chair must stand.

Raising an exception for the continuing breach

The timeliness requirement carries a big exception that centers on what's called a *continuing breach* of the rules. If the violation of the rules involves one of the following situations, a point of order can almost always be raised at any time:

>> Adoption of a main motion that violates your bylaws

>> Adoption of a main motion that conflicts with a previously adopted main motion, unless the vote was by the margin required to *Amend or Rescind Something Previously Adopted* (see Chapter 12)

>> Violation of procedural rules in any law governing your organization

>> Anything done in violation of a fundamental principle of parliamentary law, even if agreed to unanimously, such as the rules that

- Allow only one question to be considered at a time

- Limit the right to vote to members present at the time the voting occurs in a regular or properly called meeting

>> Anything done in violation of a rule protecting rights of absentees or the basic rights of the individual member, such as

- Quorum requirements

- Requirements for previous notice

- Rules in the bylaws requiring a secret ballot vote

- Actions to prevent a particular member from having full rights to participate in a meeting except after proper disciplinary proceedings (or under provisions of properly adopted motions to limit debate, close the polls, and so on)

REMEMBER

Anytime one or more members are improperly denied the right to vote (or even denied the right to attend a meeting in which a vote occurred), and the denial of those rights could have affected the result of the vote, a point of order can be raised at *any* time. The vote must be retaken if the point of order is ruled well taken.

Anytime a vote included votes cast by nonmembers, multiple votes cast by a single member, or votes cast by absent members and these votes could affect the outcome, a point of order can be raised as long as the action decided is still in force and effect. If the point is well taken, or sustained on appeal, the action is null and void.

If the executive board takes action that exceeds its authority or that is contrary to action of the membership, a point of order can be raised anytime. If the point is well taken or sustained on appeal, the action is null and void. The point of order may be made at a board meeting or at a membership meeting. Depending on the wishes of the membership, the action can be nullified, or ratified and made valid.

Looking back in time: Precedent

The presiding officer is charged with the duty to make rulings on points of order. That gives the presiding officer a lot to say about how things get decided in the future. The record of presiding officers' rulings comes in handy when points of order are decided in the future. Those rulings become precedents that can be persuasive in deciding how to handle something today.

If your secretaries have followed the rules for what to include in the minutes (see Chapter 17 for the complete list), you'll be able to look back and see the presiding officers' rulings on points of order in the past. Properly written minutes contain all rulings on points of order and the chair's reason for the ruling. That information can carry a lot of weight on how something is handled today.

Rulings on points of order and appeals aren't binding, though. A ruling today may be different from one last month. As they say, "Your mileage may vary!"

WARNING

Just as precedent-setting is a decision of the assembly on a point of order. So is the assembly's decision on an appeal (see following section) that overturns a chair's ruling.

REMEMBER

Always include in your minutes the details on how the chair ruled and the reasons stated for the ruling. Minutes also must include how the assembly decided on any point of order submitted to it and record any appeal from a chair's ruling.

TIP

An assembly can challenge precedents established by rulings of the chair or the assembly at any time, usually by just adding a rule or making a change in an existing rule. Adding to or changing your rules can eliminate doubts about how to proceed in problematic parliamentary situations.

Six key characteristics of Point of Order

The motion *Point of Order*

» Can interrupt a speaker who has the floor.

» Doesn't need to be seconded.

» Isn't debatable (unless the chair refers it to the assembly, in which case it is debatable under the same conditions as an appeal).

» Can't be amended.

» Is decided by the chair (or by majority vote, if the chair refers it to the assembly).

» Can't be reconsidered (unless decided by the assembly).

Sorry, but I Disagree: Appeal

Even the most highly studied, best prepared, and extremely popular presiding officer can make mistakes. When one of those mistakes involves a ruling on a matter of parliamentary procedure, any two members can require that the ruling be decided by the membership through the process called appeal.

The appeal of the motion to Appeal

Robert's Rules says that disagreeing with the chair is no different from disagreeing with a member in debate, and you're given a way to do it without getting personal. In fact, if you don't appeal from the decision of the chair, Robert says that you don't have any right to criticize the ruling. Knowing how to use this incidental motion is important, in case the chair doesn't make the correct ruling on your point of order. And the chair needs to know how to use it as well because it's often the best way out of a sticky wicket!

Appealing (from) the ruling of the chair

When a presiding officer makes a ruling and a member dis-agrees, the proper action to take is to rise and say, "Madam President, I appeal from the ruling of the chair." If another member seconds the appeal, the procedure is rather simple: Madam President puts the question to the members, who decide whether to sustain her ruling. But under Robert's Rules, the presiding officer gets to speak first and last in any discussion about the appeal or her decision. Other members can speak only once on the appeal.

TECHNICAL STUFF

It doesn't matter whether the ruling is on a point of order made by a member or the ruling is made simply because the presiding officer recognizes that some procedure or motion is not in order. Her job is to rule on parliamentary procedure, to keep things moving along and to ensure that the rights of the minority aren't trampled.

So when you move, for example, to amend a motion to spend $500 to have a picnic on the Fourth of July by striking out "have a picnic on the Fourth of July" and inserting "buy the secretary a new desk," the chair may likely rule your amendment "out of order" because the chair decides it isn't germane to the original motion. When she rules your motion out of order, she's expected to explain her ruling. In this case, the chair makes the ruling because she considers the main motion to be about having a social event, not about buying furniture.

But you're not focusing on the picnic. You're thinking about the $500, and you think that if the group spends $500, it should be on the secretary's desk. And maybe in place of the picnic, you can have a watermelon roast sometime during the summer where everybody brings their own watermelon (and less money is spent). Your option, then, is to say, "Madam President, I appeal from the decision of the chair." If your appeal has any support, someone will second it, and you're on!

Because the motion to *Amend*, on which the ruling was made (and from which you're appealing), is debatable, you can seek recognition to speak to your appeal. You explain that your amendment is germane to the spending of the money, and that's why you appeal. You ask the members, when deciding whether to sustain the decision of the chair, to consider that this amendment is completely germane to a question on spending $500.

Stating the question on the appeal

The chair thanks you and, realizing that it's no big deal (this isn't about her being right — it's about what the members want), welcomes the opportunity to let the members decide. The chair puts the question to the membership by saying, "Shall the decision of the chair be sustained?"

Deciding the appeal

If the members agree with the ruling of the chair, they vote "Aye" to *sustain the decision* of the chair. If they want to consider your amendment, they vote "No" and *overrule* the chair. If they sustain the chair's ruling, your amendment is out of order. Otherwise, your amendment is in order, and the chair is expected to entertain discussion on the amendment. The appeal doesn't decide whether the amendment is adopted — only whether it's in order to come before the membership.

Applying the motion to appeal

An appeal can be applied only to a *ruling* of the chair, not to an opinion, such as is a response to a *parliamentary inquiry* (discussed later in this chapter). Nor is the declaration of the result of a vote subject to an appeal. To challenge the result of a vote, you call for a *Division of the Assembly* (discussed in the section "Let's Be Sure about the Vote: Division of the Assembly," later in this chapter) or you move to have the vote counted (see Chapter 8).

REMEMBER

If the chair makes an error in declaring the result of a vote because they don't apply the correct threshold — as can happen, for example, if the vote required is a two-thirds vote, but only a majority have voted in favor and the chair declares the motion adopted (or when the vote required is a majority, but the chair declares it failed because of not getting a two-thirds vote) — then it's in order for the chair to rule on a point of order. An appeal can be made from the chair's ruling.

Six key characteristics of Appeal

An appeal from the ruling of the chair

>> Can interrupt a speaker who has the floor.

>> Needs to be seconded.

>> Is debatable unless the immediately pending question isn't debatable or it's about either violations of the rules for speaking (including indecorous behavior) or the priority of business.

>> Can't be amended.

>> Requires a majority vote in the negative to overturn the decision of the chair.

>> Can be reconsidered.

We Can't Let That Stop Us: Suspend the Rules

When I was a junior in high school (way back in the middle of the 20th century), my English teacher asked me to take some photographs to the yearbook sponsor's classroom during a class period. It was against the rules to be in the hall during class periods, but the teachers had the ability to suspend that rule by giving a hall pass. If I got stopped and questioned by another teacher or a hall monitor, I just showed my hall pass and continued on my mission.

In your organization's meetings, sometimes you need to take care of some business that normally violates your rules. When the circumstances warrant an exception, and if making the exception doesn't violate any of the rules listed under "Knowing when you can't suspend the rules" later in this chapter, the incidental motion to *Suspend the Rules* is your hall pass.

Moving to Suspend the Rules

The motion to *Suspend the Rules* is often used in conjunction with the motion to do whatever you're trying to do that's against your rules. Because the adoption of the motion (requiring a two-thirds vote) would certainly be followed by a vote to do that for which the rules were suspended, the motion to suspend the rules isn't considered a violation of the "one question at a time" principle of parliamentary law (see Chapter 3).

Suppose you want to have a professional parliamentarian preside at one of your meetings at which a divisive issue, like whether to fire your executive director, is on the agenda. Your rules, however, require your president to preside at all meetings. But the president has strong feelings about the issue and just can't do the job impartially yet objects to allowing someone else to serve as a temporary presiding officer. What can you do?

If you can get two-thirds of the members present and voting to approve a suspension of the rules, you can have the parliamentarian handle the meeting. The motion is made by saying, "Mr. President, I move that we suspend the rules and authorize the parliamentarian to serve as presiding officer for the meeting." If the motion receives a second and can muster a two-thirds vote, the rules are suspended, and your professional parliamentarian can preside over the meeting.

REMEMBER

If the president and vice-president *don't* object, the assembly can authorize the parliamentarian to preside by only a majority vote.

Sometimes the motion to suspend isn't combined with the motion it affects because it's not so clear that the original motion will pass, even if the suspension of the rules to consider it is authorized. This situation is illustrated by a common application of suspending the rules when an agenda item is taken out of its regular place on your agenda.

For example, consider the earlier example in which the parliamentarian has been placed in the chair. Everybody is ready to get on with the debate on the controversial issue, but on the adopted agenda, that issue is way down in unfinished business. Nobody really cares about the committee reports right now. So to get started on the hot item, somebody has to move that "we suspend the rules and take up the question on firing the executive director." With a second to the motion and a two-thirds vote, you can move right into debating the fate of your executive director.

TECHNICAL STUFF If I were your professional presiding officer, I may even get straight to that point by *assuming the motion* (see the nearby sidebar for more information) and *asking for unanimous consent* (see Chapter 8). That's every bit as good as having a motion, a second, and a two-thirds vote!

ASSUMING A MOTION

A presiding officer who knows when and how to *assume* a motion has a great time-saving tool in their arsenal.

Incidental motions sometimes lend themselves well to this technique. When the chair detects that the members will follow some course of action that may well be moved, seconded, and stated by the chair, they save a lot of time by assuming the motion and asking for general consent.

Examples of this presiding technique appear throughout this book. *Assuming a motion* is most often used when a particular item of business is already on the agenda, such as specific motions scheduled to come before the membership by previous notice.

To assume a motion, you just assume it. For example, you simply say, "Are there any corrections to the minutes?" Nobody has to make a formal motion. Assuming a motion is completely proper if it's clear that the motion is in order and that the membership intends to debate and decide it.

REMEMBER

In this case, suspending the rules to consider the question doesn't mean you've decided to fire the executive director. It just allows you to temporarily skip past all the routine business on your agenda and get right to the big debate.

Knowing when you can't suspend the rules

I have a friend who says that you may as well not have rules if you can suspend them anytime you need to. But really just the reverse is true: Unless you provide a rule to allow you to make exceptions, you probably don't want to have any rules at all.

But my friend is right in one respect — some rules *cannot be suspended:*

>> **Constitution and bylaws:** Your bylaws are a contract between members, and they can't be suspended, no matter how great a vote to suspend them may be. Nor can they be suspended because the rule is just too inconvenient.

However, if a bylaw provides for its own suspension, it can be suspended. Also, if a bylaw is "clearly in the nature of a rule of order," it can be suspended. A *rule of order* is a rule dealing with the "conduct of business in a meeting or the duty of officers in that connection." Examples of bylaws fitting that description include bylaws that define the order of business for meetings, or those that specify that in meetings, the president serves as the presiding officer and the secretary takes the minutes.

>> **Procedural rules prescribed by statute:** If the law of the land says, with respect to some procedure, that the procedure is required, that the procedure is prohibited, or that it must be done some particular way, you can't suspend those rules — unless, that is, the law itself allows you to do so.

>> **Fundamental principles of parliamentary law:** Such principles can't be suspended, even if the membership unanimously agrees to a suspension. Fundamental principles include those that

- Allow only one question to be considered at a time

- Limit the right to vote to members present at the time the voting occurs in a regular or properly called meeting

>> **Rules protecting rights of absentees (unless no member is absent) or the basic rights of individual members:** These rules include

- Quorum requirements

- Requirements for previous notice

- Rules in the bylaws requiring a secret ballot vote

- The right of any particular member to exercise full rights to participate in a meeting (that is, attending, voting, speaking, making motions, giving notice, and so on), except after proper disciplinary proceedings (or under provisions of properly adopted motions to limit debate, close the polls, and so on)

>> **Rules applicable outside meetings:** Policies and procedures not having to do with meeting procedure during a meeting aren't suspendable. They can be changed by rescinding them or amending them, but *Suspend the Rules* is all about meeting procedure, not how the organization operates day-to-day.

>> **Rules that have effect beyond the current session:** For example, the rule that prohibits postponement of a motion beyond the next regular meeting, or beyond a quarterly time interval, if the next meeting is later than that, cannot be suspended.

Six key characteristics of the motion to Suspend the Rules

A motion to *Suspend the Rules*

>> Can't interrupt a speaker who has the floor.

>> Needs to be seconded.

>> Isn't debatable.

>> Can't be amended.

>> Requires a two-thirds vote. (But if you're suspending a rule protecting a minority less than one-third, the rule can't be suspended if there is a negative vote as great as the number protected by the rule. A *standing rule* — a rule that isn't in the nature of a rule of order — that's applicable in meetings can be suspended by majority vote.)

>> Can't be reconsidered.

Oh, Come Now! Objection to the Consideration of a Question

Any original main motion that you just think is such a bad idea that it should never even be discussed is a fair target for *Objection to the Consideration of a Question*. This incidental motion is in order until the members begin to consider and debate the main motion. In fact, if there's no discussion of the main motion and any subsidiary motion (see Chapter 9) (except *Lay on the Table*) is proposed, *Objection to the Consideration* is still in order until the chair states the proposed subsidiary motion.

After discussion begins, it's too late, no matter how lousy the idea. You can't stop it with this motion then; you can only kill the motion by moving to *Postpone Indefinitely* or by voting it down. In short, if you miss your chance to kill it by objecting to its consideration, you have to at least listen to the maker give his pitch because he's entitled to recognition to speak first to his motion.

**TECHNICAL
STUFF**

Objection to the Consideration of a Question can be applied only to an original main motion. I discuss the difference between original main motions and incidental main motions in Chapter 6.

Objecting to Considering a Question

The following example isn't the only situation in which this motion comes in handy, but it's one of those common scenarios that lends itself to describing the motion's use.

If you're an active member of an organization and you participate regularly in its meetings, you've no doubt encountered Stumpy Neverstops — you know, the guy who shows up at every meeting making the same motion that gets argued and finally voted down. Every meeting, Stumpy batters the hull of his ship. Every month, he persists in introducing his motion, trying to get the group to do something it just doesn't want to do and isn't likely to want to do anytime soon.

After a few meetings like this, you're at your wit's end. And there's no end in sight because Robert's Rules allows Stumpy to make his motion again at every new meeting, even if it failed at a previous meeting — and Stumpy knows no shame. Well, that can all end now. In the following sections, I tell you how to send Stumpy sailing around the reef in his lifeboat while you enjoy a calm sea for a change.

Objection initiated by a member

To use *Objection to the Consideration of a Question*, get to your feet quickly (hopefully as soon as the undesirable motion rolls over the lips of the person offering it) and say, "Mr. Chairman, I object to the consideration of the question."

Because this motion decides whether to summarily dismiss a motion without consideration, it doesn't even need a second. The chair just responds with, "The member objects to the consideration of the motion. All in favor of considering the motion will rise. [pause] Opposed, rise. There are two-thirds opposed to considering the motion, and it will not be considered." It's all over, Stumpy. Sit down!

Finely tuned quick-draw skills help you any time you need to use *Objection to the Consideration* because it's too late to object to consideration of a motion once debate has begun or if any subsidiary motion (except Lay on the Table) has been stated by the chair.

Objection initiated by the chair

If the chair has a good sense of members' limits when it comes to likely intolerance for some motions, the chair may want to offer (on his own initiative) the members the opportunity to object by saying, "It is the sense of the chair that the consideration of this question may have objection. Shall the motion be placed before you for your consideration?"

REMEMBER

If a motion is outside the scope of the purposes of the organization, conflicts with the bylaws, or is otherwise deemed out of order to be considered, then objection to the consideration of the question is itself out of order. When this incidental motion is used incorrectly in this manner, it's treated as a *point of order*, with the chair ruling the motion objected to as out of order.

Six key characteristics of the motion to Objection to the Consideration of a Question

The motion *Objection to the Consideration of a Question*

>> Can interrupt a speaker who has the floor (until debate has begun on the motion to which it is applied).

>> Doesn't need to be seconded.

>> Isn't debatable.

>> Can't be amended.

>> Requires a two-thirds vote against consideration to sustain the objection.

>> Can be reconsidered only if the objection is sustained.

Too Much in One Fell Swoop: Division of a Question

Sometimes a single motion is made that proposes several different actions, each of which could stand alone as a separate motion. In one case, all the different proposals are related and involve the same subject matter. In another case, several unrelated actions are made under the same motion. In either case, you may want to vote in favor of some of the proposals and against some others, but because everything is wrapped up in one main motion, the multiple-choice option isn't available to you.

Or is it? Thanks to the incidental motion *Division of a Question*, you may have some choice after all. If the individual proposals are related, you can move a *Division of a Question*. If it's seconded and passed, you now have a series of individual motions for your group to consider. If the proposals are unrelated and are simply lumped together under the same motion, you can simply demand the division of the question all by yourself, and the division has to be made.

TECHNICAL STUFF

For a motion to be subject to use of the motion to divide the question, the parts have to be capable of standing on their own. A motion to purchase a television and give it to the school can't be divided because, if you don't purchase the television, you can't give it to the school. Furthermore, motions to amend that would change the same word or phrase throughout a motion can't be divided. (These motions are called conforming amendments.)

As an example, suppose you have a long resolution on the floor that sings the praises of a successful reality series called *The Amazing Meeting* and mentions the name of the program often. Then somebody who doesn't know beans from baseballs moves to strike all the instances of *The Amazing Meeting* and insert at every such place *Celebrity Parliamentarian*. Well, no matter how much you want to make everybody vote for each such change separately, it's not in order to move to divide the question for that purpose.

Using Division of a Question

The motion *Division of a Question* applies to two unique situations.

On a single-subject motion

Suppose that Ninny Nora, the prissy board member everybody loves to mock, moves to hold the annual teetotaler tea at Tabitha's Tearoom, and to invite the pastor of the Powerhouse Church of the Assumptuous Presumption to present the program.

Now, you're all for holding the tea at Tabitha's Tearoom, but you really don't want to hear from this pastor. So you second the motion, and as soon as the chair states the motion, you move to divide the question: "Madam Chairman, I move to divide the question to first vote on holding the tea at Tabitha's and then on the question of inviting this pastor to present the program."

Madam chairman, eagle-ear that she is, hears somebody in the back row mutter "Second," being her cue to continue, "It's been moved and seconded to divide the question into two parts first to decide whether 'to hold the annual teetotaler tea at Tabitha's Tearoom,' and then to decide whether 'to invite the pastor of the Powerhouse Church of the Assumptuous Presumption to present the program.'" Then she asks for general consent instead of taking a vote; hearing no objection, she declares the motion divided and puts each question separately. You vote to have the tea at Tabitha's, and you wind up getting the second motion amended to provide that Bella le Biché, the Prelate of Pandemonium be invited to present the program.

On a motion covering several unrelated items

This situation often arises when a committee reports multiple recommendations on several different matters referred to it, and after presenting the report, the reporting member moves adoption of "the recommendations contained in the report."

Suppose that you're considering the report of the dress code committee, and you hear all the different proposals they've recommended. One of their recommendations is that the assembly adopt distinct dress codes for each biweekly meeting of the year. Another is that the committee's budget be increased. Another is to buy Mr. Finkblossom a new bow tie. The first you think is a great idea. The second, you know is not feasible. But the last one is an absolutely brilliant idea. In this case, you can just rise and say, "Madam Chairman, I call for a separate vote on the recommendation to buy Mr. Finkblossom a new bow tie." (Because you know that everything else the committee recommended is likely to go down the tube, you want to have at least *some* chance to help your membership chair look a little better!)

In this scenario, the chair *must* take up that question separately. She may even get smart and divide out the other recommendations on her own motion, but she doesn't have to. She just has to take a separate vote on the bow tie recommendation.

The same principle applies if someone offers a list of amendments to a motion (or a primary amendment) that are all over the place, proposing changes to this, that, and the other. Although it may be a good way to clean up a lot of technical problems, any member can keep it from being an all-or-nothing proposition. If a member thinks that one of the amendments needs to be carved out and voted on separately, they can insist that the chair divide the question and take a vote on one or more of the amendments on the list.

Six key characteristics of the motion Division of the Question

The motion *Division of the Question*

» Can't interrupt a speaker who has the floor.

» Needs to be seconded.

» Isn't debatable.

» Can be amended (regarding how the question is to be divided).

» Requires a majority vote (but if the parts of the motion to which it is applied are unrelated, one member may demand the division of the question).

» Can't be reconsidered.

Going Over This Carefully: Consideration by Paragraph

Your bylaws committee has finally finished its revision of the bylaws, and the special order of business for today's meeting is to consider the revision. You're interested in tweaking a couple of words here and there, and a few other folks have some last-minute suggestions to improve readability and maybe clear up an ambiguity or two.

The proposed bylaws revision is about three pages long. If you want to save time and avoid the confusion of skipping around the revision trying to deal with all the final edits, use the motion to *Consider Seriatim,* or *Consider by Paragraph.*

Considering by paragraph

You can use this motion anytime your parliamentary situation has you considering a long report or a motion with many parts, and you want to be able to discuss and amend each part in a logical sequence before finally considering the document as a whole.

Moving for consideration by paragraph

In most situations where this procedure would be in order, your presiding officer likely will just handle the subject matter by *seriatim* (section by section) anyway. But if not, you can make the motion yourself by saying, "Mr. Chairman, I move to consider the bylaw revision by paragraph." The chair will probably handle your motion by asking for unanimous consent, but it's just as proper for the chair to call for a voice vote.

Following procedure for consideration by paragraph

Your group has come to the point in the meeting when it's time to consider whether to adopt the revision of the bylaws, and you've adopted the motion to consider it by paragraph.

In this case, the chairman of the revision committee presents the first section. The presiding officer of the assembly then asks for discussion or amendments on that section. The process for debate and amendment is handled like it is for any other motion, and when you've finished with the first section, you move on to the next one.

After you've gone through the whole document and amended everything to your group's satisfaction, the chair opens the entire document to amendment. It's the group's final chance to make changes.

As with any main motion, you can debate and amend anything about the document. When you get to the point that nobody wants to make any more changes and everybody has had a say, the group votes on the amended revision, and the chair announces the result.

Considering as a whole

Sometimes the report or revision has been so overworked that the membership is ready to just adopt everything the way it is; the members don't really care to go through it by paragraph. In this case, the motion to consider by paragraph may fail, or if the presiding officer starts to consider by paragraph, somebody may move to *Consider As a Whole*. This motion requires a second, and if such a motion passes, you can still debate and amend the report or revision, or just proceed directly with the vote on the report or revision. The motion to *Consider as a Whole* is governed by the same key characteristics as *Consideration by Paragraph or Seriatim*.

REMEMBER

Whether or not you consider a motion by paragraph depends on the pleasure of the group. But *seriatim* (point by point) consideration is definitely the way to go if you intend to review the item systematically and thoroughly as a group.

Six key characteristics of the motion Consideration by Paragraph

The motion *Consideration by Paragraph*

>> Can't interrupt a speaker who has the floor.

>> Must be seconded.

>> Isn't debatable.

>> Can be amended to consider by section or by article instead of by paragraph, or even to consider as a whole.

» Requires a majority vote.

» Can't be reconsidered.

Being Sure about the Vote: Division of the Assembly

I've been in more meetings than I can count in which the oh-so-few opponents of a motion were able to shout their "No!" votes so loudly that, if you didn't know better, you'd think they were in the majority.

The side that hollers the loudest isn't always the majority; sometimes they fool the chair. If you doubt the result of a voice vote (or a vote by show of hands), you have the right, as a single, lone member, to use the motion *Division of the Assembly* and demand that the vote be immediately taken by rising vote so everyone can see just which side is really in the majority.

Using Division of the Assembly

In any situation where you're in doubt of the result of a voice vote or a vote by show of hands, be quick to your feet and say (loudly enough to be heard by the chair), "Division!" or "I call for a division!"

Division on demand of a member

If a member demands a *Division of the Assembly*, the presiding officer must immediately retake the vote: "Those in favor of . . . will rise. [pause] Be seated. Those opposed will rise. [pause] Be seated." The chair then declares the result based on the rising vote.

REMEMBER

If a member is still in doubt after the rising vote, the member may move for a counted vote. But this motion requires a second and a majority vote of the membership to order the vote be counted. However, if the chair remains in doubt about the result of a rising vote, they may proceed to order a counted vote on their own initiative.

Division on the initiative of the chair

The chair may not even wait for a call for a division. If the chair can't be sure of a majority based on the voice vote or show of hands, the chair may retake the vote by a rising vote by saying, "The chair is in doubt as to the result. Those in favor of the motion will rise. [pause] Be seated. Those opposed will rise. [pause] Be seated. Thank you. The affirmative is in the majority, and the motion is carried."

Six key characteristics of the motion Division of the Assembly

A motion for *Division of the Assembly*

» Can interrupt a speaker who has the floor.

» Doesn't need to be seconded.

» Isn't debatable.

» Can't be amended.

» Requires no vote to be taken.

» Can't be reconsidered.

Deciding How to Decide: Motions Related to Methods of Voting and the Polls

Several methods of voting are possible other than by voice vote or rising vote, both of which are the usual methods of voting on motions (depending on the threshold required for a motion to pass).

Whenever you want to vote on a motion using another method of voting, you use a *motion related to the method of voting.* And whenever you want to specify when voting will take place, you use a *motion related to the polls.*

Using motions related to methods of voting and the polls

Motions related to the method of voting or the polls are in order as incidental motions when an election is pending or when a vote is about to be taken on a motion. These motions can't, however, be applied to another motion related to methods of voting and the polls except for a counted vote, which can be applied to anything except a motion for a counted vote. They can also be used to retake a vote by another method. These are incidental *main* motions if no other business is pending, such as when they are used to select a method of voting or details for the polls in advance.

Selecting a method of voting

As is the case with many incidental motions, the method for voting often can be decided informally by general consent. A good presiding officer sometimes simply calls for a ballot, which is approved by unanimous consent, or can exercise a chair's prerogative to call for a counted vote. But if, for whatever reason, you want to use one of these forms or another voting method, such as a roll call, a signed ballot, a counted standing vote, or even by the use of black and white balls, you can make the motion upon obtaining recognition by the chair. If you want the vote to be by ballot, say, "Madam Chairman, I move that the vote on this motion be taken by ballot." I discuss the different methods of voting in Chapter 8.

Opening or closing the polls

Usually associated with balloting, the motion to close the polls is best left to be handled by the presiding officer. Seeing that all who want to vote have done so, the chair simply declares the polls closed.

But if someone comes into the meeting who hasn't voted, and if the votes haven't been counted (and the results haven't been announced), it's perfectly permissible to allow latecomers to vote. But if the polls have been formally closed either by motion and vote or by declaration of the chair, they can be opened only by majority vote (or unanimous consent) to permit the latecomers to cast their ballots. You can find important general information on voting in Chapter 8 and on elections in Chapter 14.

Sometimes a group's bylaws prescribe that a vote be by ballot. In this case, changing the form of voting is not in order because even the unanimous consent of everyone in the meeting can't compromise a member's right to secrecy. Similarly, an election that's required to be conducted by ballot can't be held by a voice vote even if there's only one nominee or candidate (unless the bylaws provide an exception for this case) because such a change compromises a member's right to cast a write-in vote.

Ballot voting obtains the truest expression of the will of your membership on a question, so when it's prescribed, it must be used.

Six key characteristics of motions related to methods of voting and the polls

A motion related to methods of voting and the polls

>> Can't interrupt a speaker who has the floor, but a member can claim preference in recognition for moving to retake a vote or to move for a counted vote.

>> Must be seconded.

>> Isn't debatable.

>> Can be amended to the extent that amendments are for changing the times at which the polls are to be opened, reopened, or closed. If multiple methods of voting are suggested, this is handled like filling blanks, with the vote taken first on the method taking the longest time.

>> Requires a majority vote (except for closing the polls, which requires a two-thirds vote).

>> Can be reconsidered if it's a motion related to methods of voting, or a negative vote on a motion to reopen the polls, or an affirmative vote on a motion to close or reopen the polls at a specified time if the order has not yet been carried out.

Coming Up with Candidates: Motions Related to Nominations

Several possible methods exist for taking nominations for the offices and positions elected by your membership. I cover these in detail in Chapter 13.

Whenever you need to specify a way to come up with nominees, as you probably will for situations your bylaws don't cover, you use a motion related to the method of nominations. And whenever you want to specify when nominations can be made, you use a motion to *open* or *close* nominations. Collectively, these motions are known as *motions related to nominations.*

Using motions related to nominations

I cover the different methods for nominations, as well as the procedures for opening and closing nominations, in detail in Chapter 13. But the motion to specify a particular method for nominations or to open or close nominations is about as basic as it gets.

Method of nominations

This example is based on moving to have nominations by committee, but the form is essentially the same for any of the methods. You simply say, "Mr. Chairman, I move that the chair appoint a committee of three to consider and make recommendations on the replacement of Mr. Finkblossom, who has resigned as chairman of the membership committee." Whatever nomination method you propose, be specific.

In case different methods are proposed, make it easy on your group and take the vote on the methods in the order that the methods are listed at the beginning of Chapter 13.

Motions to open or close nominations

A motion to *open nominations*, when made by a member, is usually a motion to reopen nominations after they have been closed.

(The chair usually just announces the opening of nominations at the appointed time when they are in order.)

Members rarely move to *close nominations* because it's never in order to make this motion as long as anyone wants to make a nomination. Also, members rarely move to close nominations because, whenever no further nominations are offered, the chair usually just declares, "Hearing no further nominations, nominations for the office of [name the office] are closed."

REMEMBER

Even if nominations have been closed at a previous session, your presiding officer properly will call for further nominations at the election meeting.

Six key characteristics of motions related to nominations

A motion relating to nominations

>> Can't interrupt a speaker who has the floor or a member making a nomination.

>> Must be seconded.

>> Isn't debatable.

>> Can be amended.

>> Requires a majority vote (except the motion to close nominations, which requires a two-thirds vote).

>> Can be reconsidered except for the motion to close nominations or an affirmative vote to reopen nominations.

I Can't Take It Anymore! Request to Be Excused from a Duty

Sometimes membership requirements involve more than just paying dues. You may be required to complete a service project, serve on a committee, or attend a minimum number of meetings to maintain your membership. If you're an officer or committee chairman, your bylaws probably define some specific responsibilities and duties for you.

When it becomes difficult or impossible for you to fulfill an obligation imposed on you as a member, you can *Request to Be Excused from the Duty*; if the other members agree (and if the bylaws don't provide otherwise), they can grant your request.

Requesting to Be Excused from Duty

If you want to be excused from a duty, you may ask for unanimous consent, or the request may be handled by motion and vote. It's generally in order to make this request anytime a motion is being considered that's connected with the duty you're expected to perform.

If you've accepted an office or other position of responsibility, such as that of a committee chair, and you find yourself unable to properly perform the duties of your office, you can use this motion in the context of a resignation.

Resigning from office

A *resignation* is a form of request to be excused from duty. The rules for resignation from office require you to not abandon your duties until your resignation has been accepted or until the members have had a reasonable opportunity to accept it.

Resigning from membership

Resignation from membership is also a form of this motion, but it can't be used to avoid obligations already incurred. If you've paid your dues, you can't be required to continue membership if you choose not to. But if you owe back dues, resignation doesn't relieve you of the obligation to pay amounts that you owe, and the members aren't under any obligation to accept your resignation until you're current in meeting your obligation.

WARNING

If you aren't in good standing and your resignation isn't accepted, it's possible for additional charges to accrue against you.

Tendering your resignation

Resigning is properly accomplished by delivering a written resignation to the secretary (or whoever may have appointed you to your position). Resignations can also be made orally (or in writing) at a meeting. If you resign during a meeting, and the assembly put you in the position from which you are resigning, the presiding officer can assume the motion to accept the resignation, and the assembly can excuse you from your duty by accepting the resignation either by voting or by unanimous consent.

Six key characteristics of the Request to Be Excused from a Duty

A *Request to Be Excused from a Duty*

» Can interrupt a speaker who has the floor if the request requires immediate attention.

» Must be seconded (but a motion to grant someone else's request doesn't need to be seconded).

» Is debatable.

» Can be amended.

» Requires a majority vote, but is often granted by unanimous consent.

» Can't be reconsidered if it's an affirmative vote and the member who wants to be excused from the duty has been informed of the result of the vote.

Is It in Order To . . . ? Parliamentary Inquiry

You may have the sense that something isn't being done according to Hoyle (er, Robert), but you don't want to tip your hand (or embarrass yourself or your presiding officer) by raising a point of order until you're sure. Or you may want to understand the parliamentary situation better so you can decide whether to make a particular motion. Or you may want to know the effect of the pending motion.

When you want to know the answer to these kinds of questions, or just whether something going on (or being contemplated) is in order, you make a *Parliamentary Inquiry.*

Making a Parliamentary Inquiry

To make a *Parliamentary Inquiry,* just stand up and state, "Madam President, parliamentary inquiry, please."

Madam President then stops and asks you for your question: "The member will please state his question." You may respond, "Madam President, is it in order to amend this amendment?"

Whatever you need to know, just ask. That's the parliamentary inquiry.

REMEMBER

A *Parliamentary Inquiry* elicits an *opinion,* not a ruling, from the chair. Thus, the chair's answer isn't subject to appeal.

However, if the member, having received the answer to his question, then raises a point of order, the decision, or *ruling,* of the chair is subject to appeal.

Six key characteristics of Parliamentary Inquiry

A *Parliamentary Inquiry*

>> Can interrupt a speaker who has the floor if immediate attention is required.

>> Doesn't need to be seconded.

>> Isn't debatable.

>> Can't be amended.

- » Requires that no vote be taken.
- » Can't be reconsidered.

Needing to Know More: Request for Information

You get to your lodge meeting, and the Grand Prancing Reindeer has finished the Oblations to McGillicuddy ritual and moves the admission to the lodge of six new inductees. But you're a practical young buck, and you know that the admission ritual costs the lodge about $100 per person (to pay for the chocolate syrup and marshmallows for the inductees' candy coating prior to their taking the oath, of course). Before you vote, you want to know how much money is left in the treasury.

Whether it's asking for the cash balance or for some other piece of critical information to help you understand something related to the business before your group (but not related to procedure), you can make a *Request for Information* by addressing the chair.

WARNING

For years, Robert's Rules has referred to this request as a "point of information," and for as many years, people haven't figured out that it's intended as a means for a member to *obtain* information, not to *provide* information! Robert's Rules now gives this device a much better label. You may still hear people rise to a "point of information," but no matter how they say it, under the rules, it's still not an opening line for a diatribe in debate. Its only purpose is to afford you a means to get some information that can help you and your fellow members make the best decision, knowing all you need to know.

Using Request for Information

A *Request for Information* needs to be addressed to the chair or through the chair. Following the previous example, you rise and say, "O Great One, I rise to request information."

The Grand Prancing Reindeer replies, "The young buck will state his point." You say, "O Great One, your humble supplicant seeks to know how much fodder remains in the manger before we vote on admitting the fawns into the barn."

In this case, you're really asking the Exalted High Grainkeeper (treasurer), but the correct form for the inquiry is to direct your question to the chair. The chair properly responds here with, "The Exalted High Grainkeeper will report the height of the grain in the bin."

Another example would be when a member needs to ask a question of someone speaking to a motion. If the speaker agrees to yield for a question, you may ask the question, but the time used to ask and answer the question is chargeable to the speaking member's time.

In any event, the goal of this motion is to get information. When you have the information you seek, business can proceed.

Six key characteristics of Request for Information

A *Request for Information*

» Can interrupt a speaker who has the floor if immediate attention is required.

» Doesn't need to be seconded.

» Isn't debatable.

» Can't be amended.

» Requires no vote be taken.

» Can't be reconsidered.

Making Other Requests

The last incidental motions in the list make it possible to handle, in an orderly manner, just about anything that's requested. Robert's Rules covers two specific situations, which I discuss briefly in the sections that follow:

» Request for Permission to Withdraw or Modify a Motion

» Request to Read Papers

Any other requests, such as a request to address the membership when no other business is pending, are generally best handled informally by unanimous consent. But the members always must be allowed the final say on whether to grant any request.

What was I thinking? Request to Withdraw or Modify a Motion

A time may come when you make a motion that turns out to be just a bad idea; you don't really want it to be considered, but the chair has stated the motion, and it now technically belongs to the group. In situations like this, a special request is available only to you, as the maker of the motion. You can request that the motion be withdrawn (or changed).

The Request to Withdraw or Modify a Motion

You take advantage of this privilege simply by getting the recognition of the chair and making your request: "Mr. Chairman, I request permission to withdraw (or modify) my motion."

The chair then needs only to announce that you have made the request and ask for unanimous consent.

If someone objects, the chair can put the question to a vote, or you or any member can move that the assembly grant the request to withdraw the motion. Then the chair puts the question to a vote just like any other motion.

Additional information

If your request to withdraw your motion is granted, the parliamentary situation is no different than if the motion hadn't been made in the first place, so you, or any other member, can make the motion again at the same meeting.

Just let me read this: Request to Read Papers

As a means of protecting a group from any member who wants to read a lengthy item in connection with debate on a motion, it's out of order to "read papers" if anybody objects, unless the permission of the group is obtained.

Robert's Rules recognizes that sometimes a quick excerpt of some factual material may be pertinent and acceptable, so reading papers isn't expressly forbidden. But it must be done with the consent of the members.

The Request to Read Papers

If you think that the members need to have some information that requires you to read something, state that you have something you want to read "if no one objects." Be sure to tell the group what the material is and how long it is.

If someone objects, the chair asks the members, "Ms. Smart would like to read [state the item]. What is the pleasure of the assembly?" If the members agree to listen (by either unanimous consent or majority vote), read your material. If they don't agree, don't try to force it. It's just not worth the price of their goodwill.

Additional information

This rule can't be used to limit the ability to have material that is before the group for adoption read during consideration. Reading from papers generally refers to reading material with the purpose of bolstering a position in debate. If the question is on the adoption of a report or resolution, expect to have the report or resolution read aloud so you know exactly what you're voting on.

Six key characteristics of other requests

A request to withdraw a motion, to read papers, or for any other privilege

» Can interrupt a speaker who has the floor if immediate attention is required.

» Must be seconded (but a motion to grant someone else's request doesn't need to be seconded).

» Isn't debatable.

» Can't be amended.

» Requires a majority vote (but is often done by unanimous consent).

» Can be reconsidered except for an affirmative vote on a request to withdraw a motion.

made decisions

» Removing motions from the hands of committees

» Taking motions off the back burner

Chapter **12**

Looking At Motions That Bring a Question Again Before the Assembly

No matter what your group's final vote is on a motion, sometimes you have second thoughts. In some cases, you want to revisit a decision made during a current meeting. Other times, you want (or need) to take a second look at something decided several months ago.

But although your group needs to be able to change or reverse its decisions, you don't want to make the process too easy. After all, everyone would get very frustrated if the votes of one or two members kept your group forever voting and revoting, going back and forth so that nothing ever really got settled.

Luckily, Robert's Rules has a set of motions designed to let you revisit decisions without letting those revisits get out of hand. Throughout this chapter, I discuss the *Motions That Bring a Question Again Before the Assembly* (that's a mouthful!) and explore how to use them to reexamine decisions in an efficient and orderly way.

Been There, Done That! Preventing Revoting on Motions

Among all the rules in Robert's Rules, few are more important than rules that prevent somebody from incessantly requiring your group to vote over and over on essentially the same motion.

Imagine how little you'd ever get done if, right after you spent an hour discussing your organization's budget and voted to adopt it, a member (who tried to second-guess the finance committee on every third line item) made a motion that the budget be opened back up for discussion and required you to take your time going over every second line item this time around.

Or suppose you've just voted to refer a motion to reroof the clubhouse to committee to get bids and report recommendations back in two months. After all is settled, a member remembers that their cousin is a roofer, and the member wants to make a motion to just let their cousin go ahead and fix the roof next weekend (because he needs the work and is available). If members could get away with making motions that require you to rehash a decision you just made, you'd never get anything done.

These examples illustrate the need for a couple of basic principles of parliamentary law aimed to keep the minority from controlling matters by wearing down the majority:

>> After you've disposed of a motion (Motion A), it's not in order to entertain another motion (Motion B) that pro-

poses essentially the same question as the one already decided (Motion A) unless you're using one of the procedures I discuss in this chapter.

>> Changing something that the assembly has already decided shouldn't be as easy as making the decision in the first place. Depending on the situation, Robert's Rules places restrictions on who can ask that a decision be revoted on in the same meeting, and the parliamentary authority requires a higher vote, a notice, or maybe both a higher vote *and* a notice for motions revisited in later meetings.

Whatever the situation, most of the time when you decide something, you've done all the talking you need to do and you're ready to move on. But that's not always the case.

Later in a meeting, new information may come up that affects a decision your group has already made. Or something may change over time, and old procedures just no longer work.

Robert's Rules gives you a way to revisit the questions and change your collective mind. General Robert was an engineer, and he wisely provided a means for your group to dig itself out of a hole without getting too muddy in the process. Whatever the situation, you can find the right tool in the *Motions That Bring a Question Again Before the Assembly.* These motions are as follows:

>> *Reconsider*

>> *Rescind or Amend Something Previously Adopted*

>> *Discharge a Committee*

>> *Take from the Table*

Table 12-1 provides a short rundown of situations in which you use these motions.

I discuss each of these motions in detail in the following sections of this chapter.

TABLE 12-1 **When to Use the Motions That Bring a Question Again Before the Assembly**

If You Want To . . .	Then Use . . .
Revote on something you voted on in this meeting	Reconsider
Repeal (or strike out) a motion that has been adopted	Rescind Something Previously Adopted
Make a change to (or amend) a motion that has been adopted	Amend Something Previously Adopted
Take a referred motion out of the hands of a committee	Discharge a Committee
Resume considering a motion you laid on the table	Take from the Table

Having Second Thoughts: Reconsidering

You've probably been in a meeting in which the group voted and disposed of a motion, but even though you voted the way of the majority, that little voice inside started nagging at you. Maybe the group made the decision without enough information, or perhaps it just didn't think it out. The group may have made the decision because it was just in too much of a hurry. Whatever the reason, you realize that it's a good idea for the group to take a second look at that motion.

If you voted on the prevailing side in a case like this, you can ask the group to revisit the same motion in the same meeting by making the motion to *Reconsider.* If the majority agrees to discuss the original motion some more, it adopts the motion to reconsider. At the appropriate time, the chair opens the floor for debate on the original motion as if the group had never voted on the question.

Understanding "Reconsider" as a parliamentary term

All the motions in the class of motions that bring a question again before the assembly assist your group in revisiting previously considered motions. For this reason, you may find that members talk about reconsidering a motion when they really want to rescind or amend something previously adopted. Or they may just want to renew a motion that failed in an earlier meeting (or that didn't get a second in the current meeting). Using the word *reconsider* in a generic sense in a parliamentary situation can cause problems.

REMEMBER

The motion to *Reconsider* is a distinct parliamentary motion! When you use the word *reconsider* in a parliamentary situation, it refers only to this specific motion.

The motion to *Reconsider* poses the question, "Shall we give further consideration to a motion already voted on?" The motion is subject to some unique limitations:

>> It must be made on the same day as the meeting in which the motion to be reconsidered was decided (or on the next day business is conducted, if the session is more than one day).

>> It must be made by a person who voted on the *prevailing* side of the motion to be reconsidered.

REMEMBER

The motion to *Reconsider* is *not* the same as the motion to be reconsidered. The former is the parliamentary motion that's the subject of this section. The latter is the motion that's the object of the motion to reconsider.

Using the motion to Reconsider

Suppose your business networking group voted earlier in your meeting to bestow its coveted Silver Tongue Award on Farley Motormouth, the local radio announcer known as the Voice of the Hometown Niners, your city's minor-league baseball team. What an honor! You were among the rather large majority who voted in favor of giving the award to Motormouth.

Then, during a short recess in the meeting, Charlie Frumpdiddle hands you the evening paper. There on the front page is a photo of ol' Farley being hauled out of the baseball stadium in handcuffs. He's accused of saying something nice about the Swamp City Puddle Jumpers, the archrival of the Hometown Niners.

You like Farley, and he may be a fine guy, but if he says something nice about those no-good Puddle Jumpers from across the county line, he's not gonna get that award if you have anything to say about it.

When the meeting reconvenes after the recess and the president starts to recognize the next speaker on whatever business is pending, you take the first opportunity available to stand up and get recognized by the chair. You say, "Mr. President, I voted with the prevailing side for the motion to give the Silver Tongue Award to Farley Motormouth, and I move to reconsider the vote taken earlier this evening." Of course, your friend Charlie Frumpdiddle hardly misses a beat when he calls out, "Second!"

Notice that you voted on the prevailing side. In this case, if you had voted against the motion, you wouldn't be allowed to make a motion to *Reconsider*. That rule keeps the losers from just using the motion in a dilatory manner to wear down the majority.

Knowing the rules, the chair says, "The motion to reconsider the vote awarding Farley Motormouth the Silver Tongue Award has been made and seconded. Discussion on the motion to *Reconsider* isn't in order at this time, but the motion to *Reconsider* can be called up when no other business is pending." So the chair doesn't ask the members to vote on whether to reconsider just yet. Instead, they proceed with the pending business. Later, when nothing else is pending, you or someone else can *call up* the motion to *Reconsider*.

Anytime a motion to *Reconsider* is (properly) made, all action authorized by the motion being considered is suspended until the motion being reconsidered is finally decided.

Calling up the motion to *Reconsider* (that is, debating and voting on whether to reconsider in the first place) has to take place in the current session or the next session, unless the next session isn't going to occur within a quarterly time interval. In that case, it has to be completed by the end of the current session.

Otherwise the motion to be reconsidered goes into full effect as adopted.

Waiting for the right time to reconsider

Because of the nature of the motion to *Reconsider,* it's not always appropriate to discuss or vote on it at the time it's made. But it *is* important for the members to know that someone has had second thoughts even though the time may not be right for a discussion. As a result, you can make the motion anytime within the time limits for making the motion (as I discuss in the section, "Understanding 'Reconsider' as a parliamentary term," earlier in this chapter), but you can't discuss or act on the motion to *Reconsider* until no immediately pending motion is on the floor. That's because if the motion to *Reconsider* is adopted, the motion being reconsidered becomes the immediately pending motion.

REMEMBER

When the motion to *Reconsider* is applied to subsidiary, privileged, and incidental motions while a main motion is pending, the motion to *Reconsider* becomes the immediately pending question if no motions are pending that would take precedence over the motion to be reconsidered. If motions are pending that would take precedence over the motion to be reconsidered, the motion to *Reconsider* becomes the immediately pending question when the motion to be reconsidered would be in order.

Calling up the motion to Reconsider

Your motion to *Reconsider* is *called up* by any member at any appropriate time (and doesn't need to be seconded) by saying, "Mr. Chairman, I call up the motion to reconsider the vote on bestowing the Silver Tongue Award on Farley Motormouth."

TECHNICAL STUFF

Even though anyone can call up your motion to *Reconsider,* you're entitled to have the reconsideration called up at whatever time you think best, as long as no one else has the floor or another question is pending and you're not acting in bad faith or just trying to delay other business unreasonably. Robert's Rules gives you that privilege.

Whenever the motion to *Reconsider* is called up, however, that's when you have the chance to speak about Farley's indiscretion and why you made the motion to reconsider. But you need to be prepared for the possibility that other members may want to leave the matter as it is and, therefore, may argue against reconsideration.

Even so, the point to recognize here is that the purpose of the motion to *Reconsider* is to decide whether to reopen the question on giving the Silver Tongue Award to Farley. You're discussing whether to open the question, but discussion can also go into the merits of giving the award to Farley.

Knowing when not to use "Reconsider"

As you see in this section, a motion to reconsider a vote is a motion limited in both the time it can be made and the person who can make it. But even when the motion to *Reconsider* isn't in order, there's no reason you can't revisit a motion, adopted or not, at your next (or any future) meeting.

Renewing a motion

Robert's Rules refers to this procedure as "renewing" a motion. According to the General, any member can offer again a motion that failed in an earlier session. In fact, if a motion is made at any meeting and doesn't get a second, it can even be renewed at that very same meeting.

Rescinding or amending something previously adopted

This procedure has its own section in this chapter ("Rescinding or Amending Something Previously Adopted"), but I mention it here because it's the way you deal with undoing or changing something you've already done (usually at a previous meeting).

Avoiding reconsideration when it's not in order

The motion to *Reconsider* is out of order when the motion to which it's applied can be *renewed* or when the desired result can be achieved with some other, less complicated parliamentary motion.

It's also out of order if it's applied to a negative vote on some motion that would at the time be out of order because it conflicts with something already adopted, or would conflict with any other motion that is pending or temporarily disposed of and still under the assembly's control.

Of course, if a motion has been adopted and any part of the motion's provisions has been executed, it's too late to reconsider the vote.

REMEMBER

The point of all these rules about reconsidering (and renewing and rescinding and amending something previously adopted) is that the group has an orderly way available to take a second look at almost anything, as long as you use the right procedure.

Most of the time, your group can save a lot of time if members use the right motion instead of thinking of every second look at something as being a "reconsideration."

TO RECONSIDER OR NOT TO RECONSIDER . . .

You plaintively exclaim, "We want(ed) to reconsider something voted on at our last meeting, but were ruled out of order because the person who moved to reconsider hadn't voted on the winning side!"

"But of course!" I think, "You want to reconsider something! So naturally you invoke the motion to *Reconsider*. Makes perfect sense. No matter that the motion *to Reconsider* isn't the right tool.

(continued)

(continued)

Misunderstandings about the motion *to Reconsider* spring from confusing the parliamentary motion "to Reconsider" with the plain-English verb "to reconsider."

Your experience was Horrible (with a capital H). Bringing the question again before the assembly failed because nobody knew the rules or the options.

With apologies to the meter muse, here's a ditty explaining your options under Robert's Rules:

When you've decided a problem-bound measure

And now to make changes would give you great pleasure,

To reconsider this now-past decision,

Remember these options (avoiding derision).

If the motion was passed in a rush just today,

The *motion to Reconsider* might be the best way

To get to the question again the same day

Before you adjourn, but if not, what the hey?

Next meeting your options exist just the same,

Except *Reconsider* is not the right game;

You bring back a motion and vote once again,

By using the motions *Rescind* or *Amend*.

If your problem-bound measure originally failed,

Then your options are different but can be availed.

Reconsider is still not the right thing to do.

Instead, start all over! The term is *Renew!*

Using a special form of Reconsider: Reconsider and enter on the minutes

Suppose a motion is made in a meeting in which the group in attendance isn't at all representative of the usual attendance. Maybe you're near the end of the meeting, and several members have left. You still have a quorum, but the usual minority is now in the majority. Your favorite malcontent moves to direct the treasurer to transfer the group's funds to their investment brokerage company. You, along with the few good members who know better, are appalled, but you don't have the votes to stop the motion. What do you do?

By using the motion to *Reconsider and Enter on the Minutes*, you can prevent the motion (if it's adopted) from being put into effect until the more representative membership is again present to make a final decision.

As with the basic motion to *Reconsider*, you need to have voted on the prevailing side to make the motion to *Reconsider and Enter on the Minutes*, so you may have to hold your nose and cast your vote in favor of the motion. And you still need a second. But after you make this motion, the action to transfer the money is on hold, and the other members have a chance to be informed of the issue so they can arrange to attend the next meeting. At that meeting, you can call up the motion to reconsider and hopefully undo the little shenanigan.

In a few departures from the usual rules for *Reconsider*, the motion to *Reconsider and Enter on the Minutes*

>> Can be moved only on the same day on which the motion to be reconsidered was voted upon.

>> Outranks the regular motion to *Reconsider*.

>> Can be applied only to main motions finally disposed of, such as main motions that were adopted, or that failed, or that were postponed indefinitely (see Chapter 9).

>> Can't be applied to a motion if the object of the motion would be harmed by the delay of a day (for example, a motion to hire a limousine to pick up the guest speaker at the airport tomorrow morning).

>> Can't be moved at the last meeting of a session if the next business meeting won't be held within a *quarterly time interval* (see the Appendix).

>> Can't be called up on the day the motion's made, unless it's made on the last day of a session and called up at a later meeting on that same day.

More considerations on the motion to Reconsider

You need to know a few more details to properly use the motion to *Reconsider:*

>> **Applicability to motions originally adopted by unanimous consent:** If the motion you want to reconsider was adopted by unanimous consent, anybody who was present when it was adopted can move to reconsider it because of a presumption that all the members who were present were on the prevailing side.

>> **Suspension of action authorized by a motion to be reconsidered:** As long as a motion to *Reconsider* is made, even if it hasn't been called up and acted on, it suspends any authority to carry out the action ordered by the motion to be reconsidered. But it must be called up within certain time limits or the suspending effect ends. I discuss those limits in the section "Using the motion to Reconsider," earlier in this chapter.

>> **Rules for debate on a motion being reconsidered:** Debate on a motion being reconsidered is subject to the following rules:

● If reconsideration of a motion is taken up on the same day, members who used all their debate time when the original motion was considered can't debate without permission of the group. (But because they can debate twice on the motion to Reconsider, they'll probably have had their say anyway!)

- If reconsideration of a motion is taken up on the next day, a member's right to debate isn't affected by their participation in previous debate.

>> **Using the motion to *Reconsider* in committees:** A motion to *Reconsider,* when used in a committee

- Isn't subject to the usual time limitations. It can be made at any time, even several days or weeks later. A motion also can be reconsidered as often as the committee chooses.

- Can be moved by any committee member who didn't vote on the losing side.

- Requires a two-thirds vote to adopt unless all the members who voted on the prevailing side are present or were notified that the motion to *Reconsider* would be made.

Identifying six key characteristics of the motion to Reconsider

Here are six important characteristics of the motion to *Reconsider.* The motion

>> Can interrupt a speaker who has the floor before they begin to speak, but calling it up can't interrupt a speaker who has the floor.

>> Must be seconded.

>> Is debatable if the motion to be reconsidered is debatable.

>> Can't be amended.

>> Requires a majority vote.

>> Can't be reconsidered.

Rescinding or Amending Something Previously Adopted

Nothing is forever, and that saying is especially true in the world of clubs and organizations. Last year's good idea can turn into this year's problem. But thanks to General Robert's wisdom and foresight, you always have a way out!

As I discuss in the following section, by using the motion to *Rescind* or to *Amend Something Previously Adopted*, you can undo or change any decision your group made in the past:

>> The motion to *Rescind* (or repeal or annul) is used to cancel a motion altogether.

>> The motion to *Amend Something Previously Adopted* is used to make a change to a motion either by making a simple change or two or by substituting something else in its place.

Using Rescind or Amend Something Previously Adopted

Motions to *Rescind* or to *Amend Something Previously Adopted* are more common than you may think. More often than not, they're used to make policy changes. After all, policy is adopted by motion and vote, so if you want to change the policy or vacate it, you need to do so by motion and vote. When using the motions to *Rescind* or *Amend*, keep these points in mind, which I discuss in greater detail in the following sections:

>> The vote required, which is determined by whether there has been previous notice of the motion

>> Whether any proposed amendments are within the scope of your notice

Vote requirements

Three possible variations of vote requirements allow you to rescind or amend something previously adopted:

>> **Two-thirds vote without previous notice:** Suppose your organization adopts a budget proposed by the finance committee, which provided for an increase in the salary of your executive director. Then later, when new business is being considered, Ernest Pennypincher proposes to roll back all spending to last year's budget amounts. Because this motion would have the effect of rescinding the budget just adopted, it requires a two-thirds vote.

>> **Majority vote with previous notice:** But what if, instead of making the motion during this meeting, Ernie just gives notice that he'll make the motion at the next meeting? Well, when the motion comes up at that later meeting, it can be adopted by a majority vote.

The switch from a two-thirds to a majority vote may make a big difference because it could be easier to get a majority vote than to get a two-thirds vote. The equalizer is the requirement for notice. Because both sides of an issue have the chance to rally their troops and campaign for the result they want, the factor of previous notice reduces the requirement for a two-thirds vote.

>> **Majority of the entire membership:** In a situation in which there's no notice, a motion to *Rescind* or to *Amend Something Previously Adopted* can be adopted if it receives the affirmative vote of a majority of the entire membership.

You may be thinking that receiving this type of vote is an impossible requirement anyway, so what good is this last option? After all, you've probably never even had a majority of the entire membership attend a single meeting at the same time anyway. But consider the option's application in a small board. Suppose that you have a board of 15 members, and 13 are present at your meeting. A two-thirds vote requires 9 affirmative votes if all 13 cast a vote, but a majority of the entire membership (being 15) is only 8. So sometimes it's easier to achieve a majority of the entire membership than it is to get a two-thirds vote.

TECHNICAL STUFF

In a committee, you can rescind or amend a committee decision by a majority vote if all the members who voted in favor of the motion to be rescinded or amended are present or received adequate notice. Otherwise, the two-thirds vote requirement applies to the vote to rescind or amend committee action.

Scope of notice

Suppose that your group decides to raise the amount of annual dues (which, in this example, isn't fixed in your bylaws, but rather is decided from time to time by the membership). To keep from having to meet a two-thirds vote requirement, you gave previous notice at the last meeting (or in the call to the meeting) that this meeting would see a motion to raise the dues to $50 per year (up from $35).

When you gave the notice to make a motion to raise dues to $50, your notice covered any increase you may actually wind up with, up to $50. Any number over $35 and up to $50 is said to be within the *scope of the notice* and can be adopted by a *majority vote* because notice was given to raise dues to $50. But raising the dues any higher than $50 (or lowering them below $35) doesn't qualify as being within the scope of notice. So you need a two-thirds vote to change the dues to some amount less than $35 or greater than $50.

WARNING

Some rules carry stricter requirements for amending or rescinding. According to Robert's Rules, amending bylaws or special rules of order requires previous notice *and* a two-thirds vote. This requirement is based on the premise that rules like bylaws and special rules of order must, by definition, be very stable from session to session. Members are entitled to notice of any proposed change and are entitled to have rules that can't be changed in the face of opposition from a minority greater than one-third.

Knowing what motions you can't rescind or amend

Some motions can't be amended or rescinded, such as:

>> **Motions subject to the motion to *Reconsider:*** Calling to rescind or amend is unnecessary if you can simply call up the motion to *Reconsider,* which has been previously moved.

>> **Motions that have already been carried out and that cannot be undone:** If you voted to repaint the church, it's too late to rescind the motion after the church has been repainted.

>> **Motions that have been adopted to accept resignations or actions electing or expelling a person from membership or office** (if the member is present or has been notified): After a resignation has been accepted or a membership terminated by expulsion, the resigning or expelled person can be reinstated only by following the procedures for membership admission or election to office. Rescinding an election requires either a provision in the bylaws or specific procedures for removal from office, which I cover in Chapter 18.

Identifying the six key characteristics of this motion

Here are the six characteristics for a motion to *Rescind* or to *Amend Something Previously Adopted*. The motion

>> Can't interrupt a speaker who has the floor.

>> Must be seconded.

>> Is debatable.

>> Can be amended. If the proposed amendment is to change the motion to *rescind* to one of *amend something previously adopted* (or vice versa), you must propose the change by offering a primary amendment to substitute the preferred form for the other.

>> Requires a two-thirds vote without notice, a majority vote with notice, or a majority of the entire membership with no notice.

>> Can be reconsidered if it fails.

Discharging a Committee

After your group refers a matter to a committee, the matter is no longer in the hands of the group, but rather is under the committee's control. According to Robert's Rules, it's not in order for your group to act on business referred to the committee that's currently in the committee's hands.

But sometimes the group needs to take charge again. The motion to *Discharge a Committee* is the way to bring the motion back to the assembly for further action. These sections examine the lowdown on what it means to Discharge a Committee.

Using the motion to Discharge a Committee

The motion to *Discharge a Committee* is used in two general situations:

>> When the committee to which a motion has been referred has failed to report as instructed or in a timely manner

>> When the matter referred to the committee needs immediate action by the entire group

In the first case, the committee can be discharged with a majority vote without notice, Otherwise, the motion to *Discharge a Committee* requires a two-thirds vote without notice, a vote of a majority of the entire membership, or a majority vote with previous notice. (The motion to *Discharge a Committee* is similar to the motion to *Rescind* or to *Amend Something Previously Adopted*. See the section "Rescinding or Amending Something Previously Adopted," earlier in this chapter.)

TIP

When it's possible to reconsider a vote referring a matter to a committee, it's more efficient to use reconsideration and simply reverse the motion to *Commit* because reversal can be achieved by majority vote. (For more information on the motion to reconsider, flip to the section "Having Second Thoughts: Reconsidering," earlier in this chapter.)

Depending on whether you're dealing with a special committee or a standing committee (see Chapter 16), you make the motion to *Discharge a Committee* by using the following forms:

>> **Special committee:** "Madam Chairman, I move that the special committee to plan a spring picnic be discharged."

>> **Standing committee:** "Madam Chairman, I move that the meeting arrangements committee be discharged from further consideration of the proposed conference in July."

Adopting a motion to discharge a committee, when the motion referred by adoption of the subsidiary motion to commit, immediately places the referred motion on the floor by saying, for example, "There being two-thirds in the affirmative, the committee is discharged. The question is on the motion to have a club picnic this spring. Is there discussion?"

After a special committee makes its final report (discharge is automatic, in this case — no motion is required) or is discharged by motion by your group, the committee ceases to exist. The matter it was handling, provided that it was a motion referred to the committee by means of a subsidiary motion to *Commit*, is then immediately in the hands of your group, unless the motion to *Discharge the Committee* established a particular time to take up the committee's report and recommendations.

Identifying six key characteristics of the motion to Discharge a Committee

A motion to *Discharge a Committee*

>> Can't interrupt a speaker who has the floor.

>> Must be seconded.

>> Is debatable.

>> Can be amended with respect to the time when the assembly will consider the business that was in the hands of the committee, or by substituting an instruction to the committee to report instead of being discharged.

>> Requires a two-thirds vote without notice, a majority vote with notice, or a majority of the entire membership with no notice.

A committee can be discharged by a majority vote without notice if the committee has failed to report by the time required in its instructions, or whenever the assembly is considering its partial report.

>> Can be reconsidered if it fails.

Examining What's Left on the Table — Taking from the Table

In Chapter 9, I discuss the motion to *Lay on the Table,* the highest-ranking subsidiary motion. This motion is used to temporarily set aside a pending main motion, permitting something else to be addressed or done.

In most cases, the "something else" carries a sense of urgency, such as the need to allow your guest speaker to address your group at a particular time without compromising his schedule. However, whatever the reason for placing something on the table, after the more urgent matter has been attended to, it's in order to take the motion from the table and resume consideration of it at the point where you left off. But taking the motion from the table requires a motion and a second; otherwise, the chair may properly advance to the next item of business.

If no motion to *Take from the Table* is made, or if the chair doesn't assume the motion and obtain unanimous consent to resume where you left off, any member can move to *Take from the Table* any item that lies on the table. The motion to *Take from the Table* remains in order at your group's next regular business session until that session adjourns (but still only when no other question is pending), provided that your next regular business session takes place within a quarterly time interval. If your next regular business session takes place outside of that time limit, the motion to take from the table must be made and seconded before your current session adjourns.

The following sections take a closer look at this motion and explain how this motion can be used.

Using the motion to Take from the Table

Suppose you're in a meeting of your professional association, which is considering a resolution to take a position in support of increasing statutory continuing education requirements being considered by your state legislature. Your group's debate has been heated and has gone on longer than you anticipated, and your guest speaker is running on a tight schedule. You aren't finished with the debate on the motion, but you need to let your speaker make their presentation. So you adopt the motion to *Lay on the Table* the question on the resolution.

Making the motion

The speaker concludes their presentation, and the president announces the next item of business on the agenda. If you're ready to get back to work on that continuing education resolution, rise and say, "Mr. Chairman, I rise to move to take from the table the resolution on continuing professional education."

It is in order, and remains in order, to move to *Take from the Table* as long as you haven't yet moved on to a new class of business (such as going from "Reports of Officers, Boards, and Standing Committees" to "Reports of Special Committees"). But it is in order to move to *Take from the Table* during "Unfinished Business," "General Orders," or "New Business"). But if you wait too long and have moved on from the class of business that gave rise to the motion, and you're not engaged in one of the three classes of business indicated above, you can take the resolution from the table only at the appropriate time in the next business meeting, or by moving to *Suspend the Rules and Take from the Table* (see Chapter 11 for information on this incidental motion) to take something out of its proper order.

Obtaining recognition

Because this motion to *Take from the Table* enables the assembly to resume consideration of an undecided question, and because time limits on its use are in place, whoever rises to offer the motion is entitled to preference in recognition by the chair.

You can claim preference for recognition to make the motion to *Take from the Table.* You can seek recognition at any time until the chair states the question on another item of business.

TECHNICAL STUFF

The presiding officer needs to give you preference in recognition for the purpose of making this motion because it's generally desirable to finish dealing with a motion that hasn't been disposed of before going on to something else. But after consideration of another motion has begun (as stated by the chair), you must wait for the next lull in the proceedings before you can move to *Take from the Table*.

REMEMBER

Even though a motion that's laid on the table dies, if it's not taken from the table by the close of the next regular business session, it can be brought up again by just renewing the motion. Therefore, if you can't get back to a motion that lies on the table via the motion to take from the table, it's not usually a big deal except when time is critical.

Understanding when you can't take from the table

It's generally in order to move to take a motion from the table just about any time motions in the same class are in order, or when Unfinished Business, General Orders, or New Business is in order. But if a series of motions needs to be handled, the motion to *Take from the Table* can't be made. This situation may occur in these cases:

>> When you've voted to suspend the rules to allow the introduction of another main motion

>> When a motion has just been laid on the table expressly to allow consideration of another motion

>> When your group has rescinded a previous motion to allow a conflicting motion to be made and considered

>> When a main motion has been voted down because a member said that if it was voted down, he'd offer a particular motion to handle an issue in a better or more acceptable way

Knowing what's before the assembly when a motion is taken from the table

When you adopt the motion to take from the table, you resume consideration of the motion taken from the table in the same posture as it was when it was laid on the table. If an amendment was pending when the motion was laid on the table, you're back to considering the amendment. If a motion to commit was before the group, then it's before the group when the motion is taken from the table. If multiple subsidiary motions were in play when the motion was laid on the table, all those subsidiary motions remain with the motion.

TIP

Your secretary has their work cut out when a motion is laid on the table with adhering motions. Skill in the art of minute-taking is a big plus when motions are laid on the table (or postponed to a certain time) with one or more subsidiary motions hanging on for dear life. The assembly, along with the presiding officer, depends on the secretary to know exactly where things stand when consideration of the motion resumes.

Identifying the six key features of the motion to Take from the Table

A motion to *Take from the Table*

>> Can't interrupt a speaker who has the floor.

>> Must be seconded.

>> Isn't debatable.

>> Can't be amended.

>> Requires a majority vote.

>> Can't be reconsidered.

3

Getting Involved in Leadership

Follow nomination procedures properly.

Choose and implement the best election procedures for your group.

Understand the roles of officers and directors.

Form and participate in committees.

Take minutes and file accurate reports.

Decide how and when to discipline members.

Discover how to form new organizations.

Organize a convention of delegates.

Chapter **13**

Who's Going to Do the Work? Following Nomination Procedures

Getting the right leaders for your organization isn't always easy. One of the biggest problems in this area is that the person who's great at getting elected isn't necessarily the best person for the job.

Your membership has to live with its mistakes, even if that means operating with poor leaders. The best way to avoid this type of mistake, however, is to have a system for selecting leadership that puts the right people at the front of the line.

In Robert's Rules, *nominations* are the tools for setting up that system. The types of nominations in Robert's Rules are

>> Nominations by the chair

>> Nominations from the floor

>> Nominations by a committee

>> Nominations by ballot

>> Nominations by mail

>> Nominations by petition

I go over nominations in detail throughout this chapter, and I help you determine which types to use in certain meeting situations.

TECHNICAL STUFF

If you're conducting an election by ballot or roll-call vote, nominations are technically unnecessary because any voter can vote for any person eligible to serve. The real benefit of providing some kind of nominations procedure in those kinds of election is that it enhances the likelihood that voters will cast a vote for one of the nominees. Just think how long it would take to pick the president if no nominations were taken and every member simply voted for the person sitting in the next chair!

I list the six nomination methods in the order Robert's Rules provides for them to be voted on if all six were proposed in a motion to prescribe a method for nominations. Even though I've never run into such a situation, I want to cover that arcane point of order just in case you're on a big-money TV quiz show and the question comes up.

Nominations by the Chair

This method is used whenever the membership wants to rely on the presiding officer to recommend candidates but also wants to reserve for itself (or its designee, such as the board of directors) the approval of the nominee. This method is applicable when

>> Appointing members to committees, if specified in the motion creating the committee, or if prescribed in the bylaws

>> Electing a presiding officer in a mass meeting

A member who wants to use this type of nomination method includes it in the motion to establish the committee — for example, "I move that the chair nominate a committee of five members, whose appointment shall be subject to the approval of the membership, to study and recommend on the contract."

An example of a bylaw prescribing the method may read, "The president shall appoint the members of all the standing committees (except the nominating committee), subject to the approval of the board of directors."

Nominations from the Floor

Sometimes called *open nominations*, this method is probably the most familiar. It's used in the vast majority of situations when members elect their officers at a meeting. Even if a nominating committee is in place, under Robert's Rules, nominations from the floor are in order at some point before the election is pending.

The following sections explain the process of nominations from the floor from start to finish — opening nominations, closing nominations, and everything in between.

Opening the floor for nominations

Your group's rules and customs determine the time at which floor nominations are accepted. Sometimes nominations aren't taken until the election is pending; sometimes they're taken at other times, such as at a meeting before the election meeting.

Unless the bylaws contain a specific rule about nominations, the privilege to deal with floor nomination procedures is reserved for the assembly. The assembly may tailor its nomination procedures to any particular situation it encounters by using the procedures for handling incidental *motions related to nominations*, which I cover in Chapter 11. The assembly's privilege to determine its nomination procedure is important, and you need to keep that privilege in mind when a question comes up about whether nominations can or should be made.

Depending on your organization's bylaws, special rules of order, and the rules you decide on during any pending election, nominations from the floor may be taken either for each office just before the election for that office or for all offices before any elections take place. In either case, the default order for taking nominations is the order in which your bylaws list the offices.

To open nominations from the floor, the chair declares, "Nominations are now in order for the office of Top Banana. Are there nominations for Top Banana?"

Handling nominations from the floor

After each nomination, the chair repeats the name as having been nominated. For example, he may say, "Cletus Potzbius has been nominated. Are there further nominations?"

The process of making floor nominations is subject to the following rules:

> » **Recognition by the chair isn't required to make a nomination.** A member may call out a nomination while remaining seated. However, in larger organizations, calling nominations from your seat is usually impractical. In such cases, members may adopt a more formal nomination process either by rule or by the adoption of an incidental motion for that particular meeting or election.

> » **Nominations don't have to be seconded.** However, it's not out of order for members to second a nomination to signal their endorsements.

>> **A member shouldn't offer more than one nomination to a position if there are several seats for the same office — such as for nominees to a board or a committee — until all other members have had the opportunity to make nominations.** However, if a member does make more nominations before others have had their chance, those additional nominations aren't out of order unless someone objects to that member's actions. Additionally, it isn't in order under any circumstances for a member to nominate more persons than there are seats available. For example, if an election is to fill three seats on a board, a member can't nominate four people.

>> **If the bylaws don't prohibit it, a person can be nominated for more than one office and can even serve in more than one office, if elected.** However, if the bylaws do prohibit it, then either the nominee or the electors must choose one office among multiple nominations. I discuss the options for handling this situation in Chapter 14, where I cover the election process.

>> **Nominations are taken for successive offices in the order the bylaws list them.** If the bylaws say, for example, that the officers are a "President, Vice-President, Secretary, and Treasurer," nominations are taken in that order.

Debating nominations

Nominating speeches are almost a rite of passage in some organizations. Especially the big ones that hold razzle-dazzle conventions where the election of the Great- and Grand-Factotums are such a big deal that nobody would even go to the convention if it weren't for the parties that prospective candidates throw. But before Thaddeus Blowhard can give a nominating speech bellowing the qualifications of his candidate, Fran Fabulous, he must obtain recognition by the presiding officer while nominations are in order. After he's recognized, he may nominate Fran and wax eloquent on all the good reasons to elect her, or, if Fran has already been nominated, she can just launch into a speech extolling the virtues of the candidate. Same goes for a seconding speech.

But with the privilege of making nominating and seconding speeches comes the responsibility of adhering to the usual rules of decorum in debate, which I discuss in Chapter 7. When debating the suitability of a candidate, speeches get into the nitty-gritty details about personality. So, it's extra important to always be on the moral high ground and refrain from anything that comes close to speaking ill of an opposing candidate. In other words, instead of launching into an indictment of Freddie Feckless, a member recognized to speak during nominations should confine their remarks to the praise of another candidate.

TIP

It's not unusual for an organization that enjoys the ceremony of nominating speeches and seconding speeches to have rules in place to limit those speeches in some way as to time or number. Consider the common practice of having a rule to allow for one nominating speech and one seconding speech for each candidate for an office and to put a time limit on each. Placing limits on nominating speeches is governed by the same rules for limiting debate on any motion. It takes a two-thirds vote to limit or change the limits of debate (see Chapter 9), even when what's being "debated" is nominations.

Closing nominations

According to Robert's Rules, motions to close nominations are usually unnecessary because the nomination process simply continues until no one wants to make further nominations. When the nominations stop, the chair just declares nominations closed.

But before making such a declaration, the chair is obligated to be sure no more nominations are forthcoming. This obligation may be the source of another misunderstanding that many people have about closing nominations: All too often, presiding officers think they must call for nominations three times before declaring nominations closed. To set the record straight, *no such rule exists,* but the practice isn't completely unreasonable because it establishes a good way to make sure that no further nominations are forthcoming.

Still, some presiding officers think there's some magic to uttering the call three times, and in their partisan haste to shut down nominations for political reasons, they babble out the phrase three times and declare nominations closed all in one breath. When you hear that happening, you can be sure that the presiding officer either doesn't know the rules or is using the position to thwart the nomination process.

WARNING

From a practical standpoint, attempting to declare nominations closed if members want to continue making nominations serves no purpose. After all, nominations don't elect! So why would any self-respecting presiding officer give up the appearance of impartiality by trying to suppress nominations? Perhaps the chair just wants to make points with a large faction. But by pushing to close nominations, the chair reveals that an inability to discharge the office's duties with impartiality, which is a serious breach of duty.

REMEMBER

According to Robert's Rules, offering a motion to close nominations is perfectly permissible if an election is being delayed because nominations are being offered to honor people who are no more likely to be elected than they are to win the catch-the-greased-pig contest at the county fair.

REMEMBER

According to Robert's Rules, a motion to close nominations is out of order *as long as any member is attempting to make a nomination.*

Whether your organization goes on to an election for each office after nominations have closed for that office or takes nominations for all offices before any election begins is a matter of custom or rule of the organization. If neither custom nor rule exists covering your process, you decide how to proceed through nominations and elections by adopting a motion at the election meeting. Flip to Chapter 11 where I discuss motions relating to nominations.

HEY, DON'T SLAM THE DOOR ON NOMINATIONS!

One of the serious misunderstandings I often encounter about closing nominations is the notion that they can be closed in such a manner as to prevent any further opportunity for making additional nominations.

More often than I like to hear about, loyal supporters of a particular candidate attempt to close nominations as a strategy to keep opposition candidates off a ballot.

Even if they're successful at slamming the door on other nominees (by commanding a two-thirds vote to close and overruling the chair that the motion is out of order), these supporters can't keep a write-in vote from being entered on a ballot, so they don't accomplish much but to create acrimony. (Chapter 14 contains more information about write-in votes.)

In any event, closing nominations is out of order when anyone wants to nominate. And even when properly closed (by a two-thirds vote after no one wants to make additional nominations), a majority vote is all it takes to reopen nominations.

Suppressing nominations not only is out of order as long as anyone wants to add to the list, but it also wastes a lot of time and is a futile strategy.

Nominations by a Committee

In even the smallest local organization, the use of a nominating committee to assemble a list of willing and qualified candidates for office can greatly benefit members when the time comes to select leaders.

If the committee does its job well, the membership can enjoy some basic assurance that the candidates nominated have at least expressed interest in the job, have agreed to serve, and are qualified for the offices for which they're nominated.

The following sections explain the process of nominations by a committee from start to finish — from selecting the committee's members to the committee's final report.

Selecting the committee

The more broad-based the selection of the nominating committee, the more confidence the membership can have in its recommendations. For that reason, it's most advisable for the general membership or the executive board to elect the committee instead of leaving committee members to the president or chair to appoint.

In fact, Robert's Rules specifically advises against allowing a sitting president to have any influence over the nominating committee; Robert recommends bylaw provisions to prohibit the president from being the appointing power or from serving *ex officio* as one of the nominating committee's members.

Working on the committee

A nominating committee's service is most useful if its job is to report a single nominee for each office or position to be filled. That way, it can focus on identifying, in its considered judgment, the best available candidate to serve in a particular position.

Sometimes the bylaws require a nominating committee to nominate more than one candidate per office, probably because somebody thought there should always be a contest for elections. But a nominating committee can defeat the intent of such a bylaw by nominating its preferred candidate along with a surefire loser. So Robert's Rules calls such bylaw requirements unsound, and I agree!

TIP

If your organization uses a nominating committee, you do your group a favor by paying close attention to this section. The committee's duty is of paramount importance because its decisions can truly have the most far-reaching effects of any decision made by a board, committee, or officer.

Learning about your rules

As with any other committee, the nominating committee is subject to all the procedural rules that apply to committees. (I discuss committees in detail in Chapter 16.)

Depending on your organization's rules, the authority that created the nominating committee may have appointed the chair, or perhaps provides that the committee members will elect their own chair. If the chair hasn't been selected at the time the committee is appointed, its first order of business is to elect its chair. The chair is responsible for leading the committee in conducting its business; the new chair should become informed completely about the duties of a committee chair generally and about the committee's specific objectives to ensure that the committee can discharge its duty without ever giving any appearance of impropriety.

A nominating committee should conduct all deliberations in in-person meetings or by electronic means, which permit simultaneous communication (if authorized in the organization's rules). To afford itself maximum accord, all members should be present for all deliberations. Holding several committee meetings before reporting to the membership isn't unusual, so the first committee meeting needs to be called as soon as possible after the committee's appointment.

WARNING

Although it's possible to conduct some committee business outside of meetings and correspond by email, your nominating committee shouldn't be a "committee of correspondence." The subject of your discussions will be people and their fitness for certain jobs — take my advice and keep that out of email! The committee must maintain its integrity and hold the trust of the membership, both of which may be in jeopardy if the content of your discussions falls into the wrong hands.

REMEMBER

Nominating committee meetings may certainly be casual, but they must always be conducted in such a way that no member is denied full expression in the presence of the others.

Getting down to business

The first stage of a nominating committee's work is carried out as a series of steps:

1. Identify potential candidates.

2. Identify the best candidates.

3. Agree on a nominee and *then* determine that person's willingness to serve.

The immediate need at the first meeting is to assemble a preliminary working list of names for consideration. However, persons who are being considered for nomination must *not* be contacted until they're the first choice for nomination.

REMEMBER

If the committee is nominating to fill several seats on a board, it needs to prioritize its choices and contact them in order of preference until the number of accepting nominees is the same as the number of the seats to be filled.

WARNING

The committee must refrain from making any inquiry of any candidate or prospective candidate until the committee is in agreement that the candidate will be placed on the ballot if they accept the nomination. Courtesy inquiries are neither necessary nor appropriate; if the committee would almost certainly not recommend an individual for service, then inquiring about the person's willingness to serve is of no useful purpose.

Considering incumbents

The nominating committee's duty to the membership is to recommend the candidates who are believed to be the best for the organization. For this reason, no requirement says that incumbents must be nominated. Maturity, experience, leadership ability, good judgment, commitment to the organization, attitude toward service, ability to work with others, and personal dependability are important qualities for candidates. Unfortunately, not all incumbents will have demonstrated a capacity to serve the organization.

The same is true for members who have served in other leadership positions or been active in committees. The nominating committee has no obligation to nominate anyone because of willingness to serve or because of a good first impression. In fact, you can probably look to your own experience to know that appearances can be deceiving, and impressive candidates have the potential to be big disappointments.

REMEMBER

The committee's obligation is to nominate people who are best suited to serve your organization. Period.

Contacting your first choices for nomination

After the nominating committee has assembled an initial list of acceptable candidates, committee members need to make the initial contacts as soon as possible. The inquiry can be short and simple: "If nominated for the office of Exhausted High Steam-blower, would you accept?"

A candidate who hasn't served before may have questions or concerns about what service involves. Your bylaws establish your meeting schedule and the duties of the different officers and directors. Information about the frequency and location of meetings is likely important to the candidate and needs to be disclosed. Also be prepared to frankly discuss the job requirements with your nominee.

Finalizing the list

At the second meeting of your committee, review each name and corresponding inquiry response. The initial list will be shortened as you remove from consideration those who declined or even those who agreed to serve but whose answers may have raised doubts about their fitness (for example, "Well, yes, if you can't get somebody else!" or "Sure thing! I'd like to let you folks know how to really run an organization!").

At each meeting, additional names may be considered for the final list, and new information or developments may be considered on names previously added or removed.

WARNING

Nominating committee members must keep *all* discussions confidential. Although they may seek advice or information from current leadership, they need to take care to avoid premature announcements or publication of your working list.

Seeking insight and advice from current and past leaders

If you're following Robert's Rules, your president will neither appoint nor serve *ex officio* on your nominating committee, and your bylaws will include provisions to ensure neither occurs. However, that doesn't mean that the committee is prohibited from consulting with the president for their advice or opinion.

The president is in a unique position to know and understand who has the qualities of leadership necessary for a particular office and, in turn, may have valuable information that the committee finds useful. Similarly, other officers, committee leaders, and members of executive management may have information about prospective candidates or the duties of the office that may be useful to the committee. The nominating committee can make effective use of this information, if it chooses, but the committee must avoid sharing information on the current status of particular candidates.

TIP

The nominating committee is free to consult with any member or officer for information or advice, but it's under no obligation to do so. Committee deliberations should take place only in executive session, because such discussions require the same environment for candid discussion as personnel-related matters.

Getting answers to questions about procedure

Be sure to obtain from your president (or executive staff, if you have one) answers to questions about your organization's procedures relating to the nominating committee's work. But in some situations, an incumbent who is eager to influence your report may taint the information. To avoid this situation, I recommend carefully preparing an extract of all bylaws and other written rules adopted by your organization that in any way relate to the work of the nominating committee. Such a document can then be furnished to the members of the nominating committee, eliminating the need for them to depend too much on the current officers for information on the procedures for carrying out their task.

Reporting your nominations

When the time to report draws near, the nominating committee can arrange a final meeting and prepare its final report. It must prepare, review, and finalize the list of nominees as the recommendation of the committee. Coordinate with your president or staff to be sure the report is submitted in time for the preparation of a ballot or other publication, if your rules require it.

TIP

Keep the report simple, listing the nominee or nominees for each office in the order the bylaws list the offices: "The nominating committee reports its nominees as follows: For president, Portulaca Grapevine; for vice-president, Hermione Frump . . . ."

Wisdom dictates that your committee report not be disclosed or circulated until it's officially presented, or perhaps shortly in advance of the election meeting. Circumstances can change, and so may your final recommendation. However, the time to release your report is generally established by custom or by rule.

Handling the committee report

In many cases, it's assumed that the nominees the nominating committee recommends will be elected. Nevertheless, the chair is mistaken if he entertains a motion to accept the committee report; by doing so, he ignores the rights of members to make nominations from the floor. Even if such a nomination is ultimately futile or is made in pointed protest, it's still in order. For that reason, the question is never on the adoption of a nominating committee's report — it's always on the election of the officer.

Even when your assembly has received a nominating committee's report, nominations from the floor must be taken for offices in the order the bylaws list the offices. And depending on the rule or custom of your organization, nominations from the floor can be taken in two ways:

>> Take all nominations for all offices and then proceed to the elections.

>> Take nominations for an office, conduct the election for that office, and then proceed to nominations for the next office.

WARNING

If the time for the nominating committee to report arrives and the committee hasn't reported, you don't want to let that fact hold things up. Robert's Rules makes it pretty clear that such a failure on the part of your nominating committee needn't stop you from moving on to take nominations from the floor.

Nominations by Ballot

This method of nominations isn't as complex as it is different. It's based on the principle of allowing *all* voters to make nominations for all offices by completing a nominating ballot.

The ballots are tallied much like an election ballot (see Chapter 14), and the report becomes the list of nominees for each office. This method gives voters an idea of the group's preferences without holding an actual election.

The election balloting then proceeds on a separate ballot, with each voter casting a vote for the nominee of his choice. Although it may seem that the nomination ballot should just be adopted as the election ballot, doing so is improper because it's no different than holding a write-in election without any nominees; the likelihood of such an election producing a winner on the first ballot is so small that it could hide under the period at the end of this sentence.

The nominating ballot system has the advantage of eliminating some of the time spent on nominations from the floor, in addition to giving information about the preferences of the other members.

Nominations by Mail

Taking nominations by mail is the same as taking nominations by ballot, except that the former is handled through the mail. Kinda obvious, isn't it? Security measures are taken to protect the privacy of the nominating ballot; each member is instructed to fold the ballot inside a signed envelope and mail it back in an outer envelope. When the nominating ballot is received, the signed inner envelope containing the ballot is logged in against a list of voting members, and the ballot is deposited in a receptacle for tallying like an election ballot.

All other procedures for taking mail nominations remain the same as for taking a nominating ballot in a meeting. The added advantage of mail nominations is that a more widespread base of nominees can be obtained. If voting is also to be conducted by mail, the bylaws must permit it. See Chapter 8 for more information on voting by mail.

Nominations by Petition

Some organizations add nominees to the ballot only if the name is submitted on a petition signed by some minimum number of members. Nomination by petition is another method of nominations by mail; the bylaws must make provisions for it, and standard forms must be provided to candidates and electors upon request.

Chapter **14**

Holding Elections and Making Appointments

O ne of the real challenges for many organizations is making the right decisions when it comes to electing officers and directors and staffing committees. Making mistakes is easy when you don't know the proper procedures or the rationale behind them. For example, take the myth that when nobody wins on the first ballot, you automatically drop the candidates who received the lowest votes and hold a run-off for the office. Truth is, taking that route instead of following the correct procedure compromises both the election and the group.

This chapter covers the default procedures for elections and appointments, as well as the other options available for selecting leaders, as outlined by Robert's Rules. If you want to make the best group decisions when selecting your leadership team, take a close look at this chapter and make some comparisons with your current procedures. You'll clearly see any changes you need to make.

TIP

This chapter may look a bit like a rehash of the material in Chapter 8, but it actually goes beyond the basic discussion of voting methods I cover there. The information in this chapter further develops the information from Chapter 8, especially as it applies to holding elections and making appointments. In this chapter, I tie the voting basics to the process of arriving at your decisions about who will serve your group in leadership positions.

Conducting Elections Like a Maestro

In my experience, the election process itself is the easiest part of deciding who handles a particular job in the organization. By the time you get to the actual election, the process is mostly (as they say) "all over but the crying." The choices are pretty well narrowed through the nomination process, and the campaigns, if any, are finished. Now's the time to see if the members have the wisdom to put the right people to work.

An election is really nothing more than the handling of an assumed motion, with the question being whom to elect to fill a position. An election can be decided by ballot, voice vote, or by roll call; the following sections take a closer look at each. You may even make your decisions by plurality or by order of preference instead of by a majority, but this must be authorized in your bylaws if applied to officer elections, or by a special rule of order otherwise.

The point of all these details is that your group has decisions to make about elections before you actually hold an election. If you want to save yourself a lot of angst around election time, you need to decide on these methods ahead of time and make necessary provisions for them in your bylaws.

Electing by ballot

I suspect that most organizations use the method of electing officers and directors by ballot. Ballot voting (see Chapter 8 for details) is by far the surest way to allow for the free expression of the will of the membership. The decision of who you trust to do the work is certainly important enough to justify the extra effort required to ensure each member a right of secrecy and safeguard both the integrity of the count and the result.

When holding ballot elections, you have two procedural options:

>> Nominations for all offices conclude before any balloting begins.

>> Nominations for each office are followed by the election for that office.

Each of these two options is unique and has advantages and disadvantages.

Closing nominations for all offices before balloting

Nominations are closed (see Chapter 13) for all offices, and balloting for all offices can take place on the same ballot. The advantages of closing all nominations before any voting takes place are twofold:

>> It saves time.

>> It permits polling outside the meeting.

When the meeting is large and time is a real factor in counting ballots, this method works best if you hold your elections early in the meeting. Doing so gives you the best chance of completing any reballoting required in case of a tie between candidates.

One of the disadvantages of this method is that unless voters plan ahead and nominate a member for more than one office before balloting begins (which is certainly permissible), the voters miss the opportunity to elect a candidate to an office voted on later if that person loses an office voted on earlier. When using this procedure, members must be instructed that a person can be nominated for more than one office and can be *elected* to more than one office. If your group does elect a nominee to more than one office and he can't accept or doesn't choose to accept both positions, you simply conduct another election for the office left empty.

If a member is absent and the rules don't allow them to serve in both offices, the assembly must decide which of the two offices the member will hold and conduct another election for the other.

TECHNICAL
STUFF

If your election procedure uses a single ballot for several offices, and a candidate is elected to more than one office on a single ballot, the candidate (or the assembly, if the candidate is absent) must then choose *one* office even if the bylaws don't prohibit the member from holding more than one office. Then another round of balloting is held for the other office and if the member is elected again, they can hold both offices (again, assuming the bylaws don't prohibit the candidate from holding more than one office).

The reason for this is that if a candidate is elected to more than one office on a single ballot, it's not clear that the voters actually wanted that member to serve in multiple offices. They may have voted for the member for multiple offices just in case that member didn't win one of the positions.

WARNING

When it falls to the assembly to decide which office to assign a candidate who has been elected to two offices on a single ballot, it's a debatable question (see Chapter 6). And the vote must also be by ballot.

Closing floor nominations for each office before balloting for that office

The main advantage of this procedure is that members can consider the election results of one office before proceeding to the election of another office.

In this procedure, you take nominations from the floor for one office and, when no further nominations are forthcoming, you then proceed to the balloting for that office. Your tellers count the ballots and report the count, and the chair announces the results. Then you do it all again for the next office.

The disadvantage of closing nominations for one office at a time is that it requires more time for the election process, making it probably best limited to smaller groups.

TECHNICAL STUFF

If you choose the "Closing all nominations before balloting" option, your ballot should list the offices to be elected in the order the offices are listed in your bylaws. If you choose the "Closing floor nominations for each office before balloting for that office," the order in which you take up each election is the order in which your bylaws list the offices.

WARNING

When your bylaws provide that elections shall be by ballot, waiving that requirement is never permissible, even if only one person is nominated or running for the office, unless the bylaws specifically provide for such an exception. A rule requiring ballots is a rule protecting the right of an individual to vote in secret, which is considered a *basic right of the individual member.*

Using write-in votes

Voting by ballot adds another dimension to an election: It enables a member to vote for a candidate not formally nominated by writing a name on the ballot and marking the name to indicate that it's the voter's choice. Called a *write-in vote,* this type of vote is always counted. A write-in vote is a legal vote unless it's unintelligible or cast for an unidentifiable or ineligible person, in which case it's counted as an illegal vote. (Flip to Chapter 8 for the lowdown on how to count both *legal* and *illegal votes.*)

Dropping the low-vote-getter? Not so fast . . .

Although the government runs its elections by dropping all comers except the top two vote-getters, or even just electing by plurality, Robert doesn't sanction that kind of decision making unless you've made a bylaw or a special rule of order to allow it. Robert is pretty much a purist with the "majority rules" concept — even with elections.

In other words, without a bylaw that provides for election by plurality or some form of preferential voting, nobody gets elected to an office until one candidate receives a majority. A candidate can't be forced out of the race just because they're in last place, as long as a seat remains open and nobody has a majority vote. Needless to say, that means that you'll sometimes find yourself having to ballot multiple times, with the same result: no winner. It happens.

COMPROMISING ON THE DARK HORSE

The practice of holding a run-off between the top two vote-getters when neither has a majority is *not* proper under Robert's Rules. Nor is the practice of limiting voting to the top two nominees on a nominating ballot.

Even though these options seem like good ideas, the rule states that you continue to vote *(reballot)* until someone receives a majority of the votes cast. Sometimes reballoting takes a lot of time, but unless the candidates consistently drawing the low votes withdraw from the contest, they have every right to be listed on the ballot.

The advantage to this voting rule is that, more often than you may think, Mr. Listbottom may just be the ideal compromise candidate that the two hopelessly deadlocked factions can agree on. When people start to realize that they aren't going to win, but they still don't want to vote for their candidate's archrival, they begin to see the benefit of voting for that third name on the ballot that's consistently drawing some pretty good numbers.

As these stubborn voters warm up to the dark horse candidate, they begin to realize that, by switching to this candidate, they may be able to hold together an organization in danger of splitting if the members are forced to choose between two sharply contrasted candidates.

So the next time you're tempted to call for a run-off, consider compromising on the dark horse instead of barreling toward deadlock. You may be really glad you did!

But few trees are likely lost to the paper used for reballoting. The fact that it's a real drag to have to keep voting is just the motivation to get voters to rethink their positions and maybe find a low–vote–getter who's acceptable to a majority when none of the top vote–getters ever will be!

WARNING

Unless a bylaw provides as much, an assembly may not declare an otherwise qualified candidate to be ineligible to run or receive votes in an election just because she's a low-vote-getter in a round of balloting.

TECHNICAL STUFF

Adopting a special rule of order (see Chapter 2) or suspending the rules (see Chapter 11) can allow a group to drop a nominee with fewer votes from later ballots. But only a bylaw can make that nominee ineligible for election to the office or prevent members from voting for her in the future rounds of balloting.

Electing by voice vote

If your bylaws don't require you to conduct an election by ballot, and if candidates are unopposed or there's no major contest for an office, an election by voice vote (or *viva voce*) may save you some valuable time. In fact, when there's only one nominee and you're not required to elect by ballot, the chair need only announce that the nominee is elected.

The procedure for a voice-vote election is fairly simple. After nominations are closed, the vote is taken on each nominee in the order in which they were nominated.

For example, suppose the nominees for the office of treasurer are Mr. Spender, Ms. Froogle, and Mr. Dazzler. The chair begins by saying, "If there are no more nominations for the office of treasurer, we will close nominations and proceed to elect a treasurer. Are there further nominations? [pause for additional nominations] Hearing no further nominations, nominations for the office of treasurer are closed."

The chair continues, "The nominees for treasurer are Mr. Spender, Ms. Froogle, and Mr. Dazzler. All those in favor of electing Mr. Spender to the office of treasurer, say, 'Aye.' Opposed, 'No.' The noes have it, and Mr. Spender is not elected."

The election's not over yet — you have two more candidates to consider.

The chair proceeds to the vote on the candidate nominated second. The chair says, "All those in favor of electing Ms. Froogle to the office of treasurer, say, 'Aye.' Opposed, 'No.' The ayes have it, and Ms. Froogle is elected to the office of treasurer."

Now that the assembly has elected the treasurer, the question on the election of Mr. Dazzler has become moot.

The only real problem with the voice vote method is that if the members don't understand exactly how it works, the ones whose preferred candidate doesn't get voted on are likely to think something is amiss.

WARNING

Because this form of voting favors one candidate over another based on the order of nomination, avoid using it except in mass meetings or when there's no serious contest for the office and a ballot isn't required.

TIP

Depending on the group and your members' familiarity with the process, your presiding officer can avoid misunderstandings by explaining to the assembly exactly how the voice vote works. In doing so, Madam President may explain, "If you want to be sure someone down the list has a chance at being elected, you should vote *against* those higher up on the list. Your failure to cast a negative vote for candidates who get voted on before yours can actually help the fortunes of the candidates nominated before yours."

REMEMBER

If a candidate for office is unopposed and your bylaws don't require a ballot, your presiding officer simply declares the candidate elected.

Electing by roll call

If your assembly's members are accountable to a constituency, your rules may require you to conduct your elections by roll-call vote. You follow the same procedures I outline for elections by ballot (in the earlier section "Electing by ballot"), as far as arriving at the point of the election is concerned. But instead of casting your vote by ballot, each member announces his vote when the secretary calls that person's name. The secretary repeats the vote after recording it, to ensure accuracy. I cover roll-call voting in Chapter 8.

Determining who wins

Elections of officers are decided by majority vote unless your bylaws provide differently. For non-officer elections, a special rule of order will suffice to elect by plurality or preferential vote.

Viva voce elections

As far as elections by voice vote are concerned, a majority elects anyway because all you can discern with a voice vote is win-or-lose, and you stop when you have a winner. Tie votes are unlikely in viva voce elections; if you do encounter a tie, you solve the problem by division of the assembly (see Chapter 11) or even by switching to a counted vote or a ballot vote.

Ballot elections

When it comes to ballot elections, your election isn't complete until a position is filled — and a position is never filled until a candidate receives the threshold number of votes required for election. In most cases, the threshold is a majority of the votes cast. If you have only two candidates and the vote is a tie, you repeat the balloting until one candidate receives a majority.

Follow the same practice even if more than two candidates are on a ballot for one position. If no one receives a majority, you vote again. See "Dropping the low-vote-getter? Not so fast . . ." earlier in this chapter.

WARNING

Balloting must continue until a candidate receives a majority. Dropping the candidates who receive the lowest vote totals from a ballot is never proper unless they withdraw voluntarily. Run-offs, then, are just plain out of order. The requirement for election by ballot is a majority, and a candidate has no obligation to with-draw just because he polls low numbers. In fact, your members may wind up voting for Mr. Low as the compromise candidate.

TIME TO COUNT THE BALLOTS

In Chapter 8, I cover in detail how ballots are counted and how voting results are determined. But a couple of points about counting ballots in elections are relevant here:

» When you have several seats to fill on a board or a committee, a voter doesn't have to vote for more than one person for the office in order for the ballot to count. However, a blank ballot doesn't count at all.

» When you're tallying the votes, if more candidates than the required number of positions to be filled receive a majority, the winners are determined by ranking the total votes received. If some but not all seats are filled on a ballot, the candidates who receive a majority are elected, and you reballot to fill the remaining positions.

MAIL BALLOTS

Mail ballots (which your bylaws must authorize) can be a great way to elect leaders of organizations that have a large membership spread over a wide area. But they have one major drawback: When no candidate receives a majority, the price of reballoting can really bust the budget! Take a look in Chapter 8 for details about conducting a vote by mail.

TIP

To make sure you don't have to reballot when holding an election by mail, authorize in your bylaws that mail ballot elections can be decided by plurality or preferential voting. (I cover both of these methods in Chapter 8.) When making these rules, be sure you also provide for tiebreakers. Coin flips or drawing straws are the most common methods for breaking ties, but you could also use arm-wrestling or pie-eating contests.

Contesting an election

When it comes to determining election results — well, you know about the hanging chads of the infamous 2000 U.S. presidential election. Rules for contesting elections are something this country is all about. All that counts is how you handle the challenge. Robert's Rules has just the answer: more rules! It's a good thing, too. When you have an election to challenge, it's good not to have to decide at that point on the rules for challenging it.

Ordering a recount

Sometimes the solution is easy. If the election just took place and members are still in their seats, you can resolve any question about the actual vote count by ordering a while-you-wait recount. Everything else pretty much gets put on hold when that happens. It's okay — now is the best time to stop and be sure.

If you can't resolve the count issue with a recount, you're probably still okay to retake the vote using another method (unless you've gone on to the next item on your agenda and are involved in that). You'll want to follow the rules in Chapter 8.

Challenging by raising a point of order

The way to challenge elections that your organization has held generally adheres to procedures for raising pints of ardor — or, rather, *points of order* (I prefer the former but can discuss only the latter here).

Usually, you have to catch the error when it happens — and speak up right away — if it's to make a difference in the outcome. But in a few cases, you can make the challenge anytime, and it has to be dealt with then — whenever it is! Those circumstances are as follows:

>> **The individual who was elected doesn't meet qualifications for office.** Just ask President Myrtle what happened when she forgot to pay her dues and her membership lapsed. She then wasn't a member anymore, so according to the bylaws, she wasn't entitled to serve in *any* office — certainly not as the president. The vice-president automatically become the president and didn't even know it! Myrtle never forgot to pay her dues again. But it didn't matter, because she never got elected to anything again, either.

TECHNICAL STUFF

According to Robert's Rules, unless some qualification for holding office is established in the bylaws, the members can elect anyone they choose to any office. If the bylaws establish qualifications for holding an office, the qualifications must be met. So if the bylaws provide that officers must be members to hold office, then officers must be members to serve in that office.

>> **You already conducted a valid election for the same term.** Believe it or not, if you revote something against the rules, that result probably isn't valid. In this case, whatever you did in the first place still stands.

>> **The votes of nonmembers or absentees affect the result.** Whether it's zombies in New Orleans voting for years after they died or just the folks who live in St. Tammany parish voting in St. Bernard parish, if the result changes when you eliminate ineligible votes, the election outcome changes. If the ineligible votes can't be identified, and enough of them were cast to affect the result, the election has to be redone. That's because the offending votes, being unidentifiable, can't be thrown out.

>> **An election took place to fill a vacancy without proper notice.** Everybody remembers the story that went something like, "Hey, let's elect Figero before Alexander and Cicero figure out what we're doing."

>> **Disenfranchisement of members changes the result.** All it takes for this situation to happen is for the treasurer to have an incorrect membership list and find out later that eligible people weren't allowed to vote. Guess what! It's probably not too late to fix it, and the way you do that is to hold a new election.

Making it final

Elections are a big deal. But going on and on arguing about who won keeps the real work from getting done. At some point, the body doing the electing has to elect somebody who can serve so that everybody can go home. If the assembly doesn't want to have to deal with the problem itself, it can refer the decision to a subordinate body with authority to make the final determination.

But unless the bylaws or special rules of order or direct authority from the assembly expressly grant the subordinate body the power to act for the superior body in its elections, none but the electing body can make it final. Finally!

None other than the electing body can invalidate an election. If, after the general membership's meeting adjourns, the board later discovers one of the continuing breaches previously listed under the heading "Challenging by raising a point of order," it can't fix the problem itself — it has to report it to the general membership.

Dealing with incomplete elections

Despite the best of plans, sometimes your group just can't finish its order of business in a given meeting or session. If you run out of time before you've elected all the positions you plan to fill, don't worry. It's not the end of the world — just the end of the meeting! And meetings being what they are, you can be sure you'll have another one. With that in mind, if you expect that you're not going to finish your work, you need to provide for an adjourned meeting in which to conclude your election. (I tell you how to do this in Chapter 10.) However, if your next regular meeting is scheduled within a quarterly time period (see the Appendix) and you're able to wait, you can also finish your election at the next regular meeting.

If you're wondering who your officers are either after an election or during an incomplete election, keep the following points in mind:

» Elections are final immediately upon their conclusion unless the elected person isn't present and hasn't consented to serve, or unless the elected person declines to serve when notified of the election, whether present at the time of election or not.

» An election can't be reconsidered after it's finalized.

» The newly elected officer assumes office immediately unless the bylaws state a specific time for the term of office to commence.

» If the bylaws require an installation ceremony, failure to conduct the ceremony doesn't affect the time at which the term commences, nor does it prohibit the candidate from assuming the office.

WARNING

If your organization fails to complete an election for an office, the current officer might be duty-bound to continue in office until the election is complete. But that isn't always the case. The bylaws might provide for a specific term ending date, term limits might kick in, or the current officer might just have had enough and decide to step down. In any of those cases, a vacancy in office exists and you will have to check your bylaws or other rules to know what happens when such a vacancy occurs. Read the next section for more on that subject.

Filling Vacancies

Just when you think you have everything under control, somebody quits or dies, or you have to throw someone out. It's not that big a deal to have to fill a vacancy if you've just had all that fun throwing out dead weight; that's just the next item of business on your meeting agenda. But unless your group has authorized a subordinate board to fill vacancies in the positions that your big assembly normally elects once every year or two at the big event in the big city, your board can't fill the vacancy. To fill that vacancy, you have to go through the election procedure all over again.

Fortunately, Robert's Rules and common sense allow that if you want your executive board to fill vacancies in office between big meetings, you can set it up that way. All you have to do is write a bylaw, enact a special rule of order, or even just adopt a motion at the close of the meeting to refer the decision to your board or a committee. For more on filling vacancies, see Chapter 15.

Making Committee Appointments

In Chapter 16, I cover committees and the considerations necessary to staff them properly. Those considerations relate to the nature of the committee, its task, the size of committee necessary to handle the task, and the members' abilities and temperaments. In this section, I branch out to explain the procedures for committee selection.

Exploring the methods of appointing committees

The two most common methods of selecting committee members are

» Appointment by motion

» Appointment by the chair

Appointment by motion

This method is pretty self-explanatory: The suggested appointees are simply named in a motion.

In many cases, the motion is the same as the motion establishing the committee. For example, a member may say, "Mr. Chairman, I move that we refer the pending motion to contract out the landscaping of our main entrance to a committee of three members to seek bids and to review and recommend to the membership at our regular meeting in two months, and that the members of the committee be Hector Knuckles, Shirley Buckles, and Luther Chuckles."

You can instead make the appointment in a second motion that follows the committee's establishment. In this case, a member may say, "Mr. Chairman, I move that Hector Knuckles, Shirley Buckles, and Luther Chuckles be appointed as the landscape proposal bid review committee just established."

Members may want to add other names for consideration for appointment to a special committee with a fixed number of members; those names are taken as nominations, and the motion is treated in the same way that nominations and an election are held. (Turn to Chapter 13 for details on handling nominations from the floor.) Alternatively, while you're still in the meeting, you can adopt a motion to reconsider the motion establishing the committee (see Chapter 12) and change the number of members to serve on the committee.

The motion to appoint specific members to the committee may also name a chair for the committee. If a chair isn't determined in this manner, a separate motion can appoint the chair, or the motion can authorize the committee members to select their chair from among themselves. If no chair is named and no provision is made for selecting the chair, the first person named to the committee calls the committee together and serves as a temporary chair until the committee elects one.

Direct appointment by the chair

Many organizations allow the chair or president to appoint committees. In fact, a group's bylaws may make the appointment of most, if not all committees an express responsibility of the president. In those cases, members don't have any power over the appointment of committee members; they can only hope that the president heeds their recommendations. When bylaws give this kind of authority to a president, they should also provide for necessary exceptions where presidential control is not desirable, such as is the case with a nominating committee.

If the bylaws don't state that the president shall appoint all special and standing committees, the group can charge the presiding officer with the task in two ways:

>> Add the task to the motion creating the committee, as in, "I move to create a committee of five members to be appointed by the president, to gather information about a new place to hold our meetings and to report back to us next month." This method delegates any authority to select the committee members directly to the president.

>> Give the president the authority to appoint members to a committee is to make a separate motion following the adoption of the motion establishing the committee. The member taking this approach then says, "Mr. Chairman, I move that the members of the meeting location committee just established be appointed by the chair."

Finding more ways to appoint committee members

When it's time to appoint members to committees, you have four methods to choose from, in addition to the ones described in the previous section. Although these methods aren't used nearly as often as the others, they are nonetheless available and sometimes are established in bylaws or special rules of order as a particular method to use for certain committees. These methods are listed here:

>> Ballot election

>> Open nominations

>> Nominations by the chair

>> Appointment by definition in bylaws

Ballot election

Ballot election is the procedure most often used to staff important standing committees that have great power and authority. Whenever a group wants members to select the appointees and wants to afford members the benefit of the secret ballot, ballot election is the way to go. I cover the procedure in the section titled "Electing by ballot," earlier in this chapter.

Open nominations

Selecting members of a committee by open nominations is a procedure in which the presiding officer takes nominations from the floor (see Chapter 13) for potential committee members. This method gives control over appointment to the membership but doesn't carry the requirement of a secret ballot.

If the number of members nominated is no greater than the number of committee members to be appointed, the nominees can be declared appointed. Otherwise, the chairman calls for a voice vote on each nominee in the order nominated until the required number is elected. You can find more information on this kind of voting in the section "Electing by voice vote," earlier in this chapter.

Nominations by the chair

Using this procedure, you can take advantage of the chair's knowledge of the strengths and capabilities of members as they relate to the requirements of service on the committee, but you ultimately reserve the final decision for your group.

The chair offers their nominees and puts the question as follows: "The chair nominates Hoss Traynor as chairman, and Ben Dare and Don Daat as members. Shall these members be appointed to the committee?"

You can propose a veto of any member nominated by moving to strike out one or more of those named. Your chair handles such a motion as a subsidiary motion to *Amend* (see Chapter 9). But when appointing committees by nominations from the chair, you can't offer a replacement. Instead, the membership votes on your motion to strike out. If it passes, the chair offers other nominees. If it fails, the question is again raised on whether to approve the chair's nominees as members of the committee.

Appointment by definition in the bylaws

Some committees are appointed as directed under specific provisions of bylaws. (I cover bylaws in Chapter 2.)

By way of example, consider a standing committee appointed under the bylaws by a combination of several of the methods listed in this section. The bylaw for such a committee may read, "The finance committee membership shall consist of the treasurer, the chairman of the audit committee, the chairman of the budget committee, the executive director, two members appointed by the president, and three members elected by the membership at the annual meeting."

Chapter **15**

Running the Show: Officers and Directors

Your organization can't reach its full potential without the right leadership. Nothing can help an organization achieve its purpose like the right people in the right jobs. And nothing can cause it to fail like a person who is interested only in having a title.

Choosing your leaders can be a challenge. If you want to see the right results, you need to keep one key thought in mind: The ability to get elected isn't the ability to do the job. I've seen organizations with the best bylaws, the finest members, and the most noble of purposes become totally ineffective because they wind up with a president who thinks his job is to control the members, or with directors who think they own the club.

A leader's job is to fulfill the duties of office, acting for the good of the group. But to fulfill your duties, you have to know what they are. This chapter gives you information on the various offices in any organization and lays out the standard responsibilities for each officer.

Perfecting Presidential Presence

Serving as president (or grand factotum, or whatever title is given to the presiding/chief executive officer) gives you the unparalleled opportunity to make a difference in your group's work. However, before you ever think about buckling down and implementing your bold ideas, you need to get familiar with the basics, which I discuss here.

Preparing to lead

I list ten tips for presiding officers in Chapter 22, but your success as president depends on your willingness to absorb a lot in a short time. You need to take these actions before you call your first meeting to order:

>> **Get a *current* copy of your group's adopted parliamentary authority.** If that authority is Robert's Rules, be careful not to buy one of the many knock-offs of the title or an early edition that authorized revisions have long since superseded.

The current (12th) edition of *Robert's Rules of Order Newly Revised* is the only book containing the name "Robert's Rules" in its title that the Robert's Rules Association, the National Association of Parliamentarians, and the American Institute of Parliamentarians recognize as authoritative.

>> **Read and understand your organization's charter, bylaws, special rules of order, and standing rules.** You've probably already read these documents at least once if you're a member of the organization, but read them again as if it were your first time. Pay attention to any of your rules that seem to be in conflict with the way things have been done lately, and set a course to do things according to the rules under your leadership.

STAFFING YOUR ORGANIZATION

A common misconception is that officers have to be members of the organization. That's really not the case unless you establish membership qualifications for officers in your bylaws.

In reality, members are free to elect whomever they choose to serve in their offices. Adopting limiting qualifications diminishes this freedom. I'm not saying you shouldn't limit who can be an officer, but when you consider the option, keep these two points in mind:

- Sometimes a nonmember is better for the job.

- If the ultimate decision rests with the members anyway, why limit your choices?

Consider these examples of nonmembers serving as officers:

- **Secretary:** Often a board elects a staff member to this office.

- **Treasurer:** How many times has a member's spouse who is a service-minded accountant been roped into doing this job? Plenty, I assure you.

- **Directors:** It's not unusual to see boards made up of interested and well-connected members of the community who aren't members of the organization.

- **President:** Look at the United States Senate — its presiding officer is the Vice President of the United States, not an elected senator. Your group may choose a professional presiding officer to serve as presiding officer at all your meetings, and you may want to staff a paid manager to handle operations between meetings.

Whether you put membership qualifications on officers is up to your membership. Although there's nothing wrong with setting limits, no rule says that your officers must be selected only from within your membership.

Members have a right to have meetings run by the book, and these documents are your book! (See Chapter 2 for more information on bylaws and the like.)

>> **Read Parts 1 and 2 of this book.** The first two parts of *Robert's Rules For Dummies* contain the fundamental knowledge necessary to fulfill your duties as a presiding officer in meetings. Pay special attention to the rules for recognizing members and assigning the floor, as well as other principles of debate (see Chapter 7). Also get a firm handle on ranking motions in Chapters 9 and 10.

When you're reading this book, familiarize yourself with the corresponding sections of your adopted parliamentary authority. You'll find expanded information there. Your adopted parliamentary authority is binding on your group, and it's your duty to know how to find and apply the rules as your parliamentary situation may require.

Presiding with pizzazz

Although the information in Chapters 5 and 7 covers much of the details related to presiding in meetings, I outline some of the more basic principles you need to master in the lists that follow.

REMEMBER

During meetings of your organization, your presiding officer has these duties:

>> Determine whether a quorum is present and call the meeting to order (see Chapter 4).

>> Bring business before the meeting according to your order of business (see Chapter 5).

>> Recognize members who seek and are entitled to the floor (see Chapter 7).

>> Put all legitimate motions before the group (see Chapter 7).

>> Enforce the rules of debate, and grant all members who want to speak in debate the opportunity to do so, subject to the rules and limits of debate (see Chapter 7).

- » Conduct the votes on all questions, and determine and announce the results (see Chapter 8).

- » Rule improper motions out of order (see Chapter 7).

- » Decide questions of order, or ask the members to decide, when you're in doubt (see Chapter 11).

- » Respond to parliamentary inquiries or points of information (see Chapter 11).

- » Conclude the meeting by declaring it adjourned when voted by the members, when the appointed hour for adjournment arrives (see Chapter 10), when an emergency arises and safety demands it, or, if it's an ordinary local group that usually finishes its entire agenda, when the order of business is complete and no more business is forthcoming.

Along with polishing up your presiding skills and techniques, you can adopt a few practices to ensure the quality of your meetings. The tips that follow are recommendations for producing effective meetings that run smoothly.

TIP

- » **Keep your rules handy.** You never know when you'll have to stop and check on a rule from your bylaws or rules of order. Have a copy of your bylaws, special rules of order, and parliamentary authority with you at every meeting.

- » **Plan your meeting.** You know from everyday life that it's easier to go from one place to the next if you plan well and know how to get there. Make your meeting journey simpler by using a working agenda. I cover this subject in detail in Chapter 5 and give you a sample you can download online at www.dummies.com/go/robertsrules4e.

- » **Insist on following fundamental procedures.** Remain in control of the floor. For example, don't let members disrupt the meeting by calling out motions without being properly recognized. Except in limited situations, members have to be recognized before making a motion. Know which motions can interrupt a speaker, which ones are debatable, and which ones are amendable. Help members frame their motions correctly; even if they make the wrong motion but it's clear what they want to do, announce the motion as the one they're really trying to make. I'm not recommending that you be a bossy control freak: In fact, a key to successful presiding is knowing when it's appropriate to relax formalities (as long as it's not at the expense of member rights).

>> **Make sure the members know what they're voting on.** Before you take a vote, repeat the motion in understandable terms. For example, you may say, "The question is on adoption of the motion to purchase a new computer for our staff secretary at a cost not to exceed $700. [pause] Are you ready for the question? [pause] Those in favor say 'Aye,'" and so on.

WARNING

>> **Avoid the temptation to say, "You've heard the motion. Those in favor say 'Aye.'"** Much of the time, the members *haven't* heard the motion, and confusion will inevitably erupt — if not before the vote, then right afterward. Save the time wasted by confusion and outbursts, and be clear about the exact wording of the question that the next vote decides.

Maintaining magnanimity

If there was ever a key to success as a presiding officer, *maintaining the appearance of impartiality* is it. Members may know that you have an agenda for the organization. In fact, you were probably elected because you have some vision and ability. But when you're presiding over the meeting, leave it to your members to do all the debating; step back and let things take care of themselves. You'll sink your ship of state if you attempt to throttle members unjustly or take advantage of their ignorance of proper form or procedure.

Some of the best presiding officers I've known have also been some of the most opinionated. But they knew how to lead by participating in working committees and helping move their program by selling members on it, not forcing it on them. A reputation for giving full sway to the minority when debating contested issues gave these leaders the respect of all the members.

Conversely, the worst presiding officers seem to have as their hallmark the propensity to keep members who disagree with them from speaking at meetings. These leaders (in name only) almost gleefully rule a motion they disagree with out of order based on any hair-splitting technicality they can get away with.

WHEN PRESIDENTS SHOULDN'T PRESIDE: PUTTING A NONMEMBER ON THE PODIUM

When an issue has divided the membership, inviting a nonmember who's skilled in the art of presiding to chair the meeting can benefit the assembly and the decision. In fact, the stronger the commitment of the opposing members, the better off the meeting will be if the presiding officer doesn't have a dog in the fight!

Who hasn't seen an otherwise good and effective president morph into a George Gavelhammer when some issue arises for which George is particularly well known for his recalcitrant and impassioned position?

Fortunately for George and the rest of the members, Robert's Rules makes it easy enough for George to participate like any other member, and for a knowledgeable and impartial nonmember to preside over an assembly in which contention is the dominant vibe.

Without objection from the president or vice-president, the membership may, according to Robert's Rules, authorize a non-member to preside even if the bylaws provide for the president to preside over all meetings. It's as simple as it can be, and it can be done by a majority vote.

However, if the president or vice-president objects, the vote required to empower another to preside is a two-thirds vote. That's because doing otherwise requires a vote to suspend the rules that empower the president to preside at the meetings.

So when George Goodguy becomes his evil twin, George Gavelhammer, you can be ready and prepared to propose that Frank Fabulous be handed the gavel and give the members the opportunity to send George down to the floor to debate his heart out.

Many professional parliamentarians offer services as professional presiding officers. You can find qualified professionals through the National Association of Parliamentarians and the American Institute of Parliamentarians. I provide information on these organizations in this book's Introduction.

REMEMBER

The presiding officer who helps the assembly arrive at its true deliberative will is the winner on all counts.

Rounding out the job

As your group's president, you're more than likely also the chief administrative officer. You have to countersign checks and attest to resolutions published as extracts of the minutes (such as those furnished to banks when opening or changing info on accounts). If your group buys or sells any real estate or enters into any contracts, your signature is the seal of the organization.

CHOOSING A PRESIDING OFFICER

According to Robert's Rules, a presiding officer needs to be chosen primarily for the ability to preside.

That's one of those rules that needs to be taught in kindergarten, along with 2 + 2 = 4. The rule is so fundamentally true that it'd be great not to have to wait so long to discover it.

Most presiding officers get their training by ordeal. They get elected because they know how to get elected. Understanding the organization, the bylaws, and the rules for presiding is rarely important until they have one of those meetings that motivates them to call a parliamentarian and take a private lesson in procedure before the next meeting.

You'll probably never change the world by making it your personal policy to support presiding officers on the basis of the ability to preside impartially, knowledgeably, and skillfully over debate on a controversial subject. But by doing so, you may make a big difference in your own organization.

You'll never be better off in a meeting than when you have a presiding officer who takes the time to learn how to do the job right. The best presiding officer obtains the skills and techniques required to assist the assembly in arriving at its will efficiently, orderly, and with goodwill on all sides of controversial issues.

Your bylaws may also assign other duties to the president. You may be considered a member of all your standing committees, and you probably have some responsibility to make committee appointments.

WARNING

You serve the members, not the other way around. I get a good bit of mail from members telling me about how their president orders people around and keeps people from exercising their rights. I tell them about the procedures in Robert's Rules that allow them to adopt motions without worrying about whether the presiding officer likes it, remove a presiding officer from the chair during a meeting, or get rid of the presiding officer altogether. It usually comes as a big surprise to a presiding officer to have the last 26 pages of Robert's Rules (where you can find the procedure for removing a presiding officer from the chair) thrust in front of their face. The unsuccessful presiding officer likely wouldn't have wound up in such an embarrassing situation if they'd read some of the other pages first.

Playing (Not-So) Second Fiddles

An orchestra has only one first-chair violin, but it takes the entire ensemble to fill the hall with music. Similarly, although the presidency is a key leadership position in any organization, a successful organization is one that has a good leadership team working in concert. Other officers, especially people in key administrative positions, such as the ones listed in this section, have responsibilities that are just as important as the duties of the president, and they may take as much or more time to do well.

If you accept an election or appointment to serve as an officer, you can't go wrong if you spend as much time as the best president would in studying your bylaws and rules of order. Knowing your job and your organization's structure and rules is the first step to a successful term of service.

Waiting in the wings: Vice-president

The one function of a vice-president as provided in Robert's Rules is to serve in the absence of the president and to automatically succeed to the office of president in case of that officer's death or resignation, unless the bylaws provide something different, of course. In fact, members can't elect a new president to fill a vacancy in that office unless the bylaws expressly call for it. Thanks to the automatic succession rule, you never really have a vacancy in the presidency. With the vice-president's automatic succession the vacancy immediately becomes one in the office of vice-president (unless, of course, the offices of president and vice-president become vacant at about the same time).

You may have several vice-presidents in your organization. You know, a first vice-president, a second vice-president, a third vice-president, . . . a 29th vice-president (just kidding), and so forth. Unless the bylaws provide otherwise, succession to the presidency is in order of vice-presidents, with the last vice-president's position being the one vacated as they move up the food chain. Your bylaws should be specific in all matters regarding the office of vice-president unless you're satisfied with the standard provisions in Robert's Rules. Mostly, that deals with the automatic succession if your president checks out.

WARNING

Your bylaws may dictate other specific duties for a vice-president and often authorize the board or the president to assign certain duties. For this reason, it's a good idea to know just what your bylaws say about the office of vice-president before accepting the position.

REMEMBER

Robert's Rules provides several important things to consider about the role of the vice-president(s) in your organization.

>> In addition to the automatic succession-to-the-presidency rule, Robert says the vice-president "serves in his stead" if the president is absent or otherwise vacates the chair. That includes presiding over business meetings.

>> The vice-president is likely to be the appointed chairman of a committee of the whole (so it's a good idea for a vice-president to have some understanding of how a committee of the whole operates). See Chapter 3 for a quick reminder of what that's all about.

>> When presiding in the place of the president, the vice-president is properly addressed as Mr. President or Madam President. But if the president is hanging close by

and such address is apt to confuse all but the uncaring, it's cool to use Mr. Vice-President or Madam Vice-President.

>> If your organization is a constituent unit of a larger organization, your vice-president is considered an alternate delegate to the president if the president is automatically a delegate to the superior organization's convention.

>> The power to appoint committees granted to the president doesn't flow to the vice-president even if they're serving in the absence of the president.

>> If the president's report at a meeting is being handled by the vice-president, the vice-president has no authority to make any change to the report. It's still the president's report.

>> When several vice-presidents are established for an organization, when any vacancy occurs, all the vice-presidents move up one to fill the vacancies created. The vacancy thus remaining is filled by the body that elected all the vice-presidents (unless the bylaws provide some other rule). However, if the bylaws provide specific administrative duties for each vice-president, it's a good idea for the bylaws to provide a specific method for filling any vacancy in a vice-presidential office.

>> No matter how customary it is to elect the vice-president to the presidency at the end of the current president's term, it is by no means requisite to do that. Your membership is free to elect the president of their choice at that time. Fact is, Freddie Feckless might have seemed like a good candidate for vice-president when he was elected, but time proved that he lived up to his name and you're ready for Fran Fabulous to strut her stuff.

Keeping jots and tittles: Secretary

The secretary is one of the two officers your organization absolutely can't do without. It needs a presiding officer and a recording clerk to conduct a meeting and have a proper record of it, and the secretary is the recording clerk for the assembly.

REMEMBER

If any office is more important to the smooth functioning of your group, I don't know what it is. The work of the secretary is absolutely essential, and it takes a special person to do it correctly and do it well — not because the work is difficult, but because it's so important. Dependability, organization, and the ability to refrain from editorializing are the key attributes of a successful secretary.

Under Robert's Rules, a secretary's job description includes the following duties:

>> **Take minutes at all meetings and submit them for approval to the membership at the following meeting.** Minutes are the record of the proceedings in your meetings and become official when approved (see Chapter 17).

   If your meeting is more than a quarterly time interval away or the term of some or all the members are expiring, you should appoint a committee to approve the minutes. (That's to ensure you have approved minutes as soon as possible. Any problems can be corrected later when your next regular meeting occurs.)

>> **Serve as custodian of your organization's records (except records specifically assigned to other officers), including minutes; reports of officers, boards, and committees; and official correspondence.** The secretary also certifies copies of these documents when necessary.

>> **Make sure the official bylaws, special rules of order, standing rules, and current minutes book are available for reference at all meetings.** When somebody raises a point of order or has a question about a past action, you'll have the information you need.

>> **Make the organization's records available to members, in accordance with your rules.** If you don't have rules about when and where record-access requests can be accommodated, adopt a policy at your next opportunity. It will help you keep officers if there's a rule that lets them fend off Noisy Nellie when she contacts the secretary Sunday afternoon demanding a copy of last month's treasurer's report.

>> **Keep the official membership roll.** Sometimes this duty is specifically assigned to the treasurer or a staff member because the roll is often updated frequently based on dues payments or lapses.

>> **Ensure that officers, committee members, and delegates are notified when elected or appointed, and are given credentials and any necessary papers.** They're going to need to know they've been appointed, to be able to prove their authority, and if their charge requires it, review any documents essential to their task.

>> **Issue the notice (or call) of meetings, and serve as a correspondence secretary unless a separate position is established for that function.** These two duties are essential to the operation of the organization.

>> **Prepare the order of business for the presiding officer, showing everything known to be up for consideration at the meeting.** Your minutes of the previous meeting will tell you what business was postponed or delayed.

>> **Preside over the election of a temporary chairman for a meeting if the president and vice-president are absent.** You may never have to do this, but you need to know how if you do. Check out Chapter 14 for information on holding elections.

TIP

If you're the secretary, don't wear yourself out trying to write (into the minutes) everything everybody says in meetings. In fact, it's actually improper to do that. Chapter 17 contains detailed information about your minutes should and shouldn't include, but it boils down to this: Minutes are the record of what is *done* in the meeting, not what is *said*.

REMEMBER

The secretary's duty includes the duty to make available to members, at reasonable times, the records of the organization. But the members' right to inspect the records doesn't include the right to abuse or annoy the secretary. Whether you're the secretary or the member wanting to see the records, a sincere respect for each other's time and effort benefits all concerned.

Balancing the books: Treasurer

You've got a big job on your hands if you're the treasurer. Before you accept this position, find out exactly what it entails. Regardless of the size of the organization or the number of figures to the left of the decimal on your group's bank balance, your basic job description includes the following:

>> Serve as custodian of the funds of the organization, keeping careful records of all receipts and making no disbursements without the authority of the assembly (including established authorizations found in the organization's rules).

>> Prepare financial statements and report to the board and members.

>> Take responsibility for any and all reports required by taxing authorities.

That list may look like a short one, but each of the three items can carry a pretty significant workload. Fortunately, the bigger the job, the more likely there are to be sufficient resources to do a little outsourcing. In other words, if the membership is small and the budget isn't very big, you probably won't be faced with more transactions than you can handle. But if you're dealing with a large membership and tracking dues and a major budget, you'll probably have some professional help. In any event, when it comes to taking care of somebody else's money, you definitely need to know what's involved before you agree to take over the position.

Robert's Rules suggests that any officers who handle an organization's money be bonded at the expense of the group in an amount large enough to protect it from loss. The decision to obtain a fidelity bond is one for your membership, and the choice depends on the group's actual finances.

WARNING

Small organizations don't necessarily have inconsequential finances as far as the Internal Revenue Service (IRS) is concerned. You're mistaken if you think your group is automatically a nonprofit or tax-exempt organization because it isn't organized as a business. The point? If you're the officer responsible for taking care of your group's money, don't assume anything.

Before you sign any checks, ask a professional if your organization is required to file any kind of tax returns, and get the answer in writing. Whatever the professional says, be smart and take the advice.

Tackling Other Tasks

Besides the offices of president, vice-president, secretary, and treasurer, Robert's Rules lists a handful of other offices often established in different types of organizations, based on need. The name of each office suggests the general duties. For the most part, you define the specifics in your bylaws, depending on the needs of your group.

Managing the business: Directors

Your *directors* (also known as *trustees, managers,* or *governors*) are the people seated on your executive board. The directors' duties depend on the authority of the board, which is established in the bylaws.

Keeping the peace: Sergeant-at-arms

A *sergeant-at-arms* (also known as a *warden* or *warrant officer*) usually has the duty of acting on the orders of the chair to preserve order. Other duties related to the security of the floor may be assigned depending on the needs of the organization. Some organizations establish deputies or assistants who serve under the sergeant-at-arms and who may also be referred to by the same title.

Guarding the gate: Doorkeeper

If your organization closes its meeting hall to nonmembers or verifies membership credentials for admission, you may have a *doorkeeper* (also known as a *guard* or *tiler*). This officer often is responsible for closing the hall.

WHEN IS AN OFFICER NOT AN OFFICER?

Robert's Rules uses the term *officer* generically. Any set of duties assigned to an appointed or elected individual is generally understood to be an *office,* and the person elected or appointed is an *officer.*

But it's not uncommon to see the term *officer* used to define a specific subset of officers as defined in Robert's Rules. For example, *bylaws* may refer to "officers and directors," while Robert's Rules lists *directors* among "other officers."

But the terminology needn't be confusing if you simply stick to the context of the respective document. A director, in the most common sense of the word, is an officer. But your bylaws may define the president, the vice-president, the secretary, and the treasurer as officers. To thicken things, add the consideration that if those officers are on the board of directors, they're directors, too!

So when the bylaws say something about "The officers shall . . . ," the context tells you whether it means to include the directors. And if it isn't clear, let your membership handle the interpretation.

Take it from somebody with experience: Try not to get too hung up in that kind of terminology wrangling. If anything in your bylaws is too ambiguous for you to know exactly what it means, interpret it or clarify it by amending it, and move on.

Continuing the saga: Historian

Your group may maintain a written historical record (other than official minutes and reports) of the activities and accomplishments of your organization during a term. In this case, you probably have an official *historian.* Some historians simply prepare a journal, which the members adopt for entry into an official history journal. Other historians work with a standing committee and publish a yearbook.

Shelving the tomes: Librarian

If your organization maintains a collection of books, publications, films, or other cataloged media resources, the officer in charge of taking care of this property and making access available to your membership is your *librarian*.

Stowing the scepter: Curator

Some organizations possess valuable items and objects of important symbolic or historical significance. Custody of this property is vested in a *curator*, whose duty is to preserve these items.

Speaking words of wisdom: Chaplain

The *chaplain* is responsible for leading your group in its opening prayers or invocations and closing benedictions at any meetings and functions where they may be included. Some organizations, especially those of a fraternal, religious, or charitable nature, may require the chaplain to be available for personal counsel to members, and perhaps to recommend on benevolent disbursements.

Managing the staff: Executive director

An executive director (also known as an *executive secretary* or *chief executive officer*) is usually a full-time, salaried employee of a large organization that manages and administers the day-to-day business operations of the organization. Depending on the organization, this officer usually serves under contract and is selected either by the board or by the membership.

The executive director almost always serves under the direction of the board or executive committee and usually has the authority to hire and fire staff members and set their salaries. Your bylaws should specify the duties of this officer, method of selection, and term of service.

Advising on procedure: Parliamentarian

While many organizations either elect or authorize their presidents to appoint a parliamentarian from among their members, this function may also be handled by a professional who can render advice and opinions without having an interest in the outcome (other than that it be an orderly process, of course). Smaller organizations rarely need a parliamentarian. Even so, consulting a credentialed parliamentarian for help is wise when you have serious questions about member rights and procedures, or when you decide to make substantial changes to your bylaws.

In any case, the parliamentarian's role in a meeting is to advise your presiding officer on matters of parliamentary procedure. He doesn't make rulings, but rather is a consultant only. Rulings are the sole responsibility of the chair.

If you want to get the most out of your parliamentarian, involve him in the planning and preparation of your meetings. In fact, most of the work of a professional parliamentarian is actually done outside the meeting.

TIP

Because it's critical for your presiding officer to have complete confidence in the parliamentarian, it's a good idea for your group to authorize your president to appoint a parliamentarian of her choice.

WARNING

Your group may choose not to hire a professional parliamentarian, but rather to elect a member to the position. The member parliamentarian has a big decision to make when accepting an appointment to the position. Because of the complete impartiality required, they're duty-bound to forego completely their right to vote on any question at any time, unless the vote is by ballot (and they can therefore vote anonymously).

Filling Vacancies in Offices

Don't get too comfortable! Just when the members are doing what they're supposed to do and everybody is getting along, an officer resigns for some personal reason. Or maybe you have to throw out a bum officer. (You find out how to do that in Chapter 18.) No matter how good or bad things are, vacancies in office occur.

Robert's Rules helps a lot when the vacancy is in the office of the president. Unless you've decided something different in your bylaws, the vice-president automatically becomes the president if the president dies or resigns. The vacancy then arises in the office of vice-president. But when the vacancy is in any other office, some direct action is required to fill the vacancy.

Vacancies can be filled in these ways:

>> By the membership that appointed or elected the officer, unless the membership has delegated that authority exclusively to its executive board or established some other procedure.

>> By an executive board that the membership has authorized to fill those vacancies. That authorization is implicit when the bylaws provide that the board has "full power and authority" to handle the affairs of the organization between membership meetings, provided that the membership has not reserved the ability to fill of one or more of such vacancies for itself.

>> By an executive board, or committee, when the board or committee has been specifically authorized to fill the vacancy.

TIP

Many organizations are small and meet regularly and don't even have an executive board. For those groups, it's easy enough to fill the vacancy at the next membership meeting.

Other organizations have infrequent membership meetings and have an executive board that's authorized generally to tend to the business of the organization between membership meetings. For these groups, filling a vacancy in an office is almost as easy because the authorization I mentioned earlier normally permits filling a vacancy on the strength of the general authorization given to the board.

But without such a provision or a more specific provision establishing details for filling vacancies, the power to accept a resignation and fill a vacancy lies exclusively with the same body that gave the officer the job, and no other action can validly fill the vacancy.

The power to appoint or elect is the power to accept a resignation and fill a vacancy. The authority to fill a vacancy can be extended to a subordinate body only by an act of the superior body.

Regardless of whether the body filling the vacancy is the membership or the executive board, proper notice must be given to the members entitled to vote in any meeting to decide on filling a vacancy.

Defining Terms of Office

Just because your bylaws define a term of office as some specified number of years, the actual term might be more or less than the exact time. Good bylaws provide, for example, "Officers shall serve terms of one year or until their successors are elected and assume office."

Those are good reasons to provide for terms of office with "or until . . ." provision. If your bylaws just provide that "Officers shall serve for two years," you're in trouble if you need to remove an officer, or if the election meetings are more or less than exactly two years apart, or if an election meeting can't be held.

Therefore, prescribe the length of terms so that there's never a doubt as to when, for example, the president becomes the past president, and to ensure that if something causes the delay of an election meeting that you're not without officers.

Robert's Rules provides some rules about what constitutes a full term. If a vacancy occurs and the remainder of the term is at least half of the defined term, then the person filling the vacancy who serves the remainder is charged with having served a full term. If it's less than half of the defined term, the person filling the vacancy isn't charged with serving a term.

Why is this important? Bylaws frequently have some limits on the number of consecutive terms one may serve in any particular office. For example, "No member is eligible to serve in the office of president for more than two consecutive terms without a lapse of at least one year." Under such a rule, the person filling the vacancy with more than half the term remaining is eligible to re-election one time and then becomes ineligible to serve in the office for a year after the term to which they were elected is over.

Bylaw provisions that afford term limitations in private-sector organization are useful in that they allow members the freedom to not serve, and they keep others, who would enjoy too much the control they might have in an organization, from becoming inextricably entrenched in an office. You probably know a Helpful Harold, who has served as the secretary forever because he just can't say no to a membership who takes advantage of him. Give him a break! And don't feel bad if you don't know Myrtle Maniac, the treasurer who did a great job for six terms until a new treasurer was elected. Myrtle refused to turn loose the club's financial records and sign off the account at the bank, forcing the organization to seek a court order to get the bank to remove her name from the account and to have the sheriff go to her house to seize the club's filing cabinet with all the financial records.

Chapter **16**

Gearing Up for the Real Action: Committees

I n all but the smallest of organizations, committees are the organizational units in which the real work gets done. I seldom run into someone who really likes three-hour board meetings, but I find plenty of dedicated members who don't mind devoting considerable time to their respective committees, focusing on specific projects or goals they find especially interesting.

This chapter focuses on helping you and your group understand the value of using committees to achieve group objectives. And the best part about committees is that they help you reach your goals without spending tremendous amounts of time in regular meetings, going over the minute details of every idea that every member may offer.

In this chapter, I cover the technical aspects of committees as subordinate groups, each with a limited focus on a particular subject or aspect of your organization's operation. I cover different types of committees and the ways in which members are appointed to committee posts. Finally, I give you some tips about how to effectively work on committees.

Defining the Ordinary Committee

According to Robert's Rules, *ordinary committees* are regular committees that you establish either in your bylaws or as needed to consider various items of business and operational matters outside the organization's regular meetings.

TECHNICAL STUFF

The term *ordinary* distinguishes the two usual types of committees from the *committee of the whole* and the *quasi-committee of the whole*, (which isn't a full-fledged committee) both of which I discuss in greater depth in Chapter 3. These non-ordinary committees are created when an entire assembly decides to relax its rules to consider some item of business; the assembly changes itself into a committee of all the members of the organization who are present.

Ordinary committees comprise the two types of committees listed here, and I describe them in the sections that follow:

>> **Standing committees** are committees that have perpetual existence in your organization.

>> **Special committees** are committees established for a specific purpose (sometimes called *ad hoc* or *select committees*). They cease to exist after the task assigned to them is completed and the committee makes its final report.

Standing committees

Usually standing committees are established in your bylaws to serve a permanent and continuing function for the organization. Your membership can create additional standing committees if authorized by the bylaws. Consider some of the more common examples of standing committees:

>> **Auditing committee:** Even an organization with limited funds should appoint members to review the treasurer's financial records for accuracy, with an eye on whether the funds are disbursed as the members authorize. This committee, often appointed by the chair or the executive board, generally reports at the annual meeting. The treasurer shouldn't be a member of this committee because the committee reviews the treasurer's records.

>> **Membership committee:** Many organizations provide for a committee to consider and recommend on membership recruitment and retention, or even on the admission of prospective members. The chair or the executive board commonly appoints this committee.

>> **Finance and budget committee:** The necessity of this committee depends on the needs of the organization, but a finance and budget committee does what its name suggests. This committee is expected to consider the financial resources and obligations of the organization, establish a budget, and recommend on financial matters for the benefit of the executive board and the membership.

The list of an organization's standing committees depends largely on the group and its needs. Neighborhood associations may have standing committees on beautification, security, zoning, and deed restriction enforcement; professional associations may have a legislative affairs committee. The variations are endless.

TIP

Whenever an organization faces a continuing need to focus on some particular subject matter, the membership can benefit from establishing a standing committee to deal with that issue.

AUTOMATICALLY REFERRING BUSINESS TO A STANDING COMMITTEE

In some cases, bylaws (see Chapter 2) may provide that certain types of motions or items of business be referred automatically to a particular standing committee (or to the board). In such cases, the membership may not consider the motions or items in question until the assigned committee has reviewed and reported on them.

Problems with a rule such as this may arise if it's used to keep legitimate business from coming before the assembly. Take care when you're writing bylaws for your group — make sure that automatic referral doesn't necessarily preclude consideration of a motion that a committee (or a board) hasn't *approved* first.

You may like the idea of rules that can keep troublemakers from wasting the group's time. But if a faction of so-called troublemakers gains control, the same rule that protected the rest of the group may have the opposite effect and put the rogues in almost total control of your organization. They have the ability to turn the automatic referral rule against you, blocking *your* motions from being considered. Let this be fair warning: It's usually best to make sure your entire membership has the final say on any motion made.

If you decide to require that all motions first go before a committee, don't box yourself in by requiring that committee's approval. All you really need is its report and recommendation; let the membership have the right to make the final decision.

Special committees

Special committees are formed by motion and vote anytime your group needs to delegate a task or carry out some function not covered by the existing standing committees. These special committees exist only as long as it takes for them to complete their work and report back to the members.

Creating a special committee

To create a special committee, a member may say, "Madam President, I move that a special committee of six members to be appointed by the president be created to research the possibility of our organization's purchase of the vacant property next to our meeting hall." Another example of a motion to create a special committee is, "Mr. Chair, I move that the motion to buy a sailboat for our president be referred to a committee to investigate the costs involved and report back to the membership next month."

The first example creates a special committee by making a main motion (see Chapter 6). The second example uses a subsidiary motion (see Chapter 9) to *Commit* or *Refer* and creates a special committee to look into the details of enacting a motion on the floor. In both examples, the committee ceases to exist after it completes its task and reports back to the group. After the report, the committee has no function.

Saying "Goodbye" to a special committee

Special committees exist only as long as the committee needs to do its work and make its report. But that doesn't mean they go on forever if the committee never reports! When, for whatever reason, special committees wind up accomplishing about as much as standing water, you can count on Robert's Rules for a few hints on how to make them evaporate. A special committee ceases to exist in these cases:

>> When it completes its assigned task and makes its final report.

>> When it is given walking papers from the assembly that created it. We parliamentarians make it sound nicer than saying "You're fired" by calling this procedure *discharging a committee*. But the result is the same: When that happens, it's all over. That's it. *Finé, kaput.* Flip to Chapter 12 to find out more about how to throw this switch.

EXCEPTION

>> When the term of the body (like the board or the convention) that created it ends. An exception arises if the committee was created to report to a future such body (like next year's board or convention). If it doesn't do its job and give its report by the time the next board's term ends (or the next convention adjourns), it's a gone goose for sure.

A COMMITTEE OF SPECIAL STANDING

A *standing committee* is defined as one established in your bylaws and having perpetual existence. Generally speaking, a standing committee reports to the membership. So what do you call a committee that's established in your bylaws and has perpetual existence but, instead of reporting to the membership, reports to the *executive board?*

The only committee mentioned in Robert's Rules that meets these conditions is the *executive committee.*

The reason behind establishing an executive committee is to grant to a small but trusted group of officers the authority to make any critical decisions (usually reserved exclusively to the board) between board meetings. It's not uncommon to give an executive committee almost all the power of the board, yet make the committee's decisions subject to the board's ultimate approval.

Because an executive board can't delegate its authority to a subordinate body without the approval of the general membership, an executive committee can't be created or appointed unless your bylaws expressly authorize it.

Hence, as a permanent committee established in the bylaws by the membership, but one that is completely subordinate to the board, the executive committee — given the parliamentary definitions — is neither *special* nor *standing.* In fact, it's not really a committee at all. It's what Robert's Rules calls a board within a board.

If you utilize an executive committee, use it wisely because it gives a small number of people a considerable amount of power.

Taking Stock of Committee Appointment Methods

When the time comes to get specific about who's going to serve on a committee, Robert's Rules gives you six different methods for deciding exactly who you want to do what. Each method is particularly well suited to a different situation (but is by no means exclusive to that situation).

I list the appointment methods, brief descriptions, and their customary uses here (you can find a more detailed discussion of all these methods in Chapter 14):

>> **Appointment by motion:** This method is most often used to appoint special committees. Using this method, either you name the prospective committee members in the motion that establishes the committee or you name them in a separate motion after you adopt the motion to create the committee.

>> **Appointment by the chair:** This method is also commonly utilized to appoint special committees, but it can also be used in the appointment of standing committees. To use this method, you can either specify appointment by the chair as part of your motion creating the committee, or you can use a separate motion to appoint using this method. Appointment by the chair is also commonly established in bylaws (see Chapter 2) to prescribe that a group's president appoint standing committees listed in the bylaws.

>> **Ballot election:** Generally used to appoint members to important standing committees, this method is used when a group wants to select the committee members with the benefits of a secret ballot.

>> **Open nominations:** This method is used any time the members want to elect members to a committee but don't require a secret ballot. Using this method, nominations (see Chapter 13) are taken from the floor, and election is usually by voice vote. See Chapter 14 for details on the election process.

>> **Nominations by the chair:** When you want to take advantage of the chair's knowledge of individual members' capabilities, you can use this method. The chair offers her nominees, and the membership votes on each, usually by voice vote. See Chapter 14 for the specifics.

>> **Appointment by definition in the bylaws:** Some committees are established with the bylaws (see Chapter 2) prescribing details on who serves. For example, a bylaw defining a finance committee may read, "The finance committee membership shall consist of the treasurer, the chair of the audit committee, the chair of the budget committee, the executive director, two members appointed by the president, and three members elected by the membership at the annual meeting."

Appointing Committee Members

A committee is only as good as the members you appoint to it. Appointing committee members involves two steps:

1. **Decide which of the six methods for appointing members is appropriate for your specific situation.**

2. **Consider the committee's task, the size necessary to handle that task, and members' abilities and temperaments.**

For information on the first step, refer to the previous section or to Chapter 14. For information on the second step and how it applies to committees with specific functions, read on.

TIP

A committee may have members (or even a chair) who aren't members of the parent body. But unless the bylaws or other rules of the organization specifically authorize the chair to appoint nonmembers to a committee, the membership has to approve such appointments. But when the organization's members are creating a committee or naming members to the committee, no special authority is required.

Making appointments for the right reasons

Committees are formed for the purpose of getting things done, and it's never a good idea to saddle the willing and able with a fellow member who never participates except by standing for recognition at the end of the job.

WARNING

If you're operating under the notion that any good is served by making committee appointments either as patronage to pay off political favors in your organization or to *honor* an appointee, distance yourself and your organization from that kind of thinking as quickly as possible! I've seen committees crippled by the inability to achieve a quorum because members were appointed for those reasons.

Appointing special committees for investigations or deliberations

Special committees intended to handle investigations or deliberations should be large and should include anyone likely to have a lot to say about the matter referred to it. (Following this general guideline saves you a lot of time in your regular meetings.) The goal of a committee like this is to arrive at a report that best reflects the will of the entire organization. Therefore, if the committee is one-sided and doesn't include all factions in the committee discussions, then more than likely nothing will get accomplished.

Limiting participation to one side probably just ensures an acrimonious debate when the committee reports its recommendations.

For example, consider a special committee to revise bylaws. If you exclude members who always have a lot to say about how things should be done just because they're always oppositional, you only postpone the inevitable; any work you do in your committee may just become a lost motion.

TIP

By including these opinionated members in the committee's work, you're more likely to wind up with most of what you want, and you may also have their support when the time comes for the rest of the members to vote on the revision. If you argue and compromise in the committee, you have a better chance of successfully passing an acceptable revision.

Picking the right mix for committees carrying out a specific task

Some committees produce better results when they include representatives of all factions. On the other hand, a special committee tasked with carrying out an order of the membership should be limited to those in favor of the task and should have no more members than are necessary to get the job done.

Robert's Rules advises that if a committee member doesn't agree with the goals, they should ask to be relieved from the appointment.

Selecting ideal members for standing committees

Appointments to standing committees must take into consideration the abilities of the prospective members and their willingness to actively serve. These committees must be of sufficient size to handle the volume of work reasonably anticipated to come before them during their term.

Following Committee Procedures

Your committee meetings are subject to the same rules as your organization, but you have some flexibility if you plan ahead. Your organization's rules can provide for committees to adopt its own rules, as can instructions from the organization in specific cases.

WARNING

Your organization's rules can authorize your committee to meet virtually using electronic means, but it takes some form of authorization for that to happen. When the committee is established in your bylaws, the authorization must come from the bylaws. But if the committee isn't specifically established in the bylaws, the authorization can come from the standing rules of the parent body. It can also be granted in the motion creating the committee, by the motion referring a matter to it, or even later on the parent body's specific authorization. See Chapter 3 for a bit more focused info on virtual meetings.

Using small board rules

You probably won't need to concern yourself with special rules in your committee because Robert's rules that are applicable to committees are thankfully quite adequate for committee work. That's especially good news because small committees generally can use the same informal rules that are applicable to small boards. (Flip to Chapter 3 for that list.)

WARNING

The parent body can nix the ability of even a small committee to use the informal rules afforded to small boards. All it takes to require standard formality is a majority vote of the parent body.

Unfettering the discourse

Because a committee has a duty to give the organization the benefit of its thorough consideration of the matters referred to it,

>> Motions to *Reconsider* aren't bound by the same limitations on who can make them or when they can be made. Head to Chapter 12 for details on using the motion to *Reconsider* in committees.

>> Motions to *Rescind* or to *Amend Something Previously Adopted* can be adopted by a majority vote if all the members who voted in favor of the motion to be rescinded or amended are present or received adequate notice. Look in Chapter 12 for details.

>> Motions to limit or close debate aren't permitted, but if Alex Antagonist abuses (to the detriment of the meeting) the rule allowing unlimited debate, they can be removed from the meeting. Other remedies include reporting their bad behavior to the appointing authority with the hope they'll get the boot.

Similarly, the organization needs the latitude to give proper consideration to the committee's report. So, even though the organization might have finalized some amendment to a motion before submitting the motion to a committee, the committee is free to report amendments of its own, and the assembly is free to act on those recommendations despite what it might have "finalized" before the motion was referred to the committee.

Easing up on minutes

Unless the committee is large and practically its own organization, you don't have to keep formal minutes. But having some record of what happened can be useful, depending on the committee. In most cases, the chair serves as the secretary. But in larger committees, you may want to elect a secretary to prepare meeting summaries for the benefit of the committee.

Hearing from the masses

If your committee is charged with bringing a recommendation on an important matter where facts need to be gathered or the opinions of your organization's members need to be taken into consideration, you'll probably find it prudent to hold a meeting open to the membership for the purpose of hearing those opinions. Of course, it probably goes without saying that noncommittee members who attend such a meeting are subject to any rules applicable to the hearing and have no right to be present during the committee deliberations. But just to be sure, I said it anyway.

Working on a Committee

Successful organizations contain effective committees made up of dedicated members who give generously of their time. However, dedicated members with time to give aren't a dime a dozen. As a good leader, you must make committee service meaningful for members and see that committee tasks are completed.

Just as important, committee members need to participate, and each must pull their own weight and accept an individual share of the work.

Hearing from the secretary

When a committee is appointed, your organization's secretary has a specific duty to make sure that everyone appointed is notified of their appointment and to get a list of the members to the chair. The secretary must also provide the committee with the wording of any referred motion and any necessary documents essential to the committee's work. (I cover the basic duties of the secretary in Chapter 14.)

When a committee decides it needs something from the organization's records to do its work, the chair should make a request of the appropriate officer. If that officer has any qualms about furnishing the requested information, their duty is to confer with the organization's president about the matter.

Presiding over a committee

Successful committees are ones that get to work quickly. Your first duty as chair is to call a meeting of the committee. If you fail to do so quickly, you run the risk of losing members whose schedules may be overloaded if they have to do too much at the last minute. Set the tone for success by establishing a time and place for the first meeting of your committee and call the meeting to order on time.

WARNING

If the chair fails to get the committee up and running in a timely fashion, Robert's Rules permits committee members to call a meeting. Unless the bylaws, other rules, or instructions given to the committee require (or allow the committee itself to require) a larger number, any two committee members can call the meeting and get things going.

As far as notice and quorum are concerned (see Chapter 4), your committee meetings are subject to the same general rules as any other meeting. Your committee members are just as entitled to reasonable notice of committee meetings as they are for meetings of the membership. And just like in boards or small assemblies, you can attend a committee meeting by teleconferencing or videoconferencing, but *only* if the bylaws, or in some cases, other rules or actions of the parent body specifically authorize it.

If your committee is small, your role as chair probably includes the responsibility to serve as the committee's secretary, too. But if you have a big committee, you probably have enough to do already. That's when it may be appropriate to ask Marvelous Mel (the meticulous minutes-maker) to serve as a committee secretary and to make good notes. Good notes can be as helpful as regular minutes when you or Snoring Sam needs help recalling what you did in earlier meetings.

TIP

For all but very large committees (where size demands the same degree of formality as any regular assembly), committees can conduct their business meetings using considerably relaxed rules of procedure. I discuss those procedures in detail in Chapter 3.

Participating as a committee member

In the section, "Making appointments for the right reasons," earlier in this chapter I make the point that committee membership means work, and wisdom dictates that appointees be those who are willing to do what it takes to get the job done. Unless your only goal is to line up with the glory hounds for recognition when your committee makes its final report, you'll make *"Participate!"* your watchword. Make it your business to do the following:

>> **Take an active interest in your committee's work.** You don't have to be one of those eager beavers who wears out everybody with overkill in the enthusiasm department, but avoid being a bench warmer, too.

>> **Think creatively about the task at hand and offer suggestions for effective ways to achieve the objectives of the committee.** Offer your committee the benefit of your experience. Don't be a complaining naysayer. Instead, help find ways to solve problems and make things work.

>> **Do your share without waiting to be asked.** No matter what tasks are necessary to achieve the committee's goals and purpose, shoulder some of the load. Committee work is hands-on and usually involves some grunt work. Don't be too good for getting your hands dirty. In fact, the higher you think your station is, the more valuable others will see your willingness to roll up your sleeves and wield the proverbial shovel.

>> **Show up for all meetings and be on time.** Everybody is busy. Your time is no more valuable than any other member's time. If you don't have time to serve on a committee, don't accept the appointment. If you accept the appointment, set an example by being a loyal, working member of the team.

>> **Be nice.** When you go to a committee meeting, you're there for in-depth exploration of ideas so that your entire membership doesn't have to figure out all the details and possibilities at membership meetings. As relaxed and informal as committee meetings can be, molehills can become mountains, and tempers can flare. But there's no provision in Robert's Rules for relaxing the rules of decorum. In fact, when committee members become disorderly to the extent of interfering with the work of the committee and its ability to complete its assignment on time, the committee can require the offenders to leave the meeting.

Adjourning committee meetings

Unless your committee is holding its final meeting before making a final report to the assembly, you can simply adjourn with or without setting a time for the next meeting. You may have established a regular meeting schedule or the time for the next meeting. If you haven't done either, then your committee meets again on the call of the chair, who needs to give you (and everybody else on the committee) reasonable notice of the when-and-where (if they expect to get anything done, that is).

If your committee didn't set a time for that next meeting and your chair drops the ball and fails to call it, then the rules allowing committee members to call the meeting (see the "Presiding over a committee" section) still apply.

Don't use the motion to adjourn if yours is a special committee and you're in your final meeting, having concluded your work. Instead, use the motion to rise and assign one of the members or the chair to present the report to the appointing group. The motion to rise signifies that your committee has completed its task. The more seasoned you become with all this meeting stuff, the more you'll come to learn that rising is much more fun than simply adjourning!

Chapter **17**

Reporting to Your Organization

R obert's Rules contains a basic premise that I don't think has ever been reduced to words until now: When all is said and done, there's still the paperwork!

It's true! The only way you can really let your members know what's going on in the day-to-day operations of your organization is to prepare and present reports at meetings. Newsletters may generally inform members about pertinent matters, but the official reports of officers, the board, and committees are critical to your operation as an organization. After all, your reports recommend action and furnish the necessary information on which sound decisions are based.

Paperwork is a necessary evil, and everybody hates it — at least, to a certain extent (although not many people complain when it comes to having to endorse their paychecks and make out deposit slips).

Nor do many folks complain when they don't have to wade through a lot of superfluous information to get exactly what they need to make good decisions.

In this chapter, I share the information necessary for proper and informative reporting to the membership, including details about form and content of the minutes, treasurer's reports, and reports of officers, boards, and committees. I also provide tips on how to advance the recommendations contained in those reports, including the proper methods for taking action on such recommendations.

You'll still have to deal with paperwork after reading this chapter, but if you make good use of the information here, you may get away with less of it — and what paperwork you do have may be more concise and better organized.

Making Minutes Minute

Minutes need to include only what was *done* in the meeting, not what was *said.* That rule doesn't seem to get the widespread coverage it deserves. Considering how meticulously some secretaries try to record every word spoken, I can't help but wonder if they wouldn't prefer to write short, concise minutes that leave no doubt about the final results on all the motions.

Recording all the discussion that occurs in a meeting is a time-consuming and frustratingly tedious task, but unfortunately, that's what constitutes the minute books of so many of the organizations I encounter. So when I hear or read minutes prepared by folks who don't know that, I do my best to tell them about the "include what's done, not what's said" rule. It's sure to be some of the best news they've ever heard!

The following sections explain what you need to know about your minutes. That is, what to include (and not include), how to prepare them, how to sign them, and how to get them approved.

Styling your minutes

Minutes are important because they're the only surviving record of what done at the meeting. They can be dry and boring. In fact, it's probably a good sign if they are! Most importantly, they need to be informative and easy to navigate for whatever the reader needs to know six months from now.

When you call a parliamentarian and ask for help, they're going to want to see the minutes, and they're going to need to find something important — maybe the exact words of a bylaw amendment that was officially adopted, or a tellers' report that furnishes details on the vote tally. Simple organization of the facts and use of unpretentious language are the best attributes you can give your minutes.

TIP

Even General Robert was tired of the hackneyed phrase "Respectfully submitted" that adorned all the poetic 18th- and 19th-century-style minutes. It's okay to use that if you're going to write the entire minutes in similar form. But why do that? Writing like Ben Franklin isn't easy. And if you're going to work that hard, you can surely find a way to get paid more.

TIP

You want your minutes to be readable, but you must be precise in the information you give. Your minutes provide the record of the action taken at the meeting, so they need to clearly memorialize the facts.

You can write good minutes without a lot of angst if you just write in plain English, using simple sentences and including adequate information. Good form for the body of the minutes requires you to separate subject items into paragraphs.

Composing your meeting's minutes

To save you time and unnecessary work, Robert's Rules spells out exactly what needs to go into your minutes. If you want to regularly include something in your minutes that's different from the things Robert's Rules provides, you'll need to adopt a special rule of order (see Chapter 2). But if your group just wants to include something supplemental in the minutes of a single meeting, you can do that by a majority vote.

Good minutes have these characteristics:

>> Have meaningful headings to help the poor souls who actually read them

>> Are organized with separate paragraphs for each subject item

>> Are written using plain English and simple sentences

>> Contain adequate (but not too much) detail

>> Avoid the phrase "Respectfully Submitted" (it's now considered passé)

These sections explain specifically what to include in your meetings.

The first paragraph

The first paragraph needs to include this information:

>> The kind of meeting (regular, special, annual, adjourned regular, adjourned special, and so forth)

>> The name of the organization and whether the meeting is a meeting of the organization or its board

>> The date, time, and location of the meeting (don't list the location if it's always the same)

>> A statement confirming that your organization's regular presiding officer and secretary are present (or giving the names of the persons substituting for them)

>> A mention of whether the previous meeting's minutes were read and approved (and the date of that meeting, if it wasn't a regular meeting)

Corrections to minutes are entered in the minutes being corrected; they're not detailed in the minutes of the meeting at which the corrections were adopted. (The minutes of the meeting at which corrections were made should merely state that minutes of the previous meeting were approved as corrected.)

The body paragraphs

The body portion of the minutes needs to include this info:

» All main motions (except, in most cases, those that are withdrawn), along with the name of the member making the motion (but not the name of the person who seconded the motion). Chapter 6 defines main motions.

» The final wording of the motions, either as adopted or as disposed of. If it's appropriate to include mention of the fact(s) that the motion was debated or amended (or both), you can note these items parenthetically.

» The disposition of the motion. If the motion is temporarily disposed of, also include any adhering secondary motions.

» Information about the vote (take a look at Chapter 8 for details about the kind of votes listed here).

  • **Counted vote:** If the motion was decided by a counted vote, the minutes include the number of votes on each side. But if the motion is one that you wouldn't enter into the minutes in the first place, include neither the motion nor the numbers.

  • **Roll-call vote:** If the motion was decided by a roll-call vote, the minutes include the name of each member who votes and their response, even if the member abstains by simply saying "Present" when their name is called. If too many members give you the silent treatment when you call on them for their votes, you need to include some record of their presence so that, when the minutes are read, folks won't be wondering whether the meeting had a quorum when the roll-call vote was taken.

  • **Ballot vote:** Report of the tellers committee in full.

» Secondary motions (see Chapters 9 through 12) not lost or withdrawn, where necessary for clarity (example motions include *Recess, Fix Time to Which to Adjourn, Suspend the Rules, Postpone to a Certain Time, Ballot Vote Ordered,* and so on). Allude to the adoption of secondary motions by saying, "A ballot vote having been ordered, the tellers . . . ."

>> Notices of motions.

>> The fact that an assembly went into quasi-committee or committee of the whole (refer to Chapter 3), and the committee's report.

>> All points of order and appeals (see Chapter 11) and their subsequent dispositions, with reasons given by the chair for the ruling. (Rulings often establish precedent, so a careful record here is important.)

>> The full text of any report that the assembly orders to be entered into the minutes. This situation doesn't happen often because a reference to a written report is usually sufficient for the record.

>> Any of the juicy and disorderly words that a member has said that get him "named" by the chair for being disorderly (see Chapter 18 for the lowdown on the shame of being *named*).

The last paragraphs

The last paragraph of your minutes needs to include the time you adjourned. And that's it! Well, except for the following additional notes to keep in mind when finalizing your minutes:

>> The proceedings of a committee of the whole aren't included in the minutes, but you do need to include the fact that the move into committee occurred and also include the report of the committee.

>> When a question is considered informally, the same information should be recorded as in regular rules. Informality is permitted only in allowing additional opportunities to debate.

>> The full text of any report is included in the minutes only if the assembly so orders. Because written reports become part of the organization's records when they're received, it's a rare case where it's appropriate to make the actual report part of your minutes.

WARNING

Avoid minute entries that state that a report is "attached." That statement makes the report itself part of the minutes. According to Robert, the correct minute entry form for most reports is "The ice-cream social committee report was received and placed on file." That's all you need in your minutes. The report stands filed without being an actual part of the minutes.

>> Record the name of any guest speaker and the subject of presentation, but make no summary of the speaker's remarks.

Signing the minutes

Minutes are to be signed by the secretary and, if customary, may also be signed by the president. Minutes are your group's legal record of its proceedings, and the secretary's signature establishes evidence of the original document's authenticity.

REMEMBER

You can write good minutes without a lot of grief if you remember to keep it simple and understand that what's important is what was *done* in the meeting.

Approving the minutes

The minutes of one meeting are normally approved at the next regular meeting, following the call to order and opening ceremonies. I cover minute approval procedure in detail in Chapter 5.

If the meeting is an adjourned meeting (see Chapter 3), you approve the minutes of your previous meeting (the meeting that established the adjourned meeting) before taking up business where you left off in that meeting. Also, the minutes of the adjourned meeting need to be approved at the next adjourned or regular meeting.

If the minutes are those of an executive session (see Chapter 3), their approval must be done in executive session. But if the things decided in the executive session aren't secret, the minutes can be approved in a regular session. What's critical in deciding when to approve minutes of an executive session is the need for secrecy. If your board voted to purchase a building, the minute entry for that action would not be a secret, so the minutes could be approved in regular session. But the discussions about the deal that took place in the meeting must remain a secret.

TIP

When your assembly won't meet again for a good while, such as occurs when the meeting is an annual meeting of the membership where a board is elected to take care of all business for the next year, appointing a minutes-approval committee to approve minutes as soon as they can be prepared after the meeting adjourns is a good idea. The membership can still correct minutes approved by such a committee, but in the interim, the organization has legally approved minutes of its annual election meeting.

TIP

If it appears that the draft minutes need a lot of work before they're ready for approval, entertain a motion to postpone the approval of minutes to a certain time. Refer to Chapter 9 where I cover the motion to *Postpone to a Certain Time* or *Postpone Definitely.*

When you hold a special meeting, the only business in order is the urgent business for which the meeting was called — the business that can't wait until the next regular meeting. For that reason, the minutes of your regular meetings aren't brought up for approval at a special meeting (unless the approval of minutes is the urgent reason you called the special meeting). The minutes of a special meeting are approved at the next regular meeting.

REMEMBER

Minutes drafted for distribution and review in advance of the meeting at which they'll come up for approval aren't the official minutes *until the members approve them.* Because changes may be made in the minutes before they're approved, it's good practice for the secretary to note somewhere on the distribution copy that it's a "draft for approval."

When minutes are approved, the secretary annotates the original file copy with any corrections in the margin or retypes the minutes to include the corrections. The secretary then writes "Approved" on the minutes, initials them, and adds the approval date.

Publishing a record of proceedings

Your organization may like to capture a written record of your meeting's proceedings, creating pages upon pages of word-for-word from gavel to gavel. But compiling such a tome is no substitute for proper minutes for your records. Minutes have a completely different purpose: They exist for you to know exactly what you did in the meeting. Transcripts, on the other hand, exist for you to be able to relive the entire meeting by reading every utterance of everybody who had anything to say. They're not minutes — they're hours!

Preparing a transcript of the proceedings for publication makes for one onerous task for the secretary. Fortunately, Robert's Rules recognizes that if you're going to go any further and really publish the proceedings *in full,* you should probably have a stenographic reporter as an assistant secretary. Robert's Rules also reminds the presiding officer that clearly identifying all speakers is essential to an accurate report. When you're reading one of those monstrous transcripts, it's no fun to go back and try to remember who said what. Also note that publishing in full means that you include all the reports that were given at the meeting, too.

Even if you don't have a stenographic assistant, but rely instead on an overworked secretary with a tape recorder and a lot of time to type to create the transcript, the secretary has to still prepare *minutes* as described in the previous section.

REMEMBER

Minutes are a record of what was done. They are completely different from that fat published book that nobody ever reads again anyway unless the meeting was especially heated and nothing entertaining is available on television or the Internet.

First Things First: Filing the Treasurer's Report

The treasurer generally reports basic financial information at every regular meeting. Today's accounting-made-easy software allows a treasurer to pretty easily print a report that shows receipts, disbursements, and cash balances. But for organizations with simple and uncomplicated finances (maybe they have just a cash fund or a checking account), all that's really necessary is a simple, single-page report that shows the opening balance, the itemized receipts and disbursements, and the closing balance. In fact, most members want and need only that basic information to make decisions.

You can find a sample treasurer's report online at www.dummies. com/go/robertsrulesfd4e; detail beyond what's represented there is usually just a waste of the members' time. The treasurer's job mostly involves working behind the scenes to take care of the funds. The audit committee has the task of examining financial records in detail at sufficient intervals; the committee's goal is to alleviate any concerns members may have about the details of the fund management. If any member requires more detail than what appears in the treasurer's report, that member needs to make arrangements to meet with the treasurer outside the meeting to go over more detailed records.

After it's presented to the membership, the treasurer's report is simply filed, and no other action is necessary. The time for formal action on your financial reports is when you receive your audit committee's report on the treasurer's annual report. (More information on meeting agendas and the order of business is available in Chapter 5.)

TIP

No matter what the official procedure is for filing a treasurer's report after presentation, every meeting has its own Millie Motionmaker who loves to move to accept the treasurer's report. If you know Millie, remind her (and your presiding officer) that the proper way for the chair to handle the treasurer's report after it's presented is to say, "Thank you. The treasurer's report will be filed. The next item of business is . . . ."

Next Up: Hearing Reports of Other Officers

Other than the treasurer's report and the secretary's report, which is distinguished from the reading and approval of minutes, and will include, perhaps, a report of correspondence received, other officers don't usually make regular reports.

From time to time, other officers may have information that needs to come before the assembly, and motions may arise out of the presentation of such information. An officer's need to make a report is usually of sufficient importance to justify priority placement in the order of business. (Robert's Rules endorses this practice, in case you're wondering.)

When an officer makes a report that contains recommendations for action, a member other than the reporting officer should make any motion tied to the report.

For example, imagine that the president receives an offer of ten tickets to the Lake Wassamatta Submarine Races for the organization to raffle. After the president makes his report recommending that the organization accept the offer, you agree and say, "Mr. President, I move that we accept the offer of the tickets and that you be authorized to appoint a raffle committee to make arrangements for a raffle and report back to us its plan at next month's meeting."

TIP

Don't just move to accept the report or adopt the recommendations. Your motion in the example is precise and to the point; you make very clear exactly what the members are being asked to decide.

Wrapping Up Reporting: Boards and Committees

In well-run organizations, the executive board (if there is one) and committees are loaded with work between meetings of the assembly. These subordinate bodies need to keep the general membership informed of their activities and recommendations, and they do so by furnishing reports to the body to which they're accountable.

REMEMBER

Reports should certainly be made when there's business to report or recommendations to make, but not just for the sake of giving a report. Boards and committees don't have to furnish reports if they haven't done anything since their previous report. No rule in Robert's Rules requires your committees or boards to automatically add to the profits of the paper mills just because you're having another meeting.

These sections delve deeper into the basics of reporting for boards and committees. I discuss not only the reports and the info they need to contain, but also how to handle motions arising from the reports.

Hearing from the executive board

Your executive board is charged with much of the management of your organization that's necessary between membership meetings. The board commonly reports its accomplishments at the end of its term (at your big election meeting, whenever that is). But if you hold membership meetings more frequently than annually, your board may also report to the membership at other times when important matters require membership attention or when the membership has requested a report on a particular matter.

The executive board may select the person or persons to draft the report, but the president or secretary may be assigned this duty by custom or rule. The board considers the draft for adoption and amends it at its pleasure, and the report is then presented to the membership.

Handling committee reports

The nature of any committee makes it a subordinate body to the group or person under whose authority it is appointed or elected. Therefore, the committee's ultimate product is a report back to that authority. Its report must contain its findings, the results of its actions in carrying out the task assigned to it, its recommendations, or all this information.

Here I list some basics about preparing and presenting reports from boards and committees. The whole reason for these reports is to convey information that the members need to have and to make a permanent record for future reference. No one I know ever complained about having well-prepared written reports in their organization's records.

Writing the committee report

The committee's report should always be submitted in writing, unless it's so brief that its entire substance and content can be easily entered in the minutes from an oral report. Generally, committees like to elaborate on their work, so reports are often too lengthy to report orally. But committees can give oral reports occasionally, especially when a motion has been referred for a recommendation and the only report is, for example, a recommendation on how to dispose of the motion. No need for a written report there!

When creating your written committee report:

>> **Do identify it as the report of the committee, not of the committee chairman, even if the chairman presents the report.** In other words, be specific with the report title "Report of the Communications Committee" should be at the top of the report, with a minute entry something like, "Foghorn LeFebvre, committee chairman, presented the report of the Communications Committee.

>> **Do write in the third person.** "We recommend" or "The committee recommends . . . ." Never "I recommend," or "It is recommended that you . . . ."

>> **Do identify the committee.** For example, say, "The committee appointed to report on the advisability of purchasing the vacant lot next door reports that . . ." or "The Legislative Affairs Committee reports that . . . ."

>> **Do ensure that the report is signed by all the committee members who concur, or by the chairman alone, if authorized by the committee.** In that case, the chair includes the title *Chairman* next to his name as a means of certifying that the entire committee adopted the report.

>> **Don't address or date it.** After all, the report's recipient is the group to which it is presented, and minutes already reflect the date of the meeting in which it's presented.

>> **Don't include the words "Respectfully submitted" before the signatures.** This closing is no longer customary and is actually considered superfluous (if not altogether passé).

Covering recommendations for action in committee reports

Most committee reports contain some sort of recommendation, especially when motions and amendments are referred to a committee. In those cases, the committee is usually called upon to report its recommendations on the motion's disposition. It may recommend amendments to the main motion or recommend that a pending amendment be defeated. Reports with recommendations of this kind really just return the motion to the hands of the members.

After the committee makes its recommendations on a motion referred to it, the chair restates the motion in its original form (as it went to the committee); if the committee's recommendation is to be advanced, either the committee or another member makes the appropriate motion, and the discussion begins again.

Some special committees simply report the results of an investigation or their findings on some matter. (Flip to Chapter 16 for a rundown on special committees.) Their reports may require no action because the information they provide adds to discussions on some question or issue of concern or interest to the members. When no action is required, the chair responds to the committee report by saying, "Thank you, the report needs no action and will be placed on file" or "Thank you, the next item of business is. . . ."

Organizations sometimes improperly handle reports from nominating committees. Moving to adopt the report of a nominating committee as a means of electing the slate proposed is never in order. After a nominating committee presents its report, the chair proceeds directly to take nominations from the floor and continues doing so until no further nominations are forthcoming. You can find the complete procedural guidelines for this committee in Chapter 13.

Knowing What to Do with Reports and Recommendations

Consider yourself a prisoner of your words. When the time comes to present a report to your organization, be sure you use terms correctly and in the proper context — you don't want to do or say something you wish you hadn't! To avoid a lot of unnecessary trouble and confusion, keep the following points in mind:

>> **Reports are received when they're presented.** Motions to receive reports after they're read make no sense because the report has already been received. The only time a motion to receive a report makes sense, or is even in order, is when you want a report to be presented at some time other than when reports are in order according to your agenda.

>> *Adopting* **(or accepting) a report from officers, boards, and committees is problematic.** The odds are good that you don't want to adopt the whole report. If anything, you probably want to adopt only some of the motions or resolutions recommended in the report. The only time it really makes sense to adopt a report is when you want to endorse the entire contents of a report that was prepared for adoption as the report of the group. For example, when a board makes its annual report to the assembly, it is always adopted by the board that presents it. But if the parent assembly wants to publish that report in the organization's name, the assembly must adopt it to make it

the report of the entire organization. Only when the assembly *adopts* the annual report of its board does that report become an official report of the assembly.

WARNING

Adopting (or accepting) recommendations rather than taking up the recommended questions (or motions or resolutions) can create considerable confusion. If a committee recommends a resolution's adoption, you don't want to consider a motion to adopt the recommendation — the question instead is directly on the adoption of the resolution. Think about the trouble you run into if you need to amend the resolution: Just how do you amend a resolution if the motion is to adopt the recommendation?

Sometimes a report contains a recommendation on which the members absolutely need to consider and take action, but which isn't presented as a motion. Take, for example, a committee report that concludes with a recommendation that the club immediately hire a lawyer to defend the club in a lawsuit. But instead of saying, "On behalf of the committee, I move that the club immediately hire a lawyer to defend us in the suit that Tom Trubble filed against us," the reporting member just sits down after reporting the recommendation. At that time, any member might rise and make the motion to make the purchase. But if the club is the Society of Seriously Shy Sword-Swallowers, it's likely that nobody will take a stab at making the motion. In that case, even if it isn't customary for the presiding officer to do so, it's completely appropriate for the presiding officer to *assume* the motion and say, "The question is on the club hiring a lawyer to defend us in the lawsuit that Tom Trubble filed. Is there any debate?" I discuss assuming a motion in Chapter 11.

Recognizing Members' Rights to Consult the Records

Over the years, the minutes, the treasurer's financial reports, and other reports of officers, boards, and committees become an important archive for your organization. All these reports constitute your organization's records and generally must be accessible to the members. If your group is incorporated, members may even have a legal right to inspect any of these records (and more) at any reasonable time.

Robert's Rules recognizes, however, that an assembly's records aren't open to inspection to the extent that members wanting to view records can excessively pester the secretary or other custodian.

A few basic rules apply to the availability of some records:

REMEMBER

TECHNICAL STUFF

>> **Assembly minutes are available only to members of that assembly, unless the group has authorized nonmembers to view them.** This rule applies to boards, too, and means that you're not automatically entitled to view your board's minutes if you're not on the board. However, if the assembly superior to the board orders the minutes to be made available to the members, the board must follow orders.

Members of the board are free to share information from the minutes with anyone unless the content is under the protection of the secrecy of executive session. Flip to Chapter 3 for information on executive session.

Ordering the board's minutes to be read at a meeting of the membership requires a two-thirds vote, a vote of a majority of the entire membership, or a majority vote with previous notice.

>> **You don't necessarily have unlimited access to membership information.** You *probably* have the right under rule or law to view or copy basic member contact information on your organization's membership list, at least for personal use in making contact with other members. But a membership list is probably considered proprietary information to the group, and your right to the list isn't a right to furnish the list to others outside the group.

>> **Your organization's records belong only to the organization, which can and should devise policies concerning the permitted use and access to the records.** Consulting with an attorney is the best way to know whether any of your records are subject to public inspection or to inspection by the members, regardless of internal policy.

When it comes to the minutes, financial reports, and reports of boards and committees, you have to balance the rights of members with the rights of the organization as a whole. You can save a lot of worry and trouble by putting in place a standing rule to establish a privacy policy regarding the availability of your records to members and to the public.

Chapter **18**

Disciplining and Removing Officers or Members

P eople behave themselves most of the time, but sometimes members and officers alike get the urge to create problems or make a scene in meetings. However infrequent they may be, you need to know how to deal with problem situations when they occur.

And not all problems crop up in meetings. Even outside the meeting milieu, a member may act in a manner inconsistent with the standards your group requires of those who want to maintain an association with your organization. This chapter gives you information on how to deal with situations that shouldn't occur but, unfortunately, do.

Dealing with a Dictator

Has your presiding officer donned the crown of King Kong? Do they refuse to allow your proper motion to come before the membership because of their obvious effort to maintain and protect their own personal agenda or faction? If so, they're violating their duty to the assembly to maintain an impartial bearing in the chair.

Not to worry. You can exercise some options, which I discuss here, that may just cause her the utmost astonishment.

Putting a question from your place

Suppose that the presiding officer is blocking your (non-dilatory) motion by refusing to let it come before the membership for consideration, or even by refusing to recognize you when you're entitled to the floor. Your first line of defense in this sort of passive-aggressive attack on your rights is to raise a *Point of Order* (see Chapter 11) and to *Appeal* any ruling that's wrong or self-serving. If the chair refuses to entertain your Point of Order or your Appeal after you've repeated it a couple times, you get to have some fun and put the question from your place.

Putting the question from your place means you can simply ignore the chair's recalcitrance and announce to the members that the chair's unwillingness to put the question on your appeal entitles you to place before them the motion you originally wanted to make. Go for it! The rules are on your side. By this time, King Kong has probably lost some serious brownie points and may be close to having their name changed to Gorilla B. Gone.

WARNING

To put the question from your place, you need to know your political situation. You can't get far if you aren't confident that the majority is on your side. And if you are actually the problem and are just being a pill, challenging the presiding officer can't help you.

Removing the presiding officer from the chair

If King Kong continues to abuse the rights of the members, you have another weapon in your arsenal. You can move to suspend the rules and remove the presiding officer from the chair (for the current meeting or session) with a two-thirds vote. (For information on the incidental motion to suspend the rules, see Chapter 11.) When your gruesome gorilla is out of the way, the vice gorilla takes over unless your motion names another, or, if the vice gorilla isn't present, elect a temporary gorilla and contemplate the more permanent solution of busting the big ape down to a little monkey.

Removing an officer permanently

A good number of my consultations address situations in which a president decides that the membership exists to serve their personal agenda, and sorry is the poor soul who dares to suggest an alternative approach to anything.

Before you and your fellow members just give up and abandon your treasury to the control of King Kong and their minions, you may want to consider the alternative action: Remove the mighty monkey from office. Removing someone from office isn't necessarily easy, but if your bylaws include a provision that the members can remove an officer, then you can do it without much ado as long as you get a two-thirds vote on the proposal. (You can actually accomplish the removal with a majority vote if you've given notice, or if you have the votes of a majority of the entire membership.)

WARNING

You may encounter a couple of stumbling blocks in your quest to make your meetings once again safe for democracy. If your bylaws say nothing about members removing officers, you can follow the procedure I outline in this section only if the bylaws provide that the officer's term of office is "for [a certain length of time] *or* until a successor is elected and assumes office."

If you see that terminology in the bylaws, the membership can remove your officer from office by adopting a motion to that effect. That motion requires a two-thirds vote without notice, or a majority vote if proper previous notice was given, or the affirmative vote of a majority of the entire membership.

If you don't see that *or* in your bylaws but find an *and* in its place, then to bring down King Kong, you can remove them only for cause. Doing so involves charging the officer with neglect of duty or unfitness to continue in office and holding a trial. I cover the steps for this procedure in the section, "Holding a trial," later in this chapter.

TIP

The officer-removal process is the same even if you're not particularly motivated by the desire to defeat a despot. You can attempt to remove an officer for any good reason (it has to be good if you expect to reach removal through a trial), such as when Member Meanswell gets elected but has attended only one meeting in the past year since being elected. In fact, if your bylaws provide for removal or if your term-of-office clause has that little *or*, then you can remove from office any officer at any time for any reason. Not that you'd want to, but it's good to know you can!

If formal disciplinary procedures are required, an officer can only be removed for cause, that is, misconduct or neglect of duty in office.

Disciplining Members Who Shame Your Group's Name

Your bylaws may include sections on discipline and list offenses and remedies along with a procedure for dealing with them. But even if your bylaws don't address these issues specifically, you're not obligated to allow a person to continue as a member if they behave in a way that injures the work or good name of your organization. When undesirable behavior occurs outside a meeting and the entire membership doesn't clearly witness the facts and circumstances, a formal process for preferring charges and permitting the accused an opportunity of defense is essential.

Trials and disciplinary proceedings are probably quite rare in most small deliberative assemblies. In groups where it may be more common, such as professional or trade associations, bylaws or special rules of order usually define specialized procedures. However, every group needs to have a basic procedure for handling members who disregard group standards, and Robert's Rules provides you with one.

WARNING

Robert's Rules advises that you limit a president's authority to appoint members to committees formed to investigate or manage disciplinary matters. Your bylaws need to include this limitation as an exception to any authority of the president to appoint committees. Some organizations have standing committees on discipline. Not unlike nominating committees, committees that are set up to investigate and deal with disciplinary matters are best appointed by the membership, not by an officer who may have some direct personal interest in the committee's decisions.

It's important for the organization to be able to protect its interests, but it's also crucial that the rights of members are protected. To balance these competing interests, Robert's Rules permits the society to discipline members, but only after a thorough process.

CONSIDERING THE RIGHTS OF ALL

Robert's Rules requires that any disciplinary proceedings brought against a member for offenses outside a meeting be brought and considered in executive session. Allowing this kind of business to be made public and discussed outside the organization is a mistake. The rights of your group and of the accused depend on this principle of privacy, and violating the secrecy of executive session is generally considered grounds for expulsion.

Your group has the right to insist that members meet certain standards for membership. When your group decides that a member must be held accountable for unacceptable behavior, it's in the interest of both your group and the accused member to proceed carefully and fairly before making any decisions that may unfairly or wrongfully expel or otherwise penalize a member.

Checking out the facts first

Suppose that someone in the group discovers a problem that may cast a shadow on a certain member's reputation in connection with the organization. The first action to take is to have the membership appoint a committee of people whose integrity is irreproachable and give those members the task of investigating the allegations before any formal charges are mentioned.

In all cases, the details of the allegations must be excluded from the formal motion to appoint such a committee. It's sufficient to move "that a committee of [some number] be [appointed/elected] to investigate certain allegations that, if determined to be true, would cast doubt on the wisdom of retaining [insert member's name] as a member of our organization."

REMEMBER

An *individual* should never initiate a resolution directly charging a member with an offense — you need to start with an investigative committee charged with determining if sufficient cause exists. If the committee declines to prefer charges, the assembly may still do so. Even then, it's never appropriate to offer a resolution that *reveals the nature of the offense or suggests that certain allegations are true.* The group has nothing to gain and everything to lose by making the rush to judgment that these kinds of motions suggest.

The appointed committee's job is limited to conducting a basic investigation of any allegations that underlie the proceedings. The committee may not compel anyone to come forward and give information, but it must make a concerted effort to gather facts. Any confidential information it obtains may not be used in any trial that it may recommend. But that information may be useful to the committee in making its final determination.

When the committee arrives at its conclusion, it reports its recommendation to the membership, either by offering a resolution formally charging the member with a specific offense or by declaring the allegations unfounded.

Depending on the committee's findings, it may be a good idea to engage the subject of the investigation in a private and frank discussion and hear the member's spin on the spam. At this stage, a trial may still be avoidable. The accused may see the wisdom in resignation if they're likely to be removed from membership when formal charges are brought and a trial is conducted. Conversely, they may shine the light of truth on their innocence and show their accusers to be in error or improperly motivated.

Reporting findings of cause

The foundation for a trial is established by adopting the investigating committee's report that the allegations have merit and that facts exist to substantiate formal charges. The assembly must then make some specific decisions about the following items, which, ideally, should be the subject of the committee's recommendations and should appear in a series of resolutions. These decisions determine the following:

>> The date and location of the trial, affording reasonable time (Robert's Rules states that 30 days from the time the notice is sent to the accused is reasonable) for managers to prepare to present the case and for the accused to prepare for the member's defense.

TIP

If you're going to conduct a trial, devote an entire meeting to the process — maybe even schedule a special meeting for the event, Even if your bylaws don't authorize special meetings, a special meeting for this purpose is permissible.

>> Whether the trial will be conducted by the entire membership or by a committee.

>> The *charges* (the offense) and the *specifications* (the actions of the accused that give rise to the offense). Charges must cite the violated standards that give rise to penalties.

>> Selection of the *managers,* members who will present the case against the accused.

WARNING

Managers aren't prosecutors, and they should never act as such. Their role is to present the evidence and to do it in such a way as to illuminate the truth and enable the a just result.

>> Optionally, a resolution to suspend the accused of some or all of the rights, duties, and authority of membership or office (except those relating to the trial) until the trial is concluded.

>> The *citation* of the member, requiring the member to appear and show cause why the penalty being sought shouldn't be assessed based on the charges and specifications. The citation must include the details of the penalty, charges, and specifications. Further, the notice must include the following:

- The date, time, and location of the trial

- An exact copy of the charges and specifications, including when they were adopted

Holding a trial

The trial for a disciplinary matter of a deliberative assembly has many parallels to trials with which you may be more familiar. However, this type of trial is a *private* proceeding in the nature of a *formal hearing*, and its result is but a *judgment of your assembly* on the fitness of the accused to continue holding office or to remain as a member of the organization. At all times during the disciplinary process, proper precautions must be taken to provide the accused with proceedings that are irreproachable in their fairness.

Basic considerations for fairness in the trial include the following:

>> The accused is still afforded the right to defense counsel, and the defense counsel may be an attorney. But any defense attorney must be a member of the organization, unless the trial panel (or assembly, if the membership is conducting the trial) agrees that a nonmember attorney may be admitted.

>> The accused may call witnesses in their defense.

>> Nonmembers may be called as witnesses, but their presence may not be permitted in the trial except when they're giving their testimony.

The trial is the final step in disciplinary proceedings. The procedures are described in full here, from the opening statements to the determination of the verdict.

Opening the trial

The trial begins when the chair opens the meeting and addresses preliminary matters. Here are the steps:

1. **The chair calls the meeting to order and gives immediate notice that the meeting is in executive session.**

   Moving to executive session means the proceedings are secret and may not be disclosed to nonmembers, under penalty of expulsion.

2. **The secretary reads all the resolutions adopted in the preliminary proceedings and verifies the service of the citation on the accused.**

3. **The chair announces the names of the managers and asks the accused whether counsel is representing them.**

4. **The secretary reads the charges and specifications.**

   The accused enters pleas of *guilty* or *not guilty* to each specification and then to each charge.

Only a guilty plea to all of the charges makes a trial unnecessary. A member might plead guilty to a specification but not to a charge. For example, Sal Stooge might admit to the specifications that he removed money from the vending machines at the clubhouse and that he went home with the vending-machine keys that he took from the secretary's desk, but steadfastly maintains his innocence of the charge that his acts constituted theft. In such a case, a trial must still be held.

Similarly, if multiple charges are preferred, the member might plead guilty only to one of the lesser charges, and a trial for the remaining charges will still be necessary.

Trying the case

In each of the following, the managers present first, followed by the defense in this order:

>> Opening statements

>> Witness testimony

>> Witness rebuttal

>> Closing arguments

During the trial, cross-examination, redirect, and recross examination are permitted, and witnesses may be subject to recall. No persons other than the managers or the defense may have the floor during these stages of the trial. Other members may, however, submit motions and questions in writing to the chair and may also address the chair for an appeal. The only motions in order during a trial are privileged motions (flip to Chapter 10 for information on privileged motions) and motions dealing with the trial meeting. Decisions and rulings are made by the chair subject to undebatable appeal, but the chair may put them to a vote without debate.

Deciding the verdict

Generally, the rest of the trial is downhill. The managers and the defense counsel (if members of the organization) remain and participate in the discussion; only the accused and any nonmembers present must leave the room during the deliberations.

At the outset of deliberations, the chair states the question on the guilt of the accused as follows: "The question before you now is, 'Is [member name] guilty of the charges and specifications as follows?' [Read each charge and specification.]" Each charge and specification is debatable, amendable, and voted on separately, and a ballot vote *must* be taken if any member demands it. If the accused is found not guilty of all the specifications applicable to a particular charge, they are automatically not guilty of that charge and no vote is taken or any vote taken is ignored.

In some instances, in light of facts brought up in the trial, the assembly determines that the accused is guilty of a lesser charge than the one originally preferred. Adopting a finding of guilt to the lesser charges is permissible, but those lesser charges must be consistent with, and within the scope of, the charges with which the accused was noticed and tried.

If the accused is found not guilty of any charges, they're exonerated. If they're found guilty, one of the managers customarily makes the motion for the penalty (but any member may offer a penalty motion). The penalty motion is debatable and amendable, and any member may demand a ballot vote. The accused is immediately notified when the deliberations are complete and the results are determined.

A member who is found not guilty of the original charges might *not* be exonerated. A lesser charge might be preferred.

When the trial panel isn't the assembly itself, but rather an appointed committee, the panel's decision is framed as a recommendation to the assembly, which must act on the recommendations. In this case, the assembly must consider the recommendation in executive session, and, unless the committee has exonerated the accused, the accused must be given the opportunity to rebut the committee's findings. After the rebuttal, the accused must remove themselves from the room, pending the final decisions of the assembly.

The assembly may choose to decrease the recommended penalty or even decide to impose no penalty. But the assembly may not increase the penalty, and if the accused has been found not guilty, the assembly may not impose a penalty at all.

Maintaining Order in Meetings

You find problem people in all walks of life, and they're in no short supply at meetings. Consider, for example, the member who's a sore loser or the member who likes attention so much that they're willing to create a scene over any little thing. People who behave this way are everywhere, and you may have little choice but to put up with them if they're your customers, coworkers, or neighbors. But you don't have to tolerate them in meetings.

Although you can take action when Gordy Flackflinger tunes up for a tirade, you shouldn't really have to if your presiding officer takes advantage of this section's techniques for taking care of problem people.

Understanding rights of the group

When you're in a meeting, the right to say who can be present is completely within the control of your group. This right doesn't mean that you can arbitrarily exclude a member who has a right to be there, nor does it mean that you can fail to comply with provisions of a public meeting law.

But your assembly has the absolute right to eject a member if that member becomes of sufficient annoyance that the proceedings of the meeting can't continue peacefully. Same goes for a nonmember in a meeting of a public body — subject, of course, to provisions of your local laws regarding ejecting disruptive attendees.

Knowing what's expected

As a member of an assembly, you have a duty in your meetings to respect the position of the presiding officer. You're expected to generally obey their orders, but you have the right to appeal any decision in a polite and proper way.

Your presiding officer has a corresponding duty to refrain from shouting down a member or otherwise being drawn into a fracas. The chair who allows a ranting member to fizzle out usually has the most success in bringing an assembly back to order. It's generally best for the presiding officer to remain calm and deliberate and ultimately let the membership decide questions of discipline.

Managing misbehaving members

Minor breaches of order, such as wandering beyond the bounds of the question under consideration, interrupting a speaker who has the floor, or speaking without recognition, can usually be handled by simply reminding the member of the proper way to do things. The presiding officer may say, "The member will please confine their remarks to the subject under discussion," or "The member will please address their remarks to the chair."

However, sometimes in the thick of it all, ol' Gordy Flackflinger goes beyond the bounds of propriety and questions the motives of another speaker or commits some other breach of decorum (see

Chapter 7). When that happens, the group can turn to a nice, polite little procedure called *calling a member to order.*

Calling the member to order

When Gordy Flackflinger goes off (as he's prone to do) and starts talking about this or that, or maybe launches into some diatribe, the chair first warns Gordy that he needs to confine his remarks to the motion under consideration. But if Gordy ignores this warning, the chair may say, "The member will come to order and be seated." This approach is the nicest way to tell Gordy to sit down and shut up. Hopefully, he gets the message.

If the chair doesn't act quickly enough, or if a member believes the chair needs to call Mr. Flackflinger to order, the member may, without first being recognized, call out, "Ms. Chairman, I call the member to order." The chair proceeds to handle the situation as described earlier in this section. However, if Gordy has been properly assigned the floor and the chair isn't convinced that the complaining member's point is well taken, she may ask the group whether Gordy should be allowed to continue speaking. A voice vote can decide that question.

"Naming" the offender

If Gordy doesn't take the hint and continues on his errant path, the chair may direct the secretary to note the breach in the minutes. The chair can then take direct official action against the member by *naming* him and saying something like, "Mr. Flackflinger, the chair has asked you thrice now to refrain from personal attacks on members, yet you persist in refusing to obey the orders of the chair and continue in your conduct in a manner wholly unacceptable to the chair and the assembly."

If Gordy doesn't sit down and shut up, it may be time to demand an apology or even ask him to leave. But the chair shouldn't attempt to take such action by herself. The membership gets to decide Gordy's fate now. If you're lucky, when things get this far, Gordy apologizes and sits down, and the chair accepts his apology and continues with the meeting. But Gordy has a way about him that may mean you need to take the matter to the limit and turn to the membership.

Penalizing the offender

At the point the chair has reached the end of her rope in her dealings with Gordy Flackflinger, her last option is to ask the group what to do about Gordy. Should he be censured? Should he be removed from the meeting until he apologizes? Should he be expelled from membership?

If the situation has gone this far, the chair may say, "Members, the chair is at wits' end. I regret to put the question now before you, but I find I must prepare you to speak to the question of whether Mr. Flackflinger shall be removed from the meeting. Before we consider the question, however, I ask Mr. Flackflinger, 'Sir, do you wish to make a statement to the membership before I place the question on your removal?'"

Your chair should give Gordy a final opportunity to comply or at least speak in his own defense. But if Gordy doesn't straighten out fast, any of the remedies mentioned is possible.

TECHNICAL
STUFF

If it's necessary, you can even remove Gordy from the hall while you consider a final penalty. A motion to remove a Gordy-Gone-Wild while it considers the final penalty may be assumed by the chair and is undebatable, unamendable, and requires a majority vote for adoption.

The hard truth is that if Gordy can't behave in a meeting, you don't even have to allow him to continue his membership. But terminating his membership requires a two-thirds vote, unlike other remedies that require only a majority vote. In any case, any member can demand that a vote on such a decision be taken by ballot.

Removing nonmembers from the hall

You have the right to conduct your meeting without the presence of nonmembers. To that end, the chair has the authority (on her own initiative) to require nonmembers to leave the meeting. She should be ready to use this authority in the event that the peanut gallery (or any individual peanut) becomes rambunctious. Just to make sure that the chair doesn't act in opposition to the will of the assembly, however, any member may appeal the chair's order for nonmembers to leave; the question then becomes one for the members to decide. Such an appeal is undebatable.

After a removal has been ordered, whether it's removal of a member or a nonmember, the chair may exercise whatever reasonable means necessary to execute the removal. If the members who were removed don't leave of their own accord, she may appoint a committee to escort them from the meeting, or, if necessary, the chair may summon peace officers to remove the offenders and restore peace to the assembly.

Chapter **19**

Starting a New Association

Sooner or later, you'll find a cause that needs the collective effort of a group of people with the same or similar objectives. If you're someone who sees what needs to be done and sets out to do it, then you're inevitably one of the key players.

For instance, imagine that you're a new homeowner in your newly developing subdivision, and you see two houses going up that are already in violation of the roofline setbacks. You think, "Now may be the time to organize to keep our neighborhood up to the standards we agreed to when we bought our property." You're instrumental in getting things moving to accomplish the mutual goals of the group. In short, if you're not destined to be *the* leader, you're certainly a power behind the throne.

Starting a new organization isn't terribly difficult, but don't undertake it unless you're committed to spending a good bit of time making it happen. Like anything else covered in this book, starting a new organization is all about procedure. It can get technical, but it's procedure nevertheless. That's not to say you can't succeed without a sense of community, mind you — but you can't get *that* out of any book.

When you have a cause and have gathered others who share your vision, follow these steps to create your new association:

1. **Decide to organize, and prepare for an organizational meeting.**

2. **Invite prospective members.**

3. **Hold the first organizational meeting, during which you:**

   - Elect temporary officers.

   - Adopt a parliamentary authority.

   - Adopt a resolution to form a new organization.

   - Appoint a committee to draw up bylaws.

4. **Draw up your bylaws.**

5. **Hold a second organizational meeting to approve the bylaws.**

6. **Enroll members.**

7. **Hold your charter meeting and elect permanent officers.**

TECHNICAL STUFF

The organizational meetings leading up to the creation of a new association are representative of a particular form of deliberative assembly (see Chapter 3) known as a *mass meeting*. A mass meeting is a meeting of an unorganized body of people with a common goal.

This chapter describes a mass meeting of people with a goal of forming a new association. But a mass meeting may just as easily be called to start a petition drive to oust your mayor or to organize a one-time event, such as a rally to support lower taxes. In a mass meeting, anybody who attends who sympathizes with the common goal is a member — and no matter how many people show up, you've got a quorum. A group's mass meeting status ends when it achieves its goal. In this chapter, the mass meeting status ends when the new organization adopts bylaws and members officially join the new association.

Preparing for an Organizational Meeting

No doubt your heart wouldn't break if you never had to attend another meeting, but here you are getting ready to start a new organization — a new group that adds another monthly meeting to your already busy agenda. But you're dedicated, right?

REMEMBER

When you and your friends get together to plan your first organizational meeting, you need to make some decisions:

>> Where and when will the meeting be held?

>> How will you publicize the meeting?

>> Who will chair the meeting?

>> Who will start the meeting and nominate the chairman?

>> Who will nominate someone to take minutes? And who will that minutes taker be?

>> Will you adopt Robert's Rules as the authority for the meeting?

>> Who will make the presentation to the attendees about why you've called the meeting?

>> Who will propose a motion to organize a formal association?

If prearranging things makes your meeting sound like a put-up deal, well, it sort of is. You don't have an association yet. You're just a host in a room full of guests. Read on for an explanation.

Inviting Prospective Members

When you've decided when and where to hold your first organizational meeting, you have to inform the folks you want to attend — the people you think will be interested and in agreement with your goal.

The best way to get the word out is to prepare a written notice and distribute it to the people you want to come to the meeting. The following is a notice for a neighborhood meeting to get folks together to form a neighborhood civic association:

> ### Notice of Meeting
>
> *A meeting will be held for Elm Acres homeowners who are interested in forming a neighborhood civic association. The meeting will take place at the Oak Tree Branch of the Public Library at 7 p.m. on Monday, March 4. If you're interested in forming an association to benefit our community, you're invited to attend.*

REMEMBER

The first organizational meeting is a meeting to form a new association instead of a meeting of an existing group; the only rules you have to follow are the ones the people who attend agree to. It's your meeting, and until the meeting begins, you control the hall. You get to say who can attend, and you don't have to invite or put up with anybody who doesn't agree with you on the basic goal to form a new association. (But don't abuse your power. You can't have a group if no one wants to join you.) After the meeting begins, however, it's the assembly's meeting, and the assembly that controls the hall.

Until you have bylaws and permanent officers, the assembly can remove anyone who puts up too much fuss. Also, the chair, subject to appeal, can remove someone deemed to be a nonmember (that is, at cross-purposes with the purpose of the meeting).

Holding the First Organizational Meeting

You read that heading correctly — the first meeting is just the first. You'll have another meeting before you wind up with your new organization. Remember that this is all a process. Meetings, although sometimes unsavory, are necessary for making group decisions, and as great as email and chat programs and other technology tools are, there's still no substitute for getting together at the same time in the same room and hashing things out.

No matter how things were in 2020 when virtual meetings were used to simulate the deliberative process, and no matter how lucky you may have been in making group decisions using the more popular virtual meeting platforms available at the time, some serious deficiencies remain in those platforms that hinder the ability to reach the deliberative will of the assembly. Take note that the steps here for forming a new organization call for some dynamic interaction that the current offerings can't yet accommodate. I discuss virtual meetings in more detail in Chapter 3.

In this section, I run through the tasks you need to accomplish during your first organizational meeting. When you've finished all this business, you can move on to the next step in creating a new group.

Electing temporary officers

After you've called the meeting to order and given a brief talk about the purpose of the meeting, offer the responsibility for chairing your meeting to an individual elected by those in attendance. (Turn to Chapter 14 for details on how to conduct an election.) If you've been the moving force so far in pulling things together, expect to receive the chair position. The person elected as chair is known as the *chair pro tem* of this organizing assembly. After you elect the chair pro tem, the next order of business is to elect somebody to take minutes. (See Chapter 17 for more info on minutes.)

These temporary officers serve only until the election of permanent officers takes place (which occurs only after you write and adopt your bylaws). (Don't worry, you don't write or adopt any bylaws tonight.) Your chairman pro tem presides at all meetings of the organizing association, and the secretary pro tem records all the proceedings.

For this kind of meeting, getting some kind of attendance record is a good idea, but it's not a requirement. If all the folks present can comfortably sit around a table, the secretary can easily make note of who's there. Otherwise, set up or pass around a sign-in sheet to collect names and contact information from the attendees.

Adopting your parliamentary authority

Before you get into the thick of it (and it's not a foregone conclusion that it will get thick), if wisdom prevails, you'll adopt a parliamentary authority to have something to go by should questions of procedure arise. If you're comfortable with the guide in this chapter, you'll be comfortable adopting the current edition of *Robert's Rules of Order Newly Revised* as your parliamentary authority. That would be the 12th edition, published in 2020.

Adopting Robert is fairly straightforward. One of the sponsors can offer the motion right after the secretary is elected by saying something like:

> "Madam chairman, we have prepared our plan for bringing our new organization into existence using the steps provided in *Robert's Rules. Particularly,* the 12th edition, titled *Robert's Rules of Order Newly Revised.* Therefore, I move that we adopt the 12th edition of *Robert's Rules of Order Newly Revised* as the parliamentary authority for the meetings we are holding to form our new organization."

There you have it. After the motion is seconded, the chair can state the motion, call for debate, and when the moment is right, call for the vote. It's not likely to be controversial, and Madam Chairman may find it quite easy to use unanimous consent to let Robert be the go-to source for any questions on procedure during the organizational meetings. See Chapter 6 for the eight steps in handling a motion. And you can find the lowdown on how to adopt a motion using unanimous consent in Chapter 8.

REMEMBER

When you adopt Robert's Rules, you get a built-in safety valve in that you can suspend the rules or even modify specific rules and add other rules. You probably won't need to do much of that in your organizational meetings, but you can if you need to.

Adopting the resolution to form the association

When you get the organizational meeting underway, your next goal is to get agreement on the idea that you need an association for whatever reasons you've determined. Have someone lined up to give a short talk about the reasons behind the call to form an association. After explaining the whys and wherefores, you can expect the group to ask questions and offer opinions.

TIP

Your presiding officer may need to brush up on how to assign the floor and how to keep Longwinded Joe from holding forth after every other speaker takes a turn. I cover these issues in Chapter 7.

When the time is right and the sense of the meeting is clearly on track to form an association, one of the sponsors offers a motion on the adoption of a resolution to form a permanent association.

If you've planned well, you have a resolution ready and one of your friends is on standby to make the motion when the time is right. Here's how the Elm Acres gang went about it:

> I think that we're hearing a lot of good ideas and that it's a good time to get this show on the road, so I move that this group adopt the following resolution:
>
> *Resolved,* that it is the sense of this meeting that a neighborhood civic association be formed.

The chair's job is easy at this point — it's a matter of handling a motion. After the group adopts the resolution to form a permanent association, you're on your way to the next step: defining the proposed organization by coming up with a set of bylaws for your group's consideration.

Appointing a committee to draft bylaws

In Chapter 2, I explain why you need bylaws and how important they are to your organization. You don't really have an organization until you define it by adopting bylaws. And producing the right bylaws for your unique group requires a good deal of focus.

So when you reach the point in your organizational meeting at which everyone has agreed to form an association (refer to the previous section for an explanation), the time has come to authorize and appoint a committee to put together a set of bylaws for your organizing group to consider and adopt.

This committee does some important work that has far-reaching effects. Your committee volunteers need to commit to several regular meetings, because the job can take a while.

TIP

A parliamentarian is a valuable consultant at this stage of the organizational process. You can save yourself and every member of the bylaws committee countless hours by getting some professional assistance for this part of the process. Help is available from the National Association of Parliamentarians (`www.parliamentarians.org`) and the American Institute of Parliamentarians (`www.aipparl.org`).

TIP

If you want to make the best decision when selecting members of your bylaws committee, include on the committee all your best thinkers and writers. Just as important, make sure you include anybody who will probably have a lot to say about all the rules and details that go in bylaws. Get those people to the committee meetings and put them to work. Otherwise, they'll wear you out at the meeting in which the bylaws are up for official adoption. Agreeing to build a new organization is one thing; quite another is agreeing on all the details of how the group needs to operate.

Taking into account the ideas and concerns of anybody interested at the committee level can actually help you develop a good set of bylaws that doesn't tie your hands at inappropriate times or leave you open to the whims of bothersome members after you nail things down.

Before you call it a day . . .

You may think your organizational meeting is ready to adjourn, but you've got a little housekeeping to take care of at this point. Put these four tasks on your checklist and deal with them in the order listed.

1. Set your next meeting.

Decide on a time and place to reconvene and hear the report of the bylaws committee, or just plan to adjourn to meet again at the call of the chair. Make sure your bylaws committee organizes quickly and develops a schedule that affords a report at a reasonable date, although the schedule shouldn't compromise the bylaws because of a mistaken notion that this must be a hurried job.

2. **Authorize the bylaws committee to provide copies of its report, with expenses to be reimbursed.**

    Somebody just needs to make a motion to authorize reimbursement of copy expenses.

WARNING

If your great idea to create this new organization crashes and burns, the folks in the room must be prepared to cover reimbursement of the copy expenses. You don't want to leave a few of your friends holding only a copy-shop receipt for all their trouble.

3. **Take some time to discuss your aims and purposes.**

    Your bylaws committee needs guidance to know what direction the membership prefers to take with the association. In neighborhood civic associations, for example, these discussions center on knowing some of the specific needs of the individual association so that the size of the board, its authority, the nature of standing committees, and so on may be assessed generally. However, you don't want to go into too much at this stage of the game. You're much better off saving discussion of details for the committee.

4. **Adjourn to a new time or to meet again at the call of the chair.**

    Everybody likes to adjourn. It's usually the favorite part of meetings. But adjourning has rules, too, and I cover them in Chapter 10.

Drawing Up Your Bylaws

As you can read in Chapter 2, your bylaws are the rules you make for and about your own unique organization. They define how the organization operates, and, properly constructed, they protect the rights of absentees and minorities of various sizes, even down to a minority of one. Bylaws that are too easily amended (or are amendable despite the opposition of a large minority of more than one-third) are an invitation to trouble. At worst, they can be the cause of an organization's dissolution, or perhaps they enable an unrepresentative group to split off and take over a large treasury. The most important investment of time and effort for a newly forming organization lies in careful consideration of its bylaws, which I discuss in greater detail here.

Getting down to bylaw business

In your first bylaws committee meeting, you have one main objective: to talk about how you want the organization to run.

You may find it useful to obtain examples of bylaws for organizations of the same type as the one you're forming. Then spend some quality time talking as a group about how you want *your* organization to operate.

In this meeting, you need to talk about details like how often you want all the members to meet to make decisions and whether you want to have a board that does most of the work. You need to discuss the ongoing work you want the group to accomplish so that you have some idea of what kind of committees to set up. Keep in mind that ambitious projects cost money. For example, setting up a security patrol committee is unnecessary if you can't gather enough money to cover a related cost.

Appointing a subcommittee to write the first draft

At the bylaws committee meeting, you need to appoint a member or two to prepare a first draft of bylaws, with the general provisions reflecting the overall sense of the discussions you've had (see the previous section). For good measure, have these members read Chapter 2, too, so that they're more familiar with the ins and outs of bylaws.

And if I haven't said it enough already, you can't go wrong involving a parliamentarian in this critical work. A professional parliamentarian can help you include in your bylaws all the points you need to address and, at the same time, ensure that you avoid ambiguous provisions that can cause serious problems down the road. You can get referrals for professionals from the two national associations mentioned earlier in this chapter.

Reviewing the first draft

After the drafters have pulled together a document, the full bylaws committee gets back together and tackles its real work. Take your time! Pay close attention to every detail of the drafted bylaws as your committee goes through the document and prepares to nail things down for the full membership to bring the organization into existence.

You're a committee, and this first draft is just a starting point. Look at each provision closely and critically. Consider the long term and think about how each bylaw will work as you have it written. Work through each article and section individually, and examine each as if it were unchangeable. Right now, you can change them to your heart's content.

REMEMBER

Keep reviewing the bylaws until you're satisfied that you've set up an organization that will work. The important point is to take your time and get it right.

When you have a set of bylaws your committee is satisfied with, you're ready to report to the organizing membership. Call your chair pro tem and let them know you're ready so they can schedule the second organizational meeting.

Holding Your Second Organizational Meeting

The big day has arrived. Your committee to draft a set of bylaws has it all figured out. Everybody who's anybody has weighed in with the committee, and it's time to make your new organization a reality. The following sections examine what you need to do.

Calling the meeting

Your temporary chair's duty is to notify everybody who attended the first organizational meeting and let them know that the bylaws committee is ready to report. The secretary pro tem is responsible for sending the notice, because the list of attendees should be on record in the secretary's file. Even though you want a big turnout, you don't have to worry about how many people show up. Because you're conducting what Robert's Rules calls a *mass meeting* (see Chapter 3), you technically don't have a membership yet. The only members you have are ones who are in favor of the original goal and who show up for the meeting. So the *quorum* (see Chapter 4) in this kind of meeting is the number of people who actually show up.

Approving the minutes

Just as in any other meeting, after your second organizational meeting is called to order, the first item to get out of the way is the reading and approval of the minutes. Flip to Chapter 5 for more detailed instructions on this step.

Adopting the bylaws

When you're adopting initial bylaws for a new organization, you proceed by paragraph, or *seriatim*. You read the bylaws article by article, discuss each one, and make any changes article by article and section by section. When you finish the whole document, you decide whether you want to go with it. Check out Chapter 11 for more details.

If you don't like your committee's draft and you can't figure out how to amend to your satisfaction in this meeting, send the document back to the bylaws committee for more adjustment and meet again when the committee has a new proposal. If, on the other hand, you've worked out any problems and nailed down any details the committee missed, you're ready for the final vote on adoption of the bylaws. Because they're new bylaws of a brand-new organization, only a majority vote is needed to adopt them.

REMEMBER

This vote is pretty significant because, as soon as you adopt bylaws, you have a brand-new, shiny, out-of-the-box organization, and the bylaws are in effect immediately upon their adoption. No changes now without previous notice and a two-thirds vote!

Holding Your Charter Meeting

For all but the smallest organizations in which everybody who is going to enroll does so at the second organizational meeting, your next step is to conduct a third meeting, known as a *charter meeting*. The following section discuss in greater detail the charter meeting, which is actually the first official business meeting of the new organization.

Enrolling charter members

Just for the sake of encouraging you to think in terms of success, I'm assuming that you adopted the bylaws. If so, you're almost home. If you constructed your bylaws correctly, you've specified dues amounts and defined member eligibility. Your new organization doesn't have any members, though, until you enroll them by collecting dues and obtaining from each member a written agreement to abide by the new bylaws. After you've adopted bylaws, the remaining task is to officially enroll members in your new organization.

WARNING

Because from the moment you adopt bylaws you need to be an enrolled member to vote on anything, your new organization stands in immediate recess to enroll members.

You can't enroll new members without enrollment agreement forms containing a statement that the undersigned agrees to abide by the bylaws. Signing an enrollment form becomes a commitment to pay the dues and any initiation fee. The recess to enroll members may last only a few minutes if everybody planning to join is at the meeting. If not, you can adjourn to meet again in a third and final meeting, and you can take a day or two (or more) to distribute bylaws and enrollment agreements. During this longer recess, you can specify some particular date for the charter meeting, at which all the newly enrolled members have the right to vote on the election of permanent officers.

Electing permanent officers

After completing the enrollment of charter members, you have an organization — finally! Now you need to elect your permanent officers, according to the details your bylaws outline. Your temporary chairman presides over this meeting until you have a permanent president. For information on how to nominate and elect your officers, look to Chapters 13 and 14.

Handling other essential business

The countdown is on to adjournment of your new association's organizational session. But before you adjourn, you may have some final details to address. Maybe you just need to fix the time for the next meeting (your bylaws should state it). But you may have other, more important issues to wrap up. For example, the new president may have the duty to appoint committees and may have already made some decisions. Now's the time to address these details.

Adjourning

When all the work is finished, it's in order to adjourn the meeting. Future meetings are held in accordance with your bylaws. The end of this process is the beginning of your new organization. Congratulations are in order — you've just started a new organization. Now get ready: The real work is ahead of you!

Chapter **20**

The Convention of Delegates: A Special Kind of Assembly

I f you've never been a delegate to a convention, then you've probably heard about only the fun part. You may think that a convention is all about trading pins and patches, wearing funny hats, and waving flags. You may even think it's mostly about dodging balloons and confetti while a band plays the theme from *Rocky*, after which everyone parties until all hours of the night.

Now, I don't want to dash any of your illusions; some conventions are really like that. But if you've ever been to a convention as an official delegate representing your local or state unit, you know that everything's not all fun and games. Work needs to be done to establish your organization's direction for the next year (or two, or four).

Conducting business in a convention mostly works the same as in regular meetings. Despite its size and specialized structure, a convention of delegates is, after all, still a deliberative assembly (see Chapter 3). All the usual rules about meetings, motions, voting, elections, and so forth still apply.

However, some important differences need to be recognized. The organization of a convention is unique and is distinguished in several ways from the run-of-the-mill annual general meeting of an organization. These differences create the need for some special rules to make the convention an efficient and proper operation. And you're in luck — this chapter covers those special rules for properly conducting and participating in conventions.

Defining the Convention of Delegates

A *convention of delegates* is an assembly of representatives from smaller constituent groups of a larger organization. Commonly, the convention is an annual, biennial, or perhaps quadrennial meeting of an international, national, or large state organization that makes its decisions by assembling representatives from different areas or constituencies.

The organizations that meet in conventions usually have such high total numbers of members that the only hope for making decisions as a membership body is to assemble a representative group of members from local units or constituencies.

Assemblies of this type include conventions of political parties, professional and trade organizations, and fraternal lodges. They may bear names such as house of delegates, representative assembly, convocation, general assembly, or, the most common name, convention.

Serving As a Delegate

A convention can be a real test of endurance. You have to get up early, go to meetings, and eat rubbery chicken at the president's luncheon. And unless your convention-planning leadership has figured out how to make your meetings interesting, you may even have to endure hours of boring reports while seated on a stadium seat or on one of those meagerly-padded-but-soon-rock-hard institutional chairs, given respite only by the privileged motion to *Recess* (see Chapter 10).

Your election or appointment as a convention delegate is based on the rules and qualifications for delegates as established in your organization's charter or bylaws. The organization holding the convention lays out details establishing the number of delegates from a constituent unit and the method of selection (including any provisions for alternates). The local bylaws may also specify procedures for selecting delegates at the local level.

REMEMBER

If you're a delegate, your duty is to represent your constituency in accordance with the rules of your organization. You're expected to attend the meetings of the convention. You're free to vote as you see fit on any matter to come before the convention, unless you have been instructed by legitimate order of your constituent unit to represent your membership's interest in a particular way.

Organizing the Convention Assembly

Even though the organization remains in place when the convention is over, the convention of delegates exists only for the term of the session. Its membership consists of the delegates sent by the local constituent units, and the delegates have to self-organize before they can address the real business of the organization.

To accomplish the basics of self-organization, a convention requires three essential committees (normally appointed by the organization's leadership well before the convention) to do some advance work so that, as soon as the convention is called to order, the necessary decisions can be made to ensure a successful session. The following list and sections contain the three main questions that need to be answered and identifies the committees responsible for making such decisions:

>> **Who says you can vote?** Credentials committee

>> **What rules do we follow?** Committee on standing rules

>> **What do we do, and when?** Convention program committee

WARNING

Before you adopt a credentials committee report, you don't know for sure just who are the voting members of the assembly. You can't, therefore, properly vote on much — except questions of procedure — before the credentials committee report is presented. Of course, you can vote on the credentials committee report itself, or on motions that are in order in the absence of a quorum (flip to Chapter 4 to look at that list).

Deciding who can vote: Credentials committee

Before you ever get started with a convention of delegates, you have to know who has a right to vote. That determination is made by adopting a report of the *credentials committee* as the official roll (or list) of the voting delegates at the convention.

The credentials committee is charged with making sure the people permitted to vote are there by right. In a convention of delegates, not just any member of the organization can vote. Only the delegates authorized by their constituent units have that right.

This committee's job is never really complete until the convention adjourns. Its duties include knowing who to expect before registration begins, registering the delegates and validating credentials when they arrive, and keeping up throughout the session with how many and which convention delegates are entitled to vote. The committee issues supplemental reports containing changes to the roll of voting members; these revisions are subject to adoption by the convention.

The credentials committee's work starts well in advance of the convention. In many cases, an organization's paid staff, not regular members, takes care of many of the preliminaries. The appointed members of this committee may even include staff members in addition to members of the organization.

In advance of the convention, the committee does the following:

>> Sends to the constituent units the necessary information concerning their selection of delegates. This information includes the forms necessary for the local unit to certify the delegates and alternates who are authorized to represent the unit at the convention. When the credentials committee receives the completed forms from the constituent units, it verifies the eligibility of each delegate as much as is necessary or required under the bylaws and other rules of the organization (see Chapter 2). If a delegate is deemed ineligible (perhaps because dues haven't been paid, for example), the committee must let the unit know and determine which alternate is to be admitted.

>> Prepares the master list of who is entitled to register as a delegate and makes arrangements for actual registration of the delegates at the convention.

As the convention gets underway, the credentials committee has these tasks:

>> Registers the delegates upon arrival and verifies that they're properly authorized to serve as delegates.

>> Reports to the convention the roll of the then-registered delegates, with information on their number and other statistics that are customary or necessary to inform the body of its makeup.

>> Makes supplemental reports, usually at the beginning of every meeting or meeting day in the session. These supplemental reports present revisions in the roll of voting delegates and are accepted by way of a motion to adopt.

> However, in this case, even though the motion is technically amending something previously adopted, only a majority vote is required to adopt a revised credentials report. Unless the seating of one or more delegates is challenged, these reports are usually adopted by general consent.

TECHNICAL STUFF

The work of the credentials committee is essential to calculating a quorum for the convention. For business to be conducted in a convention, a majority of the total number of persons who registered in attendance at the convention constitute the quorum (unless otherwise specified in your organization's bylaws or the convention's standing rules). Consider it this way: If exactly 1,000 delegates show up for the convention and register as attending, a quorum is 501, even if some of those 1,000 delegates leave the convention to take a riverboat cruise. If another 100 delegates register as attending, the quorum goes up to 551 even if a few dozen more depart for a cross-country balloon ride. Chapter 4 discusses the concept of *quorum* in greater detail.

Establishing some rules: Committee on standing rules

Because each convention is a unique assembly, you need to have some ground rules tailored especially for your convention. It's the job of the *committee on standing rules* to propose these rules.

REMEMBER

Until you've adopted rules for this convention, you've pretty much got to rely on looking up rules in Robert's Rules. Doing so is always fun if you're a parliamentarian. But if you're not a parliamentarian, you'll be glad to get down to adopting your convention standing rules.

Defining convention standing rules

Convention standing rules are really a mixed bag; the delegates are free to adopt whatever rules they care to make for the convention, as long as those rules don't conflict with the bylaws. Some convention standing rules are, in every respect, *special rules of order;* others are more like regular standing rules.

Special rules of order are rules that modify an organization's parliamentary authority. *Standing rules,* on the other hand, speak to matters of policy. An example special rule of order is a rule that limits debate to two speeches of three minutes each on each side of an issue. An example of a standing rule is a rule requiring all delegates to wear identification badges while on the convention floor. (You can learn more about the different classes of rules by taking a look at Chapter 2.)

But no matter what kind of rule they resemble, the important point to remember is that the convention standing rules expire at the close of the convention. Over time, your organization may develop a set of convention standing rules that vary only slightly (if at all) from one convention to the next. But the rules still must be adopted at each convention because the assembly is a different group than the one that met before.

Go to www.dummies.com/go/robertsrulesfd4e to download an example of convention standing rules, in the form of a report of a convention's committee on standing rules.

Adopting convention standing rules

The job of developing convention standing rules is assigned to — yep, you guessed it — the convention's committee on standing rules. This committee's duty is to draft these basic rules under which the convention will operate and present the proposed rules for adoption by the delegates right after they adopt the credentials committee's report.

The recommended procedure for bringing convention standing rules before the convention for adoption has two main steps:

1. **Print and distribute the proposed rules to all delegates no later than the time they enter the meeting hall.**

2. **At the appropriate time, the reporting member of the committee reads the proposed rules in their entirety and then moves their adoption.**

EXCEPTION

Skipping the reading of the rules in their entirety is okay when they're substantially similar to the rules used before and all the delegates have been timely furnished a printed copy of the rules.

Voting to adopt convention standing rules

Although convention standing rules are offered as a single motion, they really are a number of separate questions, as many as there are rules on the list. But although it's not in order to consider them one by one, if any member wants to have a separate vote on any one of the rules, the demand must be met. If such a demand is made, the vote is taken first on all the other rules as a group; then a vote is taken on the separated rule or rules.

REMEMBER

The chair isn't obligated to read the rules when putting them to a vote, but if the rules haven't been read and a delegate demands they be read before the vote, the chair must read the proposed rules. And even if the rules have been read before, any rule that has been amended since being read is subject to being read as amended on the demand of any delegate.

TIP

Being nice is important. The delegate who wants the rules read need not say, "I demand the rules be read," Instead, they should say something like, "Madam Chairman, I call for a reading of the proposed rules in their entirety before we vote." Or, for the amended rule, "Madam Chairman, I call for a reading of the rules that we have amended before we vote."

REMEMBER

A two-thirds vote is required to initially adopt the convention standing rules as a group if they contain any rule which, if adopted singly, would require a two-thirds vote. Usually convention standing rules contain such rules. For example, rule that limits debate in some way are quite common for conventions. After all, having everybody speaking twice for ten minutes per speech can make completing the agenda in a timely fashion difficult. But any rule that's not of the nature of a special rule of order can be adopted individually by majority vote. However, convention standing rules are rarely controversial; in most cases, they can be adopted by unanimous consent (see Chapter 8).

Voting to rescind, amend, or suspend convention standing rules

During the convention, if you want to change one of the adopted convention standing rules, a two-thirds vote (or the vote of a majority of all the delegates who have registered) is usually necessary. But if a convention standing rule requires only a majority vote for adoption, it can be amended by a majority vote with at least one day's notice. A majority vote, however, is all that's required to suspend such a rule for a particular purpose if the suspension has the effect of reverting to a rule provided in the parliamentary authority. In other cases, the suspension requires a two-thirds vote as usual. However, a motion to suspend a rule for the duration of the convention, or a motion to suspend a rule that has application in only one situation, is not in order. In such a case, the appropriate thing is to move to amend or rescind the rule.

WARNING

A convention standing rule prescribing the parliamentary authority may not under any circumstances be suspended.

Knowing when to do what: Convention program committee

After you've decided who can vote and what the rules are, it's time to get down to the real business that the delegates have assembled to conduct.

Because conventions typically are burdened with a heavy workload that must be handled in a relatively short time, planning is critical for success. That's where the *convention program committee* comes in.

Planning the program

The task of planning a convention's schedule of meeting times and events falls to the convention program committee. But this task isn't as simple as it sounds.

A convention program committee not only has the duty to provide a schedule for meetings, meals, entertainment, and the like, but also must do so while considering the membership's need to review its recent accomplishments and consider its plans for the future. The convention can't be all fun and games, after all.

The successful convention program committee begins its work at the end of one convention and really never stops until a new committee takes over at the end of the next convention. The delegates, however, may see the results of all this work only in the schedule of events, including the order of business, which they're asked to adopt (following adoption of the credentials committee's report and the convention standing rules) at the opening session of the convention.

Agreeing to the committee's program is usually critical to the success of the convention and, ultimately, to the success of the organization. For that reason, the convention program committee must be selected with great care and deliberation. Past convention experience with the organization is always a plus.

Adopting the program

A tentative convention program may have been published well in advance of the convention to inform prospective delegates about the plans in the works. But such plans usually change as they become finalized.

On the day of the opening session, the program to be adopted should be distributed to the delegates. Any changes to this edition can be noted when the convention program committee reports and moves the adoption of the program.

The convention program committee reports immediately after the convention standing rules are adopted. The motion to adopt the program is debatable and amendable, and it requires a majority vote. Changes after adoption require a two-thirds vote or the vote of a majority of all the delegates who have registered. Most of the time, however, the convention program and later changes are adopted by unanimous consent (see Chapter 8), to save time.

Understanding Other Convention Committees

The credentials committee, committee on standing rules, and convention program committee are indispensable in bringing the convention assembly into existence. But they're not the only committees necessary to produce the convention or to help process the business as your organization works through its agenda.

In addition to those three committees (and any other specialized functioning committees your own organization may constitute for your convention), Robert's Rules discusses two committees that are common to nearly all conventions:

>> Convention arrangements committee

>> Resolutions committee

Getting down to details: Convention arrangements committee

The unsung heroes of a successful convention are the people who work behind the scenes in concert with the board and the executive staff to pull together all the details of the convention. These folks help make it an event to remember: They're the members of the *convention arrangements committee.*

This committee is usually a standing committee of the organization rather than a committee of the particular convention. It often includes members with prior convention experience, as well as members who are constituents of the local units where the convention is to be held.

The convention arrangements committee often is appointed *with power* to contract with meeting planners or deal directly with hotels, meal functions, social functions, meeting facilities, speakers, entertainment, transportation services, or any of the many integral components necessary for a large group to comfortably accomplish its work.

TECHNICAL STUFF

If this committee isn't specifically empowered to act, the executive board is forced to give specific authorizations to contract in the name of the organization. This approach is often impractical, so you may also find that key members of your organization's paid staff often work in close association with the convention arrangements committee to secure all the services necessary for the convention.

In addition to the basics mentioned earlier in this section, the convention arrangements committee sees to details such as the following:

>> Arranging hotel accommodations for guests

>> Receiving visiting dignitaries upon arrival

>> Providing all printed matter, including local maps and locations of meetings and events, and information about the attractions of the area

>> Directing the seating arrangements, platform setup, audiovisual equipment, and other details related to the meeting hall and staging areas

>> Providing for communications needs, such as telephone services, Internet access, and radio communications

>> Staffing an information desk and perhaps creating press releases in connection with the event

Screening proposals for action: Resolutions committee

A convention usually has many essential objectives that must be met in a short time, and when that is the case, it becomes necessary to screen any original main motions (except for motions that have been screened by other committees) that delegates may want the convention to consider.

Members usually have the right in meetings to make main motions without notice, but in a convention of delegates, motion screening is necessary because of the sheer numbers of delegates and program time constraints. The convention rules or bylaws need to address how to handle original main motions through automatic referral to the *resolutions committee.*

Defining the procedures for handling motions and resolutions

The timing and frequency of the resolutions committee's reports depend on the number of sessions and the times or opportunities available for members to submit original main motions to come before the convention.

Whether an original main motion is made as a formal resolution (being a *form* of main motion) or simply as a main motion without any particular formality, the usual and proper use of the resolutions committee is to have all original main motions referred to it for review and recommendation. (See Chapter 6 for more information on main motions.)

If you've properly defined your resolutions committee in the bylaws and established good rules for its use, its primary purpose is to review all original main motions (except for those reviewed by another committee) before they're placed before the membership for consideration.

A resolutions committee can be authorized to put motions and resolutions in the proper form to ensure that it really proposes what the mover intends. Sometimes the committee needs to deal with multiple motions on the same subject and can be authorized to offer a single motion, to avoid duplication. The committee is often authorized to discuss and consider the merits of the motion and report its recommendations to the convention.

Establishing the role of the resolutions committee in your organization

The role and authority of a resolutions committee can vary from one organization to another, and much depends on the organization's needs and customs.

WARNING

For obvious reasons, a resolutions committee generally shouldn't be empowered to keep a motion or resolution from being considered unless it's clearly dilatory or improper. I've seen enough problems created by a well-intended resolutions committee that's perceived to be using its power to silence members with whom committee members disagree or just don't like. Your committee can be empowered to hold motions from consideration, but it rarely bodes well for a select few to be able to keep a motion off the floor, no matter how the members of the committee may feel about the idea. Be judicious in your rules for the resolutions committee regarding what and how it must report, and make provisions for the membership to require the committee to report a resolution, even without a recommendation and even if the committee otherwise wouldn't be so inclined.

Acting on a resolutions committee report

When a resolutions committee reports, the chair handles the motions independently of the committee's recommendation.

For example, when the committee reports a member's proposal that dues be increased, it may recommend unfavorably. The chair mustn't offer the motion to "adopt the committee's recommendation," but rather should offer the motion itself: "The resolutions committee reports the motion of Mr. Money to raise the dues by $10 per year and recommends it be rejected. The committee's recommendation notwithstanding, the question is on the adoption of the motion to increase the dues. Those in favor of increasing the dues will say 'Aye.' Those opposed, say 'No.'"

The Part of Tens

4

Chapter **21**

Ten (Plus Two) Meeting Procedure Myths

I n my experience, most members and presiding officers really do have an interest in conducting business according to Robert's Rules. The real trouble is that, more often than not, they've never actually *read* Robert's Rules — or even a book like this about Robert's Rules. The trouble is, when you haven't *read* the rules, but instead just operate based on what you've *heard* are the rules, you unknowingly help to create or strengthen a procedure myth. Unfortunately, Robert's Rules is often misinterpreted, and a lot of common meeting procedure myths are floating around.

This chapter dispels the myths and reveals why some things really need to be done a certain way. If your goal is to have good meetings and avoid wasting time, you'll be glad you read about these ten (or so) myths, and you'll see how things actually ought to be done according to Robert's Rules.

TIP

To do things "by the book," you have to know what the book says! Get the right book, and read it before you go off pontificating about procedure.

Robert's Rules Is Just a Guide You Don't Have to Follow

Bzzzzt! Sorry, no prize for you! (This one has to be the mother of all myths — it's completely baseless!) If your bylaws provide that Robert's Rules is your parliamentary authority, then the rules are binding on your group.

Most of the time, people who say this don't know the truth, or just don't think about it. Only rarely are they trying to manipulate the organization or take advantage of the members' lack of familiarity with the rules.

I can't argue that Robert's Rules doesn't contain a lot of guidance. It does! With all its "should" rules, it offers members and leaders alike plenty of advice and solid recommendations based on common sense and logic. But as helpful as it is as a guide, when you've adopted it, Robert's Rules is the definitive authority for decisions on parliamentary procedure.

REMEMBER

If you adopt a parliamentary authority, its rules are binding on the organization, insofar as they don't conflict with the bylaws or special rules of order the organization adopts.

Only One Motion Can Be on the Floor at a Time

Robert's Rules establishes that it's a *fundamental principle of parliamentary law* that only "one question can be considered at a time." I'm not arguing. You can consider only one *question* at a time. That question is referred to as the *immediately pending question.*

The myth arises because the actual rule is often misstated. Several pending motions can actually be on the floor at one time when you include any *secondary motions* that may be made during the handling of a main motion.

REMEMBER

These motions can be made while another motion is pending, subject only to their particular rules of applicability and precedence. They're added to the stack of pending motions as they're made, and they're voted on (or considered) one at a time, from highest ranking back down to the lowest ranking, in their proper order. Flip to Chapters 9 through 11 for a more in-depth discussion of secondary motions.

For example, imagine that a motion is made to hire a management company to handle your condo association's business dealings and physical building maintenance. A member then moves to amend the motion in some way. While the amendment is being discussed, someone moves to refer the motion with the amendment to a committee to report back next month. While the motion to refer is being discussed, someone moves to limit the debate on the motion to commit to ten more minutes and then take a vote.

Your parliamentary situation is that you have four motions pending, or *on the floor,* at one time. But you can *consider* only one question at a time. In this case, the immediately pending question is whether to limit debate and decide it before you get back to the motion to commit. Then the motion to commit becomes the immediately pending question. If the motion to commit fails, you go back to considering the amendment, which becomes the immediately pending question. After you decide the question on the amendment, you're again able to consider the original main motion.

REMEMBER

Many *pending motions* can stack up during the course of a discussion, but only one *question* can be considered at a time — known as the *immediately pending question.*

The Presiding Officer Can Vote Only to Break a Tie

This popular myth, and its variation that the chair *must* vote to break a tie, are more common than ants at a picnic. And it's simply not so!

Robert's Rules says that the presiding officer (if a member) votes with the other members when a vote is by ballot. For other forms of voting, though, the chair's duty to maintain the appearance of impartiality while presiding should convince him to refrain from voting, except when their vote will affect the result. (Chapter 8 contains more information on voting procedures.)

The myth comes about because of two misconceptions:

>> **The first is based on the misunderstanding that a tie vote isn't decisive.** On the contrary, whenever a majority vote is required to adopt a motion, a tie vote *is* decisive; a motion that fails to achieve the majority vote necessary to adopt it *fails*.

If the vote is tied, the presiding officer doesn't need to vote unless they want the motion to be adopted. They can then vote in the affirmative, and the motion passes.

WARNING

The presiding officer doesn't get to cast a second vote. If you're voting by ballot for an election and the result of a ballot is a tie, everybody just votes again. If you're voting by ballot on a motion and the result is a tie, the motion fails.

When you're not voting by ballot and the vote isn't tied, but the affirmatives outnumber the opposition by one vote, the chair doesn't need to vote unless they want the motion to fail. They can then cast a vote in the negative, creating a tie and causing the motion to fail.

>> **The second misconception comes from the failure to consider that the chair's vote can also affect the outcome when the threshold for adoption is anything other than a majority.** For example, if a motion requires a two-thirds vote to pass, the chair's vote can make a difference if it causes the motion to reach (or not reach) the two-thirds threshold. In either case, the chair can vote if they want to affect the result.

REMEMBER

The chair votes along with other members whenever the vote is by ballot; otherwise, they vote only when they want to use their vote to affect the result.

REMEMBER

The chair of the committee or small board is free to speak in debate, make motions, and vote in all cases. I cover this in more detail in Chapter 3.

The Parliamentarian Makes Rulings

Some presiding officers like to pass the buck when it comes to handling points of order and parliamentary inquiries. They say things like, "The parliamentarian just ruled that . . ." or "The parliamentarian says you can't [or can] do such-and-such."

But a presiding officer who knows their stuff stands in control of the meeting. They assume the responsibility incumbent upon them after consulting with and paying heed to the parliamentarian's opinions on matters of procedure.

REMEMBER

The parliamentarian's job is to advise the presiding officer and give an opinion when asked. But the sole responsibility for ruling on a point of order or answering a parliamentary inquiry lies with the chair.

A Motion Not Seconded Is Void

The purpose of the requirement for a motion to be seconded is to avoid wasting your group's time on a motion that no one other than the person who makes the motion wants to discuss. If the members debate an unseconded motion, vote on an unseconded motion without debating it, or adopt it by unanimous consent, the motion is adopted, being presumed to have a second because members discussed it or acted upon it.

REMEMBER

A point of order that a motion isn't in order for lack of a second must be made before any discussion or vote takes place on the motion.

Abstentions Count As Yes (or No) Votes

One of the most frequent questions asked of parliamentarians is "How do we count abstentions?" The answer is simple: You don't. Abstentions are *not* votes. They're instances of members choosing not to vote.

The confusion probably comes from the fact that voters who abstain typically do, by their abstention, influence the outcome of a vote. For example, if the requirement for adoption is a majority vote, abstentions have the effect of a vote for the prevailing side. By not voting, members have helped the winner.

On the other hand, if the vote required for adoption is the affirmative vote of the majority of the members present, an abstention has the same effect as a negative vote. But in any case, abstentions never count toward a certain side, even if the fact that a member doesn't vote has a direct effect on the outcome.

REMEMBER

A member has a duty to vote, but they can't be compelled to vote, because they also have the right to remain neutral on a particular question. Therefore, requiring a motion to be decided based on the number of members present usually isn't a good idea; this arrangement denies a member the right to be neutral on the question. (I discuss abstentions and vote-counting procedures in Chapter 8.)

The Chair Must Ask for Unfinished Business

You're not alone if you or your fellow members think that *unfinished business* is that part of the agenda where you rehash old ideas that never went anywhere. Those who have knowledge of the term but have never considered its true definition under Robert's Rules perpetuate the myth.

Unfinished business is business brought over from an earlier meeting. It consists of motions (except for special orders) pending when the meeting adjourned or which were on the agenda or order of business, but not reached before the meeting adjourned. As a class of business, its items are determined based on what happened at the prior meeting. Unfinished business isn't the place for members to bring up old ideas that never took off.

REMEMBER

The presiding officer and the secretary aren't doing their jobs if neither knows whether the group has any unfinished business. If the presiding officer does know, they need to announce the first item in the class as soon as the meeting reaches the point in the order of business when unfinished business is addressed.

The Chair Must Call for Nominations Three Times

This myth seems to have a life of its own, like some kind of urban legend. It rivals the myth that all a member has to do to stop debate is to holler "Question!" (I discuss that mistake in Chapter 21.)

Perhaps this myth has its foundations in a reasonable policy that some judicious presiding officer once adopted to be sure that nominations weren't closed as long as there was a member who wanted to make a nomination from the floor. They may have thought, "If I call for nominations once, hear none, and declare nominations closed, somebody is sure to say, 'Hey, wait, you can't just close nominations like that!' If I try again and call for nominations a second time, members who didn't hear me the first time are likely to react the same way. So I'll just ask three times before I say, 'Hearing none, the chair declares nominations are closed.'"

This logic is reasonable, and it's certainly not a bad policy. But it isn't a rule.

REMEMBER

The motion to close nominations is never in order as long as anyone wants to make a nomination. In fact, the motion is rarely even necessary. Upon determining that no further nominations are forthcoming from the members, the chair simply declares nominations closed.

If the Winner Doesn't Serve, Second Place Can Take Over

This myth is one of those misconceptions that sounds reasonable until you give it some thought. The second-place candidate is either the loser of a two-candidate race or one of several people the members rejected in favor of someone else. In the first situation, the candidate was rejected outright; in the second situation, no one knows how the members would've voted had the original winner not been on the ballot. You can't assume that the second-place candidate would have been the winner if all the members who voted for the actual winner had voted for someone else.

Sorry, but if the winner declines the office after being elected, you have what Robert's Rules calls an *incomplete election* (see Chapter 14). To resolve the incomplete election, you need to reopen nominations and have another try at it. If the winner fails to serve out the term of office, you're left with a vacancy, and you need to follow the rules in your bylaws for filling the vacancy. Depending on the particular office and your bylaws, you may have to hold another election or your executive board may be able to appoint someone to fill the vacancy. If your bylaws say nothing about filling vacancies, you hold another election for the office.

REMEMBER

Except when your bylaws provide expressly for filling a vacancy *in the office of president,* if your president dies or resigns, the vacancy actually occurs in the office of vice-president, who automatically becomes the president. You then fill the vacancy in the office of vice-president.

REMEMBER

If the winner of an election declines to serve, the election is incomplete. Vote again! Otherwise, vacancies in an office are filled either according to the bylaws or rules of order, or by the electing authority if no applicable rules are in place.

Officers Must Be Members

If your organization follows this policy, it's not because of anything in Robert's Rules. The only way you can properly put a limitation on whom to elect is to establish that qualification in the bylaws. If you don't have this kind of limitation, however, Robert's Rules recognizes the complete autonomy of a membership body to select anyone it wants to serve as an officer.

Organizations frequently rely on nonmember officers. A treasurer may be an accountant who's not a member but who does the organization's bookkeeping. Similarly, a secretary (or even the president/CEO) may be an employee of the organization but not a member.

If your group wants to limit its own power to decide who serves by adopting a bylaw requiring officers to be members, that's fine. But Robert's Rules sees this action as a limitation on the right of the membership itself to make the final decision on whom it wants to elect to serve.

Ex Officio Members Can't Vote

Now that's just plain silly. Of course they can vote! They're members, aren't they? *Ex officio* simply refers to how they came to be a member: They hold membership *by virtue of some office.* Members can always vote, no matter how they come to be a member, unless some concrete rule in the bylaws restricts the voting rights of a particular class of members.

Motions Don't Take Effect Until Minutes Are Approved

If this statement were true, you could never even have approved minutes, because minutes of one meeting wouldn't be officially approved until the minutes of the meeting in which they were approved got approved, and those minutes wouldn't be approved until the next meeting, and so on. You'd have a never-ending wait for approved minutes.

Motions are in effect upon adoption, unless the motion provides for some other effective date. The fact that minutes aren't yet approved has nothing to do with whether a motion is in effect. Approving minutes approves only the record of the adoption of the motion, not the motion itself.

Chapter **22**

Ten Tips for Presiding Officers

Whether you're presiding over a meeting of 2,500 members or a small board or committee meeting, your job is the same when it comes to the goal of successfully managing a meeting. And to ensure that you manage successfully, consider these tips to help you establish yourself as a knowledgeable, well-organized, and helpful leader.

Know Your Rules

One of the best ways to establish your credibility as a leader is to know your rules. If you don't know your rules, your members will know it, and you'll come to a sudden understanding of how it probably feels to be a deer staring into oncoming headlights. (I was there once — caught unprepared, that is, not staring into oncoming headlights. But I don't ever intend to be in that position again.)

No feeling is quite as bad as standing in front of a room full of people who know more about your job than you do. For what it's worth, General Robert was in that position once, too. After his experience, he wrote a book on the rules!

TIP

To avoid being caught unprepared, make sure you're well read on your group's charter, bylaws, special rules of order, and parliamentary authority. No one other than a person who has held your office before you (and your parliamentarian) should know as much about these rules as you do.

Plan Your Meetings

Nothing benefits you and your group as much as being prepared for your meetings. Planning your meeting in as much detail as possible gives you the best chance of completing the agenda within the time available (or at least knowing whether you'll need to hold an adjourned meeting to finish your business).

The process of planning your meeting so that you can cover everything you need to cover is much easier if you follow these tips:

>> **Make it everybody's responsibility to know the agenda.** Use the minutes from the last meeting as your primary planning and management tool. Distribute the minutes and reports in advance of the meeting. The more everyone knows, the better you can budget your time.

>> **Call on your officers and committee chairs to submit their reports early.** You need to know the recommendations contained in the reports before the meeting so that you know what motions the committees will be making or that are likely to arise from the report.

>> **Call on members to advise the presiding officer of motions they know they intend to introduce.** With advance info on motions, you're in the best position to see that motions are drafted well, saving lots of time on technical amendments during the meeting.

Start Your Meetings on Time

People have busy schedules. Your time is valuable, but it's no more valuable than that of the members who have arrived on time and are ready to start at the appointed hour.

I've been to too many meetings where the presiding officer waits too long after the scheduled time to accommodate members who are late. In my opinion, aside from a few minutes delay in the event a quorum isn't present, starting late is a big mistake. An effective presiding officer accommodates the members who arrive on time and insists that the habitual latecomers adjust to everyone else instead of making everyone adjust to them.

REMEMBER

Nothing you do commands the respect you must have as the chair as much as starting your meeting on time. Your members know you mean business, and that's fine, because that's what you're all there for.

Use Unanimous Consent

I discuss the concept of *unanimous consent* (when the chair declares a motion to have passed without taking a vote and instead asks simply if there's objection) in Chapter 8. And in several places throughout this book, I mention its use in handling particular motions.

Unanimous consent is a remarkable tool for handling any motion for which it's clear and obvious that the assembly's will is to pass the motion.

The most recognizable situations in which unanimous consent is used are in approving minutes and adjourning a meeting. But unanimous consent is just as useful even if the question is on a bylaw amendment, as long as no opposition is apparent. Members rarely object to unanimous consent when they know that opposition is so minimal that it won't affect the outcome.

REMEMBER

If you ask for unanimous consent and a member objects, you simply take the vote. Otherwise, it's a great timesaver, and members really do respect presiding officers who know how to save them time.

Use Committees

Encourage new proposals to be brought through your organization's committees. Members often have good ideas, but those ideas sometimes need some work before they're ready for a vote.

Teaching your members how to take their ideas to committees can have great benefits for you and your organization. But members need to have confidence in their committees' willingness to help them with their ideas. Take a look at Chapter 16 for more discussion about how to create effective committees.

Let members know that they can save time in general meetings by perfecting their ideas in committees. Saving time increases your own stock as a leader. Committees will be respected for making solid recommendations, helping to get motions easily decided.

REMEMBER

If your committees are set up well, everybody who's really interested tackles the discussion in the committee meetings, and the rest of the members know that the committee's recommendations are based on sound reason. But good committees go to waste without a strong leader to make efficient use of them — that's you.

Preside with Impartiality

Nobody expects you to actually *be* impartial. You were probably elected or appointed because you have an overall agenda and a program you hope to advance. But when you're presiding during your meeting, you must put aside your personal agenda and help the assembly make the decisions. You can't lose if you do this, because ultimately, the decision belongs to the majority anyway.

You're far better off being known as a leader who ensures that the minority has a full opportunity to present its case than as one who uses the power of the chair to thwart the minority's efforts to be heard.

As I explain in more detail in Chapter 7, the presiding officer must leave any personal or political agendas to those members on the floor that support the same program. As presiding officer, you really only control the floor (and you're expected to follow clear and definite rules about how the floor is assigned — I discuss these rules in Chapter 7). Everything else is really in the members' hands. It's always in your best interest to be known as a leader who helps the minority make its case — and to do so no matter how you personally feel about its position.

To preside with impartiality, follow these tips:

- **»** **Don't enter into debate.** When a member concludes their speech, don't rebut them, argue with them, or explain why they're wrong. Say "Thank you" and recognize someone on the other side of the issue.

- **»** **Don't gavel through motions.** What clearer indication can there be that you don't have any respect for the minority?

- **»** **Don't vote (except by ballot) unless your vote will affect the result.** You don't need to make your preferences known unless it's going to be the deciding vote.

- **»** **Don't refuse to recognize someone just because you don't want a certain member to be heard.** Instead, take extra care to assist all members in their efforts to be heard.

The chair of a committee or small board is free to speak in debate, make motions, and vote in all cases. I cover this in more detail in Chapter 3.

The surest road to your success as a presiding officer is to take the position that the members control the decision, and you're there to help them do just that.

Never Give up the Chair

Although at first this tip may appear to be an elaboration on my previous tip to maintain the appearance of impartiality, it's a little more than that.

WARNING

No matter how strongly you feel about an issue, your job is to preside. True enough, Robert's Rules provides that if you can't preside impartially because you feel too strongly about an issue, you must step down and let someone else preside until the vote is taken. But I caution you to always consider whether giving up the chair is really wise. Also consider that the person who takes the chair may not gracefully return the position to you! That can get mighty uncomfortable. Take my advice: Don't give up the chair.

Don't Share Your Lectern

Put simply, never share your lectern with other speakers. Instead, provide a separate and distinct station for other officers and committee chairs to use when giving their reports.

During a business meeting, your duty requires that you stay in control of the floor, and you can't be in control of the floor if you can't use your station to address the assembly without moving somebody else out of the way.

When officers and committee members make their reports, motions may arise, and questions may come up. Having two lecterns allows you to manage the discussion from the chair and keeps the reporting member available to respond to questions as the chair requests.

REMEMBER

Members always address their remarks and comments to the chair, and the chair recognizes members to speak and ask questions. It's your job and your station. Make the place from which you preside yours exclusively.

Keep Your Cool

Sometimes presiding over a meeting just isn't easy. When disorder erupts, no amount of hammering a wooden mallet on a sounding block is going to do anything but aggravate an already bad situation.

When a bombastic member decides to ignore the rules and fly off into 17 different disorderly rants, calmly rap the gavel once and ask the member to come to order. If they ignore your request, the most effective thing you can do is stand firmly at your station. Don't allow yourself to become engaged personally with the member. Instead, calmly entreat them to come to order.

In my experience extremely difficult situations — when an entire assembly erupts in disorderly demonstration — often come about as a reaction to perceptions that the chair is being partial to one side. Whatever the reason, sometimes it's just best to wait until the inevitable silence finally falls and then ask for unanimous consent to a recess so that tempers may ease. If you make mistakes that give rise to disorder, meet with those members in a position to assist you in reestablishing the respect due to the chair so that the meeting can either continue or adjourn.

Use a Parliamentarian

In the world of Robert's Rules, you don't have to go it alone. Regardless of the size of your organization, when you have problems or questions, you can seek out the services of a professional parliamentarian. Resources are available online to answer questions, and local units of parliamentarians exist all over the country. Check out the website for the National Association of Parliamentarians at www.parliamentarians.org or the website for the American Institute of Parliamentarians at www.aipparl.org.

Small local organizations sometimes engage parliamentarians to assist with particular problems or with bylaw amendments and revisions, but your board doesn't need to have an extremely large budget to have a professional parliamentarian serve regularly at your meetings. With a little planning, you can afford the assistance more than you probably realize, especially when you break down the real cost per attending member and the benefits of the assistance.

REMEMBER

The parliamentarian's job is to make you look good in the chair. Much of your parliamentarian's work is done outside the meeting, helping you prepare for your meeting and know your rules. But when it comes time for the meeting, nothing beats the confidence you feel if you have a parliamentarian there to advise and assist you.

Chapter **23**

Ten Motion Mistakes to Avoid

Robert's Rules are rules designed to facilitate the transaction of business by your group, not to hinder it. Nitpicking on minor technicalities is against the rules. Robert's Rules warns that calling attention to purely technical errors when no one's rights are being violated is a mistake. If you're going to be effective in meetings, you must know the right and wrong ways to use parliamentary motions.

You can find details for using all the basic motions in Part 2 of this book. The purpose of this chapter is to clue you in to the more frequent and obvious places where some members reveal their ignorance by trying to prove that they know so much.

"Reconsidering" a Vote

The motion to *Reconsider* is often a problem not because of the complexity of the motion itself, but because of the verb *to reconsider* finds broad use outside its parliamentary context. Under

Robert's Rules, however, the motion to *Reconsider* (a vote) is a specific parliamentary motion with a specific and limited application.

Frequently, someone moves to reconsider a vote taken at an earlier meeting. However, the correct motion in this case is either *Rescind* or *Amend Something Previously Adopted (when a motion was adopted at a previous meeting)*, or, *renewing* that motion. Renewing a motion is simply making the motion again at a future meeting. In short, a motion to Reconsider the vote on a motion that occurred in an earlier session is not in order. The choice of the proper motion to use in the new meeting depends only on whether the motion you're trying (incorrectly) to reconsider passed or failed, respectively.

WARNING

The problem is compounded when a presiding officer allows a motion to reconsider a vote from a prior meeting and applies the rule that only a person who voted on the prevailing side is entitled to offer the motion. On the contrary, any member can move to rescind or amend something previously adopted, or renew a motion that failed (in a prior meeting) at a new meeting.

REMEMBER

When it comes to parliamentary usage, *Reconsider* is something you can do *only with respect to a decision made in the current meeting* (or on the next day, if the session lasts more than one day). See Chapter 12 for discussions of all these motions.

Speaking without Recognition

First, and most important, just shouting out a motion is a mistake. Indeed, it's a mistake to make just about any motion without first being recognized by the chair. You've probably heard folks shout out motions at meetings. The world would be a calmer place if they would only learn a little meeting etiquette and refrain from calling out their motions (except for points of order and a few others) until they have the recognition of the chair.

Don't make the mistake of being one of those rude people. Rise and address the chair (say "Mr. President" or "Madam Chairman"), and seek recognition in proper form. You don't always get the first shot, but you're entitled to preference in recognition way ahead of all those others who just shout out their motions. Take a look at Chapter 7 for more information on getting the floor in meetings.

REMEMBER

The chair's recognition isn't required for the subsidiary motions Call for the Orders of the Day and Raise a Question of Privilege (see Chapter 10), the incidental motions Point of Order, Appeal, Objection to the Consideration of the Question, and requests and inquiries (see Chapter 11).

Moving to "Table!"

In too many meetings, when anything controversial comes to the floor, somebody calls from their place, "I move to table!" In addition to the offense of speaking without recognition, the member is misusing one motion in an attempt to accomplish the object of a completely different motion.

You and I know that the offending member is opposed to the pending main motion and wants to kill it. But you also know that a member doesn't kill a motion by moving to table it (refer to Chapter 9) — at least, not if the group follows Robert's Rules. The motion to "table" is actually the motion to *Lay on the Table*, and you use it to temporarily set aside a pending motion to take up something else more pressing or urgent. If you want to *kill* a main motion, you move to *Postpone Indefinitely*.

In situations like this, I generally advise the chair to ignore a motion to "table" unless it's made after a speaker is recognized. If the speaker has properly obtained recognition, the chair must discern whether the speaker's intent is to lay a pending motion on the table or to kill the main motion. If it's the latter, I suggest that the chair put the question as the motion to *Postpone Indefinitely*, which is how you decide whether to kill a motion under Robert's Rules. You find more information about motions to *Lay on the Table* and *Postpone Indefinitely* in Chapter 9.

Calling the Question

When members get tired of hearing the same arguments go back and forth on a pending motion, they get impatient. Inevitably, somebody calls out, "Question!" or "I call the question!" Like the call to "table," (see the previous section), the member adds to their misuse by not seeking recognition of the chair before speaking.

Sometimes the fact that no one else wants to speak is obvious, and the chair can simply say, "If there's no one else who wants to speak, then, without objection, we'll vote on the motion." But your presiding officer may prefer to take the opportunity to tell the members that *calling the question* actually requires a formal motion from a member after being recognized by the chair. See Chapter 9 for the complete details on this motion (*Previous Question*). A presiding officer needs to help members understand that it's his job to offer the members the opportunity to vote when it's clear that no one else wants to speak; calling out "Question" without first obtaining the floor is just plain rude.

Tabling It until Next Month

This attempt at a motion is yet another misuse of the word *table*. The member who makes this proposal really wants to *Postpone to a Certain Time*, not *Lay on the Table*. You may be thinking, "Why all this emphasis on the correct words if you know what the member is trying to accomplish?" The reason has a lot to do with the order of precedence of these motions and the rules covering whether the motion is debatable, amendable, and so forth.

A motion to *Lay on the Table* outranks the motion to *Postpone to a Certain Time*. *Lay on the Table* is neither debatable nor amendable (either a motion is going to be laid on the table or it's not). *Postpone to a Certain Time* is both amendable as to time and debatable on whether to postpone. All these factors influence the decision to be made, and one of the chair's many duties is to make sure the question sought by the member is the one put before the members.

Offering a Point of Information

For years, Robert's Rules provided a motion known as *Point of Information*. But Robert intended it to allow members to ask questions, not to add to the debate. Still, way too many people think it means they can get the floor to *give* information. When the chair doesn't know any better, misuse of this motion is often a sneaky way for a member to inject themselves into the debate even after they've exhausted his right to speak.

REMEMBER

Robert's Rules has renamed *Point of Information* as *Request for Information*, to clarify its proper use.

Next time Knotthead Know-It-All seeks recognition for a point of information so that they can inform the assembly of their opinions, take a minute and let them know that it's now a "request for information" and ask them what they need to know. Knotthead, knowing everything, should just sit down.

REMEMBER

A *Request for Information* is made to enable the member to *request* information, not to give them an opportunity to speak again.

Offering Friendly Amendments

Most everybody has encountered a well-intentioned member who offers, "I want to make a friendly amendment." As if! General Robert never even used the term *friendly amendment*. The term finally showed up in the tenth edition of Robert's Rules, only to explain that it's not what everybody thinks it is.

The term is often used as a means of asking permission of the motion's original maker to add the amendment. Ol' Schmedley doesn't want people to think that they doesn't like Ernestine's idea. They're just trying to help! But the fact is, when a motion is on the floor, the maker of the motion no longer owns it. Whether Ernestine accepts Schmedley's amendment is of no consequence. Any motion to amend a main motion depends on the acceptance of the assembly, not the person who made the original motion.

If Schmedley offers his friendly amendment before the chair states Ernestine's motion and Ernestine accepts Schmedley's change, the chair states the motion as changed, and there's no need for the members to vote on the so-called friendly amendment. It's part of Ernestine's motion from the start.

Offering a friendly amendment is really patronizing. The best thing to do is to simply get recognition of the chair, move your amendment, and tell the membership why you're offering the amendment. Believe me, Ernestine's feelings won't be hurt. She'll probably be pleased that you cared enough to help perfect her idea. Chapter 9 covers amendments in greater detail.

Making Motions to Accept or Receive Reports

The belief that you need to do something official with a report presented to your group is pretty widespread. But except in some specific situations, which I list here, the chair doesn't entertain motions to *accept* or *receive* reports after they're presented. Instead, the chair simply thanks the reporting member and goes on to the next item of business.

If anything besides "Thank you" needs to be said, stick to something like, "The report requires no action. The next item of business is . . . ." The chair can acknowledge a written report by simply saying, "The report will be placed on file." Sometimes a report contains recommendations or suggests the need for the group to take some specific action. In those cases, the presiding officer states the question *on the motion that arises* from the report, not on whether to adopt the recommendations contained in the report, nor on whether to receive, adopt, or accept the report.

The only situations in which it's proper to accept or adopt a report are when a particular body wants to make a report its own, as in the following situations:

>> When a board or committee wants to adopt a draft of its own report, which is prepared by members of the board or committee for the purpose of reporting to the general membership.

>> When the assembly wants to endorse every word of a report, such as in these examples:

- **An auditor's annual report of the financial records of the treasurer.** Endorsement relieves the treasurer of further liability, except in the case of fraud.

- **A convention credentials committee report.** Endorsement establishes the membership of the convention.

- **A convention standing rules committee report.** Endorsement adopts the convention standing rules.

- **A convention program committee report.** Endorsement adopts the convention agenda.

- **A report to be published in full in the organization's name.** Endorsement makes the report an official statement of the organization.

WARNING

Two situations in which adopting or accepting a report is never proper arise in the case of a nominations committee report, which is always followed by nominations from the floor, and a treasurer's report, which is simply filed. Generally, it's only the audited annual treasurer's report that is filed for audit.

Dispensing with the Minutes

You don't want to dispense with the minutes; if anything, you want to *dispense with the reading of the minutes* — for now, at least! In parliamentary terms, you make the correct version of this motion to enable your group to handle the approval of the minutes at a later time, out of the regular order of things. It absolutely does *not* equate to approving the minutes.

I've attended many meetings in which moving to dispense with the minutes has become quite the custom. For example, "Approval of Minutes" is on the agenda. Fonquetta J. Figaro famously does their duty and offers, "Madam President, I move we dispense with the minutes." Madam President dutifully responds with, "If there is no objection, we will dispense with *the reading of* the minutes [pausing in case someone objects]. Hearing none, the reading of the minutes is dispensed with. The next item of business is . . . ."

Do you think the minutes are approved? Maybe Fonquetta does, and maybe Madam President does. But unless the question is on the *approval* of the minutes, they haven't been approved. Instead, they've just been formally ignored.

REMEMBER

Minutes must be approved before they become the official record of the assembly's action. Dispense with their reading, if you must, but ask for corrections and approve them at some point so that you have a complete and official record of your meetings.

Wasting Breath on "I So Move"

Oh, come on now! What's your motion? State it! When the presiding officer says, "The chair will entertain a motion to take a recess," say, "I move we take a recess for ten minutes." If you just say, "I so move," you haven't actually made a motion. You've only confused half the members and bumfuzzled the rest. Whatever possessed you to think that it's okay to make a motion that doesn't propose any action? Think of it like this: The chair says, "Ms. Portulaca moves 'so.' Those in favor of 'so,' say 'Aye.' Opposed, say 'No.' The ayes have it, and we will 'so.'" Obviously, this doesn't make any sense because you need to know what "so" stands for, but this is what happens when you say, "I so move."

Chapter **24**

Ten Custom Rules to Consider

I f your organization has adopted Robert's Rules as its parliamentary authority, you've got a good rule for just about anything that comes up. However, Robert's Rules doesn't try to be one-size-fits-all when it comes to individualizing your own rules. Robert's Rules encourages you to make your own specific rules and provides you with good information to help you fine-tune your rules as needed.

This chapter lists some of the ideas that parliamentarians frequently recommend on the topic of special rules and bylaws. The list is far from exhaustive; in fact, it probably barely scratches the surface. But it's a start, and the recommendations come with a lot of 20/20 hindsight. I certainly didn't think of the items on this list all by myself, but I've had clients who wished they'd thought of them before they were forced to pay me to help straighten out their messes!

Changing the Ten-Minute Speech Rule

Robert's Rules provides that each member may speak twice per day to a motion, and each speech may last up to ten minutes.

Even though members rarely claim the right to a full ten minutes, speeches can be time consuming if members do speak that long. And when speech time becomes an issue during a meeting, changing the limits requires a two-thirds vote. Getting that vote takes time — and unless it's done on a particular topic before members begin to speak, the first speakers will have been able to speak longer than the members who speak after the limit is adopted.

TIP

If you want to save your group some time and trouble, you can consider what limits your group may prefer to work under and adopt a *special rule of order* (see Chapter 2) to provide a time limit of less than ten minutes for a member's turn at speaking in debate.

Defining Your Quorum

Robert's Rules defines a *quorum* as the number of members that must be present to conduct business (and Robert's Rules recognizes only one type of member — the type that has full voting rights). If your group hasn't defined its quorum, Robert's Rules does it for you. For most organizations, quorum is a majority of your members. For more detailed information on quorums, see Chapter 4.

A majority quorum is fine if your group is small. But if your organization is large, and especially if most people join for the benefits and don't care about the meetings, you may find yourself unable to conduct business. As the number of members increases, you'll encounter problems in obtaining a quorum. Making reasonable quorum provisions in your bylaws is the best way to prevent this problem.

According to Robert's Rules, a quorum should be set as the largest number of members that can be reasonably expected to attend meetings except when extraordinary circumstances take place, like when the weather is too bad, or the bridge into the city shuts down. I tend to believe that it's best to set quorum levels by number rather than by percentage, especially if the membership level is stable. But whether you set a count or a percentage isn't as important as giving careful thought to your quorum and defining it in your bylaws.

Establishing Rules Related to the Quorum

No matter how carefully you consider and define a quorum (see Chapter 4), membership numbers can change quickly and outpace your ability to reach a quorum under your current rules. If your group faces this problem, you'll be glad you considered the following rules to help make things easier.

Authorize your board to fill its vacancies to achieve a quorum

Organizations with small boards usually have bylaw provisions that authorize the board to fill any board vacancies that occur between election meetings. This provision is fine unless too many people resign from the board at one time. When that happens, the board members who are left need to have the power to fill the vacancies. But they can't take official action if their number falls below the quorum established for the board.

A good way to make sure the board doesn't become powerless in this situation is to make a bylaw provision stating that if the number of board members falls below a certain level, the remaining members may accept resignations and fill as many vacancies as necessary to again have a quorum (allowing it to act as a board again).

Alternatively, remaining board members need at least temporary authority to do whatever is necessary to call a special meeting of the membership to elect replacement board members.

Authorize a mail or Internet vote to change an impossible quorum

Suppose your organization is one whose quorum is expressed as a percentage or is defined by Robert's Rules as only a majority of the membership. What if you find one day that your membership has grown so large that you can't possibly achieve the quorum?

You have a real problem! If you can't achieve a quorum, you can't do anything! You can't change the quorum to a reasonable number, and you can't even take action to dissolve the organization.

The solution? Foresight! Place a provision in your bylaws that if your group is unable to achieve a quorum within a specific time and after taking some specified action (such as sending a notice of the problem to the members and attempting a second meeting), the quorum can be amended by snail mail or secure Internet ballot. I cover mail and Internet balloting in detail in Chapter 8.

WARNING

When making provisions for these ballots, clearly state what vote is required for any issue to be decided in that manner. Also make clear that you have no quorum requirement for votes conducted by mail or Internet balloting.

Electing by Voice instead of by Ballot

A bylaw providing that a vote shall be by ballot is designed to protect the single member's right to cast their vote in any way they choose without revealing their vote to the other members.

Nevertheless, even in groups where it's abundantly clear that only one candidate is seeking an office and that candidate is practically guaranteed election, *a ballot must be taken unless the bylaws make a special provision allowing a voice vote.* For details on general voting by ballot, flip to Chapter 8. For specifics on ballot elections, take a look at Chapter 14.

TIP

If your group wants to require ballot votes except when you have only one candidate, it can do so by adopting a bylaw similar to the one used in a local parliamentarians' unit of which I'm a member): "Votes for officers shall be by ballot unless there is only one nominee for office. In such case, the chair may declare the sole nominee elected."

Adopting Special Vote Thresholds

Robert's Rules is not just about majority rule. It's also about protecting the rights of the minority. You can see this exemplified in the two-thirds vote requirement applicable to rescinding or amending things previously adopted. The two-thirds vote threshold in these cases is about protecting a minority of more than one third.

Other situations exist where provisions need to be made to protect even smaller minorities.

One such situation is when an assembly is responsible to an interested constituency and the roll-call vote is important in putting the vote on record. Robert's Rules discusses the wisdom of providing for a low threshold of voters to be able to require a roll-call vote because a majority is usually unlikely to require itself to go on the record. (Flip to Chapter 8 for details on roll-call voting.)

Another case where this principle may apply is in ordering a ballot vote or a counted vote. Without providing otherwise in your bylaws or adopting a special rule of order, the voting threshold necessary to order a ballot vote or a counted vote is also a majority. However, as with roll-call voting, you can eliminate some anxiety if the requirement for these votes is lower than a majority, too. Although you can use a percentage, I recommend adding a specific number. Generally, votes requiring a percentage can become cumbersome, in that you need an exact count of the attendance.

The specific number method finds good use in one of my state's political parties, whose bylaws provide that a roll-call vote must be taken in the demand of ten members. This rule makes it pretty easy to decide whether the vote must be by roll call.

On the other hand, the percentage method works efficiently for a professional association I once worked with. Its bylaws provide, "A ballot vote may be ordered by 10 percent of the members registered for the meeting." They have varying levels of attendance, depending on the meeting's program, but they always know the number of people actually registered at any given meeting, so they don't have to stop and count the members present to figure out what number is represented by 10 percent.

Authorizing a Committee to Adopt Its Own Rules

Robert's Rules allows an executive board to adopt special rules of order if they don't conflict with the organization's other rules (bylaws, special rules of order, parliamentary authority, or standing rules). But that doesn't hold true for committees. Unless your bylaws, rules, or motion creating a committee provide that your committees can adopt their own rules of procedure, Robert's Rules prohibits them from doing so. They're then completely bound by the organization's bylaws, standing rules, special rules, and the other default rules found in Robert's Rules. This rule is fine for smaller organizations, but it can be problematic for large organizations — especially those with large committees.

If your committees work mostly as autonomous bodies, it may be beneficial to make provisions in your bylaws allowing committees to adopt their own rules of procedure.

I don't know of many situations in which this change really hurts anything, but I can think of plenty of cases in which it helps. Consider a provision such as, "The auditing committee may adopt such procedural rules as it deems necessary to the conduct of the business of the committee, so long as they do not conflict with any specific provisions of these bylaws, special rules of order, or standing rules." A provision like this works well for many organizations. It really benefits a committee that's too large to effectively use the relaxed rules that Robert provides for committees and small boards. (I cover how and when it's okay to use less formal rules in Chapter 3.)

Authorizing Spending When Adopting Budgets

Your finance committee probably takes great pains to work out a good and workable budget, and you likely spend a lot of time going over the budget when it comes up for adoption by your board or organization. But adopting the budget just shows that members agree on how to spend the organization's money; it doesn't authorize the treasurer to write any checks. For that, the treasurer needs some sort of disbursement authorization.

I provide a sample proposed budget report online at www.dummies.com/go/robertsrulesfd4e. In it, I include a disbursement authorization as part of the language of the motion to adopt the budget. But you can achieve the same purpose by adopting a special rule of order or bylaw that makes the adoption of the budget an authorization to the treasurer to disburse the funds.

TIP

Your rule to authorize disbursement can be as simple as, "Upon adoption of a budget, the treasurer is authorized to make disbursements up to the total amount shown approved in the budget." But you may want to help the treasurer avoid problems by adding "upon the order of the president and the committee chair or officer under whose direction a particular budget item is administered."

Requiring an Adopted Agenda by Rule

Another tip that can make meetings go faster and reduce surprises from any member who likes to spring a controversial motion on everyone at the last minute is to have some special rules covering meeting agendas. See Chapter 5 for more information on agendas.

You can adopt special rules that

>> Provide for an agenda to be sent to members before the meeting.

>> Establish procedures for members to submit motions before the meeting.

>> Set a particular threshold of votes required to bring up new business that's not on the agenda.

A special rule of this kind may read, "The agenda for the regular meetings of the board shall be mailed to the board members within seven days before the meeting and shall include any items received by the secretary no later than ten days before the meeting. Additional items may be placed on the agenda for consideration during the meeting with the consent of a majority of the members present and voting."

REMEMBER

Robert's Rules provides that you can adopt an agenda at the beginning of a meeting and change it only by a two-thirds vote. By adopting the special rules suggested here, you add the benefits that come with advanced planning, yet you can still deviate from the plan if enough members want to do so.

Adopting a Customized Order of Business

Robert's Rules provides a logical and workable plan for the order of business for your meetings. I discuss it in detail in Chapter 5. However, although Robert's Rules' standard order of business is thorough when it comes to essentials, it's very basic. Your organization may want to add items to your order of business or do them in a different order. You can play around with the order of business as much as you want, but you need a special rule of order in place to make a permanent change for your meetings.

Breaking a Tie in Elections

According to Robert's Rules, an election (see Chapter 14) to office requires a majority vote unless the bylaws establish some other threshold. Under the rules, you just have to keep voting until someone receives a high enough vote for election. Sometimes a tie is the best you can do. Whether you're faced with a tie between the only two candidates for a single office or a tie between more candidates than there are seats on the board, a tiebreaker bylaw saves you time and frustration.

In one organization I belong to, we have an election for nine directors, and election is by plurality. (The winners are the nine candidates who receive the highest number of votes, even if nobody gets a majority.) We wanted a way to avoid having to reballot to break ties for the last seat or two because that usually took more time than it was worth. So we changed our bylaws to read, "In the event that there is a tie for any seat on the board, the decision shall be made by lot."

But the best way I have found to avoid (for the most part) tie votes and the consequences, when reballoting is impractical, is to use preferential voting. Just like with plurality voting, your bylaws must provide for it. I recommend preferential voting over plurality voting because preferential voting will generally elect the candidate most acceptable to the entire group. I discuss plurality and preferential voting in Chapter 8.

Chapter **25**

Ten Considerations for Electronic Meetings

R obert's Rules contains sample bylaw provisions and rules for electronic meetings of four general types. I list them here in the order of relative complexity.

» Speakerphone meetings where some members are in the same room together and others are on the phone

» Telephone meetings where all members are on a phone call

» Speakerphone meetings or telephone meetings, with Internet services used for secret voting and document sharing

» Fully featured Internet (or combination Internet and telephone) with capabilities for secret voting and document sharing

The first two types of electronic meetings are probably the ones most of you have become familiar with over the years. After all, Robert's Rules has included a requirement to make bylaw provisions allowing for meetings by teleconference since the dawn of the 21st century. As a result, many organizations have already opened the virtual door for executive boards and committees to meet by teleconference. This form is probably the easiest (though fraught with inconveniences and its own set of problems) way for small groups to conduct business meetings electronically. The lack, however, of the ability to conduct secret votes or to view documents online make this method useful only when decisions are relatively pro-forma or when they can be handled by unanimous consent. Roll-call voting is the only other option in these meetings.

The third and fourth type of electronic meetings, which involve the use of Internet platforms for voting, document sharing, and videoconferencing offer opportunities for organizations to bring together not only the small board or committee, but groups of hundreds of members. Unfortunately, the larger the group, the more complicated the rules must be if you're to ensure a meeting that protects the rights of all participants as established in Robert's Rules.

This chapter provides you with important considerations with respect to your choice of means to hold electronic meetings.

WARNING

Things can go south fast if you haven't planned well for going virtual. I urge strongly that you look to a professional parliamentarian to help you tune your virtual meeting dial so you can avoid the static and interference you might encounter otherwise.

Developing Bylaw Provisions

Among the simpler provisions are those that simply provide for electronic meetings by teleconference. A teleconference can also use videoconferencing technology as long as everybody can hear each other. But if you provide exclusively for electronic meetings by videoconference, all the participants have to be able to hear and see each other.

A sample basic bylaw that will allow your executive boards or committees to meet by teleconference might read, "Meetings of the executive board and committees may be held using telecommunications technology provided all participants have access to the designated technology platform and can hear each other during the meeting" But that's just a start.

Good bylaw provisions will address other concerns, including who can call an electronic meeting. (Is it the board? What about the president?) And if you're going to be meeting using Internet with videoconferencing, you'll need to be covering things like online voting, displaying motions, and so forth. Things get complicated fast the more virtual you try to take your meeting.

Making Members Responsible for Connection and Access

You'll want a rule that makes members responsible for their own access to the required technology. That can keep you from dealing with members who cry foul because they lose connectivity in mid-sentence. If Mona Motormouth's connection is breaking up and nobody can understand her point, the assembly shouldn't be held hostage until she can complete her speech. Of course, if the Internet platform itself goes down or loses connectivity, then it's not much different than if something makes it impossible to continue any meeting. You just have to make provisions for continuing the meeting. That means rescheduling and giving a reasonable notice for what essentially becomes an adjourned meeting (I cover those in Chapter 3).

Providing for a Quorum Call

When you're in a room all together, it's usually noticeable when attendance dwindles to the point that you may be lacking a quorum. But with an electronic meeting, especially a telephone meeting, it's not always easy to know if you have a quorum. The smaller group on the teleconference might avoid the problem by using roll-call votes, which will let you know right away if you still have your quorum. The larger groups that are meeting using Internet meeting platforms will probably have to go by the platform-maintained list of current attendees for a count.

Obtaining Recognition to Speak

On telephone conferences, members simply have to pay attention to pick the time to seek recognition from the chair. Presiding officers, then, must be alert for the voices of members seeking recognition. With sophisticated Internet platforms, however, you'll find all sorts of whistles and bells — like the chat box, for one — that can help you get the attention of the organizers and moderators. Your rules should consider all the possibilities in this regard offered by your platform and perhaps go so far as to provide for the roles of multiple meeting assistants because in a virtual meeting, everybody might be muted when another person is speaking.

Interrupting a Speaker

When everybody is in person in the same room and a controversial motion is being debated, Gordy Flackflinger can interrupt with "Point of Order," and the chair knows (or should know) just what to do. But when you're in a virtual meeting where everybody is muted except for a recognized speaker, how are you going to make sure that a point of order can be raised timely? That's dependent on the platform you're using and the availability of help in monitoring the attempts of members trying to interrupt a speaker for a legitimate reason (that is, when Robert says it's okay). A videoconferencing platform that allows participants to get a word in edgewise using a chat feature, or an attention-getting click that mimics raising hands, waving, or setting off fireworks (just kidding on that last one) can help as long as the presiding officer isn't the sole soul doing the monitoring.

You may need a professional virtual meeting service provider that staffs your meeting with persons monitoring all the members for potential interrupting motions. Those services are expensive but may be a bargain when you consider the cost of holding an in-person meeting of hundreds of members.

Establishing Requirements for Motions

When I'm in the chair, I almost always ask for main motions to be given to me in writing. This prevents me from having to ask Milton Mumble to repeat his motion, and then to repeat it again. In an in-person meeting, I can have the written motion before my eyes and thus state the motion accurately. And then I can pass the written motion on to the secretary.

But when the meeting is by teleconference, Secretary Sadie is essentially taking dictation. Maybe the motion isn't all that complex, and she copies it down as it's being made. But if it's a complex motion, it might be a good idea to have an option for the member to call in to another person who is present at the meeting so that it can be transcribed. Depending on the meeting type, you'll probably need some sort of rule on when and how to make sure motions are made so that they can be stated by the chair and understood by all the participants.

TIP

Making sure about the wording of the motion and any amendments is part of the job of presiding. It may take some time to get the motion reduced to writing, but doing so pays rich dividends in terms of accuracy, which pays back more dividends in terms of time. When you're tending to getting a motion written, you don't have to take a recess. You can just tell the assembly to "Stand at Ease" while the motion is put in writing. Nobody is likely to object to that.

Hearing "What Are We Voting on?" Less Frequently

This question plagues even the in-person meeting, so it's doubly important for the chair to make sure that they've stated the question and that the members have the opportunity to know exactly what they're voting on. If you're in an Internet meeting, displaying the motion in writing on the screen is going to be a blessing to everyone. Given the state of technology today, you can process motions and amendments using video displays even in in-person meetings.

Prudence Wiseman, a wise and prudent presiding officer, will make sure her virtual meetings take advantage of the screen-sharing so that everyone attending via videoconference can see the motion and any amendments in play. Members attending telephonically will be at a disadvantage, especially during the handling of complicated amendments. But if you've put the burden of having the right technology on the members, they'll have to make do with the technological limitations they've imposed upon themselves. Just be sure you have a rule (see the section, "Making Members Responsible for Connection and Access," earlier in this chapter).

Covering Voting Methods

Provisions have to be made for the different types of voting (I cover them in detail in Chapter 8). *Viva voce*, the most common voting method used in in-person meetings, isn't much of an option in virtual meetings. Hearing the speaker rattling as members say "Aye" or "No" probably won't provide a valid or reliable way to know who has it. Therefore, the chair may too often be in doubt.

Figuring out the will of the assembly in an electronic meeting depends a good bit on the technology. A speakerphone or telephone meeting will function best with unanimous consent or roll-call voting unless provisions are made for online voting. An Internet online meeting platform may have vote-counting features that will be of great help (except with secrecy).

But when Riley Ruckus wants to raise one over the results of a vote, only forethought and careful advance planning (along with a rule or two) will keep things civil while the chair or the tellers figure out what actually happened.

Noting Comings-and-Goings

Rules requiring members to announce their arrival and departure from the meeting are going to be critical in determining when and whether a quorum is present. It may be desirable to have the secretary keep a record of the comings and goings of the members to know who is actually in attendance at any given time, especially when a vote is taken.

Pulling the Plug

One thing anyone who's attended an electronic meeting has experienced is a sudden blast of audio when an attendee's dog sets to barking, or when a persistent child in want of attention addresses the participant. Aside from the rules already covering ejecting a member from a meeting for certain undesirable behavior, you should consider making provisions for muting a member or dropping their connection when that connection becomes disruptive. A rule can give the chair the permission to pull the plug subject only to an undebatable appeal to leave the connection intact.

Appendix

Glossary of Parliamentary Terms

absentee voting: Voting by (postal or electronic) mail, fax, or proxy by persons not in attendance at a meeting; not permissible unless authorized in the bylaws.

abstention: The result of abstaining from casting a vote. An abstention counts neither when considering the number of votes for or against nor in determining the total number of votes cast.

accept: To adopt, as in "accept a proposal." Due to the technical definition, it's usually unwise to vote to accept a report.

acclamation: An election by unanimous consent.

ad hoc: Latin meaning "for this purpose only." Used with committee. See *special committee.*

adhering motions: Pending secondary motions that must be decided before the main question can be decided and, as a result, remain pending along with the main motion when a motion is referred, postponed, or laid on the table.

adjourn: To close a meeting.

adjourn sine die: To close the final meeting of a session with no further meetings of the same group. See *sine die.*

adjourned meeting: A meeting that continues a session working through a single order of business.

adjournment: 1) The closing of a meeting, as in "Everyone left after adjournment." 2) An adjourned meeting, as in "Tonight's meeting is an adjournment of last week's meeting, at which we ran out of time."

adopt: To accept or agree to.

affirmative vote: A vote in favor of adopting a motion.

agenda: A list of the items of business to come before a meeting. See *order of business.*

alternates: Substitute delegates who serve if the regular delegate is unable to serve.

amend: (v.) To change. (n.) Name of a subsidiary motion that proposes to change a main motion (or any other amendable motion) before it's finally adopted.

amendment: A proposed change. Offered as a motion to *Amend* or, when applied to past actions, a motion to *Amend Something Previously Adopted.*

annual meeting: As provided in a group's bylaws, a meeting held once a year at which a group elects new officers and hears annual reports of officers, the board, and standing committees. An assembly that holds regular monthly or quarterly meetings may designate one of the regular meetings as the annual meeting.

appoint: To designate and authorize a person to serve in a particular role.

articles of incorporation: The terms under which an organization establishes its legal standing as a corporation chartered by state government.

assembly: A deliberative body. The membership present at a meeting.

ballot: A slip of paper on which a voter's preference is written. A ballot is always understood to be a secret ballot unless specifically qualified otherwise, as with a signed ballot.

board: A management and policy-making deliberative assembly that is either subordinate to a larger assembly or autonomous and established by law or charter.

bylaws: An organization's rules about itself that are of such importance that no change should be possible without previous notice and a two-thirds vote. In Robert's Rules, the term refers collectively to the constitution and bylaws if a society has both documents.

call (or notice) of a meeting: Written notice of the time and location of a meeting, which is sent to all members entitled to vote. Must include the specific items to be considered if the meeting is a "special meeting."

call the roll: A secretary's formal oral inquiry of each member, by name, to establish, for the record, the member's presence at the meeting or the member's vote on a specific question before the assembly.

call up the motion to *Reconsider*: The motion to *Reconsider* can be in order even if it's not in order to consider it at the time it's made. In such a case, the motion is made and works like a notice, and the actual decision of whether to *Reconsider* is made later when a member calls up the motion to *Reconsider*. If it's in order at that time, the vote on whether to *Reconsider* is taken up.

caucus: A group of members or delegates who meet to decide how they'll vote in a meeting or to plan strategy regarding items of business.

censure: Official expression of disapproval.

chair: The presiding officer, or the station of the presiding officer in a meeting, as in the reference, "The chair rules the motion out of order."

chairman: A gender-neutral title that refers to a group's presiding officer or the presiding officer of a committee.

charter: A group's articles of incorporation. Also, a document issued by a superior organization authorizing or establishing a subordinate or constituent unit or society.

close nominations: To formally end the nomination process and proceed to the election. This action isn't in order as long as anyone is actually trying to make a nomination or there hasn't been a reasonable opportunity for nominations.

close the polls: To conclude the acceptance of ballots and proceed to the count and determination of the result.

commit: To send, or refer, a motion to a committee.

committee: A group of persons (or one person) assigned to a particular task by or under the authority of a deliberative assembly.

committee of the whole: The entire assembly acting as a committee and chaired by another member who's not the presiding officer of the assembly; it operates under the rules for committees instead of the rules for regular assemblies. Operating as a committee of the whole allows the members to speak an unlimited number of times in debate on the particular subject referred to the committee, and its votes on the subject become recommendations to the assembly, which then takes the final votes.

consent agenda (consent calendar): A list of noncontroversial items of business that can be adopted all at once, saving the time that would be consumed if each item were voted on separately. The list can also contain special preference items to be considered in order at the appropriate time.

consideration by paragraph: See *seriatim.*

constituent society: A quasi-independent organization subordinate to (or otherwise operating under the authority of) a superior organization. Also known as a constituent unit.

constitution: An organizational document once used more widely than is common today. A constitution is different from bylaws only in that the constitution contains articles that rarely change, and amending it requires a higher voting threshold than for bylaws. Robert's Rules uses the term bylaws to refer to both constitutions and bylaws.

convention standing rules: Rules of order and policy that a convention of delegates adopts and that apply to the conduct of business during a complete session.

counted vote: A vote in which the prevailing side is determined by a count (conducted by the chair, the secretary, or tellers) of the number of members voting on each side of the question. It's used only when the chair or the assembly desires it; an individual member can move that a vote be counted but doesn't have the right to demand it.

cumulative voting: A form of voting used when filling positions on boards or committees or when appointing delegates. The process allows a voter one vote for each seat to be filled and permits the voter to cast all the votes in any combination for any number of the choices. Not permissible unless authorized in bylaws.

dark horse: A candidate for office who is the first choice of few but who may have wide support as a second choice. A compromise candidate.

debate: Formal discussions of the pros and cons of motions.

decorum in debate: Being nice; keeping debate on the merits of the question and not venturing into questions on the motives of members. Also refers to following the rules for debate.

defer action: The result of adopting a motion to *Postpone to a Certain Time* (or *Postpone* definitely).

delegates: Elected or appointed representatives from constituent units chosen for a single session of a larger assembly that's convened to act in the name of the entire society.

deliberative assembly: A group convened to discuss and debate action to be taken in the name of the group; it operates under the rules of parliamentary procedure.

dilatory: Intending to thwart the will of the assembly by misusing parliamentary motions.

disciplinary procedure: A procedure by which an assembly holds members and officers accountable for offenses such as serious breaches of order in meetings, or serious violations of the duties and obligations of membership and of holding office.

Division of a Question: An incidental motion that results in voting on parts of a motion separately. The parts must be capable of standing alone as complete motions.

division of the assembly: A rising vote required on demand of a single member who doubts the result of a voice vote. The chair may also call for a division of the assembly if in doubt as to the result of the vote or when an unrepresentative number of members have voted.

executive board: A body subordinate to a society that is empowered to act in a management or administrative nature in the name of the society between regular meetings of the membership. See ***board.***

executive committee: A committee (expressly authorized by the bylaws) appointed to act for or in the name of an executive board.

executive session: A session during which only members and invitees are permitted to attend and in which all discussion is to be held in confidence by those in attendance.

ex officio: Latin for "by virtue of office."

ex-officio members: Members who hold membership (on a particular board or committee, for example) by virtue of an office they hold.

filling blanks: A method of choosing by majority vote from an unlimited number of alternatives to complete a detail in a main motion or primary amendment.

Fix the Time to Which to Adjourn: The privileged motion used, while business is pending, to establish a continuation of the current meeting.

fixed membership: The number of members specifically authorized to compose a board or committee, as distinguished from the current number of members actually serving on the board or committee (when less than the total number authorized).

friendly amendment: An improper form of amendment conditioned on the approval of the maker of the motion to which it's to be applied.

fundamental principle of parliamentary law: A rule of order so basic that it's held to be inviolate and unsuspendable.

general consent: See *unanimous consent.*

general order: An item of business that, in the prior meeting, was pending when the meeting adjourned or otherwise was postponed to the current meeting without being made a special order. See *order of the day, special order.*

germane: Pertaining to the subject. Amendments are required to be germane to the motion being amended.

honorary officers and members: Persons granted a special title or membership status, but in name only and without any rights of office or membership except as the bylaws specify.

illegal vote: Refers to a ballot cast for an unidentifiable (or ineligible) candidate, a ballot with votes for too many candidates, or a ballot that's otherwise unintelligible. An illegal vote cast by a member entitled to vote, however, still counts as a vote cast when determining the number of votes required to adopt or elect.

immediately pending question: The motion that must be decided before any other pending motions may be considered further. Yields only to a higher-ranking motion.

incidental main motion: A main motion that deals with the business of the assembly or its past or future action. It can't have *Objection to the Consideration of a Question* applied to it.

incidental motion: A secondary motion that deals with questions of procedure.

incomplete election: An election not completed before adjournment, including one in which no candidate has achieved the required number of votes.

informal consideration: Occurs when an assembly suspends the rules relating to the number of times a member may speak in debate on a main motion and its proposed amendments.

item of business: A specific report or motion within a particular class of business. For example, when moving from the report of your finance committee to the report of your membership committee, the chair says, "The next item of business is the report of the membership committee."

Lay on the Table: The subsidiary motion used to set aside the pending question to handle an urgent matter. "Tabling" can't be used to kill the pending question or to postpone it to a specific time.

main motion: A motion whose introduction brings business before the assembly.

majority: More than half.

majority of the entire membership: More than half of the total membership, including absentees.

majority vote: The vote of more than half the members present and voting at a properly called meeting.

mass meeting: A meeting of an unorganized assembly that is called for a particular purpose. The mass meeting is open to invitees interested in a particular subject who are generally in favor of accomplishing the announced objectives of the meeting.

meeting: An official gathering of the members of a deliberative assembly or committee, for any length of time, to transact official business, with no break in the proceedings for more than a few minutes. Such a break is called a *recess,* not to be confused with an *adjournment.*

member: A person with unrestricted rights of participation in meetings of a society, including the right to make motions, debate, and vote.

member in good standing: A member whose rights aren't under suspension because of disciplinary action or a provision in the bylaws.

minutes: A concise and official record of the proceedings of a meeting, containing (generally) what was done in the meeting but not what was said.

motion: A proposal formally offered by a member in a meeting, requesting that the assembly take specific action.

nomination: Derived from Latin meaning "to name," a name offered as a proposal that someone be elected or appointed to an office or other service position. Nominations don't require a second.

notice: 1) See *call (or notice) of a meeting.* 2) See *previous notice.*

object: The bylaws article stating the purpose of the organization.

officer: An elected or appointed person holding office as defined in bylaws, who is assigned specific duties, responsibilities, and term of office.

old business: An improper term sometimes used in place of the term *unfinished business.* Should be avoided because it implies that it's appropriate to discuss business that the assembly has already disposed of.

order of business: The sequence in which business comes before an assembly as established by rule. An order of business in which times are assigned to the items or classes of business is commonly referred to as a program or an agenda.

order of precedence of motions: The ranking of motions so that one motion takes precedence over another, which must yield to the higher-ranked motion.

order of the day: A prescheduled item of business. See *general order, special order.*

original main motion: A main motion which, when introduced, brings before the assembly a substantially new question on a new subject that's not related to the internal business of the assembly. The motion *Objection to the Consideration of a Question* can be applied only to an original main motion.

parliamentarian: A consultant who advises on matters of parliamentary procedure.

parliamentary authority: A manual of parliamentary procedure that an assembly adopts and makes binding unless superseded by the charter, bylaws, or special rules of order of the organization.

parliamentary inquiry: A question about parliamentary procedure raised by a member during a meeting.

parliamentary law: Generally, the body of rules applicable to procedures for the conduct of business in deliberative assemblies.

parliamentary motion: Any motion relating to procedure and to the conduct of business in a deliberative assembly. Includes secondary motions (subsidiary, privileged, and incidental motions) and motions that bring a question again before the assembly.

parliamentary procedure: Generally, the rules and procedures under which a deliberative assembly conducts its business and arrives at decisions in the name of the group. The application of common parliamentary law and rules of order.

pending question: A motion currently under consideration, even if it's not the immediately pending question. A motion subject to becoming the immediately pending question whenever pending motions of higher rank are disposed of.

plurality: Largest number of votes received in situations with more than two choices. A plurality isn't decisive unless the assembly has a special rule of order (or a bylaw, in the case of officer elections) that permits it to be the basis for a decision.

preferential voting: A form of voting in which voters indicate the relative preference of each candidate. Preferential voting yields the election of the most preferable when it might be impossible to achieve a majority vote for any one candidate. Can be used for election of officers only if the bylaws permit.

prevailing side: The constituency voting in the affirmative if a motion passes, or in the negative if the motion fails.

previous notice: A notice that a particular motion will be introduced at the next meeting. The notice includes an accurate and complete statement of the motion's purport, but does not need to include its exact content. Depending on provisions in the bylaws and intervals between meetings, previous notice is given in writing with the call of a meeting or orally at the prior meeting.

Previous Question: The subsidiary motion used to close debate, stop amendments, and take an immediate vote on the pending question. Calling out "Question!" to close debate is never in order.

primary amendment: An amendment applied to any main motion or amendable secondary motion, except to another amendment. (When an amendment is applied to a pending primary amendment, it's called a secondary amendment.)

privileged motion: A secondary motion of higher rank than any subsidiary motion. Deals with the privileges of the assembly.

pro tem: Latin abbreviation for pro tempore, meaning "for the time (being)"; temporary.

program: 1) The nonbusiness part of a meeting, such as when a guest speaker makes a presentation. 2) A written schedule of events. See ***agenda.*** The order of business of a convention is sometimes called the program or is included in "the program."

proviso: A provision related to transition; a condition precedent usually to the enactment of a bylaw. Often deals with an effective date.

proxy: 1) A power of attorney authorizing a person to vote in the stead of another. 2) The person holding a proxy.

putting the question: Putting a motion to a vote.

quarterly time interval: A period beginning on the date of a meeting and extending to the last day of the calendar month three months beyond the calendar month in which the first meeting occurs. For example, if a meeting is held on the first day of January, a meeting held on April 30 is within a quarterly time interval. (Yes, that's right. The *quarterly time interval* can actually include up to four full months.)

quasi: Latin meaning "as if"; commonly used in the phrase "quasi-committee of the whole."

question: The decision to be made, as in, "The question is on the adoption of the motion to send Dan out for pizza."

quorum: The minimum number of members who must be present at a properly called meeting for business to be legally conducted.

ratify: To affirm or uphold a decision made in the name of the assembly, but without proper authority at the time the decision was made or carried out.

recess: A short break in the proceedings of a meeting during which members may leave the room. A recess doesn't end the meeting.

recognition: The chair's assignment of the floor to a member entitled to speak or propose a motion.

***Reconsider*:** The motion that, if adopted, allows the assembly to consider and vote again on a motion that was voted on earlier in the same meeting, or during the same or previous business day in a session consisting of more than one meeting, such as a convention. In a committee, there is no time limit on making a motion to *Reconsider*.

refer: To send a motion to a committee. Also known as "to commit."

regular meeting: An organization's meeting that occurs on a regular basis and is usually prescribed in the bylaws.

renew: To offer again a motion that was disposed of without being adopted or defeated. Generally, failed main motions are renewable only at a new session. Renewable secondary motions can be in order in the same meeting, as long as material debate or business has transpired making such a motion, in essence, a new question. A withdrawn main motion can be renewed (proposed again) in the same session.

***Request for Information*:** A request made to the chair for information regarding the pending business and not about parliamentary procedure. Sometimes called *point of information*.

rescind: To repeal or annul action taken by the assembly.

resignation: A request to be excused from all further obligations of holding office or of membership.

resolution: A written form for a main motion that begins with the word *Resolved,* setting forth in specific terms the action to be taken. Often, but not necessarily, a resolution is preceded by a preamble of one or more paragraphs formally stating the rationale for the resolution.

revision of bylaws: A procedure for the amendment of bylaws in which a set of amendments makes such substantive changes throughout the current bylaws that it's offered and considered as a substitution for the current bylaws.

rising vote: A vote in which members stand to express their support or opposition to a proposal. Allows for visual rather than aural determination of the prevailing side. Used instead of a voice vote when a two-thirds vote is required, or any time a member calls for a division of the assembly.

Robert's Rules: 1) (Informal) Parliamentary procedure. *Caveat:* Although the term "Robert's Rules" is often used to mean parliamentary procedure generally in casual use, parliamentarians will be careful to make the distinction between parliamentary procedure itself and a particular manual on the subject (even if it is the most widely used manual). 2) The parliamentary authority that is *Robert's Rules of Order Newly Revised.* The current title in the series of official revisions and editions of the parliamentary authority originally published as *Robert's Rules of Order* in 1876 by Henry M. Robert.

roll-call vote: Yeas and nays. A vote in which each voting member (or delegation) is called by name and a record is made of the vote. This type of voting procedure should be used only in representative or constituent bodies.

rules of order: Any written rules of parliamentary procedure a deliberative assembly adopts.

scope of notice: The range within which amendments may be applied to motions for which the required previous notice has been given. Amendments outside the scope of notice aren't in order because the notice protects the rights of absentees. In cases where previous notice isn't actually required, but giving notice lowers the threshold required for adoption, amendments outside the scope of notice are in order, but if they're adopted, the motion now requires the same threshold for adoption as if no notice was given. (Unless the effect of this would be that a vote of a majority of the entire membership is required and there are not that many members present, in which case such amendments are not in order.)

second: An acknowledgment by a second member that a motion should come before the assembly. A second doesn't imply agreement with the object of the motion; it indicates only that the seconder wants the motion to be decided. If discussion or debate ensues without a second having been obtained, the fact that there was no second is of no consequence.

secondary amendment: An amendment applied to a primary amendment.

secondary motions: A collective term for subsidiary, privileged, and incidental motions.

secret ballot: Under Robert's Rules, all ballots are secret ballots unless specifically designated otherwise, such as with a signed ballot. See *ballot.*

select committee: See *special committee, ad hoc.*

seriatim: Latin meaning "step by step." Used in the incidental motion consideration by paragraph or seriatim. A procedure for considering a document — such as bylaws — one section or paragraph at a time.

session: A meeting or series of meetings devoted to one continuous order of business.

signed ballot: A ballot that identifies the person who casts it. This voting procedure is a substitute for roll call when a record is required of who voted and how. May be advisable when dealing with a large number of voting members or when only a relatively small portion of the entire membership is present.

sine die: Latin meaning "without day." See *adjourn sine die.*

society: The entity (association or organization) that's governed by a deliberative assembly.

special committee: A committee that is formed for a specific task and that ceases to exist after the task is complete. Also known as a *select* or *ad hoc committee.*

special meeting: A meeting other than a regular meeting at which only business specified in the notice for the meeting may be considered. Special meetings usually are reserved for urgent matters that can't wait until the next regular meeting or for scheduling an entire meeting devoted to one subject, such as disciplinary proceedings against a member or officer. Must be authorized in the bylaws (except in the case of disciplinary trials).

special order: An item of business that's set for a particular meeting or a particular time in a meeting and that takes precedence over any other business, with very few exceptions. See *general order, order of the day.*

special rules of order: Rules (adopted by an assembly) related to parliamentary procedure that supplement or supersede particular rules in the assembly's parliamentary authority.

specification: In disciplinary proceedings, a statement of what the accused has allegedly done to warrant being charged with an offense.

stand at ease: A request by the chair for the assembly to pause briefly in its proceedings (but not recess or adjourn). This request may be used to accommodate the chair's brief consultation with the parliamentarian or secretary, to permit adjustment of audiovisual equipment, and so on.

standing committee: A permanent committee that performs a continuing function, usually established in the bylaws.

standing rules: Adopted rules that establish policy and usually aren't related to meeting procedures. They require a majority vote without notice to adopt. Standing rules may not be suspended unless their application is in the context of a meeting.

standing rules of a convention: See *convention standing rules.*

straw poll: An informal poll to determine voters' leanings. A straw poll is never in order because it doesn't decide anything.

subcommittee: A committee that's subordinate to another committee.

subsidiary motion: A motion that aids in the disposal of other motions.

substitute: A form of amendment whose purpose is to strike out and insert an entire paragraph (or paragraphs).

substitute motion: See *substitute.*

Suspend the rules: An incidental motion to enable action that would otherwise violate the rules of order. This motion requires a two-thirds vote and is applicable only to rules of order, not to the bylaws (unless the rule in the bylaws is clearly in the nature of a rule of order or provides for its own suspension).

tellers: Persons appointed to receive and count ballots or other votes.

two-thirds vote: A voting threshold of two-thirds of the members present and voting. This threshold is required to adopt certain motions as a means of protecting the interests of a minority greater than one-third.

unanimous ballot: A ballot cast by an officer (usually the secretary) to elect a sole candidate to office. A unanimous ballot is out of order if the bylaws require a ballot vote because the unanimous ballot denies members the right to vote against the candidate by casting write-in votes.

unanimous consent: An expedient procedure for adopting a motion or confirming agreement by the assembly to a course of action without the formality of a vote or, in some cases, even a motion. The chair obtains unanimous consent by requesting it; if no objection is raised, the chair may proceed as if the assembly had voted formally. Also called *general consent.*

unanimous vote: A vote in which all members present and voting vote the same. This term is often misused; it's never correct to declare a vote unanimous if the outcome of the ballot vote was not unanimous to begin with, unless the motion to make the ballot vote unanimous is itself voted on by ballot.

undebatable motion: A motion on which the question isn't subject to discussion.

unfinished business: Questions carried over from the immediately preceding meeting that didn't complete its order of business before adjournment. Unfinished business includes motions pending when the last meeting adjourned and any other business left on the prior meeting's agenda that wasn't reached before it adjourned (except for special orders). Unfinished business isn't an applicable order of business in meetings separated by more than a quarterly time interval. See also *general order.*

vacancy in office: Occurs when, due to death, resignation, or removal, an officer doesn't complete the term. Unless a vacancy is to be filled according to the assembly's standard procedure for appointing or electing a person to that office, the bylaws should specify provisions for filling vacancies. Under Robert's Rules, when there's a vacancy in the office of president, the vice president automatically succeeds to the presidency, creating a vacancy in the office of vice president.

viva voce: Latin meaning "with the living voice." Refers to a vote taken by voice. ("Those in favor of the motion, say aye . . .")

vote of no confidence: Not a parliamentary term under Robert's Rules. To express disapproval of an officer or adopt a motion of censure.

with power: Describes a committee that's authorized to take binding action in matters referred to it.

withdraw or modify a motion: Until the chair states a question (bringing it officially before the assembly), the member making the motion has a right to withdraw it or modify it without the permission of the assembly. Once stated by the chair, however, the member must obtain the permission of the assembly to withdraw or modify the motion. A withdrawn motion is considered one that has never been made, so it can be offered again (renewed) during the same session without violating any rules.

without objection: See *unanimous consent.*

write-in: A vote for an individual or choice not nominated or shown on a preprinted ballot.

yeas and nays: See *roll-call vote.*

Index

Q

quarterly time interval, 173, 225, 280, 484

quasi, defined, 484

quasi-committee of the whole, 62, 352

question, defined, 484

Question of Privilege motion, 143, 218

quorum call, 469–470

quorums

about, 74, 77

counting ex-officio members in board and committee quorums, 78–79

defined, 484

defining your, 458–459

determining a, 78

establishing a, 78

establishing rules related to, 459–460

handling emergencies without a, 81–82

not having a, 79–81

R

Raise a Question of Privilege motion

about, 80, 141, 212, 217–218

key characteristics of, 220

using, 218–219

raising a point of order, 321–322

ranking

privileged motions, 212–214

subsidiary motions, 178–180

ratify, defined, 484

Ratify motion, 82, 110

recapitulation, 155

recess, defined, 50, 484

Recess motion

about, 111, 212, 214, 220–221

key characteristics of, 222

using, 221–222

recognition

defined, 484

determining who to give, 134–135

obtaining to speak, 289–290, 470

seeking, 60, 137–138

speaking without, 450–451

recommendations for action, 380–381

Reconsider a Vote motion, 132

Reconsider and Enter on the Minutes motion, 132, 141, 279–280

Reconsider motion

about, 51, 128, 132, 133, 141, 271, 272

considerations for, 280–281

defined, 484

key characteristics of, 281

knowing when not to use, 276–278

mistakes with, 449–450

Reconsider and Enter on the Minutes motion, 279–280

"reconsider" as a parliamentary term, 273

using, 273–276, 361

using in committees, 361

recounting votes, 173, 321

refer, defined, 484

Refer motion

about, 177–179, 193–194

to create special committees, 355

regular meetings

about, 51–52

defined, 484

giving notice of, 70–71

relationships, defining between classes of motions, 101–102

Remember icon, 5

renew, defined, 484

renewing motions, 276

reporting

about, 367–368

boards and committees, 377–381

executive board, 378

findings of cause, 391–392

handling, 381–382

members' rights to consult records, 382–384

minutes, 368–375

nominations, 308

from officers, 377

resolutions committee, 428

treasurer's report, 376

Request for Any Other Privilege motion, 231, 232

Request for Information motion

about, 141, 231, 232, 263, 453

defined, 484

About the Author

C. Alan Jennings holds a Professional Registered Parliamentarian (PRP) credential from the National Association of Parliamentarians. He is a past president of the Louisiana Association of Parliamentarians and is a member of the American Institute of Parliamentarians.

His interest in parliamentary procedure began when he was a fifth-grader at Davis Elementary School in Jackson, Mississippi. His class learned about Robert's Rules when electing class officers. Alan confessed he was more interested in the cute class secretary (who would smile at him during the meetings, making his heart go all squishy) than he was interested in Robert or his rules.

Alan's experience as a parliamentarian began when it became his duty to establish a new local congregation of his church. As is true for most parliamentarians, his education as a parliamentarian is experiential. As he learned Robert's Rules by using the book as the guide for organizing the congregation, he applied the rules in another venue — creating an educational organization for Louisiana's notaries at civil law. From the start, Alan encouraged the leadership teams of these organizations to develop a working knowledge of the official Robert's Rules and to use it in their work with the organizations; he credits the success of the local congregation and the state notary association (both have achieved international recognition) to the leadership's consistent application of the principles of procedure and leadership found in the pages of Robert's Rules.

In 2000, Alan retired as the executive director of the Louisiana Notary Association. He currently writes for several publications in his professional fields and publishes a regular newsletter for notaries at civil law in Louisiana. He is a consultant to the director of the Louisiana State University Office of Assessment and Evaluation, which administers Louisiana's Civil Law Notary qualifying examinations for the state. Alan formerly served on the advisory committee to the Louisiana 19th Judicial District Court on civil law notary examination procedures. He is currently a member of the Louisiana State Law Institute's notaries committee.

Alan is active as a professional parliamentarian and serves as meeting parliamentarian for organizations on the local, state, and national levels. He provides consulting services year-round for clients in a wide variety of situations and specializes in bylaws and corporate documentation.

Alan and his wife, Hartwell Harris, have been married for 41 years this year. Retired from 31 years of public service, Hartwell is an accomplished photographer and artist, and is a certified hypnotherapist. Both Alan and Hartwell enjoy not only the day-to-day adventures at home in Baton Rouge (with their American Staffordshire terrier, Mr. Boo), but also their working (and vacation) travel time together.

Dedication

To all the people who attend meetings and come home thinking, "Surely, there has to be a better way."

Author's Acknowledgments

This book wouldn't be in your hands right now if it weren't for the generosity of so many. I've worried a bit that I have nowhere near the page count available to acknowledge them all if I were to start the list where it belongs, with my first-grade teacher who started me off with that big fat pencil and Big Chief writing pad. So I'll just thank Miss Hill and Miss Bradshaw for that and move on to the more immediate friends, family, and colleagues who helped me with this particular work.

First, I thank my original parliamentarian-mentors the late Eleanor Earle, PRP, and Myra Myers, PRP — who gave me so much of their time and encouragement.

I am inspired by the example of these leadership role models who exemplify such special character attributes that no one can go wrong by seeking to emulate them: the late Eileen Armstrong, NAP past presidents Loretta Simonson and Kathryn Scheld (this book's first-edition general reviewer), Judy Young, and Tommy

French. I am inspired by the skill and dedication of these parliamentarian teachers: Nancy Sylvester and Eugene Bierbaum. I am inspired by the wisdom and loyalty of friends like my late colleague, Col. Tom Austin, and I am at once inspired and humbled by the personal strength and dedication to learning of an early protégé, Rapunzel Fontenot. Finally, I am inspired by the consummate professionalism of Ann Rempel, PRP, CPP-T (one of the earlier edition's technical reviewers), and Jim Lochrie, CPP-T (an exemplary professional presiding officer).

Gratitude for personal and direct help on my original manuscript is extended to my colleagues known as the Klatched Parliamentarians, especially Rod Davidson, Kim Goldsworthy (RIP), Jonathan M. Jacobs, and John Stackpole (RIP). For the collection of notes and tips stacked in my reading files from Jim Lochrie, Teresa Dean, Michael Malamut, Dan Honemann, and Jim McCabe, I am grateful.

I am especially indebted to my friend and colleague, Shmuel Gerber. Shmuel gave me a thorough editor's pass of *Robert's Rules For Dummies,* 1st edition, first printing. His edits, comments, and quibbles gave the second printing a special luster. Shmuel is such a great writer, editor, and parliamentarian that the authors of Robert's Rules made him a member of the Robert's Rules authorship team in 2011. Thanks, Shmuel!

What self-respecting author wouldn't let the whole world know how much he appreciated the help and hard work of the editors who not only helped him find his muse, but took his manuscript and made it into the book you hold in your hands today? I don't know of anybody who'd fail to be prolific in his words of appreciation for the gang at Wiley, namely Natasha Graf, Natalie Harris, Elizabeth Rea, Michael Lewis, Tracy Brown, Krista Hansing, Tracy Boggier, Tim Gallan, Lindsay LeFevere, and Chad Sievers. To all of you, my heartfelt thanks.

The hero of this edition (as with the third edition) is Joshua Martin, the parliamentarian's parliamentarian who serves as this edition's technical editor. His excellent advice and informative notes and comments have done wonders for the knowledge this this book holds for its readers, and his edits have put a polish on the accuracy of the information that will benefit every reader. Thank you, Josh.

Publisher's Acknowledgments

Executive Editor:
Lindsay Sandman Lefevere

Project Editor: Chad R. Sievers

Technical Editor: Joshua Martin

Production Editor:
Tamilmani Varadharaj

Cover Image: © Billion Photos/
Shutterstock